THE RESTRUCTURING OF
CAPITALISM IN OUR TIME

The Restructuring of Capitalism in Our Time

William K. Tabb

COLUMBIA UNIVERSITY PRESS   NEW YORK

COLUMBIA UNIVERSITY PRESS

Publishers Since 1893

NEW YORK   CHICHESTER, WEST SUSSEX

Library of Congress Cataloging-in-Publication Data

Tabb, William K.

  The restructuring of capitalism in our time / William K. Tabb.

    p.   cm.

  Includes bibliographical references and index.

  ISBN 978-0-231-15842-8 (cloth : alk. paper) — ISBN 978-0-231-52803-0 (electronic)

  1. Capitalism—Political aspects. 2. Financial crises. 3. Finance—Law and legislation.

4. Monetary policy. 5. Banks and banking. I. Title.

HB501.T313   2012

332—dc22

                                                      2011008941

CONTENTS

I first wrote about the growth of financialization in a paper entitled "Finance and the Contemporary Social Structure of Accumulation" presented at the Conference on Growth and Crisis, Social Structures of Accumulation Theory and Analysis, November 2–4, 2006, at the J. E. Cairnes Graduate School of Business & Public Policy, National University of Ireland, Galway, Ireland. The paper was subsequently published in *Contemporary Capitalism: Social Structures of Accumulation Theory for the Twenty-First Century*, edited by Terrence McDonough, Michael Reich, and David M. Kotz (Cambridge University Press, 2010). Another formative piece was "The Centrality of Finance," written for the *Journal of World-Systems Research* 13, 1 (2007), in which I worked out the extent of financialization and its role in the contemporary world system Some of the material from chapter 9 is included in an essay I was asked to write for the Oxford University Press *Handbook on the Political Economy of Financial Crises*, edited by Gerald Epstein and Martin H. Wolfson, which is in preparation.

The social structure of accumulation and world system thinking regarding globalization are central to this book. I have been influenced by my years of teaching and thinking about American economic history and the perennial questions of money and banks, their regulation and impacts, and by teaching money and banking and industrial organization courses. The dominant literatures and theoretical approaches of these fields, and of mainstream macroeconomics, have not sat well with my understanding of the world. I have benefited over the years from conversations with Michael Edelstein on, among other topics, the role of banking in American history, with Harvey Gram on Keynes, and with Thom Thurston regarding mainstream macroeconomic theory.

My thanks go to the Warner Fund of the University Seminars at Columbia University for financial support in the preparation of the manuscript; to participants in three of the seminars—on Full Employment, Social Welfare, and Equity; Political Economy and Contemporary Social Issues; and Globalization, Labor, and Popular Struggles—for their comments; to Irene Zola and Anita O'Brien for perceptive editing assistance; Pat Perrier for masterful indexing; Leslie Kriesel for her good cheer in so efficiently facilitating the production of the book; and most definitely to my philosopher daughter Kathryn C. M. Tabb for conversations on how we know what we think we know. Specialists in the many literatures upon which this book draws may find things to take exception to and are advised to direct any criticisms to Professor Emeritus Irving Gershenberg, who resides in Berkeley, California, and is solely responsible for all remaining errors.

The title of this book as submitted to the press was "Financialization: The Appropriations of Finance and the Restructuring of Capitalism in Our Time." I agreed that the shorter, broader title could be used since, as suggested by in-house decision makers, it better conveys the breadth of coverage, going beyond aspects of financialization. I hope that the centrality of finance that I privilege remains the focus of reader attention even as other issues receive their due: globalization, shifting patterns of economic and political power in the world system, and the need for economic democracy to infuse our politics if we are to find a more felicitous outcome to the continued unacceptable economic conditions under which most Americans and others around the world live.

This book is dedicated to my wife Margaret Mikesell Tabb, for all the usual reasons, and then some.

THE RESTRUCTURING OF
CAPITALISM IN OUR TIME

The Centrality of Finance

The U.S. has the world's most diverse and efficient capital markets, which reward, and even celebrate, risk-taking.
—THOMAS FRIEDMAN, 1997

It's dispiriting indeed to watch the United States financial system, supposedly the envy of the world, being taken to its knees. But that's the show we're watching, brought to you by somnambulant regulators, greedy bank executives and incompetent corporate directors.

This wasn't the way the "ownership society" was supposed to work. Investors weren't supposed to watch their financial stocks plummet more than 70 percent in less than a year. And taxpayers weren't supposed to be left holding defaulted mortgages and abandoned homes while executives who presided over balance sheet implosions walked away with millions.
—GRETCHEN MORGENSON, 2008

Not long ago the near collapse of the financial system discredited the excessive financialization central to contemporary American capitalism. History suggests a prolonged transformative crisis, one made worse by macroeconomic policy errors, including in the handling of the debt ceiling, and by overoptimism regarding the self-healing powers of the market. As banks and the stock market recovered, the conversation moved to worrying about public debt. Financial reform was presumed to have been achieved; the financial crisis safely consigned to history. This book is a protest against this premature dismissal and suggests we need to understand the damaging role finance has assumed in the economy, the continuing problem of global capital flow imbalances, and the danger of a still worse crisis.

According to the National Bureau of Economic Research committee that dates business cycles, this severe crisis began in December 2007 and ended eighteen months later, in June 2009; the longest and, by most measures, deepest recession since the Second World War. However, efforts to bracket the period 2007–9 as the Great Recession, with a beginning and an end followed by an economic recovery, obscure the manner in which excess financialization continues to contribute to high unemployment, extreme inequality, and stagnant living standards. It also underestimates how close the world came to another Great Depression. Federal Reserve Chairman Ben Bernanke told the federal inquiry commission in a closed-door session on November 2009 that "as a scholar of the Great Depression, I honestly believe that September and October of 2008 was the worst financial crisis in global history, including the Great Depression." He estimated that of the thirteen most important financial institutions in the United States, twelve were at risk of failure with a period of a week or two (Financial Crisis Inquiry Commission 2011:354). At the time he was hardly alone in this judgment.

Three years on, however, some academics, Wall Street leaders, and a libertarian former chair of the Federal Reserve argued that the Dodd-Frank Wall Street Reform and Consumer Protection Act, signed into law in July 2010, would create regulatory-induced market distortions, be impossible to implement, and was a possible threat to U.S. living standards. That is, once the banks had been saved with multitrillion-dollar government assistance, they, and economists with strong free-market convictions, no longer saw any flaw in the system or accepted that it could be made to operate better through stronger regulation.

Although the crisis originated in the United States, expanded across the globe, and came as a surprise to many, some economists and investigators predicted such a disaster. They saw an expanding bubble that could only end badly. In 2002 Dean Baker concluded that a housing bubble was under way; he offered increasingly sharp warnings of the systemic implications of a housing collapse. In the summer of 2005 Nouriel Roubini predicted that real home prices in the United States were likely to fall at least 30 percent over the next three years. He warned that subprime lending might be the proverbial canary in the mine—or tip of the iceberg—and signal a broader economic recession with falling wealth, reduced real incomes, and lost jobs, a disaster affecting millions of households. Other respected economic observers, including Joseph Stiglitz, Robert Schiller, George Soros, and Paul Krugman, publicly predicted the crisis. And heterodox economists such as Steve Keen, Wynne Godley, and Michael Hudson early on developed models of how financial markets interacted with the macro economy to forecast a severe collapse.

Such financial and banking crises are historically not that unusual, and their consequences have often been painful. Economists at the International Monetary Fund (Balakrishnan et al. 2009) report on the medium-term impact of eighty-eight banking crises over the previous forty years in a wide range of developing and developed countries. They conclude that for the average country seven years after the crisis, the output level is around 10 percent below its precrisis trend. They find that because a crisis typically depresses investment, employment suffers lasting losses as well. Carmen Reinhart and Kenneth Rogoff (2010) show that on average a modern banking crisis is responsible for an 86 percent increase in government debt in the three years following it (important, given that overpaid government workers and welfare-state spending were to be blamed for deficits). Their examination of fifteen post–World War II financial crises in advanced and emerging market economies and three synchronized global contractions finds real per capita gross domestic product (GDP) growth rates significantly lower during the decade following severe financial upheavals. Most worrying, in past financial crises it has taken an average of seven years for households and businesses to bring their debt and debt service back to tolerable levels relative to income.

Remarkably, given the depth of the Great Recession, "large corporations had a good crisis, which they used to make their operations leaner and boost productivity while piling up cheap finance," as the *Financial Times* noted editorially (2011). But it was a bleak recovery, seen from a working-class perspective, with continued exceedingly high levels of sustained unemployment. And while job creation typically lags business recovery coming out of a recession, the manner in which societies carry out necessary deleveraging of debt varies. Daniel Costello (2011) begins a report on executive pay by noting, "Rarely has the view from the corner office seemed so at odds with the view from the street corner. At a time when millions of Americans are trying to hang on to their homes and millions more are trying to hang on to jobs, the chief executives of major corporations like 3M, General Electric and Cisco Systems are making as much today as they were before the recession it. Indeed, some are making even more."

In the years following the official end of the Great Recession, cuts in entitlements and public goods were declared necessary to bring government spending under control. The question—and it is a political one rather than simply a matter of economics—is how the shortfall should be addressed. Liberals proposed increased public spending to stimulate economic growth, and paying down the increased public debt from the increased revenues an adequate stimulus would presumably generate. Conservatives disagreed and called for cutting spending to reduce the deficit. An alternative to such austerity is to look for more income on the revenue side. For three decades and more, the share of total taxes paid by the corporate sector has declined, and tax reforms have disproportionately lowered the taxes paid by the very wealthy. Liberals argued that this would be unfair and that raising taxes on wealthy people was unlikely to lower consumption and investment much under the circumstances.

In a nine-hour filibuster on December 10, 2010, to protest a Republican demand that the Bush tax cuts to the very richest taxpayers be extended for ten years, Vermont senator Bernie Sanders pointed out that not only would this increase the deficit by $700 billion, but "right now, the top 1 percent controls more than 23 percent of all income earned in America. The top 1 percent controls more than the bottom 50 percent. It's not only that the rich are getting richer. The very, very rich are getting richer. In the last 25 years, we have seen 80 percent of all the new income going to the top 1 percent." He noted that corporations were sitting on two trillion dollars in cash waiting for demand for their products to pick up. Their current profits were high, thanks to downsizing, plant closings, and layoffs, but they saw no reason to expand production and hire more employees. Taxes collected from corporations in the United States raise only 2.1 percent of GDP (well below the 3.5 percent average for the richer countries that are members of the Organization for Economic Cooperation and Development). Closing tax loopholes and shutting down tax havens through which income is routed could further reduce the deficit. A crisis calls attention to the perceived fairness of a society's political economy.

When President Obama brokered a deal with congressional Republicans to keep the Bush tax breaks for upper-income taxpayers, only a third of Americans agreed that this was a good thing to do, according to a Bloomberg National Poll (McCormick and Goldman 2010). In a *New York Times/CBS* poll, nearly two-thirds of respondents chose higher payroll taxes for Medicare and Social Security over reduced benefits in either program. Asked to choose among cuts to Medicare, Social Security, and the military, a majority, by a large margin, chose the military (Calmes and Sussman 2011). Senator Sanders, a political independent and self-declared socialist, may have represented the views of a majority of Americans who might not know the exact numbers but feel the pain of an economy that does not seem to put their needs foremost.

The United States has experienced three jobless recoveries in a row. Between 1999 and 2009 there was no net job creation, and median household income fell 5 percent. Real wages have stagnated for four decades. During the Great Recession years, the United States lost eight and a half million jobs, far more than in the previous four recessions combined. As the recession officially ended, almost one in five Americans in the workforce, 18.3 percent, either did not have jobs or were working part-time and wanted full-time employment. An exodus of discouraged workers from the job market kept the U.S. unemployment rate from climbing, but unemployment continued to rise in the months following the official recovery date. Those who found jobs were working for lower pay. The crisis exposed underlying structural changes in the U.S. political economy and the world system, changes that interact in complex ways and suggest that American workers will experience income and employment problems well into the future, even with the worst months of the recession behind them and renewed hiring.

Further, coming out of the Great Recession and in contrast to the worsening plight of many needing work, the large banks, which were seen as having caused the crisis, fared very well. The rescue of Wall Street increased concentration in finance. By mid-2010 Bank of America, JPMorgan Chase, and Wells Fargo had a third of all U.S. deposits, up from 21 percent in mid-2007. At no previous time in history has such a rapid increase in industrial concentration in banking taken place. The crisis caused by the banks rewarded the biggest of the biggest, as they took over the industry's failed enterprises. JPMorgan Chase took over Washington Mutual, increasing its assets by 20 percent; Bank of America absorbed Merrill Lynch and Countrywide, with combined assets of nearly $1 trillion. If one adds in Citigroup, by early 2010 the assets of these three banks were up by more than 50 percent from 2007. Along with investment bankers, hedge funds, and private equity groups, these banks have changed the face the American economy in ways that create long-term structural weakness. Short-term speculative gambits, the maximization of shareholder value, and the pressure of debt on companies and households produced a growth dynamic that is not dependent on rising real incomes of American, but is built on asset bubbles, capital gains, and debt-driven consumption. Technology, globalization, and the ability of firms to reset employment contracts (so they no longer tied worker pay to productivity) caused employment to become less well remunerated and more insecure.

If economic growth were once again to lift all boats, this would have to change. I will argue that the way finance had come to dominate the economy in an era of global neoliberalism was significantly responsible for these developments, and that a crisis of faith in American capitalism, on the one hand, and suspicion of government, on the other, are changing the "normal" of the American political economy. Citizens were deeply divided as to which deserved more blame and which should be looked to for solutions. There was also awareness of the incestuous relation between the two that frustrated many. In his 2011 State of the Union message, President Obama tried to rally Americans to meet the challenges the nation faced: the need to reduce federal spending and to become more competitive in the twenty-first-century global economy. He called for increased government spending on infrastructure, research, and education. Republicans presented the president's competitiveness push as an excuse for bigger government. But active government with a transformative agenda is necessary to escape long-term stagnation. Serious reform of the financial system is a needed part of this. Serious social control of the economic surplus, channeling it away from speculation and into job creation, is essential; major redistribution of income and reorientation of priorities are required.

These political conflicts form the background to this inquiry into the role of the finance, insurance, and real estate (FIRE) sector, the need for broader restructuring of the U.S. and global economies, and why the world economy would be unable to get out of long-term crisis without new regulatory regimes for productive investment.

The Role of Finance in Our Economic System

Economists remain divided on many aspects of the Great Recession, although there is agreement around two familiar poles: "the government is to blame" and "the market did it." In the first camp John Taylor (2009:1–2) tells us that the "federal government actions and interventions caused, prolonged, and worsened the financial crisis. There is little evidence that these forces are abating, and indeed they may be getting worse. Hence, this view sees government as the more serious systemic risk in the financial system; it leads in a different direction—to proposals to limit the powers of government and the harm it can do." Those who argue that markets know what is best believe that government will be ineffective or incompetent and will do more harm than good.

However, say those who fault the market, because market participants can base decisions on misleading information and are subject to herd behavior, endogenous financial crises should not be unexpected. Hence there is need for vigilant government regulation to enforce standards of honesty and moderate procyclical developments that threaten to inflate asset bubbles. While the last of these is a difficult judgment call, it is no longer acceptable to say, as Federal Reserve chair Alan Greenspan did before the global financial crisis, that they should not interfere with the market. There is now a good deal of research that links rapid increase in credit creation in an economy with the likelihood of financial bubbles and busts. When serious economic crises occur, government intervention on a significant scale is required, as Greenspan was to acknowledge (see chapters 6 and 7). This suggests the unenviable, but necessary, task of taking away the punch bowl when the party becomes too exuberant.

From my perspective the question becomes how serious a crisis has to be before the society can successfully initiate, and effectively enforce, better norms and regulations in its members' long-term interest. In addition to the instrumentalist influence of money in electoral politics, and the staffing of key positions in revolving-door fashion by leading figures from Wall Street, there are structural incentives for regulators to pull their punches: to retain the confidence of the business community, encourage investor optimism, and support the accumulation process by not "overregulating." These are state priorities, not simply a response to money politics. Government depends on the private sector to create jobs, on business taxes to fund programs, and on economic growth to keep the electorate happy. These are structural givens. The interesting questions come over differences as to what government can do to foster growth and what kind of growth is best for the nation. What appears to one constituency to be "anti–free enterprise," government takeover, and runaway spending is seen by others as regulation to promote competition and societal investment to enable economic growth and promote stability.

Undertaking bold transformations is not usually the first choice of politicians or technocrats charged with unpopular tasks. The job of the latter is to work out details of proposals that meet political requirements of officials who want to be reelected. Technical solutions adopted by the political process are vetted by savvy policy entrepreneurs, lawyers, economists, congressional staffers, lobbyists, and others who have been around Washington for a while and are well practiced in disguising the interests of those who fund the political process. At the same time, when regulators and policy makers are seen as too generous to those they regulate, there is popular resentment. Officials are caught between powerful pressures in a politics of who will pay for crises. Although it is too rarely put this way the choice is whether the burden will fall on capital or labor. To what extent will government-provided services and the transfer payments to ordinary citizens be reduced? Will corporations

and the wealthy pay more in taxes? Do efforts to raise the taxes on corporations and the wealthy discourage investment, as conservatives stress, or are
progressive taxation and a more egalitarian distribution of income conducive
to growth, as liberals assert? Such issues are a matter of clashing political
opinions and differing economic beliefs.

There is no question that countries need healthy banks and well-functioning credit systems. There are, however, different ways to go about this. The
one chosen by the administrations of George W. Bush and Barack Obama
was to give, through a host of programs (to be discussed in chapter 6), overwhelming subsidies and guarantees to the banks to restore confidence. The
Economist (2009b:13) described this option as the "monstrous bargain that
bankers extracted from the state." It called for the government to guarantee
huge parts of the financial system to restore their profitability courtesy of
taxpayers. Once this alternative was chosen, authorities pulled out all stops.
Secretary of the Treasury Timothy Geithner and Federal Reserve chair Ben
Bernanke did an excellent job of creatively finding all manner of innovative
ways to funnel money and guarantees to the deeply shaken financial sector to
restore its viability, and so to get markets functioning, more than doubling
the Fed's balance sheet in the process and moving beyond the function of
lender of last resort, lending on sound collateral, to major investor and significant risk taking. This creates expectations that such safety nets will be as
available next time, encouraging excessive risk taking as the financial system
expands once again. Evaluation of the way the banks and other financial institutions were rescued may appear in a harsher light when the next financial
crisis comes around and the extent to which the public guarantee is judged to
have encouraged greater risk taking is weighed.

A second approach is to make bank executives, shareholders, and unsecured creditors take the losses in state-directed restructurings. President
Obama granted that European governments that had nationalized bankrupt
banks, reorganized them, and sold them off to investors as functioning entities had done a good job and saved taxpayers a large amount of their hard-
earned money; but, he said, such an approach was just not politically possible in the United States. Indeed, to face the reconstruction of finance on
a different basis would take historic imagination, courage, and the support
of a public embracing an alternative set of beliefs to those hegemonic at the
time. Secretary Geithner argued that nationalizing banks "would have been
catastrophic." Larry Summers, the head of the National Economic Council,
saw the revival of the banks and their paying back public monies they bor-

rowed as refuting the argument that "the economy would somehow be in better shape today if the government had nationalized the banking system" (Baker 2011).

The decision to support banks with every tool at its disposal was based on the administration's conviction that the best way to restore confidence was to return the financial system as quickly as possible to the status it enjoyed before the crisis. It was understood that there was no going back to the regulatory order established in the 1930s, and that the complexity of modern finance meant government could only tinker at the edges to increase capital requirements and perhaps limit leverage. The essence of the new order was making money through short-term investment strategies, often with borrowed money, and sometimes very short-term, as with millisecond execution of trades based on computer algorithms. This modern financial market had little to do with raising funds for long-term investment and socially efficient allocation of resources.

Paul Sweezy (1994:7) writes: "Finance capital, once cut loose from its original role as a modest helper of a real economy of production to meet human needs, inevitably becomes speculative capital geared solely to its own expansion. In earlier times no one ever dreamed that speculative capital, a phenomenon as old as capitalism itself, could grow to dominate a national economy, let alone the whole world. But it has." He describes how over the previous twenty years or so a relatively independent superstructure has grown atop the world economy, with its national units, and "a bewildering variety of financial assets and services, all interconnected by a network of markets, some of which are structured and regulated, others informal and unregulated. Such an entity is multi-dimensional, and there is no conceptual unit that could be used to measure its size." Sweezy's description of how the occupants of the corporate boardrooms were increasingly controlled by financial capital as it operated through the globalized network of high-speed markets, and how political leaders who were thought to wield power over their countries' fate were subject to these same constraining forces (and not just the leaders of the weaker states, but of the strongest as well), is a prescient telling of what has since come to be more widely acknowledged.

The philosophy of maximizing shareholder value had a number of elements. The dominant one was the idea that companies should not retain earnings for reinvestment, or even a cushion against unforeseen adversity, but rather return earnings to stockholders. To ensure that management maximized returns to owners, companies should load up on debt. The interest payments they needed to cover obligations would pressure managers to wring as much out of the companies as they could, cutting costs and maximizing short-term profits. The financier Felix Rohatyn tells us that until that crisis point was reached, "cash was a dangerous thing to accumulate: activist investors stalked companies, urging boards to return it to investors, to pay special dividends or to buy back shares. Ever since the 1980s the fashion has been to make companies as lean as possible, outsourcing all but your core competencies, expanding your just-in-time supplier system around the globe, loading up on debt to 'leverage' your balance-sheet." Looking at what had happened, Rohatyn offers a sobering assessment and a warning that went unheeded: "In a sense, the financial services business has been masquerading as a manufacturing industry ever since interest rates started climbing, constantly rolling new investment vehicles off its assembly line. But we are learning that these investment vehicles are not necessarily better, they're just riskier" (Rohatyn 1994:7) When economic downturn occurred, this high debt-minimal reserve position left companies in a troubled situation. It was difficult to meet interest obligations, to borrow more, or to roll over existing debt. Company suppliers had similar problems and might lack working capital to meet just-in-time production schedules. The extreme debt strategy at such a time was dangerous and painfully costly for many enterprises and the wider economy.

Financialization

Financialization can be understood to denote the dominance of the financial sector in the totality of economic activity such that financial markets determine the state of the overall economy and financial sector demands dictate nonfinancial company behavior. Finance capital, footloose and flexible, interposes itself whenever arbitrage opportunities present themselves. It represents the increased power of abstract capital as opposed to productive capital. On another level, financialization is a policy choice of governments in alliance with internationally oriented financial institutions. It is a tool of accumulation pushed powerfully by the American state and other money-center governments. Within corporations, therefore, it is the financial people, not those involved in production or sales, who set company strategies. When the financial sector moves beyond lubricating the wheels of commerce to dominate the "real" economy, problems develop. Companies are seen as portfolios of financial assets to be bought and sold, reorganized, merged, spun off, or closed down for short-term profit and tax benefits.

Financialization has become the leading organizing logic of accumulation in Anglo-American-style economies and has had impacts elsewhere to a substantial degree. In its shortening time horizons of productive capital, it allows a redistribution of profits from the realm of production of actual goods and non-financial services to speculator profits and enlarges the sphere in which money is made from money. Speculating on and manipulating the future value of financial assets implies consequences for citizens. It increases uncertainty and risk with regard to decisions about financing consumer purchases, homes, education, retirement, and other quality-of-life decisions. Internationally the rapid increase in financial flows promotes overextension of national governments in the same manner as easy credit destabilizes households and businesses.

To Gerald Epstein (2002:3), the term financialization denotes "the increasing importance of financial markets, financial motives, financial institutions, and financial elites in the operation of the economy and its governing institutions, both at the national and international levels." William Milberg (2008:5) sees the term financialization as applying to the greater share of GDP in the industrial countries accounted for by the financial sector, gross international capital flows having grown much faster than world output and trade in goods and services, and nonfinancial firms increasingly involved in finance rather than production as both a source and use of their funds. Mathew Watson (2009:258) suggests that financialization can refer to "the attempt by governments to subject the entire process of macroeconomic management to the needs of a 'finance-led growth regime,'" and the attempt by firms to enhance their standing on the stock market by engaging in "value-based management" designed to expand their asset-based wealth.

Some political economists combine phenomenological characteristics with a strong capital logic approach. Stanley Malinowitz (2009:1) understands financialization "in general terms as the increased domination of the power and logic of finance in the neoliberal period." This is a broadening of the construct so that it takes in more facets affecting the defining institutions of our era. In this regard Stockhammer writes:

> The notion of financialization covers a wide range of phenomena: the deregulation of the financial sector and the proliferation of new financial instruments, the liberalization of international capital flows and increasing instability on exchange rate markets, a shift to market-based financial systems,

the emergence of institutional investors as major players on financial markets and the boom (and bust) on asset markets, shareholder value orientation and changes in corporate governance (of non-financial business).(2008:184)

Writing during the expansion that preceded the world financial crisis, two trade union researchers discussing their industry point out that

> as "impatient" capital penetrates sectors such as food and beverages, hotels, and catering, it accelerates layoffs, casualization and outsourcing. One of the many consequences of this is that unions seeking to bargain changes in conditions, negotiate the impact of restructuring, or challenge closures run up against new financial power-holders who are not interested in arguments about improvements in production or services, increased productive capacity, new product lines, long-term viability of markets, consumer needs, etc. (Rossman and Greenfield 2006:5)

Financialization has not only changed corporate governance but proven to be a form of redistributive growth. In this regard Thomas Palley (2007:14) suggests a "financialization thesis," which is that "these developments regarding increased debt, changes in the functional distribution of income, wage stagnation, and increased income inequality are significantly due to changes wrought by financial interests."

Spreading risk does not make it disappear. It only changes who is exposed to it. There was widespread anger as many investments that were sold as safe turned out to be toxic. Local governments, pension funds, and individual investors all over the world suffered from taking on far more risk than they initially thought possible. In 2007 a remote Norwegian town north of the Arctic Circle had its moment of fame when it was discovered it had made multimillion-dollar bets on complicated financial products designed by Citigroup and sold to it by a Norwegian bank, only to watch most of the value of the investments collapse. Since then, the number of jurisdictions known to have bought derivatives that they did not understand and that would damage their fiscal health has grown remarkably.

In the wake of the financial crisis, opinion has turned against financialization to the point that some definitions include normative condemnation. In such a vein Bresser-Pereira (2010:2) writes, "Financialization will be understood here as a distorted financial arrangement based on the creation of artificial financial wealth, that is, financial wealth disconnected from real wealth or from the production of goods and services." More generally, political economists identify income and spending changes driven by financialization as underpinning a "broader distributional, ethical, and moral repercussions across society" (Lapavitas 2009:110). Deregulation of finance is the result of the influence of the financial sector on governments, revealing a process Jacoby (2008:10) has called "deregulatory capture."

Robin Blackburn (2006:42) characterizes this growing and systemic power of finance and financial engineering as "grey capitalism" because relations of ownership and responsibility have become weakened or blurred. He writes, "In the end the largest and most famous of corporations have only a precarious and provisional autonomy within the new world of business—ultimately they are playthings of the capital markets." While perhaps somewhat exaggerated in the sense that financial markets respond to and anticipate changes in the perceived values of assets, including the creditworthiness of corporations, and chief executive officers have discretion over strategic decisions in meeting market demands, these financial pressures exercise a potent influence over how success is measured. Blackburn is right as well when he suggests that investors consider the corporation itself as simply "an accidental bundle of liabilities and assets that is there to be reorganized to maximize shareholder value" (43). Investors in the era of financialization were far from the patient capital of the earlier period. Given the pressure on institutional investors to maximize short-term returns, there was a constant churning of assets and, thus, pressure on companies to maximize quarterly earnings and current stock price. The incentive structure makes this rational behavior but can produce irrational results in terms of the long-run health of companies and the system. The increase in intrafinancial system leverage, which spread danger rather than reducing risk, the complexity of derivative products, and the huge increase in trading volume relative to the rest of the economy (all to be discussed at length) raise a crucial issue, in retrospect and prospect, of whether increased financial intensity has delivered added value for the real economy.

The financial sector's impact on corporate governance and industrial restructuring increased economic insecurity and fostered a dramatic rise in inequality and stagnation of working-class living standards. It increased systemic fragility and engendered crises. Wall Street guided policy makers to embrace solutions that led to new asset bubbles. Neoliberal globalization promoted the freedom of capital movement, which intensified and spread such dangers. Economists were slow to see the downside of unregulated global financial markets and, in their claim that everyone benefited, ignored globalization's redistributive elements. Financialization expanded significantly faster than the overall growth of global GDP, with securitization, pension investments, continued privatization of public enterprises, an increase in leveraged buyout activities, and the growth in market valuation fed by income growth at the upper end of the income distribution.

The Growth of Finance

The world's financial assets include bank deposits, government debt, private debt equity, and equity securities. In 1980 the total value of world financial assets was $12 trillion, about equal to global GDP, but less than a tenth of the figure a quarter of a century later. In 2005 it was more than three times global GDP (McKinsey & Company 2006:9). Globalization and financialization profoundly reconstructed money center economies, replacing polluting industries with clean, information-based finance to drive accumulation.

The centrality of the United States to the process of greater financialization of the internationalization economy can be highlighted by a number of measures. The global share of U.S. equity securities increased from 37 percent to 45 percent between 1993 and 2003 owing to both higher earnings and, even more, the increase in price/earning ratios accepted by investors—increasingly foreign investors buying U.S. assets. The U.S. financial market is the largest in the world, with 37 percent of global financial stock, 45 percent of global equities, and 51 percent of private debt security stock (McKinsey & Company 2006:86). The share of financial-sector employment as a percentage of the labor force grew by 21 percent between 1970 and 2002 as the growth rate for the entire economy fell (Felix 2005: table 7). Corporate profits of the financial sector of the U.S. economy in 2004 were $300.6 billion, compared to $534.2 billion for all nonfinancial domestic industries, or about 40 percent of all domestic corporate profits that year. They had been less than 2 percent of total domestic corporate profits forty years earlier, a remarkable indication of the growth of financialization (President's Council of Economic Advisors 2006: table B-91). McKinsey &Company estimates that one-fourth of U.S. market capitalization is attributable to profits from foreign subsidiaries. (This is a more realistic estimate than the one offered in government reports that come from the filings by corporations for tax purposes, which inflate foreign earnings.)

Some American industrial cities were reborn as service centers and above all financial centers. As postindustrial production sites, they were not in their essentials different from older industrial ones in this new manufacturing-like activity. Writing of New York, Albert Scardino (1987:C1) explains, "The debt industry requires vast interiors where thousands of factory hands can assemble, package and warehouse their product. The industry calls them trading floors, but the activity on them resembles the scenes along the lower Manhattan waterfront a century ago, when tall-masted ships called on New York from around the world to disgorge their goods for the new American empire." He sees the telephone lines delivering "the world's cash to be remixed as if in a bottling plant, squirted into different containers, capped and shipped back out." Financial centers bought and sold paper promises, by packaging an unbelievable range of such promises as financial products and selling them to pension funds, municipal governments, insurance companies, and other investors. It was the unwillingness to slow this financial production line that led to questionable, then dangerous, and finally catastrophic consequences.

New-style bankers originated and distributed assets rather than holding them until they were paid back. The short run dominated, and not only in finance narrowly defined but in all aspects of the economy under its influence. Relational contracting and long-term, established ties gave way to spot markets and very short-term thinking. In the era of global neoliberalism, the Anglo-American version of capitalism triumphed over European and Japanese corporatist models. The autonomous role of the social partners, labor and government, was diminished. Labor's wealth was managed according to short-term financial criteria, whether in pension funds or employees' individual investments in mutual funds. The interpenetration of the various distinct financial sectors of insurance companies, investment banks, thrifts, merchant banking, and credit card companies was accompanied by increased finance-driven mergers and acquisition activity. Nonfinancial corporations came to be dwarfed by the profitability generated by their financial subsidiaries. General Motors Acceptance Corporation, which financed car sales, became more profitable than GM's car production. Sears credit cards became the key to whatever profitability Sears the retailer had. (Indeed, Sears used its cash to buy financial firms, including a major real estate broker, Caldwell Banker, and a large investment bank, Dean Witter.) General Electric's financial arm, which once primarily funded purchases of the parent company's products, became GE's dominant profit center, expanding into commercial real estate, home mortgages, and leasing. It financed mergers, and it also owned a major investment firm, Kidder, Peabody.

When the financial bubble burst, the cost of this transformation of American capitalism was more visible. In 2009, after government rescue of GE

Capital (the nation's largest nonbank financial firm), Jeff Immelt, General Electric's chief executive, gave a speech in Detroit where he said the country had to refocus its economy on manufacturing and exporting if it wished to escape from its sad economic situation. He suggested that the United States should have 20 percent of its workforce in manufacturing, double the current proportion and that the country had outsourced too much of its capabilities to make things and relied too much on finance (Bailey and Kim 2009). In 2011 President Obama appointed Immelt chair of the President's Council on Jobs and Competitiveness, which replaced the President's Economic Recovery Advisory Board headed by the departing Paul Volcker. The rebranding was part of the administration's effort to show it was serious about job creation. The choice of the head of GE was not uncontroversial. The company had cut tens of thousands of American jobs in recent years, closed plants that were moneymakers, and moved the work out of the country.

Sixty-four percent of GE's revenues in 2010 came from overseas. Its aggressive tax planning allowed it to pay zero taxes on over $14 billion in profits for 2010, a story that two months after Immelt's appointment received widespread media coverage, although not on NBC (owned by GE). Some accounts quoted President Obama, who had said when announcing that Immelt would head the Council on Jobs and Competition that the head of GE had "something to teach businesses across America about competing in the global economy." Many hoped that he did not mean how to avoid paying taxes in the United States. It was reported that "a review of company filings and Congressional records shows that one of the most striking advantages of General Electric is its ability to lobby for, win and take advantage of tax breaks" (Kocieniewski 2011).

The president's shift in focus from recovery from crisis to economic nationalism made political sense. But as Robert Reich points out, "The recession wasn't due to loss of 'competitiveness' relative to the Chinese or anyone else. American corporations are enormously competitive, racking up some of their highest profits in history. But much of their success comes outside the US. General Electric has more foreign employees than American. General Motors sells more cars in China than at home." What many were missing in this turn was the president's failure to address this "decoupling of corporate profits from jobs, and explain what he'll do to get jobs back." Reich argues that this made his plans for reviving competitiveness a distraction from the real task. Driving the point home, he adds, "Government exists to protect and advance the interests of average working families. Without it, Americans have to rely on increasingly global corporations, whose only interest is making money wherever it can be made" (Reich 2010). President Obama's focus on innovation was welcomed even if it was not clear what government could and should do, and whether innovation would create jobs in the United States in anywhere approaching the number the country so badly needed. While U.S.-based companies may produce high-value-added products, the jobs resulting from much of this innovation are in other parts of the world.

Financialization in the Long Run

From the 1970s the dominance of U.S.-based finance was a powerful instrumentality through which U.S. economic power was asserted. Ironically, for the dual nature of the new reality has not been adequately grasped, it was the expansion of financialization that also set the terms on which U.S. hegemony was to be challenged in the new century. The United States was following the path of previous hegemonic powers, which expanded the scope of financial control to extract rentier income from rising centers of accumulation. World-systems theorists point out that previous great powers—Genoa, Holland, Great Britain—when no longer paramount in product markets moved decisively to financialization (Arrighi and Silver 1999:258–64). Their loss of leadership was accompanied by the geographic relocation of the centers of capital accumulation.

The United States may be on a historical trajectory not dissimilar to that of these previous great powers. As described by Giovanni Arrighi:

> One kind or another of financialization has always been the predominant response to the over-accumulation problem of the established organizing centers of the system of accumulation. Thanks to their continuing centrality in networks of high finance, these centers have been best positioned to turn the intensifying competition for mobile capital to their advantage and thereby reflate their profits and power at the expense of the rest of the system. Over time, however, financial expansions have promoted the geographic relocation of the centers of capital accumulation by rerouting surplus capital to states and regions capable of ensuring a more secure and profitable spatial-temporal fix to the overaccumulation crisis. Previously dominant centers have thus been faced with the Sisyphean task of containing forces that keep rolling forth with ever renewed strength. (2004:536)

While the U.S. experience followed this pattern, the deep financial crisis and the increase in foreign ownership of system-significant financial institutions adds a globalization dimension to this historic pattern. The dollar as the reserve currency allowed the United States to in effect print up green pieces of paper (and expand their electronic equivalent) and exchange them for real goods and services produced abroad, and so to consume beyond its ability to produce, initially with little immediate discernible cost, and to finance wars without correspondingly taxing its citizens. Now, however, the United States, as a significant debtor nation, must take account of creditor demands and preferences. For example, Washington's hold on the International Monetary Fund (IMF) is challenged by the need of that institution to raise great sums, which can only come from nations that want greater voting strength within the organization in return. Financial claims more broadly are shifting with the rapid growth of systematically significant emergent economic powers (Tabb 2007). As Robert Skidelsky (2009:33) writes, "Every historian knows that a hegemonic currency is part of an imperial system of power relations." For Washington to end the global imbalance, it must acquiesce to a pluralistic world, give up its status as the global superpower, and accept a reconfigured system of global governance in which its role is diminished. This, as Skidelsky says, "will require a huge mental realignment in the United States." It is an unthinkable realignment for a very large number of Americans, fueling angry nationalist populism.

The noncore economies of the world system—the developing economies as they are called—accounted for 37 percent of world output by 2008 (and 45 percent of total global output measured in purchasing power parity terms). Impressively, almost 60 percent of the increase in world output between 2000 and 2008 was in these countries, half of it in the BRICs (Brazil, Russia, India, and China) by themselves. In the case of Russia, its fortune shifted with the price of oil, natural gas, and minerals and the degree to which its corruption or gangster- or state-dominated capitalism was seen as ascendant. Brazil, China, and India are expected to grow rapidly, as are two dozen other emerging market economies to varying degrees. In these countries, many of the growing companies are family managed, in need of capital infusion to go global, and ready for reorganization. U.S.-based private equity companies like Kohlberg Kravis Roberts, Carlyle, and Blackstone see major profit opportunities in the faster-growing economies of the former periphery of the world system. For such firms, foreign market profits were rising three times as fast as those from the United States in the opening years of the twenty-first century.

While financial flows a century ago rivaled those today, their composition was quite different. In the late nineteenth and early twentieth centuries, bonds and other loans for infrastructure (heavily for railroad construction) and to fund government debt predominated. In the second half of the twentieth century, foreign direct investment and portfolio holdings were more important. But the biggest difference in the era of global neoliberalism became the huge speculative transactions, currency movements, and the sale of derivatives of all kinds on the international market. A diminishing proportion of financial flows by the first decade of the twenty-first century (a trend well under way in the final decades of the previous century) went to productive investment. The dramatic increase in the use of financial instruments, from credit cards to the guaranteeing of commercial paper, occurred through money center banks, which became dominant players in local economies around the world. The strength of these large international banks of the core had been established through their capacity to develop and market new financial products as well as their presumed skill in selling their ability at parsing risk. Given the underdevelopment of Asian financial markets, it seemed efficient for surplus savings to find their way to New York, with its deep, liquid financial markets denominated in dollars, the reserve currency of choice. That Wall Street seemed to be addressing a shortage of financial capital seemed incongruous in a world in which the sheer quantity of such assets was growing so dramatically (Caballero 2006). Confidence in the capacities, reliability, and expertise of Wall Street was challenged with the meltdown of 2008.

Economists Confront Reality

When the financial system went into free fall, the economics profession was confronted with a loss of legitimacy, its failed models mugged by reality. "The credit crisis showed," *Financial Times* columnist John Authers writes, "that the most basic assumptions of the investment management industry were wrong." A leader in the *Economist* suggests that "of all the economic bubbles that have been pricked, few have burst more spectacularly than the reputation of economics itself." Adair Turner (2010a:1318), Britain's chief financial regulator, calls attention to an "over-simplistic and overconfident economics" which helped create the crisis. Lord Turner has been outspoken in his condemnation of the "quasi-religious" dogma of finance that assumes that markets are always right and regulators should allow profitable activities that have little or no social benefit, direct or indirect, and of bankers who push money around, enriching themselves in the process while sewing social distress. (Mr. Turner was hardly an uninformed critic or government bureaucrat. He became wealthy working at the consulting firm McKinsey & Company and is a past head of the Confederation of British Industry, the main business lobbying group in Britain.)

The collapse in 2007–8 was clearly inconsistent with the expectations of received doctrine. A central part of the professional consensus, that prices in financial markets reflect relevant information and so correctly allocate resources (Fama 1970:383), was found wanting. For decades it had been asserted that "there is no other proposition in economics which has more solid empirical evidence supporting it than the efficient market hypothesis" (Jensen 1978:95). After the deep financial crises it was hard to escape the conclusion that markets have not met the efficiency criteria but misallocated resources on a gargantuan scale. Economists had generally been blind to what was happening. The core approach of the mainstream had been that "progress in economic thinking means getting better and better abstraction, analogue models, not better verbal observations about the real world" (Lucas 1980a:700). But the real world ridiculed abstract models in which events so damaging to the lives of hundreds of millions were not a possibility. The approach that follows looks at different models, critiquing those that fail the test of relevancy and interpreting what happens in the real world. Better descriptive explanations fit alternative framings that privilege institutions, incentives, and the psychology of market participants. Better descriptions of the real world become the building blocks for better theory. More acute verbal observations and alternative stories encourage scrutiny of relations left unexamined by mainstream modeling.

Neoliberalism had both a negative moment of destruction of the old national Keynesian order and a positive moment of the creation of new institutional forms and social relations. In chapter 2 a social structure of accumulation (SSA) framework is developed to compare and contrast the institutional norms of the post–World War II period and the era of global neoliberalism. Observers living through transitional periods can fail to see how tensions inherent in an SSA's undoing are necessary preludes to the emergence of new social elements that will begin to transform one SSA into its successor. Thus, initially many analysts saw neoliberalism as an effort to turn the clock back to a kind of capitalism that no longer exists. There was reluctance to see the new world of greater risk and destabilization of postwar accommodations as anything but an era of crisis. Andrew Gamble (2006:21) notes that it took some time to appreciate that neoliberalism "did have some distinctive new features as the prefix 'neo' implied, and was an integral part of the re-organization of capitalist relations which was taking place." While contradictions within an SSA grow over time and eventually undermine its capacity to reproduce its stabilizing features, the transformative role of financialization for global neoliberalism brought a specific dynamic into play.

Finance has always been central to capitalism, primarily as a servant of development by mobilizing savings held by some individuals and relending them to those wishing to borrow. But finance has two moments that need to be distinguished. One is the traditionally stressed function of collecting savings of those without immediate need to make purchases and channeling the monies to investors, to businesses, to governments, and to individuals who desire to increase immediate expenditures (and who commit to paying back the loans over time). This function is crucial to the growth prospects of society. The other is the buying and selling of risk, an arena in which speculation dominates and mechanisms that allow the purchase of insurance against some occurrence, a presumption of certainty for a price on some transaction that will take place at a future date, can become predominantly vehicles for gambling with other people's money and the society's future. In contradistinction to the mainstream finance theory that claims expectations are rational and financial markets are efficient and best left to regulate themselves, theorizing explanation of endogenous financial crises in chapter 3 draws on an alternative approach offered by Hyman Minsky (who remarkably wrote during a period of financial stability). His understanding of the incentives of speculators and of financial cycles explains the way expectations can become self-reinforcing and then suddenly reverse, consonant with the stress by Frank Knight and Maynard Keynes on uncertainty, to explain financial cycles. Minsky's contribution was to understand that when the economy appears to be expanding smoothly and optimism prevails over a long period, a contraction is likely to follow. The time to start worrying is when there are expectations of cloudless expansion. Cycles are endogenous to our capitalist economy.

Banks at the heart of the system traditionally acquire short-term deposits and make long- term loans. This duration mismatch is inherent in the nature of banks. A loss of confidence can lead to problems if there are large withdrawals of short-term liabilities since long-term assets are heavily illiquid. In the United States the Depression era created the Federal Deposit Insurance Corporation (FDIC), protecting depositor money. The demise of the 1930s regulatory order and the failure to modernize regulation allowed a pattern of accumulation that was both necessary, in the sense that without it the surplus capital would have had no place to go, and at the same time dangerous, as the world found out in that it greatly increased short-term borrowing by financial institutions supported by collateral subject to sudden repricing. The deregulation of financial markets allowed the dramatic growth of a shadow financial system of special investment vehicles, highly leveraged hedge funds, and private equity, as discussed in chapter 4.

It will be argued that any analytic separation of a regulated banking system from a shadow system should be entertained with caution. It was the commercial and investment banks that, as heavy users of the overnight repurchase market, were in the most serious trouble when their lenders refused to roll over short-term loans, with immediate and system-threatening consequences. When caught in a credit squeeze, these borrowers who are experiencing difficulty meeting obligations produce knock-on impacts because of the chains of interdependent obligations in a highly interconnected financial system. While regulators were well aware of this phenomenon, they were, and remain, hesitant to demand of the banks much more in the way of long-term capital since this could lead activity to gravitate away from the regulated banking system even more. The banks' problems were ignored partly because modern finance theory supported risk-management techniques that use historical volatility as a proxy for risk. It was presumed that a fall in volatility meant less risk.

In its discussion of the factors that led to the near collapse of the financial system in late 2007, chapter 5 recounts events that are not unfamiliar to those who have followed accounts of the Great Recession. What stands out in this telling is the extent to which illegality and opportunism were not marginal to these events, but central, requiring fundamental qualification or correction to conventional wisdom on finance and the macro economy. The economic collapse brought awareness that the American financial system was far more corrupt than it appeared in economists' modeling, and that credit flows needed to be explicitly modeled. Unless the extent of opportunism and even outright fraudulent practices are acknowledged, along with system fragility caused by interdependent loan commitments, there is likely to be inadequate regulation. Each credit bubble reveals the extent of corporate hubris and mutually supportive webs of collusion among rating agencies, banks, lawyers, regulators, accountants, and others. Unlike approaches that attempt to isolate the economy from politics, this work considers the relation be-tween the state and the market and privileges the psychology of economic actors, revealing a full set of actions, including "to lie, cheat, steal, mislead, disguise, obfuscate, feign, distort and confuse" (Williamson 1985:51). Oliver Williamson's economic man, who exhibits "self-interest-seeking-with-guile" (198), is hard to model rigorously and so has tended to fall by the wayside in mainstream modeling. But it is essential to understanding behavior in fi-nancial markets. The faith many economists have in the efficiency of markets obscures features often present in their actual operation. In no area is this as true as in finance, where market failure proves so costly.

Political economy as deployed here understands possible incentives of mar-ket participants to include rational decisions to break the law, trade on insider information, and withhold or distort information. Criminal cooperation (in-cluding by so-called gatekeepers whose reputation for probity in transactions is presumed to guarantee the integrity of an exchange and the proper valu-ation of assets), circles of collusion, and fraudulent practices are revealed in downturns when looting strategies are made public. These are connections that prove difficult to fit into deterministic models. The insistence on separat-ing the economic moment from the political (and the criminal), each best left to specialists, reduces the practicality of the advice offered to policy makers by economists, who are frequently seen as political innocents. In the wake of scandals, there are demands for serious enforcement of ethical norms and for new laws to close loopholes. Yet proposed measures to limit structural danger provoke warnings of the harm that will be done by "excessive" regulations, and legislators are urged not to go "too far," stifling innovation, imposing "unreasonable" costs on firms, dampening economic growth, and inhibiting the ability of American firms to compete internationally.

Negotiations over seemingly technical matters are politically contested. The investment theory of government embraced here suggests that powerful, fi-nancially well-endowed individuals and business interests invest in politicians, expecting a return to their campaign contributions and lobbying, and that elected officials, given the expense of running for office, are often influenced by such investors to adopt legislation and regulatory enforcement preferred by these interests. What is impressive in debate over financial reform, discussed in chapter 6, is the degree to which regulators had accepted theories of how markets naturally operate to produce efficient allocation. These proved flawed, yet it was difficult to envision an alternative regulatory structure sufficient to protect the economy from a new, and perhaps more painful, financial crisis.

As the importance of globalization became evident, attention at first focused on the impact of trade in the restructuring of national economies. It took some time for the awareness to grow that globalization and the deregulation that accompanied it made possible a three-stage process in which different aspects were sequentially dominant: first trade, 1950–1970; then foreign investment, from the late 1960s; and finally financial liberalization, from the early 1980s. The importance of the third financial stage, as Deepak Nayyar (2006:145) notes, "had two dimensions: the deregulation of the domestic financial sector in the industrialised countries and the introduction of convertibility on capital account in the balance of payments." He also calls attention to the fact that globalization, "at a scorching pace since the mid-1980s, is not unrelated to the dismantling of regulations and controls."

Financialization has occurred in a context of globalization, and there has been growth in the importance of finance within countries. Between 1990 and 2006 the number of countries whose financial assets exceeded the value of their GDP more than doubled (from thirty-three to seventy-two). By 2006 all the industrial economies and the largest emerging market countries had financial markets at least twice the size of their GDP (Farrell et al. 2008). At the peak of the financial bubble (2006), the value of the world's equities was rising by $9 trillion or 20 percent a year (at constant exchange rates). It was also in 2006 that China became the world's largest exporter of capital. In mid-2007 the value of euros in circulation exceeded that of U.S. dollars for the first time. While the focus of this study is on the United States, financialization in other countries is discussed, as are imbalances in the world system, in chapter 7.

Chapter 8 is devoted to consideration of the lessons to be learned from the Great Recession and economic policy debate over the future of the United States. The argument in the first half is that there is a path forward toward more effective understanding and regulation of finance, but that there are enormous obstacles standing in the way. The second part considers what might be done to improve the state of the U.S. economy and by extension, other countries' economies in the face of the realities that have been discussed. Between here and there the project is to interpret the role of financialization in the global financial crisis that still affects our lives and in creating the contemporary economy and its ongoing tensions. The task of mobilizing productive assets both for job creation and to address the obvious needs of people and the planet is daunting because it involves major redistribution of political power and greater government initiative in directing the use of the social surplus.

2

Financialization and Social Structures of Accumulation

Financial investors are not only claiming ever higher returns for their assets; they are changing the social framework and environment for all economic and increasingly parts of social activity, putting them under enhanced competitive pressure and forcing them to subordinate every tradition, social relationship and activity under the imperative of rapid return to investment.

—JÖRG HUFFSCHMID, 2008

. . . a new aristocracy of finance, a new sort of parasites in the shape of promoters, speculators, and merely nominal directors; a whole system of swindling and cheating by means of corporate juggling, stock jobbing, and stock speculation. It is private production without the control of private property.

—KARL MARX, 1894

The social structure of accumulation (SSA) framework suggests that periods of growth require a coherent set of mutually reinforcing institutions favorable to capital accumulation. These involve the creation of relatively lasting accommodations between contesting social forces, including stable understandings between capital and labor, the United States and the rest of the world, capital and the state, capitalists and other capitalists, and citizens and their government. Institutional stability provides conditions under which the behavior of others, the meaning of events, and the likely outcome of actions can be predicted over the relevant planning horizon with enough confidence to provide consistent expectations, and so encourage investment and promote growth. Such institutional understandings and practices take on a certain solidity so that expectations stabilize, and people can act with confidence that mutually understood rules and norms will be followed. The SSA framework gets at this essential feature of the growth of capitalism: that despite its continuing dynamism, there is a relative stability to institutions over an extended period, during which regime norms allow for predictable system reproduction (McDonough 2010). The breakdown of such once mutually reinforcing accords or understandings of relationships between key constituencies, so that existing expectations of stability no longer govern, signals a crisis of the SSA. Over decades, one SSA gives way as contradictions and conflicts grow, and eventually a new set of accommodations come into being. Transitions from one SSA to another take time. Transitions are periods of disruption and slow growth in which issues of distribution of economic adjustment burdens become highly politicized. Following the Great Recession, the United States entered such a period.

The SSA Transition

A social structure of accumulation framework can be helpful in understanding regulatory regimes and the institutions that constrain and enable markets in particular historical contexts. Developments in the forces of production create pressure for change in the social relations of production. The accommodations of a particular social structure of accumulation come under pressure as technological possibilities change the bargaining power of economic actors relative to each other. In any given situation different outcomes are possible, depending on the political strength, consciousness, and state of organization of interest groups and class fractions. The differences between these regimes affect pricing behavior, labor's ability to influence wages and benefits, tax incidence, interest rates and their volatility, and the extent of public goods provision. These institutional relations have both micro- and macroeconomic consequences. The SSA framework and its French cousin, regulation theory (Aglietta 1976; Boyer 1990), provide a framing perspective within which isolated market phenomena and their societal impacts can be better understood.

Theorists dealing with the social structure of accumulation suggest that SSAs typically last three decades or so, followed by a period of breakdown and slow growth (although dating issues are ever present in application of such schemas). The demise of an SSA is signaled by internal contradictions, which grow to the point where once effective institutional accommodations fail, and a new set of understandings and social relations emerge to take their place. SSA theorists (Kotz, McDonough, and Reich 1994) have focused on four social structures of accumulation in the United States: (1) from the Civil War to the late-nineteenth-century financial crises, (2) from these crises to the reorganization of the banking and financial system to 1929, (3) the New Deal and post–World War II, and (4) free-market global neoliberalism. Early SSA theorists saw the stagflation period of the 1970s as a crisis of the postwar

stage of capitalism (Gordon, Edwards, and Reich 1982). Falling profits intensified international competition and dramatic inflation, and, indeed, stagflation brought the accommodations of the national Keynesian SSA to an end.
The SSA of global neoliberalism includes its free-market ideology, decline
in coverage by the social safety net, more individualistic citizen-state relationships, deregulation, harsh capital-labor relations, and reduced financial
regulation of banks.

Individual entrepreneurs led the early industrialization and growth of
American business. From around 1840 there was a growth in middle management and finally the first managerial revolution. This involved the replacement of the founders, owners, and representatives of investors with
professionals, in a context where owners did not manage building the enterprise often for no other reason than that compensation, which tended to
correlate with size, led to different sorts of misallocation of resources. Early
on, the new managers would have been engineers in manufacturing firms;
later they would have had business degrees. By the 1970s corporate restructuring began to undermine what has been thought of as the 1870s model as
lawyers became more important and finance began to dominate over production. CEOs increasingly came from the ranks of financial specialists. By the
time of the hostile takeovers in the 1980s, finance dominated. The market in
corporate control presumed that good managers could manage any firm and
that the key to good management was financial skills. The task of management was to free cash flow from the companies. In the process labor was
shed; physical assets sold; and whole units put on the block, in contrast to
earlier capitalist expansion, understood by Joseph Schumpeter, which comes
from innovation. As the business historian Alfred Chandler has stressed, the
large firm has historically been supported by patient capital.

The governing paradigm for most of the twentieth century, mass production or fordism (after the man and the assembly line manufacturing model
he developed), with its standardized product and long production runs,
replaced the paradigm of artisanal craft workers, which was dominant into
the second half of the nineteenth century. Unskilled and semiskilled hands
were part of a great division of labor bringing thousands of workers together
under one roof. Ford's assembly-line method, with its high fixed but low
variable cost structure, meant the more standardized items produced, the
cheaper the selling price. Mass production supplied the consumer market
and created the fabled American middle class, with rising income in the era
of national Keynesianism. But after the dominant industries of the twentieth

century (textiles, auto, rubber, and steel) declined in the face of mature markets at home and global production, often by U.S.-based transnationals, capital was withdrawn domestically from these industries by financiers, buyout artists, and merger activities.

To the elements discussed by SSA theorists, it is important to add another, the financial accommodations of the regulatory regime (Wolfson 1994). The financial structure in the United States in the national Keynesian SSA has been called "3-6-3" banking, so named because, in its simplified telling, it involved banks paying a regulated 3 percent interest to depositors, lending at 6 percent, and the bank president getting to the golf course by midafternoon. This orderly state of affairs was possible thanks to the separation of commercial and investment banking established by New Deal legislation, the prohibition of payments on demand deposits, the Fed's Regulation Q, controlling interest rates on savings accounts, federal deposit insurance, and relatively strict government oversight.

In the 1960s and 1970s senior management in large corporations tended to be risk adverse, maximizing growth, not necessarily profitability, retaining "free cash flow" to the maximal extent possible, and sometimes using it to buy other firms often unrelated to their prime business. "Retain and reinvest" was most strongly practiced by conglomerates like Gulf & Western and ITT, which grew through mergers and typically expanded into areas managers knew little about. Managers, by maximizing the size of their firms and minimizing risk, produced higher compensation for top executives than by being more entrepreneurial and taking risks to increase the value of stockholder equity. Poor performance eventually brought this mode of corporate leadership into disrepute. When growth slowed, with the ending of the era of national Keynesianism, principal-agent theory suggested that managers, to be rewarded for results (as measured by increased stock prices), should be paid above a base salary with stock options to align their interests with stockholders and improve performance. It was also believed that by increasing company debt levels, not only could more be paid to owners but managers would be put under pressure to repay debt obligations, and this would force them to be more effective in increasing profitability. This, as has been discussed, has been shown to be incorrect.

Finance in the current SSA is very different in relation to the economy and in the character of financial institutions and their functioning. Commercial banks depend on borrowing funds every day to be paid back the next on the repurchase or repo market (although the loans are typically renewed and in normal times represent a stable source of funding). These, rather than depositor monies, are the major source to fund mortgages, auto loans, and other consumer and business borrowing. In the United States alone, trillions of dollars are transferred between banks each day to support $50 trillion in outstanding credit (Ceccetti 2009:51). This great dependence on credit increases sales of all manner of commodities and supports speculative activity. The extent of leverage involved in the borrowing is much higher than in the era of national Keynesianism, and the centrality of the repo market characterizes the new period.

SSAs are dominated by political coalitions. The history of the American political economy suggests that between 1896 and 1932 a center-right coalition was hegemonic, and between 1932 and 1968 a left-center coalition was dominant. The first period ended as financial interests, SSA theorists suggest, gained at the expense of workers and farmers so that demand by consumers did not keep up with the capacity of the economy to produce, and underconsumption resulted. This structural imbalance led to the Great Depression. The second ended in the aftermath of the Vietnam War.

The decline of the national Keynesian SSA can be dated from the closing years of the Vietnam War in the late 1960s, or perhaps the abandonment of the Bretton Woods postwar international financial regime and the oil price increase by the Organization of Petroleum Exporting Countries (OPEC) of the early 1970s. The global neoliberal SSA only established its positive moment in the 1980s, signaled by Reagan's election. The George McGovern wing tried to move the liberal-labor alliance too far for many traditional party supporters, and the bloc fell to defection of Reagan Democrats. The ascendant right-center coalition dominated national politics through the years Bill Clinton was in the White House and weakened with the extremism of the George W. Bush–Dick Cheney administration.

In the United States neoliberalism was spherically coherent; its dominant elements, attitudes, and practices were mutually reinforcing. With regard to the state-citizen relationship, there was a rejection of the previous entitlement presumptions of welfare-state provisioning and the regulatory role of the state in favor of deregulation, contracting out, and privatization. The capital-labor discord was one of flexibility, higher cost of job loss, downward pressure on wages and benefits, individualism in place of solidarity, and a greater degree of job insecurity. The previous core-periphery relation between the richer countries of the world system and the rest, in which the former are industrialized and the latter providers of raw materials, was replaced by the emergence of newly industrializing economies and significant deindustrialization of much of the former manufacturing core. Neoliberalism proposed a trade-not-aid development approach for the poorer countries. Capital-capital relations were globalized. Complex commodity chains bespoke cooperation-competition patterns among technologically sophisticated firms and unremitting pressure on suppliers.

In each SSA there is a regime of accumulation, labor relations, taxation, spending priorities of government, and regulatory norms consonant with the composition of dominant class alliances and the ideological predilections favored by this historic bloc. There is an overlap, if not always a total coincidence, between the dominance of political coalitions and the economics of an SSA and an interdependence of the institutions of an SSA, which form its unified internal structure as overdetermined, each shaped by and incorporating elements of other institutions of the SSA with which it interacts (Lippitt 2010). For some social scientists, the systems of social relations, their patterns of roles, relationships, and forms of control can include broader categories of race, gender, religion, education, sexual preference, and more. It is possible, although political economists have declined to go this far, to build even broader models using such variables in keeping with the use of the terminology "social structure." SSA theorists from the economics discipline have been happy to leave such "sticky problems of culture" to others (Sewell 1992).

David Kotz (2010) has distinguished two types of SSAs: a regulationist institutional structure characterized by an interventionist state, cooperation between capital and labor and other accomodationist elements; and a liberal institutionalist structure in which state intervention is limited, capital is aggressively combative toward labor, and laissez-faire policy dominance reigns. ("Liberal" here is used in its pre–New Deal meaning, which is also termed neoliberal). The postwar national Keynesian SSA, with its positive role for activist government interventionism to preserve stability and promote growth and to address market failures, muted intercapitalist rivalry, encouraged cooperation between labor and capital, and fostered the Pax Americana under U.S. hegemony. It was a regulationist SSA. Based on such thinking, the financial crisis can signal the end of the global neoliberal regime's period of confident growth and a prolonged period of stagnation and uncertainty until a new SSA comes into being. These are not matters simply of economic laws, but of agency and political movement building in the face of the perceived failure of an aging SSA.

A sitting president can come to personify the breakdown of a failing SSA even as a breakthrough figure of a rising SSA is recognized for his or her game-changing policies and public philosophy. Ronald Reagan was greeted as bringing in a new era of neoliberalism with his stress on rugged individualism and condemnation of government paternalism. The new SSA he helped usher in encompassed a new citizen-state accord with its promise of opportunity and liberty; the business-government accommodation of low taxes and deregulation; a business-labor nonaccord of anti-unionism, demands for concessions, increase in contingent work; and a U.S.–rest of world framework of expanding freedom and the magic of the marketplace. George W. Bush serves as the bookend to this SSA, whose institutional priors he pursued enthusiastically, but to poor effect.

As a fiscal conservative, Mr. Bush must also be judged a failure. In 2008 the Bush administration presided over $1.7 trillion in increased spending and passed on to the new president a national debt that had almost doubled on his watch. Nor, if the yardstick is employment creation, did people gain from jobs promised as a result of the lower capital gains rate. During Mr. Bush's time in office, the economy added only enough jobs to employ 14 percent of the added number of working-age Americans, the lowest proportion of any president since the Great Depression. If the criterion is growth, the GDP grew at a lower annual rate than for any president since the end of World War II, half the rate of growth under the runner-up for worst performance, George Herbert Walker Bush. Even the stock market through January 2009, when George W. Bush's successor was inaugurated, had lost over 5 percent of its value over the previous decade (assuming reinvestment of dividends and adjusting for inflation). The country had reached the end of the regime of accumulation that started in the late 1970s and featured financialization, deindustrialization, and globalization. It was clearly not bringing economic growth. Indeed, fidelity to its ideological and institutional fundamentals was responsible for a deep economic crisis. By the end of Bush the younger's administration, such a record brought loss of faith in deregulationist, efficient market thinking and a broad openness to an alternative public philosophy and set of policies.

The SSA theoretical framework suggests that a serious economic crisis, such as the one the country encountered beginning in the final year of the Bush administration, can rupture the prevailing social and institutional order, initiating a prolonged period in which class coalitions are reshaped and power relations change, creating new institutional architecture. Such a shift does not happen immediately. Indeed a crisis caused by rigid adherence to a deregulationist philosophy and neoliberal policies and norms was addressed through intensification of these same approaches. Redistribution from labor to capital, and especially finance capital, angered many, yet in political terms the onus fell on government policy makers. The legacy of decades of anti–Big Government rhetoric was that anger was aimed primarily at incumbent politicians rather than opening a critical debate over the nature of real, existing American capitalism. The prospect of slow redistributive growth led to a circling of the wagons rather than a clear-eyed view of what the neoliberal SSA had wrought and the changes that better social regulation of capital might bring.

Disappointing overall growth and social progress during the decades of global neoliberalism contrast with the decades 1950–80, during which national Keynesianism reigned. The earlier period was more successful overall in terms of economic and social development than the three decades of global neoliberalism, during which economic growth and social progress for the majority in most countries were significantly slower (Weisbrot, Baker, and Rosnick 2005). Real global growth averaged 4.9 percent a year during the golden age of national Keynesianism (1950–73). It was 3.4 percent between 1974 and 1979; 3.3 percent in the 1980s; and only 2.3 percent in the 1990s, the decade with the slowest growth until then since World War II (Maddison 2001).

From the end of World War II until 1979, productivity and real wages had grown at roughly the same rate; economic gains were shared between capital and labor. After 1980 the growth of productivity continued, but its longtime link with wage growth was absent. The profit share in national income increased. Labor's share decreased. A substantial drop in the savings rate was evident from 1980. After 1979 household and also nonfinancial corporate debt grew dramatically relative to GDP. Before 1980 employment in the manufacturing sector grew as the economy improved and fell in recessions. The next cycle would push manufacturing employment beyond its previous peak. After 1980 expansions did not bring an increase in manufacturing employment to its previous peak. Indeed, after 1980, manufacturing as a share of total employment fell substantially. Business investment spending remained weak, and firms increasingly borrowed to buy their own stock. In the neoliberal SSA, companies issued less stock than they bought back. Buybacks seemed a sensible way to spend profits since reinvesting in greater production was not attractive. This was also in part the result of the dramatic increase in the use of stock options, which became a major method of compensating top executives; and in order not to dilute the stock price, buybacks were necessary. There was as well a secular trend of increased corporate cash holdings from 1980, with the average cash-to-assets ratio for U.S. industrial firms more than doubling between 1980 and 2006 (Bates, Kahle, and Stulz 2009).

The postwar Keynesian SSA was characterized by relatively high personal savings rates, a relatively low personal debt-to-income ratio, relatively low corporate debt-to-capital ratios, net equity issuance to finance fixed capital investment, as well as companies retaining a large part of their net profit. In addition, income inequality was low by historical measure. In the global neoliberal SSA years, all this changed. The growth in net capital stock fell; net equity issuance became negative, as corporate governance focused on maximizing short-term returns to stockholders; savings rates fell significantly, becoming negative for the first time since the Great Depression; and income inequality increased to levels not seen since the 1920s. Many scholars attributed the break between what had been a long-standing link between wages and productivity, stagnant real wages, and growing inequality to financialization and the new accumulation model premised on debt creation and asset price inflation.

Internationalization

As national Keynesianism and the (relative) domestic quiet life under oligopolistic competition came under pressure, profits from domestic production were more likely to be reinvested in financial assets rather than in plant and equipment. Weiskopf, Bowles, and Gordon (1983:389) note that increases in financial assets, as a percentage of all corporate uses of funds from less than 20 percent in the period 1959–66 had reached 25.8 percent during 1973–79. The figure was to grow far larger (Stockhammer 2004). Expansion of the financial sector resulted from the need to fund international transactions and then as a logical successor to accumulation strategy, one reminiscent of the pattern of previous declining hegemons, suggested by Arrighi and Silver. While international economics presumes separate nation-states as units of analysis, world-systems theorists have long questioned this perspective (Wallerstein 1974). A shift to a transnational perspective raises perplexing issues because the pattern is one of combined and uneven development. Rising powers outside the traditional core have different and some overlapping interests from those of traditional hegemonic elites, adding tension and uncertainty to efforts to reach accords on new international regimes, for example on currency alignment.

In the postwar SSA, economists worried about trade deficits because dollars leaving the domestic circular flow—all else equal—slowed growth. In the successor SSA, increased imports kept inflation down and allowed American workers, whose real incomes were stagnating, to live beyond their means on the money borrowed from foreigners. Household debt was a little less than half gross domestic product in 1981. It was equal to 100 percent of GDP in 2007, even as the household savings rate fell to zero. U.S. borrowing was not used to build capacity to repay the debt. It created jobs abroad and profits that were recycled to allow Americans to borrow more, producing overextension that was bound to end painfully. Increasingly U.S.-based transnationals invested abroad not only to export back to the United States but because domestic markets in these countries were growing. After 1980 U.S. trade deficits increased. Unemployment stayed higher than in the postwar period. Government policy did not see lack of jobs, especially well-paying work, as a problem as it had in the era of national Keynesianism. This was related to globalization.

A strong dollar helped U.S. transnationals to invest abroad and import goods more cheaply, even as it hurt domestic industry's international competitiveness. Trade deficits were not seen as an issue. They helped hold down inflation and in any event were the result of market forces and so were acceptable. (Palley 2007 provides detailed data on these trends.) The interaction of financialization and globalization characterized the transition after 1980, hurting American manufacturing and allowing for the growing gap between productivity growth and wage gains, thus increasing income inequality in the United States (for details, see Michel, Bernstein, and Allegretto 2007). Easy credit encouraged U.S. consumers to borrow more and spend. Buyers favored SUVs and light trucks, which used a lot of gas, swelling the coffers of oil producers and consumer-product manufacturers, mostly in Asia. Profits from these sales were lent to the United States, pushing interest rates down and not only encouraging more household spending (which rose as a proportion of U.S. GDP) but feeding asset bubbles. While the United States led the way, labor shares in GDP decreased in most economies.

The material basis for the turn to financialization was evident to observers by the late 1970s and certainly the early 1980s, and not only in the United States. In 1984 IMF director Jacques de Larosière explained:

Over the past four years the rate of return on capital investment in manufacturing in the six largest industrial countries averaged only about half
the rate earned during the late 1960s. . . . Even allowing for cyclical factors, a clear pattern emerges of a substantial and progressive long-term
decline in rates of return on capital. There may be many reasons for this,
but there is no doubt that an important contributing factor is to be found
in the significant increase over the last twenty years or so in the share of
income being absorbed by compensation of employees. . . . This points
to the need for a gradual reduction in the rate of increase in real wages
over the medium term if we are to restore adequate investment incentives. (Wachtel 1986:37)

Labor shares were not, however, the problem or the cause of the profit
squeeze in subsequent years of the neoliberal SSA.

Samuel Bowles, David Gordon, and Thomas Weiskopf (1983), effectively
in agreement with the IMF director, explain the demise of the postwar SSA
by assuming a stance essentially similar to that of Samuel Huntington's "excess of democracy" theorizing. In this view, it was the resistance of labor that
led to a profit squeeze and to the decline in the rate of productivity growth.
Companies attempted to pass these costs on in higher prices. In the era of
national Keynesianism, recessions were typically triggered by the Federal
Reserve, raising interest rates in response to inflationary developments. By
slowing growth and creating unemployment, the bargaining power of labor
was undercut, and labor cost–led inflation stopped.

As the era of national Keynesianism gave way to global neoliberalism,
bargaining power shifted. Large corporations, because they could more effectively source globally, and thanks to labor-saving technological developments, gained the upper hand. Labor in the economies of the core was no
longer able to make excessive demands on the system; rather, concession
bargaining became a general pattern. While union militants complained of
"betrayal" by their leaders, concessions resulted from forces beyond the capacities of workers and citizens to effectively prevent. From a longer-term
perspective, their inability to guide globalization toward a process of leveling up, rather than leveling down, needs to be placed in the foreground.
The recovery of Japan and Europe by the late 1960s and early 1970s stimu-
lated outward expansion of multinationals. Later the industrialization in
East Asia put still more pressure on industrial workers in the United States,
Japan, and Western Europe. To put the focus on the excessive demands of

American workers for causing the demise of the postwar SSA, as its early theorists tended to do, was short-sighted.

The perspective needs to be broadened to the forces of globalization, the centrality of financialization's short-term time horizons, and the shift from managerial capitalism to financialized capitalism, recognized at the time by CEOs of industrial firms. Consider the following revealing passage written by Edson W. Spencer (1986:20), chairman and chief executive of Honeywell:

> Many factors have turned American industry into a high-stakes poker game. Pension-fund managers, to cite one example, compete for more than $1 trillion in investments. One way they win business is to outpace each other in quarterly yields. And the importance that pension funds place on quarter-to-quarter performance is simply a reflection of the attitude the stock market in general holds toward quarterly earnings. Investors put pressure on portfolio managers and brokers who run funds to outperform averages—and one another—in order to earn their bonuses and keep their clients. Moreover, companies themselves exacerbate this focus on short-term performance by pressuring their own pension-managers to generate high short-term rewards.

Long-term growth required market expansion, product quality, research and development, and customer and employee satisfaction, the ingredients of long-term success for companies that were, in the short run, costly choices for managers given these pressures. The triumph of shareholder value maximization as the dominant ideology of corporate governance paved the way for the transition from managerial capitalism to finance capitalism.

The development of computer-assisted number crunching allowed a high degree of complexity in parsing of risk and the development of new financial instruments. The end of the Bretton Woods system of fixed exchange rates was occasion for financial innovation to hedge increased foreign exchange risk. There was also a great deal of money made in takeovers and reorganizing enterprises. Leveraged buyouts are attractive, especially when interest rates are low and liquidity abundant. Such financing provides for high returns through dramatic downsizing, exerting pressure on workers, suppliers, and others and cutting costs in such areas as research and development. The firm thus slimmed and loaded down with debt can be spun off, producing significant financial gain.

From 1980 through 2007 the world's financial assets, including equities, private and public debt, and bank deposits, almost quadrupled relative to global GDP (Roxburgh et al. 2009:9) as financialization joined globalization and neoliberalism as the key words of the new SSA. The dominance of the financial industry over other economic activity meant financial markets powerfully determine the state of the overall economy and centrally characterize the new SSA. Speculators increasingly constrained and shaped corporate strategies and the choices of elected officials. Globalization complicated and amplified financialization's impact. Financing of leveraged buyouts was made easier by the capacity to borrow in foreign currencies at low cost. Strategies like the carry trade investment of Japanese yen (available over a long period at virtually no-cost funding) to purchase assets denominated in other currencies were major factors in the buildup of debt and its vulnerability to repricing. Short-term arbitrage opportunities could suddenly disappear, producing financial turmoil. Publications of the International Monetary Fund, the Bank for International Settlements, and other regulators repeatedly warned of the dangers of foreign-exchange risk and high debt strategies (D'Arista 2006).

In an increasingly globalized labor market, American workers, who as a group had enjoyed higher living standards, found they were in a more competitive, far larger labor pool. Some economists explained the theory of comparative advantage and assured these workers that they would be better off accepting greater mobility of capital, goods, and services. Others explained the law of one price, which said that the price of goods, services, and labor adjusted for transportation cost, and differential taxation would tend to become equal in a globalized economy. This meant those more highly paid, competing with lower-wage workers at the same tasks, would see their wages fall and benefits decrease over time as transportation became less expensive and tariff and other barriers fell. For workers in the United States, lower wages were offset only to some extent by the availability of lower-cost imports. A focus on better education, certainly desirable, could help younger workers if jobs were available using their skill set, but a bachelor's degree came to be worth less in the new century, and inequality grew among those with such degrees. Younger workers as a group were not earning what previous cohorts had at the same age. Retraining older workers was, typically, for nonexistent jobs and generally more of a cooling out mechanism than an effective reemployment strategy. Less-educated workers and those whose skill set was either outmoded or available at lower cost elsewhere did especially poorly. Their suffering was widely seen—by some who were not themselves suffering—as something the government could not do much about.

Financialization and Commercial Banking

Dramatic increases in the size and scope of the financial sector have accompanied major periods of economic restructuring. This is the case for at least four reasons. Major expansions typically cannot be funded internally but require significant borrowing or equity funding, premised on expected earnings. Second, such an optimistic context attracts and provides some cover for inflated claims, opportunistic behavior, and dishonest dealings. Bubbles can develop through mutual reinforcement by key actors and gatekeepers: accountants, bankers, stock analysts, and media hyping sales of new financial claims and innovative instruments. Third, when the scope of the market expands geographically, as happens when innovations in communication and transportation reduce costs to distant markets, there is accelerated merger and acquisition activity as companies bulk up to exploit economies of scale. This happened with the development of oceangoing ships, with the railroad, and, in a more generalized form, in the current wave of low-cost information processing. Finally, many firms that had been competitive under earlier conditions no longer are in an environment of technological and product innovation, drawing the interest of financiers to restructure them.

The financial services sector was itself affected by technological changes in information processing and computer capacity innovation, which increased the capacity of nonbank financial institutions to compete with commercial banks. Money market funds drew away large depositors, and the development of the commercial paper market allowed established corporations to bypass banks in lending and borrowing. Such innovations cut deeply into the basic business model of large commercial banks.

The financial sector between 1978 and 2007 quadrupled its borrowing relative to the real economy, and its profits rose by 800 percent, adjusted for inflation, between 1980 and 2005 (compared to 250 percent for nonfinancial sector profits), indicators of this dramatic change. The economy's rate of growth over these years resulted from a substitution of debt for labor income. This is reflected in the nature of growth in these years. The neoliberal era experienced three long expansions (1982–1990, 1991–2000, and 2001–2007). In each, output per hour rose substantially more rapidly than the real earnings of nonsupervisory production workers; profits rose rapidly relative to wages; and labor's share of national income fell as income inequality increased substantially, reaching levels not seen since before the Great Depression. Household debt rose as a percentage of disposable income from

59 percent in 1982 to 129 percent in 2007 (Kotz 2009). These developments changed the nature of accumulation in the U.S. economy, which was less dependent on saving and investing and profit generated from the production of goods and nonfinancial services and more the result of the growth of net worth through capital gains and debt-fueled consumption.

Between 1973 and 2007 real wages went down by 4.4 percent, in contrast to the 1947–73 increase in real wages of 75 percent. In the years of the global neoliberal SSA, income inequality climbed (Wolff 2010). The number of better-paid jobs and the level of benefits declined with trade union density. Concession bargaining and pay freezes became more frequent even before the Great Recession, which intensified pressure on workers for concessions. More jobs were converted to contract work or part-time employment. Income precariousness and job precariousness grew. Large numbers of workers were excluded from unemployment benefits, and many exhausted these benefits. Severance pay became less substantial or was nonexistent. A major source of debt creation was stagnant real wages, as the cost of job loss resulted in borrowing to maintain consumption levels.

Stagnation of wages and loss of purchasing power from labor market churning came in part as a result of restructuring pressures imposed by financial markets on U.S. companies. Globalization and movement of jobs offshore put further pressure on workers. The share of U.S. national income going to wages and salaries reached its lowest recorded level (until then) in 2005–6. Corporate profits, which were 7 percent of U.S. GDP in 2001 (at the start of a cyclical upturn), were 12.2 percent at the beginning of 2006 at their peak, while by this later date median income was 3 percent lower in real terms. American families added to their debt between 2001 and 2005 at a rate 60 percent greater than the growth of the overall economy. As the era of global neoliberalism wound down, American workers had the unenviable position that despite the highest output in the world per hour, they put in the longest hours while their real wages had stagnated for thirty years. Average household debt had risen from three-quarters of annual disposable income in 1990 to nearly 130 percent on the eve of the crisis.

Private college loans, which amounted to $2 billion in 1996–97, grew to over $17 billion a decade later. Borrowing to pay for health-care expenses increased as well. Banks looked for customers who could not pay back debt, customers who would stay perpetually behind, providing a continuing source of interest and fee income. Julie Williams, the chief counsel of the Comptroller of the Currency, explained in a March 2005 speech: "Today the focus for lenders is not so much on consumer loans being repaid, but on the loan as a perpetual earning asset." At the end of 2008 household debt was $13.8 trillion, and the total debt of the financial sector was $17.2 trillion. Government debt was less than either, although after that, as it stepped in to make good private-sector bad debt, it rose dramatically. Importantly, while half a century earlier three-quarters of financial sector debt was on the books of banks, savings and loans, and finance companies, by 2008 these traditional financial institutions were responsible for only 18 percent of the total.

Bank failures in the 1980s and beyond rose remarkably compared to the postwar period. Bank profits fell by the mid-1980s, until the large banks discovered the marvels of leverage, which soared so that return on equity increased. Bankers at the top received huge bonuses, not for increasing profitability on a risk-adjusted basis, but for taking on greater and greater risk, thanks to deregulation of U.S. banks by the Depository Institutions Deregulation and Monetary Control Act of 1980. In the neoliberal era, a major divide took place between the mega banks and the traditional smaller and midsized banks.

Growth took place in the shadow banking system, as it was called (see chapter 4), where top earners at investment banks, hedge funds, and private equity and mutual funds—the people we think of as Wall Street—are heavily represented in the top one-tenth of 1 percent of the income distribution and the top hundred thousandth of 1 percent, more than the CEOs and other top executives of nonfinancial corporations, and account for a good part of the growing inequality in the United States (Kaplan and Rauch 2009). *Forbes* surveys of how the richest four hundred Americans make their money show 8 percent in finance in 1982 but 27 percent in finance in 2007, when the financial sector harvested 41 percent of all domestic corporate profits. Few Americans would agree that this represented the contribution of finance to the well-being of the rest of America.

These were the years during which, while the economy appeared stable, the situation of individuals deteriorated dramatically. The majority of people were exposed to more risk and income decline in these years in which financialization became the dominant characteristic of the political economy (Gosselin 2008). In late 2007 a survey conducted by MetLife found 44 percent of Americans living paycheck to paycheck, and a little under half of all households having less than $5,000 in liquid assets. Millions had stopped contributing to retirement plans and delayed retirement as the nation's pension plans and 401(k)s lost trillions of invested dollars. The proportion of older Americans in the labor force grew even higher as overall unemployment increased.

Between 2004 and 2006 Americans withdrew in excess of $800 billion a year from their homes, refinancing them or taking out home equity loans. In the middle of the decade, a third of American households borrowed in these ways, pushing the nation's savings rate deeper into negative territory to fund their day-to-day spending. Increasingly through the years when financialization grew, banks expanded their campaigns to change ingrained attitudes. They cold-called homeowners to persuade them to take out home equity loans and ran extensive advertising to this end. Debt was no longer a cause for guilt but an opportunity to purchase "what one deserved," they suggested. Their advertising conveyed that people should feel good about buying on borrowed money. Given stagnant real incomes, this argument had its attractions.

Households, through these years, increased borrowing to pay for living expenses. Federal Reserve household debt service and financial obligations ratio data reveal financial obligations of households to have increased from 15.36 to 19.35 percent of disposable income between 1980 and 2007, a remarkable increase. When the Great Recession struck, many were forced to pay down debt as the value of their homes fell and job pressures reduced their disposable incomes. The pain was intense, and the deleveraging would be ongoing for some time. Associated with this increase in consumer indebtedness over the years of the neoliberal SSA was the rise in bank income coming from consumer lending from overdraft fees, late-payment charges, and credit card interest. Total U.S. late payment fees, for example, rose from an insignificant amount in 1990 to $9 billion by 2003. Citibank's global consumer division in 2006 booked over half the firm's profits on a little over 30 percent of its revenues (Dos Santos 2009:191, 194). A handful of companies dominate the American credit card market. Consumers rarely shopped for lower rates (and penalty charges) available from alternatives such as credit unions and some smaller banks.

Financial returns exceeding the rate of profit in the real economy can be realized over an extended period only if finance increases efficiency so that discounted future earnings increase. If, as is more often the case, profits are achieved by short-term expedients: squeezing wages, the prices received by suppliers, research and development expenditures, and the sale of company assets, the rate of economic growth outside of finance slows. In a basic sense these sources of financial profits come as an appropriation from the rest of the economy. By 2004 profits in the financial sector in the United States reached $300 billion, compared to $534 billion for all nonfinancial corporations that year. This was a bit over 40 percent of all domestic corporate profits. The sector's share had been 2 percent of domestic profits forty years earlier. This growth of financialization was a major contributor to growing inequality in the country. The top 1 percent of households owned over a third of financial stock, and the top 10 percent held over half of all financial stock. Between 2002 and 2006, the wealthiest 10 percent of households saw more that 95 percent of all income gains. From 2000 to 2006 the combined real earnings of the ninety-three million production and nonsupervisory workers in the United States rose by $15.4 billion, less than half the amount of the combined bonuses at the top five Wall Street firms for 2006 alone (Sum and Tobar 2008).

Whereas when Ronald Reagan took office the richest 1 percent took home 8 percent of national income, the figure was 20 percent in 2007. The last time inequality had reached this level was 1928. The average tax rate paid by the richest four hundred Americans fell by a third through the first six years of the Bush administration, and their average income doubled, according to the Internal Revenue Service. Seventy-five percent of all income gains during the administration of George W. Bush went to the top 1 percent of earners, many in the financial sector. The bottom 90 percent of taxpayers (with incomes under $126,300) received about 10 percent of the total.

The pressures the financial sector–imposed incentive structure puts on the rest of corporate America to maximize short-run profits and payouts to investors further increases inequality by its downward pressure on company workers and suppliers who are squeezed. Financialization, then, in its many manifestations, is a prime cause of the growing inequality and instability of the U.S. economic system. The incentive structure imposed by the objective function of maximizing stockholder short-term returns contributes substantially to these developments. Aligning management incentives to this goal transformed the nature of U.S. capitalism and suggests the appropriateness of one last definition of financialization as the "capacity of finance capital to take over and dominate, for a while at least, all the activities of the business world" (Arrighi 2004:230).

The total value of financial assets as a percentage of GDP grew more than twice as fast after 1980 as for the previous eighty years. In 1981 U.S. private debt was 123 percent of GDP; by the third quarter of 2008 it was equal to 290 percent of GDP. The biggest rise was in the financial sector itself (Crotty

2009b). Between 1980 and 2000 financial industry profits rose from $32 billion to $196 billion. Not surprisingly, profits in the financial sector compared to those in other sectors of the economy rose remarkably after 1980. Pay for generating these high returns grew so much that, while before 1980 average compensation in finance was similar to that in other sectors (indeed lower than in the 1950s and 1960s), more money and talent flooded into finance because pay scales rose dramatically. But executive compensation more broadly also rose substantially, and, as shall be discussed, this was tied to the increasing financialization of the rest of the economy. The wealth-to-income ratios among households grew after 1980 in part as a result of capital gains growth and from the rapid rise of top corporate executives compared to the average worker, especially from income growth at the top in finance (Bosworth and Flaaen 2009).

Stock Options' Transformational Influence

The significance of stock ownership changed substantially over the neoliberal era. The idea that there was a group of owners who acted as guardians of a company watching out for its long-term interests and as a check on management had been challenged in the 1930s by Berle and Means, who pointed out the separation of ownership from control and the resultant principal-agent problem, whereby management maximized its own interests at the expense of the principals (the stockholders). It was this that stock options were meant to address by aligning the interests of the owners' agents, the top managers, with maximizing returns for owners.

Nevertheless, to align corporate leaders with the single-minded pursuit of stockholder value, stock options became the dominant source of executive compensation. In practice this encouraged executives to maximize short-term profit and invited manipulation of earnings to coincide with cashing options and a shift in the firm's objective function to a new growth-profit combination of higher profit and lower growth (Lazonick and Sullivan 2000). Firms under this incentive structure could grow faster but chose not to because that would reduce profitability. In 1980 fewer than one in three chief executives was granted stock options. As the neoliberal era advanced, this became a more general practice and grew to remarkable heights. In 2003 options represented 23 percent of the net earnings of Standard & Poor's (S&P) 500 companies, up from 2 percent in 1996. Between 1995 and 1999 alone, the value of stock options going to executives more than quadrupled to the equivalent of one-fifth of nonfinancial corporation profits net of interest. A relatively small group of executives by 1999 were dividing $100 billion. While in 1990 only 8 percent of CEO compensation was in the form of stock, in 2001 the median CEO of a S&P 500 company received two-thirds of compensation in equity, giving them incentive to realize corporate profit at the time it served them best (Boyer 2007).

The origin of the move from salary to payment through options can be traced to the Revenue Act of 1950, which enabled executives to be taxed at the lower capital gains rate under specific conditions (later limited by the Economic Reform Act of 1981). There has been some discussion in the literature concerning the unintended consequences of congressional action, responding to earlier public outrage at the growing gap between fast-rising executive salaries and stagnant workers' income. Congress capped (at a million dollars) the part of an executive's salary for which companies could claim tax deductions. Deregulatory reform in 1992, relaxing the rules under Section 16(b) of the Securities Exchange Act of 1934, permitted officers and directors to exercise stock options and to sell the shares without holding them for the previously required six months, leading to the possibilities of timing sales (Coffee 2003:38), although exercisable incentive stock options were limited.

The larger point is that stock options, usually not treated as expenses, have often been invisible to stockholders even as equity grants are typically two-thirds of compensation. If revealed, they are typically found only by the eagle-eyed in obscure footnotes in the legally mandated reporting of corporations. John Plender (2003:13) describes this development as "probably unique in history in that it saw the arrival of a form of legal embezzlement. The growth of stock options in the boardroom was arguably a form of theft—a debt-financed transfer of wealth from outside shareholders to inside managers. In the absence of legal constraints or an active exercise of control rights by institutional shareholders, the managers extracted private benefits of control in the form of stock market windfalls." Such a harsh judgment was at odds with what millions of economics and business students were taught regarding the effectiveness of stock options in aligning the interests of executives and their equity-owning principals.

Looking at the bonuses of the rainmakers at financial firms, James Crotty (2009b:12–13) finds for 2005 that bonuses rose by almost $7 billion while profits at their companies fell by over $4 billion—hardly increased reward for better performance. In 2007 these firms collectively lost over $11 billion but paid record bonuses amounting to almost $33 billion. The next year, when Citigroup lost over $27 billion, it paid out more in bonuses than in 2006 when it generated over $21 billion in profits. Growth in bonuses since the early 1990s in finance has been larger than that of net earnings, in many years by considerable amounts.

While typically not as extreme, the situation for nonfinancial companies is not all that different in the lack of consistency of earnings and performance. It is hard to know what a CEO actually earns. They are paid in cash, in stock (the value of which may not be known for years), and in retirement benefits for decades. There are also valuable perks that may be found in footnotes to corporate reports or not disclosed. By generally agreed upon calculation in 1980, the CEOs of Fortune 500 firms were paid 42 times the average worker's wage. By 2007 they were paid an average of 364 times as much. While pay for performance requires comparison with a group of comparable companies, the peer group is often suspect, frequently picked to allow executives to clear performance hurdles. The consultants on pay for performance are paid by the firms; and wanting return business gives them an incentive to maximize CEO earnings in the same way that Enron's auditors had reason to look at things the way that the company liked. Firms themselves inflate earnings, spinning profits by estimating revenues on sales without considering returns or allowing for discounts, underestimating how much inventory becomes obsolete, forecasting unusual gains and losses in restructurings, and other accounting tricks to lowball losses and overestimate tax deductible expenses.

Each year there are new candidates for the poster CEO of a Fortune 500 company who most appears to have abused his or her position. In 2008 the winner was perhaps Aubrey McClendon of Chesapeake Energy, with total compensation of $112.5 million in a year when his company's stock fell by 40 percent. Such imbalance was not all that unusual. What placed him high on the list of CEO abusers was the company's purchase of McClendon's personal collection of antique maps for $12.1 million, after being advised that this was its fair price by the dealer who helped Mr. McClendon buy them. Stockholders, the presumed owners of the company, have little say on whether such a purchase is in their interests. In searching for a parallel to the way CEOs choose their own boards, David Owen suggests that "if the federal government worked the same way, sitting presidents would have the power to appoint members of Congress."

Stock options not only became an instrument of major redistribution of wealth but a cause of bad decision making. It is not primarily that executives are often paid too much, although they are, but that they are too often paid to do the wrong things. A mechanism that was supposed to align the incentives of top executives to those of the actual owners of a company in fact produced huge losses for those stockholders. Just like opportunism in other realms, and indeed criminal behavior of street criminals, significant numbers of people in finance responded to the cost-and-benefit calculation of evading moral and legal strictures and maximized their own welfare at the expense of their principals, the stockholders. The influence and the high status accorded to those who reach the top lead to ignoring the need to strictly enforce desirable norms on such individuals, on the grounds that with so much at stake they would not risk their reputations in this way. The lack of checks on management means they can appropriate a great proportion of shareholder value.

The extent of wealth transfer through stock options is impressive. While in 1992 corporate CEOs had held 2 percent of the equity in U.S. companies, a decade later they owned 12 percent. Over the period 1992 to 2005 (measured in 2005 dollars), the average annual compensation for the CEOs of the S&P 500 companies almost tripled, from less than $4 million to $10.5 million. Careful statistical analysis (Bebchuk and Fried 2004) confirms executive compensation to be decoupled from performance and that, rather than the arm's length bargaining model in which boards extend rewards to top executives based on increased shareholder value generated, managers influence and distort executive pay systematically, with no necessary relation to performance. It is not a matter of a few abuses, "bad apples," but systematic failure of corporate governance.

Reshaping the incentive structure to short-term orientation led to dramatic exaggeration of earnings that would catch up with the companies, but often after those responsible left with their millions. Options were often granted for absolute, rather than relative, performance so that an executive whose firm lagged well behind competitors would benefit from a rising economy and CEOs could be granted huge option benefits for poor performance. This is a reason that company profits increasingly went to buy back company stock (to reduce the amount outstanding and to drive share prices up). Much of this buying was necessary to make up for the dilution of ownership claims created by the generous option granting. They also drove up the company's stock price in the short run so that executives could cash out at inflated values. Even if the stock price fell soon thereafter, a happenstance that was not uncommon, executives were unlikely to be subject to penalties or forced to surrender any of their often ill-gotten gain.

Accounting for Corporate Profits

Companies in the 1990s learned to take "extraordinary charges" to increase their bottom lines with extraordinary regularity. These special one-time costs, which are presumably just that, a rarity, became a normal way to inflate profits. Through the 1990s and into the next decade, the gap between Generally Accepted Accounting Practices (GAAP) without such special charges and reported profits was 17 percent, on average, for S&P 500 companies. In 2001–2 the gap between the two rose to 40 percent as earnings hype increased while real profits fell. Some analysts disregarded the measure altogether and used core earnings, a more restricted and accurate definition than the one most corporations were using. Looking at core earnings reduced profits remarkably. It was not likely that company profit reports over a number of years really were represented by "the Beautiful Line," a plot of reported profits that shows a steady, unbroken, upward ascent. Even successful firms have bad years, make mistakes that go to the bottom line, and take risks that do not pay off. But, by pushing expenses to next year, booking profits early, and other ruses, the line can be preserved using structured finance in a "reclassification context."

Establishing valuations can be guesswork and numbers easily slanted. It is of course possible with great effort to sort through such ruses (Burnsa and Kediab 2008). After Enron's collapse in 2001, the field of forensic accounting, reconstructing the gimmicks used in defrauding investors, came to prominence temporarily at least, employed to put accounting practices under the microscope. It is a time-consuming and expensive business but often turns up questionable practices that shed light on the real situation. The current value of a company represents a judgment call regarding the future. The accountants' work, based on historical data, does not serve. Companies whose future profits are based on expectations are subject to wide interpretation and fluctuation.

Since stock turnover is rapid, few investors know much about the fundamental situation or have inquired into the accounting gimmicks a company may deploy. A study by Thompson Financial of the thirty companies in the Dow Jones Industrial Average found 46 percent of them just meeting the consensus forecast or beating it by a penny. This is just not plausible. Rather it reflects the ability of accountants to massage results, called "backing in" on Wall Street. One starts with the number one wants to end up with and then figures out how to get this number. Investors did not seem to care that firms do this and accepted the numbers even when they suspected they were manipulated. Companies where executives are disproportionately compensated in stock options are more likely to report earnings that meet or beat analysts' forecasts. When results have to be restated, executives do not give back the money they received for meeting target goals.

There are common techniques employed that make understanding the true state of things difficult. These include abuses of GAAP; the use of mergers and acquisitions as a tool to manipulate earnings and deductions, as, for example, taking in-process R&D charges (the estimated value of research and development at a purchased firm); pooling good will; the use of pro-forma statements to report huge profits (while later reporting huge losses to the SEC); restructuring reserves; channel stuffing (booking profits when goods are sent to a warehouse even if they will not be sold for some time or perhaps ever); vendor financing (lending companies the money to buy a company's products, loans that might not be repaid if the firms they lend to get in trouble, as happened widely in the telecom meltdown, for example); and the use of "special expenses" and of earnings before interest, taxes depreciation, and amortization (EBITDA) as a measure of cash flow (which fails to include cash costs) rather than net income. In times of an economic crisis, the illusion of accounting exactitude comes to be seen as fraud as these tricks are revealed as misrepresentations calculated to mislead investors.

When the pretense of profitability cracked and the stock market collapsed in 2000–2001, companies had to come clean on at least some of what had been done. By the summer of 2002 the Bureau of Economic Analysis's National Income and Products Accounts had revised downward the profits for the years 1998, 1999, and 2000, 11.0 percent, 9.3 percent, and 8.9 percent, respectively. Over this period there had been a threefold increase in stock options to about $200 billion in 2000. In mid-2002 a retired J. P. Morgan vice president estimated that about half the exaggerated earnings reflected the lack of recording options as expenses. The other half was manipulation of earnings. This breakdown is confirmed by a study by researchers at the New York Federal Reserve Bank who estimate that half the correction in profits came from stock options and the rest from aggressive accounting.

The backdating of options, the after-the-fact dating of their sale, and re-lated practices, which came under increasing scrutiny, led to dozens of ex-ecutives being forced to resign and to widespread restatement of earnings. By 2006 more than two thousand companies were found to have prob-ably backdated stock options to maximize top executives' incomes. Using information from the Thompson Financial Insider Filing database of stock transactions by top corporation executives, reported to the Federal Securi-ties and Exchange Commission, academic researchers examined nearly forty thousand stock grants over a decade. Based on market probabilities, they es-timated that almost 30 percent of companies had used backdated options to increase executive compensation. Looking at returns from fifteen hundred of the largest American corporations between 1992 and 2001, other researchers found that companies dispensing larger than average options to their top five executives produced decidedly lower returns to shareholders than those dis-pensing smaller option grants. One scholar characterized the practice, which she also found widespread, as "secret compensation" (Anabtawi 2004).

A Boston Consulting Group study of companies that were found guilty of fraud estimated the value of stock options granted to the CEOs of those firms in the years before the fraud was made public to be 800 percent greater than the value of those granted to CEOs in comparable firms in which fraud was not found. Nothing, it turns out, correlates as strongly with fraud as stock options. After the downturn in 2007–8, researchers found that divi-dends from 2004 through 2006, a seeming indicator of corporate profitabil-ity, were paid for in a large number of cases with borrowed money, inflating stock values and artificially increasing stock option payouts. From the fourth quarter of 2004 through the third quarter of 2008, the companies of the S&P 500 reported net earnings of $2.4 trillion but paid dividends of $900 billion and repurchased $1.7 trillion in shares to the benefit of those exercising stock options (Norris 2009). The bonuses were real, but the profits were a mirage.

From 1997 through 2008, 438 companies in the S&P 500 stock index spent $2.4 trillion on stock buybacks. Leading high-tech companies, such as Microsoft, IBM, and Intel, spent more on stock buybacks than on research and development. As William Lazonick (2009b:96) tells us, "If bailed-out General Motors had banked the $20.4 billion it distributed to shareholders as buybacks from 1986 through 2002 (with a 2.5% after tax annual return), it would have had $35 billion in 2009 to stave off bankruptcy and respond to global competition." Financial incentives in a host of ways have reduced the U.S. ability to efficiently produce goods and services and create well-paying jobs outside of finance. The use of stock options to encourage executives to maximize shareholder value weakened American capitalism to an incalculably dramatic extent. The weakening of American producers owing to the triumph of maximization of shareholder value and the short-termism it engendered, manipulated by executives eager to maximize income from stock options, is a central part of the story and a component of why, for example, manufacturing (and industrial wages and benefits) in Germany look so different.

With regard to the banks, it is commonly pointed out that the top executives at Lehman Brothers and Bear Stearns, two investment banks that failed spectacularly (see chapter 5), were wiped out when their companies went under. It is then concluded that their pay structure could not have caused excessive risk taking. Lucian Bebchuk and Holger Spamann (2009), using Securities and Exchange Commission data, however, find that the banks' top five executives did quite well. Over the 2000–2007 period, the top five executives at Bear received cash bonuses in excess of $300 million and at Lehman in excess of $150 million. These numbers are before counting what they received in sale of company shares. Unloading their banks' stock netted the ten executives $2 billion. By 2008, when the collapses came, they had sold more shares than they still retained. In selling shares they, like other executives, had incentive to maximize short-term profit in timing such sales. While the impact of financial incentives was devastating to many American companies and their employees, as a combination of extracting maximum shareholder value and the extraction of top executives removed resources from other shareholders and undermined corporate America's future prospects (see below), special notice is required for practices at financial firms.

Executives of these companies enjoyed what New York State attorney general Andrew Cuomo (2009:2) calls the "heads I win, tails you lose" bonus system. He reports, for example, that if you bought stock in a big investment bank in 1998, by early 2009 you would have lost two-thirds of your original investment. The rainmakers, as Crotty calls them (the key people in financial firms: top executives, traders, salespeople, and merger and acquisition and initial public offering teams) made billions of dollars while their activities destroyed shareholder value. The process was to use borrowed funds to buy up assets, pushing their price higher and using the assets as collateral to borrow and buy still more. The liabilities of the investment banks rose from $548 billion in 1995 to $3 trillion dollars in 2007. (Crotty 2009b:4). Rising leverage was the source of funding and of the outsized profitability until the bubble collapsed, bringing down some of these firms and requiring the government to save others.

In 2007 the large financial giants collectively lost over $11 billion, but the rainmakers paid themselves $33 billion in bonuses (more than in any other year). The collapse of Lehman Brothers destroyed $22 billion for shareholders, but compensation the year it failed was larger than in 2004 when the firm was profitable. All told in the decade to 2008, a decade in which the cumulative profits for shareholders was zero, employees were paid $55 billion. In 2008 Citigroup lost $28 billion but paid more in bonuses than in 2006 when it generated $36 billion in profits. Commenting on the data and the perverse reward structures, Crotty (2009b:11) writes "that it is rational for top financial firm operatives to take excessive risk in the bubble even if they understand that their decisions are likely to cause a crash in the immediate future. Since they do not have to return their bubble-year bonuses when the inevitable crisis occurs, and since they continue to receive substantial bonuses even in the crisis, they have a powerful incentive to pursue high-risk, high-leverage strategies." While an angry public and vocal public officials proposed various clawback provisions and vesting of earnings strategies, such incentives remain. These rainmakers control the firms they work for and run them primarily in their own interests.

The impact of this aspect of financialization is that the combination of maximizing stockholder value, the use of stock options to compensate top executives, and the stock buybacks these policies encouraged changed the direction of American capitalism. Instead of investing in the future, American corporations pulled money out as they imposed shorter time horizons on management. From 2000 to 2008 the top fifty stock-repurchasing corporations spent $1.5 trillion on stock repurchases and $876 billion on cash dividends. Together these expenditures exceeded their collective net income. In 2008, with the financial meltdown, there was an even greater net disinvestment by these firms through buybacks and dividends (Lazonick, 2009b:33). While we cannot be sure where this "free cash flow" ended up, the chances are good that the funds stayed within the realm of speculative financial investment and that the stock dividends and cashed stock options bid up financial asset prices rather than going to investment in the real economy.

Citigroup would not have needed to be saved by the Abu Dhabi Investment Authority with $7.5 billion toward the end of 2007 if it had not engaged in buybacks in 2006 and 2007. Likewise Morgan Stanley traded 9.9 percent of its equity for $5 billion from China's sovereign wealth fund after spending over $7 billion in 2006–7 on stock buy backs (Lazonick 2008). Buybacks in the pharmaceutical industry exceed R&D budgets, suggesting that the drug companies' claims that they cannot reduce the price of prescription drugs without undercutting research are suspect. The scale of corporate buybacks is a major reversal of pre-1980 patterns. Previously corporations borrowed to fund new investment. Post-1980 companies borrowed to fund buybacks. In 2006 equity purchases by U.S. companies were 44 percent of nonresidential investment spending (Palley 2007), suggesting to Michael Milken (2009:A21) that "without stock buybacks, many such companies [he listed a who's who of corporate America—from General Electric to Macy's and Motorola] would have little debt and would have greater flexibility during this period of increased credit constraints. In other words, their current financial problems are self-imposed." Again, in no industry was this truer than in finance.

The central story of the performance of the American economy in these years is that actual profits faltered. Money was made in speculation. Gains in the real economy were for the most part illusory. The exaggeration of profitability is important to our story because it increased returns to capital, which found their way into money and capital markets and underwrote new borrowing by companies buying back their own stock and their taking on of higher leverage. The short-term mentality encouraged by acceptance of shareholder value maximization, the claim to stock options, and the broader climate of neoliberalism were part of a far less regulated capitalism in which financialization became the driving force of a redistributive model of accumulation.

A change, comparable to the one Berle and Means called attention to in the 1930s (the managerial revolution), is under way. Since 1980 it is more accurate to speak of the "ownerless" corporation. Under postwar managerial capitalism the firm was understood as a single unit. In the era of extensive financialization, the firm was seen as a bundle of assets. Private firms could profitably buy and sell such pieces, restructuring companies to extract value. It paid to buy a company, break it up and sell off the pieces (helping oneself to the cash reserves of the firm and its capacity to borrow). The stock price of a potential takeover target would rise as investors, looking forward to the premium the buyout firm would offer, bid up price. Expected takeovers became a major factor driving the market. Stockholders maximizing short-term gains would dump stock of companies that took the longer view since such investment expenditures lowered short-term returns. They favored asset stripping, dismemberment, or merging companies. Managers who did not pursue short-term profitability would be replaced by new owners after hostile takeovers. They found it wise to spend these down and take out loans so that new owners would have little to walk away with after the purchase, thus discouraging takeovers. A shorter investment horizon for investors became the norm.

Whereas in 1960, on average, only 12 percent of a New York Stock Exchange–listed company's shares would turn over in a year, by 1990 turnover was 46 percent, in 2000, 88 percent, and before the crash of 2008, well over 100 percent. There were few long-term owners and much churning by institutional investors who sought higher short-term profits from trading. John Boggle, founder and former CEO of the giant mutual fund Vanguard Group, who pointed out that in 2009 the average stock changed hands two and a half times, 250 percent, compared to 20 percent three decades earlier, wrote that it did not appear to him appropriate to speak any more of an "own-a-stock" system but what had developed was a "rent-a-stock" system (Ody 2010).

Actually this does not begin to capture the brevity of the ownership period for most stock purchases. Big money on Wall Street is made in high-frequency trading done by computers, which buy and sell stock at speeds much faster than humans can process information. The Nasdaq Stock Market lets traders see orders for thirty milliseconds (0.03 second) before they are available to other investors. The hedge funds and investment banks, like Goldman Sachs, have superfast computers that process this information using powerful algorithms, or "algos," and automatically place buy and sell orders based on what they know demand will be in thirty milliseconds. This allows them to make millions of orders and while making tiny profits on each, become exceedingly wealthy. A handful of high-frequency traders who have heavily invested in what is an ongoing arms race in increasingly sophisticated software account for more than half of all trades. While celebrated as increasing market efficiency by catching the smallest discrepancies in value, program trading was accused of causing major market breakdowns from time to time by magnifying movements away from equilibrium price (Patterson 2009). The stock market is not a successful mechanism for aligning corporate decision making with long-term economic efficiency.

Financialization's Restructuring

In subsequent chapters, attention turns to the causes and significance of asset bubbles associated with recessions in the macro economy traceable to the excessive risk taking of financial institutions. It is argued that the increase in financial speculation was related to falling returns in the productive sectors of the economy and thus a lack of promising alternatives. Regulators permitted practices in these areas of financial speculation that caused damage to the economy. The greater crisis, however, is the result of the long-term weakening of the real economy to accommodate short-term profit maximizing that has hurt the long-term prospects of the economy and its workers and undermined the country's future prospects. The debt-driven redistributive growth model, featuring a harmful financialization, characterizes the global neoliberal SSA.

In the global neoliberal SSA, finance took center stage; the chief financial officer became a more prominent player, and manipulating money and creative accounting became crucial profit generators. Value-added in production actually fell more than 20 percent for the two years from mid-1997, while reported profits grew over the same period by 20 percent a year, largely based on fraudulent manipulation of the numbers. In a climate in which acknowledging lower returns would have been severely punished, all manner of creativity was used to make the numbers. Ordinary expenses were listed as capital investment. Expected profits, overly generously estimated, were booked as current earnings. Debt was moved off balance sheets. No one involved had an incentive to point any of this out. Compliant accounting firms, cheerleading stock analysts, duplicitous lawyers, and regulators chosen for the comfort with which they wore blinders all contributed to the collective project of gaming the system. Indeed, it could hardly be called gaming the system—it *was* the system, an assertion supported extensively in chapters 5 and 7. So powerful is the hold of free-market economics that externalities that are of dominant importance can be ignored and misallocation of trillions of dollars in resources can be blamed on government rather than on the influence of economic power over government decision making.

During the postwar SSA, a norm of oligopolistic interdependence had moderated price competition while stressing product differentiation and planned obsolescence. U.S. companies were unprepared when Japan and Europe recovered from wartime destruction and came back with more modern production techniques and innovative products. The roots of financialization are found in the stagnationist tendencies of first U.S. capitalism, and then other mature economies. This is a difficult idea to grasp given the prevalence of consumerism and seemingly unlimited desire for more goods and services. However, by the end of the war in Vietnam and the first OPEC price increase, American real income growth (adjusted for price changes and taxation) had for the vast majority come to an end. The expansion of debt kept consumption up for a remarkable amount of time. This postponed rather than removed the structural problems visible by the 1970s. The dominance of finance over production resulted from the difficulty of addressing these developments. Many of the iconic blue-chip firms of the twentieth century suffered from overcapacity. Some, while they remained profitable, understandably did not invest in expansion in the United States.

Hostile takeovers were possible using borrowed money, which would be repaid from the target firm's cash reserves. Holding such reserves identified a firm as a potential "cash cow." The best way to protect a company was for it to take on a large amount of debt. This represented a major turnaround in the understanding of the proper role of debt for corporations. Where managers had in previous decades identified with their firm's long-term prospects, growth, and maintenance of a margin of safety through holding a significant cash buffer, this was no longer possible under a regime of shareholder value maximization. Stockholder expectations constrained managers. The shift in emphasis coincided with globalization and the need to reorganize production. Indeed, the actual reorganization began in the 1970s when it was widely identified as deindustrialization (Bluestone and Harrison 1982). If existing management was unwilling or unable to downsize, it faced being replaced by takeover operators who would wring shareholder value out of restructuring. In the 1990s, as companies released capital (and labor), stock prices rose and resources redeployed to faster-growing parts of the economy. The fastest growing was of course finance.

Maximizing of shareholder value undercut both the capital-labor accord of the postwar SSA and the basis of productive growth long central to economic expansion. The term of art for what was demanded of workers under a neoliberal regime is "flexibility," understood in terms of static or short-run efficiency in which lower cost is the measure of success. Flexibility included the greater use of part-time and contingent employment, contracting out, worker speedup, hiring and firing at will, and hours changed as the company demands. In the context of global labor markets in which the threat to employment is real and the cost of job loss high, flexibility has meant a widespread deterioration of working conditions, pay, and security. Such flexibility can be contrasted with forms of labor-capital cooperation that primary-sector workers enjoyed in the postwar SSA when job protections, grievance procedures, unions, job ladders, health care, and defined-benefit retirement were assumed if one worked for the typical large corporation. Neoliberal demands to maximize stockholder value affected the nature of the corporation.

In the Anglo-American economies, the presumed parties of the left center took on the coloration of the SSA. In Britain "the City" (London's Wall Street) became a metaphor for New Labour as the then chancellor of the exchequer Gordon Brown aligned the interests of the purportedly working person's party with those of finance capital. Deregulation and "light touch" policies were calculated to win support from the financiers and make banking the even more privileged heart of the British economy. In the United States Bill Clinton, a leading light of the Democratic Leadership Council, reshaped American politics by moving it, as the DLC would have it, beyond the old left-right debate, galvanizing popular support for a new public philosophy built on non bureaucratic, market-based solutions. Robert Rubin, head of Goldman Sachs, raised money for Clinton's campaign from Wall Street and reigned over the administration's economic and financial policies as his secretary of the treasury. If, as it is said, the Supreme Court follows the election returns, the actions of elected officials hew to pressures originating in the rise of new, powerful economic interest groups that come to ascendency in the economy and rely on political influence to transform the rules to favor their continued growth. It is hard to see how in a capitalist system (capitalism being the name of our economic system), in which money politics is so powerful, it could be otherwise. While this is trivially obvious, it also goes undiscussed for the most part. The media being owned by large corporations and relying on corporate advertising is not a transgressive force by nature. Nor have academics been very useful in understanding the weaknesses that were building up in the economy as financialization became dominant.

The conventional story of the 1990s declared it a fabulously successful decade for the U.S. economy (Blinder and Yellen 2001). In such a telling, credit is given to Rubin for focusing single-mindedly on debt reduction, bringing interest rates down, and stimulating investment. There was a run-up in stock prices larger than in any other decade in the history of the United States. It is by this measure that fulsome praise was garnered and that the easy money policies of the Federal Reserve and the fiscal priorities of Mr. Rubin are judged remarkably successful. However, the basis of the growth in retrospect is suspect because what was created was a bubble economy that eventually came crashing down in 2000–2001. Joseph Stiglitz (2003), Clinton's chair of the Council of Economic Advisers (1995–97), speaks of the misguided "ascendancy of finance." At the time, however, the performance of traditional economic indicators suggested great success.

In the recovery from this downturn, the profits of S&P 500 companies more than doubled from 2001 to 2005. By late 2006 the Dow surpassed the previous peak reached at the height of the Internet bubble. But economic growth in the George W. Bush years was anemic, a jobless recovery. The question asked in retrospect is: how were these returns being made? Shareholder value was increasing far more rapidly than the economy was growing. The product market's success lagged behind the capital market's rate of return on capital employed, thanks to mergers, downsizing, higher debt levels, and creative accounting. By pushing stockholder value logic to the point of extracting every ounce of surplus and loading the firm with debt and not allowing it the reserves traditionally held against bad times, financialization tempted large-scale bankruptcy.

The neoliberal paradigm shift helps explain what Robert Hall (2007), chairman of the National Bureau of Economic Research's committee (which decides when recessions start and end), described as "causeless" recessions of 1990–91 and 2001. In previous postwar recessions, the Fed had raised interest rates to prevent a rise in inflation, triggering the slowdowns. It had not done so in these recessions. Their cause perplexed Professor Hall, who looked for "mystery shocks." It is now clear that they were brought on by the collapse of asset bubbles. Such collapses were clearly endogenous to the accumulation model of the period of global neoliberalism, which gave pride of place to debt creation. This is certainly the case for the collapse in 2007–8. The general problem was an overaccumulation of capital seeking higher returns in speculative investment. Funds pile into a growing economy to purchase assets—real estate, equities, and, in the most recent crisis, financial products like collateralized debt obligations and credit default swaps—until increasing risk can no longer be ignored; prices peak; and the bubble bursts. Debts then cannot be repaid, and the economy goes into crisis.

Summing Up

Financialization was a central, if not the central, feature of the social structure of accumulation, the Anglo-American model of capitalism that grew dependent on financial innovation as a major, if not the major, source of economic growth. Financialization dramatically changed the way capitalist production was organized over the decades of global neoliberalism. It also imparted a systematic problem of great significance. It promoted a particular kind of growth, and this led to a belief that the market was working well. It was thought that the new financial products must be good ones because the market, whose judgment was trusted, embraced them. Whatever the market said something was worth, that was it. The very possibility of herd behavior producing a bubble was not part of the reigning finance theory's equation.

Finance constantly seeks new speculative frontiers. As vast sums were poured into financial markets, investors sought to diversify their holdings into new asset classes. Because innovations cannot be patented, and successful ones are soon copied, there is a preference for opaque products and secretive dealings to protect rents. It is also the case that not all participants are equally skilled. The impact of others piling into an investment category can disorient markets. For example, movement into commodity markets in recent years seems to have broken the usual relation between price and demand by users of the commodities (copper, wheat, whatever). As investors entered these markets, commodity prices became increasingly correlated with each other and with stock prices (Tang and Xiong 2009). This is to say that commodities have gotten increasingly financialized, and the market has changed as spectators move in and out as part of a broader investment strategy, which is why, for example, even when demand for commodities is strong, their prices can fall, suggesting a mispricing, and influencing the allocation of real resources in a nonoptimal fashion. As this is written, banks are borrowing at zero interest from the Fed to buy and store commodities that are floating around the world on huge ships in storage awaiting still higher prices, pushing the Baltic Dry Index (which measures global shipping costs for commodities) higher than the price of commodities at present warrants, suggesting yet another speculative market in which bubbles become larger and volatility increases beyond what the supply-and-demand fundamentals would explain. There is obviously a good deal of money for those smart enough or lucky enough in such speculative activities to come out on top. Because of the acceptance of an equivalence between profit and economic utility, so central to thinking about the economy, insufficient attention is given to what economists insist on calling externalities—impacts on others who may be harmed from the consequences of such dealings. Until economists and others take seriously the need for social cost/benefit analysis of market activities, a great deal of damage will continue to occur.

This chapter suggests that a social structure of accumulation lens allows us to connect the preconditions that led to the worst economic crisis since the Great Depression with not only the decades-long excesses of financialization, which came to dominate the economy, but with a financialization that invaded other aspects of the economy and contributed to undermining the national Keynesian SSA, its labor-capital relations, citizen-state accord, and capital-capital accommodations. Of course neoliberalism was the core of the way Washington relied on global state economic governance institutions such as the International Monetary Fund and the World Bank to restructure debtor economies and other international economic norms. At a deeper structural level, financialization in the era of global neoliberalism may have changed the behavior of business cycles in which recessions have been caused by financial bubbles and have been followed by jobless recoveries. Before this SSA, recessions in American history mostly tended to be V-shaped, with laid-off workers called back to their old jobs, consumer confidence returning, and durable goods consumption resuming. The Great Depression of the 1930s is the major exception, and the Great Recession experience sheds some parallel light on why it was different.

It is good to bear in mind structural development discussed in this chapter when the events of the Great Recession and proposals for financial reform are discussed in later chapters. Whether regulators can keep financiers from putting money to use where they expect the highest returns, even if the uses chosen increase risk to the system, is a very real question. If capital markets are functioning to maximize paper profits even if this does not stimulate job creation; if the most powerful figures in the corporate world are able to enrich themselves at the expense of stockholders, including pension and mutual funds to which Americans have entrusted their savings and hopes for a more comfortable life; and if companies remain profitable but find no better use of the surplus than to buy back their own stock, why will financialization not continue to do damage to the society? In taking financial reform seriously, these deeper systemic questions should not be ignored.

3

Realism in Financial Markets

*But what is in even shorter supply than credit is an economic theory to explain
why the financial tsunami occurred, and what its consequences might be.
Over the past 30 years, economists have devoted great intellectual energy to
proving that such disasters cannot happen. The market system accurately prices
all trades at each moment in time. Greed, ignorance, euphoria, panic, herd
behavior, predation, financial skulduggery and politics—the forces that drive
boom-bust cycles—only exist offstage in their models.*

—ROBERT SKIDELSKY, 2008

*Trying to model something that escapes modelization is the heart of the
problem. We like models because they do not require experience and can be
taught by a 33-year-old assistant professor. Sometimes you need to say, "No
model is better than a faulty model"—like no medicine is better than the
advice of an unqualified doctor, and no drug is better than any drug.*

—NASSIM NICHOLAS TALEB (GELMAN 2008)

The first financial crisis in the Western world is said to have been in
1622 when the Holy Roman Empire debased its coins, bringing on
a modern-style banking crisis. This could be understood perhaps as
the result of poor monetary policy or simply the greed of an elite that did not
distinguish between the state and the self. Since the triumph of the market
system, economists with faith in the rational expectations of investors and
financial markets to produce efficient outcomes understand crises as caused
by shocks to the system coming from the outside. The most frequently
mentioned of these exogenous influences is bad government policy. Yet it
is doubtful that policy-maker error or excessive government spending had
much to do with the South Sea Bubble in 1720, or with panics in financial,
property, and commodity markets in an emergent British capitalism in 1763,
1720, 1793, 1797, 1799 or 1810, or in the United States in the nineteenth century when financial crises occurred with similar frequency.

Factors endogenous to the market itself explain quite a lot about such
events. Consider Irving Fisher's analysis of the major financial crises of U.S.
history. He saw the crisis of 1837 as connected to the lucrative investment
opportunities in the developing West and Southwest in real estate, cotton,
canal building, turnpikes, and steamboats, while the crisis of 1873 was in

railroads and farm indebtedness following the Homestead Act. The over-optimism of investors encouraged more and more speculation until bubbles burst. This is not to say that in a number of instances government cannot be found guilty of contributing to problems. Fisher attributed the overindebtedness leading to the panic of 1893 to the addition of too much silver relative to gold in the backing of the U.S. money supply (Fisher 1933:348). Were Fisher around for contemporary high-tech and real estate bubbles, he would no doubt see a continuation of a familiar pattern of successful growth encouraging speculation. Many of these episodes involve bubbles—a continuous, sharp rise in the price of a type of asset or a range of assets, with the initial jump generating expectations of further rises and attracting new buyers interested in profits from trading in the asset rather than in its use or earning capacity (Kindleberger 1987). Expectations produce momentum and a psychological propensity of investors to lose perspective in the presence of a run of encouraging news and outcomes so that they overshoot at both the top and bottom, moving prices away from their true values and producing endogenous cycles.

While standard neoclassical theory precludes the existence of asset bubbles, some economists have developed formal models that challenge the efficient market presumptions and focus attention on behavioral factors such as Keynes's animal spirits and herd behavior. They construct models of rational arbitrageurs who, while they understand that the market will eventually collapse, "ride the bubble as it continues to grow and generate high returns" (Abreu and Brunnermeir 2003:174) with the expectation of exiting to "beat the gun," in Keynes's phrase. Of course, not everyone can get out the door at the same time.

Decisions are not made in isolation from what others think, as the demand curves of mainstream economics suppose. Neuroscientists' brain studies find that people place greater value on something when other people tell them that it is worth more than they thought and downgrade their own assessments when others say something is worth less than they thought. When lots of other people agree with us, we become even more enthusiastic and have greater confidence in the expected direction that values will take. Cells in the ventral striatum, a reward center wired with dopamine neurons, respond to pleasures (sugar, sex, higher returns on investments). Activity is triggered in the insula, a section of the brain associated with heightened awareness, so our attention is grabbed and we respond (Campbell-Meiklejohn et al. 2010). Both social influences and autonomous brain circuitry thus play a part in the herd behavior associated with financial decisions, confirming Keynes's view and adding to intrinsic uncertainty in forecasting. In the matter of concern here, the speculative bubble, Robert Shiller (2003:35) tells us that it is "a period when investors are attracted to an investment irrationally because rising prices encourage them to expect, at some level of consciousness at least, more price increases." He explains that a feedback develops as people become more and more attracted and invest more, and thus prices continue to increase. When people no longer expect prices to increase, demand falls, the bubble comes to an end, and the market crashes.

This sort of understanding of market psychology is expressed with some regularity after a crisis and stands in contrast to the stories of efficient markets and rational expectations that are celebrated in expansions. Shiller (2009:9) offers the view that "to a remarkable extent we have got into the current economic and financial crisis because of a wrong economic theory—an economic theory that itself denies the role of animal spirits in getting us into manias and panics." Some monetary economists, while recognizing that bubbles are real, do not accept the endogenous financial cycle thinking implicit in Shiller's definition. Allan Meltzer (2003:27), for example, concludes that a bubble is "a name we assign to events that we cannot explain with standard hypotheses." Others have stronger reactions. Even after the Great Recession bubble deflated, the prominent University of Chicago economist Eugene Fama defended the efficiency market hypothesis, which he had a major role in promoting. When asked, "Surely, we had experienced a giant credit bubble?" he replied, "I don't know what a credit bubble means. I don't even know what a bubble means. These words have become popular. I don't think they have any meaning" (cited in Cassidy 2010:30).

Such statements illustrate a refusal by influential academics of a certain persuasion to acknowledge the historical record of bubbles and cycles. Professor Fama was so upset by the numerous times the *Economist* used the term "bubble" that he canceled his subscription. One is reminded of the most famous editor of that publication, Walter Bagehot, who canonically quoted the banker Lord Overstone's description of the stages of the cycle: "quiescence, improvement, confidence, prosperity, excitement, overtrading, CONVULSION [emphasis is Bagehot's], pressure, stagnation, ending again in quiescence." Convulsion did not catch on. "Bubble" has entered the lexicon and stands in rebuke to those who deny the existence and persistence of this all-too-familiar phenomenon associated with investors as a group suddenly changing direction.

Charles Mackay, in his 1841 book *Extraordinary Popular Delusions and the Madness of Crowds*, famously laid out the tension between greed and fear as the prime mover in the behavior of market participants in an anachronistic-sounding but surely not wrong perspective: "Men, it has been well said, think in herds: it will be seen that they go mad in herds, while they only recover their senses slowly, and one by one." Today behavioral economists observe a pattern of people dysfunctionally clinging too tightly and too long to opinions (Barberis and Thaler 2003). Information theorists identify the phenomenon of coordinated behavior premised on questionable information creating "rational" herding (Calvo and Mendoza 2000; Bikhchandani and Sharma 2001). The problem in what passes for information in financial markets is that it is based on expectations that are not verifiable in the sense economists normally mean when speaking of information. Rather, it is opinion. Investors tend to place great faith in their ability to judge the validity of information that they want to believe true. Work in behavioral economics provides a more realistic sense of how people think and act under conditions of uncertainty. Such unorthodox approaches are making inroads into the core market model priors as the standard theory comes into question more widely. The Great Recession may be forcing a basic rethinking of ideas that have been marginalized in the profession for three decades or so.

Willem Buiter (2009a), a distinguished practitioner as well as theorist of monetary policy, writes that "the typical graduate macroeconomics and monetary economics training received at Anglo-American universities during the past 30 years or so may have set back by decades serious investigations of aggregate economic behaviour and economic policy-relevant understandings." The profession increasingly accepts that the economic transactions covered by the discipline are a small subset of actual practices, which include many undertaken by opportunistic agents who lie and deceive; that market signals are wrong in important instances; that these false signals can reinforce each other, driving the economy further off course; that the complete markets at the core of mainstream theory as it continues to be widely taught do not exist; and that many deterministic linear mathematical exercises that are part of accepted theory are not acceptable, given the way market participants learn from and respond to changes in their environment in recursive fashion.

The still dominant approach is based on an understanding of rational expectations (RE), which in behavioral terms, as David Colander (2009) explains, "would imply that individuals and the economist have a complete understanding of the economic mechanisms governing the world. In this sense, rational expectations models do not attempt to formalize individuals' actual expectations: specifications are not based on empirical observations of the expectations formation process of human actors." The problem, in short, is that in attempting to be "scientific," by mimicking nineteenth-century physics, economists ignore contemporary psychology.

A second essential building bloc of the mainstream approach is the representative agent model, which, since economics is about interaction of actors with different "motives, knowledge, and capabilities," implies heterogeneity of agents. Therefore, such a modeling approach is unrealistic. It is defended on two grounds: it allows for accurate prediction, and it is mathematically tractable. The latter is certainly the stronger reason since the resulting models, by assuming away complexity, "do not pass even "a perfunctory common sense smell test." Yet it is such models, Colander observes, that are "studied ad nauseam." They are maintained despite the evidence gathered in empirical behavioral research. Mainstream finance theory is being challenged by what may be called postmodern financial theory, which is based on openness to contingency and psychological insight.

The theoretical underpinning of mainstream theory remains general equilibrium models, developed through advanced mathematics, requiring a high level of abstraction. For the math to work, market participants are presumed to hold a particular kind of rationality and access to information regarding the probable distribution of future events so that probabilities can be calculated. As Paul Davidson (2009:87–88) explains, "Since drawing a sample from the future is not possible, efficient market theorists must presume that probabilities calculated from already existing market data is equivalent to drawing a sample from markets that will exist in the future." This presumption is the ergodic axiom that, as Davidson says, is "in essence an assertion that the future is merely the statistical shadow of the past. . . . Those who claim that economics is a 'hard science' like physics or astronomy argue that the ergodic axiom must be the foundation of the economists' model if economics is to be a 'hard' science." This is also the basis of modern laissez-faire economic thinking since government policy "is equivalent to throwing something into the predetermined path of the economy pushing it temporarily off its path involving more unemployment, resource waste, et cetera."

Efficient market theory would never permit people to spend more than their income so that the debt they contract cannot be paid. Markets would not be efficient if obligations were not met. As Korkut Ertürk and Gökcer Özgür (2009:3) write, "Wouldn't credit card holders who are having trouble meeting even their monthly minimum credit card payment obligations and those mortgage borrowers who were foreclosed out of their homes be happy to know if only they had lived in a classical world of efficient markets, they would never have become entrapped in such burdensome contractual obligations?" Such cutting irony seemed very much on target in the midst of the financial meltdown, which, as it happened, took place in a nonergodic world.

It is not just that mainstream macro models cannot speak to the concerns of policy makers, "which they can't, but rather that it is difficult for anyone brought up under their influence even to conceive of such events occurring in the first place. That is why a crisis in macroeconomics is an integral part of the current economic crisis" (Laidler 2009:13). Robert E. Lucas, Jr., is considered the preeminent macroeconomist of the global neoliberal SSA; indeed, agreement over method in the profession along new classical lines, setting out the standard of what counts as good economics, is attributed to him (Chari 1999:22). For some time Lucas has been aware that "the problem is that, in the new theories, the theories embedded in general equilibrium dynamics of the sort that we know how to do pretty well by now, there is a residue of things they don't let us think about. They don't let us think about the U.S. experience in the 1930s or about financial crises and their real consequences in Asia and Latin America." Lucas goes on to say, "In terms of the theory that researchers are developing as a cumulative body of knowledge— no one has figured out how to take that theory to successful answers to the real effects of monetary instability" (Lucas 2003b:23). Laidler (2009:4), who was in the audience for Lucas's remarks, adds in response that those same models "do not help us think about the problems that are dominating the current evolution of the world economy—some residue!"

The theory of financial markets retains a basic dependence on unrealistic restrictive assumptions in describing the behavior of firms in the marketplace, as illustrated by the longevity of a model introduced by Modigliani and Miller (1958), subsequently named the M-M concept. This model was based on the assumption of perfect information and perfect competition, a well-functioning market, neutral taxes, and rational investors, allowing the conclusion that it makes no difference whether a firm invests out of retained earnings or out of debt. The value of the firm is the same either way. The lesson was applied to the real world: that the value of the firm should not be affected by the share of debt in its financial structure or by what will be done with the returns—paid out as dividends or reinvested (profitably). The M-M conditions mean that investment decisions and cash flow are independent of financial policy and leverage levels, and taxes are assumed not to be a factor. In the real world, the amount of debt held by a firm matters very much, as does the importance of tax deductibility for interest paid. Continued teaching of pure models by those unwilling to dirty their hands with real-world complications has been the hallmark of prestige to many in the economics profession.

Of course, if financial markets are competitive, always liquid, frictionless, and tax neutral, financial composition of debt-to-shares may not matter. But in the world in which we live, loading up on debt and holding minimal capital can kill a company in an economic downturn. Sophisticated economists use models as the starting point to talk about how the real situation departs from their assumptions and focus on its consequences. However, most students are taught only the pure case that abstracts from such concerns. The counterframeworks developed in this chapter and the history of crises make clear why the profession needs to revisit its core and explain the behavior of financial innovation and its consequences for received theory. The credit crunches that stress highly indebted corporations arise from excessive leverage in the financial system, and so an alternative to the M-M starting point is essential in thinking about the need for macroprudential regulation (Hanson, Kashyap, and Stein 2010).

Business schools have begun to warn students of the limits of economic models, something that had not been stressed before the Great Recession's financial sector meltdown, and less is heard of Milton Friedman's (1953) contention that speculation is always stabilizing. It is not that business programs did not have a vast literature on credit cycles on which to draw, but what was thought of as theoretical rigor took precedence, indeed eclipsing the study of the economic history in the education of economists. Charles Kindleberger (1978:2) describes many instances of "speculative excesses, referred to concisely as a mania, and revulsion from such excess in the form of a crisis, crash, or panic can be shown to be, if not inevitable, at least historically common." The fiction of ever rational investors and always efficient financial markets does not describe the real history of our economic system, prone as it is to repeated crises. In actual crises even libertarians, if they are in positions of responsibility, learn that markets endogenously produce crises.

Alan Greenspan told a congressional committee in 1998 that "at one point the economic system appears stable, the next it behaves as though a dam has reached a breaking point, and water [read confidence] evacuates its reservoir." A decade later Greenspan recanted a career's worth of belief in free-market theory and minimal regulation when he famously found "a flaw" in such thinking. Greenspan's predecessor as head of the Federal Reserve, Paul Volcker, declared, "Flows of funds and their valuation in free markets are influenced as much by perceptions as by objective reality—or perhaps more precisely, the perception is the reality. The herd instinct is strong. Only in hindsight do episodes of strong 'overshooting' or 'undershooting' become evident, and the reversals are typically sudden" (1998:1). Andrew Crockett (2001), when head of the Bank for International Settlement explained, echoing Keynes, "To an important extent value, like beauty, is in the eye of the beholder. Its assessment is subject to powerful waves of shared optimism or pessimism. Investors are prone to see new paradigms . . . individual stocks, even stock indices, can move by large amount even in the absence of significant new information."

In his 1930 *Treatise on Money*, Keynes offered an interesting wrinkle on this when he explained that bears in the financial market, not willing to take on speculative risk, lend their funds for modest interest income, but these funds end up being borrowed by bulls who use them to speculate. In the process, the more cautious fund the risk taking of others. The contemporary pattern of international capital flows, to be discussed later, can be interpreted as transferring global "bear funds" to "global bulls," the former cautious savers funding the latter leveraged speculators (Ertürk 2010:45). Different risk propensities do not inhibit speculative bubbles. Keynes wrote "each individual investor flatters himself that his commitment is 'liquid' and is willing to run a greater risk" (Keynes 1936:160), but investors are unwise to do so, for, as he wrote, there is no such thing as liquidity of investment for the community as a whole. This became painfully clear during the world financial crisis. It also should serve as a caution against the assertion that hedge-fund managers and others who say their firms did not cause the crisis or need a government bailout and so do not need stricter regulation when in fact they are extensively connected to the regulated banks that did need bailing out. They may themselves prove more intimately involved in future crises, given their importance in contemporary financial markets.

The point to be stressed is the endogenous and the subjective recursive aspects of market psychology. George Soros, a man who knows a thing or two about the behavior of speculators, reminds us that buyers and sellers in financial markets, in seeking to establish the present value of a discounted future, are part of a reflexive process since that future depends on their own decisions. That is, the shape of the demand and supply curves for the assets whose prices they speculate on cannot be taken as given because of the need to incorporate expectations about the events that are shaped by these expectations. This complicated feedback loop brings strong indeterminacy to the process. Prices, as a result, can move away from their theoretical equilibrium for sustained periods. The path away from this theoretical equilibrium affects the manner in which they will then come back or not. While economists are not ready to abandon the usefulness of equilibrium models of price determination of financial assets, Soros thinks they should do so since, "in the absence of equilibrium, the contention that free markets lead to the optimum allocation of resources loses its justification." And of course with that a great deal of economists' certainty disappears. Much of what was seen as calculable risk and deterministic becomes uncertain. Looking at this in traditional supply-and-demand terms, higher prices in asset markets call forth greater, not less, demand, unlike in most product markets.

In a 2001 letter to his stockholders, Warren Buffett, America's most successful investor, describes the essence of what occurs in the greed-fear balance when speculation is in full swing: "Once a bull market gets under way, and once you reach the point where everybody has made money no matter what system he or she followed, a crowd is attracted to the game." These people superimpose an I-can't-miss-the-party factor, "like Pavlov's dog," Buffett suggests. "These 'investors' learn that when the bell rings—in this case the one that opens the New York Stock Exchange at 9:30—they get fed. Through all this daily reinforcement, they become convinced there is a God and that He wants them to get rich." People do not connect their good fortune in a bubble situation to monetary policy makers maintaining low interest rates and easy access to speculative credit, or to runaway animal spirits. Optimism feeds optimism.

It is useful to go back to the foundational literature of the 1930s when these issues were explored in conjunction with collapsing markets. Economists bent their minds not to creating a world of zero market imperfections to mimic pure physics (as they understood physics), but instead struggled to theorize from acute observation what was happening in the real world in which they lived, using inherited models that were little help in explaining then current phenomena. In 1933 Irving Fisher published the classic explanation of how bubbles are created: "Easy money is the great cause of over borrowing. When an investor thinks he can make over a hundred per cent per annum by borrowing at six per cent, he will be tempted to borrow and to invest or speculate with borrowed money" (1933:348). This, Fisher thought, was a prime cause of the overindebtedness of 1929. "Inventions and technological improvements created wonderful investment opportunities, and so caused big debts." Fisher called attention to the specifics unique to that particular episode. For him these included the "leftover" war debts, domestic and foreign, public and private; reconstruction loans to foreigners; and England's low-interest policy starting in 1925 to help it get back on the gold standard. The specifics always differ, which contributes to people thinking that "this time it is different." But the overoptimism, overextension, breakdown, and periods of extended pessimism are the same. Fisher used the image that beyond certain limits "at first, a stick may bend under strain, ready all the time to bend back, until a certain point is reached, when it breaks." He also used the image of a ship capsizing after being tipped beyond a certain point, no longer able to right itself, bringing on calamity (339).

Fisher described the "public psychology of going into debt for gain" as going through four more or less distinct phases: (1) the lure of gain of income in the remote future from an investment; (2) the hope of selling for capital gain in the near future in a rising market; (3) "the vogue of reckless promotions," sellers taking advantage of the public's great expectations; and (4) "the development of downright fraud, imposing on a public which had grown credulous and gullible" (349). He stressed the overinvestment and overspeculation but noted that they would do far less harm if not for the accompanying overborrowing. Fisher's inclusion of the last of his four stages—the corrupt dealing that seems to grow in the final stage of a bubble—is a topic that most economists usually leave out, such vulgar dealings being beneath their attention. Mainstream macroeconomics and finance theory generally have not seen this corruption as integral to the nature of financial crises. Nor have they connected the collapse of bubbles with the impact on business decisions in the way Fisher usefully did.

Fisher pointed out that as businesses get into trouble, they sell assets to raise capital. When large numbers of firms sell assets, their price is driven down, undermining debtors' positions as remaining collateral is worth less. This pushes more assets onto the market in a destructive downward, debt deflation cycle. Homeowners, unable to pay their mortgages, default, pushing down housing prices and leading to a similar cycle. Deflation in asset prices turns into a vicious cycle. In what Fisher called "a stampede to liquidate," the economy goes into a severe economic crisis. "Over-investment and overspeculation are often important; but they would have far less serious results were they not conducted with borrowed money. That is, over-indebtedness may lend importance to over-investment and over-speculation." He added, "The same is true as to over-confidence. I fancy that over-confidence seldom does any great harm except when, as, and if, it beguiles its victims into debt."

Little needs to be added to Fisher's description of such "debt disturbances." These elements—the temptation to speculate with borrowed money, to push one's luck too far, and for investors/speculators to do this as part of a herd—produce bubbles and overreach and bring on financial crises. The role of "downright fraud" during the "vogue of reckless promotions" and the trouble businesses engaged in directly productive activities encounter in the downturn accelerate the destructive debt deflation. Downturns are made worse, as Fisher points out, by heavy leverage. These remain the essential elements for an understanding of the global financial crisis that occurred in the first decade of the twenty-first century.

John Maynard Keynes stressed the potential volatility of investment and thus the potential instability of the capitalist growth process. Many things can alter expectations regarding an enterprise's costs and revenues and affect investment decisions. These range from the degree of international competition to changes in capital-labor social relations, government policy, and financial variables (Crotty 1986). Keynes himself asserted the necessity of government intervention, not only in the short run, but as structurally necessary in the long run since there was never reason to believe that aggregate demand and aggregate supply would be equal at the full-employment level of output. It did not matter whether wages were rigid or flexible, or markets competitive or monopolistic; there was a role for government in creating and preserving full employment through activist policies.

Many introductory textbooks still contrast Keynes, as advocate of countercyclical fiscal policy, manipulating taxation and government spending to bring an economy back to equilibrium, with monetarists, who recognize the interest rate and the quantity of money in circulation as the effective policy levers. This reduction of macroeconomics to a choice of hydraulic Keynesianism (taxing and spending, more or less) versus monetarists (raising or lowering interest rates or the quantity of money) ignores, among other things, Keynes's appreciation of how finance works through a different channel and that the economy tends to fall into an under full employment equilibrium requiring continuous government activism.

Unlike most mainstream macroeconomists, Keynes understood the importance of finance as distinct from monetary economics. In his *Treatise on Money* he defines finance as "the business of holding and exchanging titles to wealth" while industry is "the business of maintaining the normal process of current output, distribution and exchange and paying the factors of production their income for the various duties they perform from the first beginning of production to the final satisfaction of consumers" (Keynes 1935:243). This is a very different understanding of the role of money in a capitalist economy from the "money as a veil" approach of traditional monetarists. Keynes also rejected the notion that economies find equilibrium only in full-employment situations but proposed that a country could go for a long period in a state of underemployment equilibrium. Because such a view does not have micro foundations in the competitive market model central to neoclassical economics, it was rejected by the counterrevolution in economic thought that came with the demise of the national Keynesian SSA (Tabb 1999: chaps. 8, 9).

Textbook Keynesian macroeconomics sees savings attributed to households coming out of the circular flow and returning through the intermediation of banks to increase aggregate demand. In reality, corporations fund investment out of retained earnings. Lending overwhelmingly goes to the financial sphere and stays there. It is used to buy assets that appreciate in value to act as collateral for more borrowing to buy more assets, in a self-generating spiral—until it happens that asset values do not rise further as expected, and debt obligations cannot be honored. In the neoliberal era, it is useful to distinguish two types of saving: the kind stressed in the textbooks by households and businesses, and the kind that comes from rentier income, most of which is reinvested in assets looking for capital gains, often leveraged with borrowed funds. In traditional terms, such saving does not increase as the value of marketed assets increases, as does debt in the system.

In *The General Theory,* Keynes defined speculation as "the activity of forecasting the psychology of markets" and enterprise as "the activity of forecasting the prospective yield of assets over their whole life." A speculator buys and sells on short-term movements. The old-style manager looks to the long-run profitability of the company. It is production that has been the subject of economics. Keynes warned of allowing the tail of speculation to wag the economic body. Such has been the influence of financialization that just such a condition had become the reality in the pre–Great Recession United States and England. Keynes spoke of the desirability of "the euthanasia of the rentier." In the era of global neoliberalism, rentier interests took over corporate decision making, as discussed in chapter 2.

In the expansion, potential credit is limited only by expectations of inadequate increases in the market price of assets. As long as their price is expected to rise, money is available to be borrowed to purchase them. Purchases further inflate the value of the assets until expectations are disappointed and the bubble bursts. Increased saving to address the debt problem reduces consumption and slows growth while deleveraging continues. The question is always, why don't people see this coming? Some do. The issue is always timing, getting out just as or slightly before the market peaks.

While money is a unit of account, a medium of exchange, and a store of value, it is a fourth demand for money—the speculative demand—that Keynes introduced in *The General Theory* and which has taken center stage. Rather than there being the socialization of investment, which he advocated so that growth would be guided by social priorities, the surplus created in production does not go to meet the public's needs or to social partners but is understood as the property of stockholders, even if they are very transient owners. The difficulties that concerned Keynes would occur when, as he famously wrote, "enterprise becomes the bubble on a whirl-pool of speculation. . . . Capital development becomes a by-product of the activities of the casino" (1936:159). This famous passage comes to prominence when asset bubbles are seen as inflating dangerously. Certainly this is a good description of the situation leading to the financial crisis of the Great Recession.

In the same year that Keynes's *Treatise on Probability* appeared, Frank Knight (1921) offered the canonical distinction between measurable risk and risk that is indeterminate and so unmeasurable, which he called uncertainty. Since the latter cannot be measured in advance, as in the case of statistical risk, it needs to be thought of quite differently. The two constructs are very different, and uncertainty cannot legitimately be reduced to statistical risk since "risk" in the second case is by definition unknowable. Knightian uncertainty is banished from mainstream economics in the assumptions of most market models. Keynes's writing on probability was devoted to understanding decision making under unmeasurable uncertainty. This aspect of his work, so central to concerns here, received little or no attention from most modern Keynesians until the severe financial crisis occurred. To Keynes, the difficulties people have in decision making leads to herd behavior. This, combined with a willingness to gamble on borrowed money, magnifies impacts, which push markets away from stable outcomes.

In an expansion, as Warren Buffett noted, everyone thinks they are geniuses. Our lack of knowledge of what the future will bring, combined with a willingness to trust untrustworthy impulses, means, as Keynes declared in his famous chapter 12 of *The General Theory*, that the "outstanding fact" is the "extreme precariousness of the basic knowledge on which our estimates of prospective yield have to be made. Our knowledge of factors which will govern the yield of an investment some years hence is usually slight and often negligible." Because investments are made based on estimates of expected future earnings, and because views on what these may be can shift dramatically, markets can become volatile in periods of great uncertainty, so that if "we speak frankly we have to admit that our basis of knowledge for estimating the yield ten years hence of a railway, a copper mine, a textile factory . . . amount to little to nothing." What is missed by the herd, because for long periods it can seem irrelevant, is that this intrinsic uncertainty of the future can mean that collective euphoria pushes values over sustained periods in wrong directions, resulting in the sudden need for painful adjustments.

Efforts to paint Keynes as out-of-date (since he could not foresee the efficient markets of modern financial systems) flounder when one considers his knowledge of financial markets and experiences as a speculator of no mean achievement. As Robert Skidelsky (2005:18) notes, "Keynes, who wrote a pioneering essay on futures markets, would have been completely at home in a world of ever more complex financial instruments designed to insure against every conceivable kind of risk. Whether he would have bought the ideology that comes with them is a different question. He would surely have recognized the systemic risks in the hedge fund culture." The point, Skidelsky maintains on behalf of Keynes, is that "we have become increasingly sophisticated at hedging risk, but uncertainty is uninsurable. We get around this awkward corner by reclassifying uncertainty as risk." For example, Keynes thought that we talk of "political risk" when we should be talking about political uncertainty. "The use of the word risk conveys a spurious precision, which comforts the market but has no basis in science."

The strength of the pre-Keynesian revival from Reagan through the administration of George W. Bush produced a generation of economists who counted on the market to do its magic, even in a depression. This was a step back even from the bastardized Keynesianism of the American postwar Keynesian-neoclassical synthesis, which had already marginalized Keynes's important insights. The version of the synthesis that reigned was one that consigned Keynes to a historical footnote while turning a blind eye to the existence of numerous market failures, which were disregarded on the assumption that they were minor in a market economy. As Joseph Stiglitz (2009:293) writes,

In the aftermath of the Great Depression, a particular doctrine came to be accepted, called the neo-classical synthesis. It argued that once markets were restored to full employment, neo-classical principles would apply— the economy would be efficient. We should be clear: it was not a theorem but a belief. The idea was always suspect—why should market failures only occur in big doses? Rather, recessions can be seen as the tip of the iceberg; underneath are many "smaller" market failures, giving rise in the aggregate to huge inefficiencies.

Actually existing capitalism left much to be desired in the inadequate number of decent jobs it created and the failure to attend to public goods preferred by a democratic polity.

Following on Keynes's insights, Hyman Minsky's financial instability the-sis suggests that fragility grows over the extended period of prosperity as risk is rewarded, leading to the taking of greater risk. Indebtedness increases as investors/speculators seek to take advantage of the good times. An extended period of prosperity can lead to greater future instability as the confidence with which a prosperous present is projected forward evaporates. At first the situation is one of what Minsky calls hedge financing, an unfortunate choice since for him hedge financing is when borrowers are able to pay interest and return principal when it is due (a different connotation from the more recent use of "hedge" as in hedge funds). Hedge financing units are those that can meet their payment obligations out of cash flow. Such a firm is able to re-duce its net debt burden. As the expansion proceeds, hedge financing gives way to speculative finance, where only the interest can be paid back, and debt is rolled over by taking on new debt. Speculative finance units can meet their payment obligations out of cash flow but cannot repay the principal out of income. There is nothing necessarily wrong with this; growing firms are typically in this position. Their debt burden, however, increases as a result. Finally, Ponzi financing occurs in which economic agents must borrow to pay interest on existing liabilities. This is a position of significant risk and financial fragility.

Since finance costs are greater than income from assets in Ponzi style, fi-nance debt increases over time. For Ponzi units, the only hope of repaying debt is an increase in the value of the underlying asset that the borrowing was used to purchase. One reason some engage in Ponzi financing is that this may not be intentional. A second is that one can control more assets us-ing other people's money. If the value of such assets rises sufficiently, Ponzi financing can turn into hedge financing. If not, it may still be possible to milk assets that one temporarily controls, as some private equity firms have become expert in doing. They may have to sell a company for less than they paid, but while in control they may loot it and so come out well ahead. It is possible that Ponzi financiers will be bailed out by the government if their failure is seen as a systemic threat, as was the case of many banks by 2007–8 (see chapter 5).

Fragility is generally the result of increased payment commitments relative to gross profits owing to the increase in short-term financing costs. The downturn comes when a high-profile borrower or borrowers cannot sustain their obligations and must sell assets and take a loss on the sale (Taylor and O'Connell 1989; Schroeder 2002). When it is seen that they are overextended, creditors wonder who else may be in the same boat. Lenders turn cautious. It becomes difficult to obtain new credit, and asset values plummet as more distress sales take place. This was the state of things in the dog days of the presidency of George W. Bush. The more speculative and Ponzi units there are, and especially units that have moved from hedge to speculative to this latter category, the worse the economic downturn will be.

The Minsky Moment

The combined efforts of lenders and borrowers expand debt to the point where borrowers have trouble paying the carrying costs of their debt and lenders become cautious. At this point, when an overleveraged system encounters financial difficulties, it has reached the "Minsky Moment," as the better read on Wall Street have come to know it. There is no comfortable return to equilibrium as textbook models propose. Instead, good times move further into the danger zone until the inevitable collapse comes. Speculative and even hedge financial units become Ponzi financing as assets are thrown on the market, and other businesses face a bleaker future in a process of cumulative causation. The collapse of speculative positions amplifies a wider instability. More hedge finance turns into Ponzi finance as the economy deteriorates, provoking a generalized panic situation—what the Germans call *torschlusspanik*, or door shut panic, words conveying that not everyone can get out the door first when there is need to dump assets quickly. Minsky does not use the phrase, but it is this relation of leverage to confidence and panic that is central to his understanding of financial crises; hence the Minsky

Moment is *torschlusspanik* time. The trigger may be a tightening by a major central bank that limits liquidity globally and affects financial markets. A rise in interest rates by the Bank of Japan means that hedge funds, which had borrowed cheaply in yen and invested in high-yield assets elsewhere, leveraging their money, are exposed to greater risk. The popularity of such carry trade in fact meant knock-on impacts for high-yielding currencies from New Zealand to Iceland. Unexpected change can produce major sell-offs with no buyers at viable prices.

A significant literature has come into existence exploring the relation of Keynes's views on crisis with Minsky's. Most obviously, financial indebtedness is at the center of the latter's thinking (Minsky 1986:172), while Keynes's focus is the disappointing of optimism with regard to return on investment, a response to awareness of change in the marginal efficiency of capital (Keynes 1936:321) after the peak of the boom passes. What is important for our purposes here is that both see cycles as endogenous, setting their approaches, which have been conjoined for this analysis, at odds with the dominant macro- and financial economics. We cannot, of course, know what Keynes would think in the present period of the dominance of a financialization decoupling finance from production. Indeed, we do not know what Minsky would think, given that his financial instability thesis was premised on overindebtedness resulting from capitalism's proclivity to growth in which it is the nonfinancial business sector that is overindebted, surely not the case in the current conjuncture (De Antoni 2010; Rochon and Rossi 2010). Whether "it has happened again" depends on how narrowly or broadly one wants to understand Minsky's approach. Kregel (2008) thinks that the declining margins of safety and Ponzi financing are not the result of the general endogenous process Minsky describes but the specific evaluation of credit worthiness in the originate-and-distribute model that banks have adopted in securitizing rather than retaining loans, which will be discussed in subsequent chapters (see also Davidson 2008).

The broad point is that policy makers wishing to prevent or at least moderate such events need an understanding of the dynamic in Minsky's words that "the normal functioning of our economy leads to financial trauma and crises" (1986:287). For Minsky, as for Keynes and Marx, whenever something approaching stability is achieved, destabilizing processes are set off. Business cycles are endogenous. That is the way a money economy works: "Each stage, whether it be boom, crisis, debt-deflation, stagnation, or expansion, is transitory" (1986:61). From such a perspective, institutions can never create more than a conditional stability, a temporary order. They cannot eliminate uncertainty. The perception that risk can be controlled encourages greater risk taking. Too much confidence is a problem. It reduces caution, which is required to limit the extent of leverage and prevent overextension. This is not, as mainstream neoclassical theorists suggest, because some exogenous event causes the crisis, although one may trigger awareness of the unsustainability of the extent of debt financing, but rather because the internal dynamics of capitalism produce crises. Proper regulation can moderate but not prevent financial cycles. As that outlaw economist Karl Marx, a pioneer of endogenous monetary theory, wrote in volume 3 of *Capital*, "In a system of production, where the entire continuity of the reproduction process rests on credit, a crisis must obviously occur—a tremendous rush for the means of payment—when credit suddenly ceases and only cash payments have validity" (Marx 1894:490).

At the level of mainstream theory, which presumes the need for micro foundations for macro models, it is difficult to include a true credit view of finance-driven bubbles. The restrictions on the acceptable priors of such models have meant that there has been little influence of Minsky or Keynes on contemporary macro modeling of credit even by academically talented future policy makers who have ventured onto the borders of this terrain (Bernanke and Blinder 1988; Bernanke and Gertler 1995). In Minskyan terms, finance does not merely act as an accelerant to underlying developments but initiates a process of self-expansion premised on speculative opportunities in expected financial asset valuations. Alan Greenspan, while he saw irrational exuberance in frothy markets, allowed the bubble to continue to inflate rather than cut off growth. Precrisis Ben Bernanke argued too that the Fed should act to control inflation but not try to manage credit. Whether and how the Fed could, if it wanted to, attempt to preemptively manage the cycles of boom and bust is not at all clear unless it were to take a more active role in controlling capital markets. Knowing when and how to intervene and being allowed to do so are enormous challenges under the accepted restrictions implicitly placed on central banks.

If one works from a Minskyan mindset, prolonged low interest rates eventually lead to a mispricing of assets, incorrect profit signals, and too much leverage and asset inflation, which must at some point end and will usually end badly. This is because the extended past and satisfactory present will be projected forward with too much confidence. Minsky's analysis suggests that an extended period of financial stability is a breeding ground for crisis and instability, the very opposite of what conventional economists typically assume.

Fed chairman Bernanke famously celebrated the years of explosive growth of financialization and high-leveraged risk as the Great Moderation, a period of relatively steady economic growth (1984–2004). In fact it was a time of growing risk taking, dangerously increasing leverage, and Ponzi financing, as well as fraudulent financial practices—even as there was contemporaneous celebration of the success of Fed policies. Bernanke, commenting on the Great Moderation and the decrease in economic uncertainty confronting households and firms and fewer and less severe recessions, attributed these fortuitous changes to improvements in monetary policy.

These years were, in short, a perfect example of the validity of Minsky's thesis that instability is created in a period of seeming stability. The extent to which Ben Bernanke was clueless regarding what was happening is indicated by an essay he published in 2003 warning that the critical problem the country faced was the threat of impending deflation (Bernanke 2003:75). His concern, as it turned, was out misdirected. It was the weakness in the quality of the balance sheets that built up along with excessive leverage that was missed by a Fed missing these indicators. The buildup of unpayable debt would lead to collapse.

For an extended period, the economic mainstream's message had been that financial problems had diminished. Economists noted that the variability of real output had decreased by half since the mid-1980s, accompanied by lower volatility of the rate of inflation (Blanchard and Simon 2001). They described the macroeconomic stability in the mid- and late 1990s as the "Goldilocks economy" (not too hot, not too cold, just right) and applauded the success of macroeconomics as a field of study (Blanchard 2008). Yet "Great Moderation" thinking had consequences seen more clearly in retrospect. The theory held that economic cycles would be milder than in the past and that investors could feel comfortable investing in higher-yielding but difficult-to-sell assets. Much smart money accepted these presumptions, leading to a great deal of money being lost when assets dropped in value. In retrospect we know that this "Great Moderation" theory was wrong. James Galbraith (2010:5), perhaps somewhat unkindly but not inaccurately, speaks of "The Grand Illusion of the Great Moderation." A Keynes-Minsky perspective explains why.

Such a description of the period is also at variance with the reality experienced by most Americans, who encountered large fluctuations in earnings. They did not enjoy the stability in their own lives that monetary economists saw at the macro level. Insecurity had grown for working people over these years, their real income stagnating and their debt levels dramatically increasing. Peter Gosselin (2008) finds that the probability of a person or a family experiencing a year-to-year drop in income of more than 50 percent almost doubled between the 1970s and the 2000s (from about one in twenty to one in eleven). The change was not caused by more family breakups, increased health costs, or any other demographic elements, but by the changing sectoral composition of the economy—patterns of stagnating real income and lower benefits.

This world of increased working-class insecurity had come into being over the three decades of neoliberalism's dominance. In these years the crisis tendencies of the SSA had become cumulatively more pronounced, yet for the most part they went unobserved or ignored by most academic economists and policy makers. For fifty years from the institution of New Deal financial reforms, there had not been crises of the sort that became frequent in the neoliberal era. With new financial products and market structure changes, the older regulatory system had become less effective. But, rather than updating financial regulation in response to risks engendered by financial innovation, decision makers embraced deregulation. With the return in academia to pre-Keynesian theories stressing deregulation of markets, and with the political establishment responding to Wall Street preferences and choosing to remove significant regulatory limits to market freedom, the older restraining norms were cast aside.

In the Matter of Fed Policy

As Keynes knew, the economy is "a system of borrowing and lending based on margins of safety." It is important to grasp the generality of this proposition. We borrow against the future when we take out a car loan or a mortgage. We could lose our job and become overextended. We might have to move to a new job and sell our house in a falling market. Companies borrow to expand output or to finance a merger in the expectation that such actions will increase future profits and generate cash flow sufficient to pay the debt and leave a surplus. It is the expected future earnings that are the security for the loan. Because economic growth is not steady, some of these expectations will not be fulfilled. Disappointments are likely to be bunched because of the waves in market psychology, accentuating cycles as economies experience periods of expansive optimism and recessionary pessimism. Financial market instability affects the rest of the economy, and, as George Soros (1997:58) suggests, its swings can act "like a wrecking ball, swinging from country to country and destroying everyone who stands in their way." The mainstream view, on the other hand, has been to embrace deregulation and let the free market restore equilibrium. Soros argues that "imposing market discipline means imposing instability."

Economists who would blame government, in the form of the Federal Reserve, for not being sufficiently promarket have a hard case to make, given Alan Greenspan's libertarian philosophy and unwillingness to regulate banks. Indeed, it was owing to these views that President Reagan appointed him to chair the Fed in 1987, replacing Paul Volker, who believed that financial markets needed to be regulated for their own good. Greenspan did not. It was Greenspan who allowed the tech bubble (which deflated in 2000–2001) and based a recovery on sustained low interest rates that gave rise to another asset bubble based on housing. Greenspan believed it was not the Fed's job to control bubbles but to allow them to run their course. For regulators to ignore asset inflation is a big mistake. It is a miscalculation that Greenspan made as chair of the Federal Reserve System and that his successor Ben Bernanke endorsed.

As the economy expanded, based on the pyramiding of debt and ultimately unsupportable leverage, Greenspan was celebrated as the maestro. The *Washington Post* featured a likeness of Greenspan in a toga and the wreath of a Roman emperor-god. Prominent economists declared that he "has a legitimate claim to being the greatest central banker who ever lived" (Blinder and Reis 2005). Christina Romer, who was later to head the Obama Council of Economic Advisers, declared in fall 2007 that "better policy, particularly on the part of the Federal Reserve, is directly responsible for the low inflation and the virtual disappearance of the business cycle in the last 25 years," a celebratory remark soon no doubt to be rued (cited in Postrel 2009:32).

It was not long before the Greenspan legacy was being interrogated quite differently. A little over a year after Romer's remarks, Peter Goodman (2008:18), reviewing current opinion, wrote, "If Mr. Greenspan had acted differently during his tenure as Federal Reserve chairman from 1987 to 2006, many economists say, the current crisis might have been averted or muted." Greenspan was remembered for remarks he made testifying before congressional committees expressing his views that "risks in financial markets, including derivatives markets, are being regulated by private parties," and "there is nothing involved in federal regulation per se which makes it superior to market regulation." When Representative Bernie Sanders from Vermont asked

Greenspan about the growing concentration in the financial sector of huge institutions whose failure would have tremendous impact on the national and global economy, he replied, "I believe that the general growth in large institutions has occurred in the context of an underlying structure of markets in which many of the larger risks are dramatically—I should say, fully—hedged." Such views were shared by Robert Rubin and Larry Summers, who warned against regulating derivatives (as the then head of the Commodity Futures Trading Commission, Brooksley Born, attempted). These men were totally wrong in their interpretation of what was going on. It should also be noted that in the light of the subprime crisis, which triggered a wider financial market collapse, Congress had given Greenspan explicit authority to examine the quality of mortgage lending in the 1990s, but he had refused to use it on free-market grounds.

As an academic economist, Bernanke wrote that "changes in asset prices should affect monetary policy only to the extent that they affect the central bank's forecast of inflation. To a first approximation, once the predictive content of asset prices for inflation has been accounted for, there should be no additional response of monetary policy to asset-price fluctuations" (Bernanke and Gertler 2001:1). Such faith comes from a larger belief that markets know what they are doing and will soon return to equilibrium if disturbed. This is antithetical to a Keynes-Minsky view of financial markets in which animal spirits lead to the "irrational exuberance" that produces bubbles and financial crises. Where once a head of the Federal Reserve could speak of the job as "taking the punch bowl away just when the party gets going," this has not been the view of the Fed for some time. In the era of global neoliberalism and financialization, the Fed encouraged new ways to expand leverage and increased systemic risk. By the end of the decade Bernanke understood things differently.

Before then, however, Greenspan and Bernanke were responsible for encouraging the high leverage and loose lending that led to the subprime mess and related excesses. After the 2001 stock market collapse, the Fed aided speculative overextension by keeping rates so low for so long. Its rescues increased moral hazard. Its implicit guarantees offered inducement for economic actors to be irresponsible, knowing that government would come to the rescue. After decades of holding to the view that regulation should be minimal and that financial markets could, without government intervention, solve any problems that arose, a contrite Alan Greenspan in October 2008 famously told a congressional committee that there had been "a flaw" in his thinking. He explained, after the bubble had burst, that "this modern risk paradigm held sway for decades. The whole intellectual edifice, however, collapsed in the summer of last year because the data inputted into the risk management models generally covered only the past two decades, a period of euphoria."

The vast increase in speculative capital and the climate of financial liberalization made crises more likely and attempts to guard against them more expensive and difficult. Unlike in Keynes's time, money managers working for large institutional entities, including pension and mutual funds (along with high-frequency traders, to be discussed), were responsible for most of the equity buying and selling. These managers faced career risk, the prospect of being caught out of step with their peers and making what turn out to be bad judgments, which cost their clients serious money. It was better to stay with the herd and be wrong than to follow one's own judgment that turned out to be wrong and out of step—or even too prematurely right. This powerfully adds momentum to stock market rallies since fund managers cannot afford to be left behind the pack. Caution exercised too soon can be a problem; hence the rationality of going with irrational exuberance and hoping to time one's exit well. Short-term incentives lead to trend-following strategies that distort markets and add to overshooting, increasing the volatility of markets over time and the amplitude of bubbles. Competition among fund managers does not deliver efficiency prices and certainly does not discipline market excesses. In the neoliberal SSA, the dominance of finance made business cycles far more financially driven.

Financial Tools and Their Misuse

Because a new financial product offers its developers opportunity for high profit until others copy the innovation and returns fall, Wall Street is constantly dreaming up new ideas and rushing them into investor hands. If the pharmaceutical industry did this and there were tragic results, elected officials would sooner or later come up with a review process run by an agency, perhaps calling it the Food and Drug Administration, which would require proof that a new product would not be harmful. Finance has not embraced the precautionary principle. While after the harm is done there are calls for "transparency" so that investors can understand what they are buying, the reason there is little transparency and it is so difficult to practice due diligence on these products is that the lack of clarity allows their sellers higher profitability and makes it more difficult for competitors to understand and copy.

As has been noted, mainstream models assume that there is a known distribution of risk, and market participants choose assets based on their willingness to accept an expected degree of risk. In the mainstream view, as opposed to the Keynes-Minsky approach, how much an outcome is expected to deviate from a neutral or average outcome, known as the variance, can be statistically estimated. Some investments are riskier than others. They have higher variance. The square root of variance or the standard deviation is the usual measure of volatility or riskiness of a particular outcome. Such an approach presumes a normal distribution of risk, the statistical properties of which are that if we go one standard deviation in both directions from the expected outcome, we will include two-thirds of possible outcomes. Two standard deviations will cover 95 percent of possible outcomes and three standard deviations nearly all—except for those once-in-a-century exceptions way out at the far ends of the distribution. However, when these sorts of very highly unlikely outcomes come around far more frequently and impose extremely high social costs, it is time to rethink the use of such a framework, including the confidence with which financial economics has used a value at risk (VAR) measure, which statistically summarizes the downside risk of a portfolio of different assets into a single number.

Financial institutions confidently used VAR as a dynamic risk measure. The calculated VAR numbers were, and are still, often disclosed to investors as a kind of assurance. This approach to risk exposure assumes that the future movement in risk factors will parallel movements in the past, that they are normally distributed, and that the variances and correlation matrices of factors affecting profit and loss do not change over time. Under normal market conditions, a bank, for example, estimates that 99 percent of the time the portfolio it is holding cannot lose more than a certain dollar amount. It is VAR that dictates active management of bank portfolios as described above and guides them to the bubble tendency described. Assets are adjusted to liabilities on balance sheets to ensure that total equity is proportional to the VAR of their assets. The presumption is that the calculation makes the strategy sound.

Banks use VAR to limit their trading risk and to help them decide how much capital they need to support their risk exposure. Every day banks look at the amount they have at risk and, if it is too high, sell off some risky assets or add to their equity. The Basle Committee on Banking Supervision, which advises national regulators, recommended placing faith in the banks' own internal risk evaluation models to set capital requirements. The banks could regulate themselves (as under Basel II guidelines to be discussed in chapter 7) because the science behind what they were doing was judged sound. However, VAR can be manipulated to reduce the amount of capital a bank is required to hold. By increasing its leverage, a bank could, so long as things went well, increase its profits on invested capital. So long as VAR was low, all would be well—until it wasn't. Because these seriously painful "tail events" happen perhaps every half dozen years or so, a banker looking toward this year's bonus is easily tempted to use a model that discounts or rather does not allow for their rare occurrence. It does mean that government (taxpayer) bailouts are needed at unpredictable but repeated intervals. The great virtue of VAR measures for the banks was that, because they used data from recent years (of an expanding bubble economy) during which losses were minimal, optimistic numbers allowed the banks to set aside minimal capital while increasing leverage.

Diversification was presumed to reduce risk, which in normal times it does. In volatile times, different asset classes become highly correlated, and so volatility of profit and loss become far greater than VAR measures suggest. In the calculations of risk, each instrument and position is tested separately. But when so many take similar risks, the situation changes, especially where pioneers do well and imitators allocate in the same manner, hoping for similar returns. The herding of investors and financiers created a situation where it was seen as foolish not to accept the risks others were taking. Again, it was rational for money managers to be possibly wrong along with others rather than to not take the same risk, earn lower returns, and be challenged by those to whom one was accountable. (Keynes described a sound banker as "one who, when he is ruined, is ruined in a conventional and orthodox way with his fellows, so that no one can really blame him.") In terms of particular asset categories, it turned out that the financial firms were using very optimistic assumptions and oversimplified data in their modeling. Top executives in the banks had no idea what the "quants" were doing, but it was impressive math, and the results were trusted until in 2008 almost all asset values fell in highly correlated fashion, and losses exceeded by huge amounts those the models predicted were probable or even possible. In the serious crisis the normal tails at the once-in-a-century territory turned out to be "fat tails" with much higher probabilities. The events that triggered these unexpected outcomes were correlated in a Soros superbubble collapse. The generalized high leverage and the presumption of low risk, thanks to the triple-A ratings given to financial instruments, disguised the reality that systemic risk had been dramatically underestimated and that the probability of serious trouble increases as a bubble inflates.

After a financial collapse, it is all well and good to point out that the Wall Street firm risk officers knew that the models were fitted from periods of low volatility when markets were rising. But these people understood that senior management preferred to take on additional risk since "if the dice came up seven they stood to receive megabonuses, whereas if they rolled snake eyes the worst they could expect was a golden parachute." The technical staff "knew which side their bread was buttered" (Eichengreen 2009:3). What the investment banks and others did (with SEC encouragement) was to take on huge leverage in the expectation that the odds worked in their favor, an investment strategy based on the high probability of modest gain and a low probability of a huge loss in any period. By taking on sizable debt, firms could leverage modest gain on invested capital into a high rate of return, magnifying gains. However, should the low probability eventually strike, it would wipe out the investor, as in fact it eventually did, and with it the financial model accepting undeserved confidence in minimally regulated financial markets as well.

Geoffrey Hodgson, writing toward the end of 2008, wondered whether skepticism of received doctrine and the relevance of alternative Keynes and Minsky framings were being rediscovered in departments of economics, in the journals, and on the reading lists. He found the overall picture in the leading journals of economics to be one of continuing secular decline in discussion of Keynes's ideas and "a relative neglect of other authors who warned of the dangers of financial deregulation" (Hodgson 2008:279). The same methods of quantitative risk analysis are still being taught in business schools. They continue to predict that what has happened could not have happened in thousands of years of financial risk taking. The difference is that in the wake of the crisis, teachers and, with a lag, textbooks warned students that these models were an input to careful decision making and not a substitute for market awareness and judgment. The extent to which such qualifications were stressed before the crisis is hard to know. It is difficult to find finance professors who do not claim they have always issued such cautions.

The Keynes-Minsky understanding of financial crises is ignored by the mainstream at the level of theory for the most part because it is at fundamental odds with efficient market theory. However, when crises strike, practitioners grudgingly accept it, at least until the crisis has peaked and recovery seems likely. In normal times, theories of rational bubbles and other efforts to make reality compatible with the conventional wisdom absorb attention. But, as Bank of England economists write, "The orthodox account of crisis is left to explain many of the most important features of the past decade as a series of exogenous shocks. This does not seem to be much of an explanation at all, especially when these exogenous shocks are also hard to identify" (Hume and Sentance 2009:6). While the two approaches are in conflict, it is possible to say that for long periods markets tend to appear rational, and only at (painful) intervals does the market psychology described by Fisher, Keynes, and Minsky become manifest in the eruption of crises. Increasingly, behavioral economists are returning to and building on their insights.

The behavioral perspective, while it has been around for decades, is increasingly making inroads into mainstream economic thinking. Akerlof and Shiller (2009) extend the definition Keynes offered of animal spirits to not only the importance of confidence issues, but fairness mattering to people, as do issues of corruption and bad faith dealings. They stress the importance on investor attitudes of the conventionally believed stories that dominate a period. These insights are especially important in explaining what has been called the Quiet Period in banking following the New Deal reforms, which led many to think that banking panics were a thing of the past. For seventy-five years there was relative calm in banking, suggesting the importance of institutional approaches in reconfiguring understanding of the constraints and enabling structural factors in theorizing crises.

New technologies, financial products, and deregulation changed the terrain. Economists have come to understand that for Lehman Brothers, Bear Stearns, and others in the period of financialization's dominance, "the best indicator of the availability of credit seems to be the growth of collateralized borrowing, and in particular the stock of outstanding repurchase agreements" (Adrian and Shin 2007). As financialization peaked between 2002 and 2008, the amount Wall Street firms put up as collateral for short-term loans in the form of repurchase agreements tripled, from $500 billion to $1.6 trillion, as firms saw their assets rise in value, encouraging them to borrow to buy more, using the assets they already held as collateral and continuing the self-levitation process. The widespread use of asset-backed securities and other nondeposit-based funds led to the questions: How is liquidity to be best measured? Were analysts keeping up with financial innovation's consequences?

The assumption for individual players is that they can sell their assets at an expected price; that is, that their assets are liquid. What is true of the individual investor or institution is not the case for investors and institutions collectively as an asset bubble collapses. Liquidity suddenly dries up. This is when the monetary authorities have to flood markets with credit, loan guarantees, and other measures to stop the downward cycle of collapsing asset valuations, raising the questions: What should the monetary authorities do in the expansion phase of the bubble? In the collapse after the bubble is popped? Traditionally they watch the money supply for signs of trouble, but unlike in the simple bank model, where the liabilities of the institutions were primarily depositor money, the shadow banking system of hedge funds and others (along with the banks) borrow funds, buy assets, and use those assets as collateral to borrow more. The conventionally measured money supply does not capture this expansion of credit. From the beginning of the neoliberal SSA, money has not been a good measure of liquidity, and the assumption that trouble always comes from outside the normal working of financial markets is less convincing. A longer-term perspective makes the key change in finance clearer.

Whereas before World War II money and credit fell significantly below trend after crises and did not recover to precrisis growth for five years or so, in the postwar period monetary authorities learned to increase the rate of money supply and financial institutions to expand credit aggregates. This made the impact of crises less severe. Real investment activity and output declines were less dangerous in the postwar period through the Great Moderation. The sense that monetary policy could head off or quickly repair downturns led, however, to greater risk taking undetected by monetary authorities, who continued to rely on monetary aggregates as predictive tools.

Bank loans have increased through monetary liabilities rather than through depositor monies, which makes the link between money and credit far looser and monetarist models less useful. Instead of watching the money supply, the Fed and other central banks should have been worrying about the dramatic increase in credit creation. They did not. Since the market was responsible for rising asset prices and markets were rational, macro theorists did not deem asset inflation in the absence of a general price inflation to be a problem. However, Moritz Schularick and Alan M. Taylor (2009:20), running a variety of models correlating credit expansion and macro stability, finds a credit boom over the previous five years, indicative of a heightened risk of financial crisis and supporting a Minskyian approach, reinforcing the view of modern financial crises as "credit booms gone wrong" (Eichengreen and Mitchener 2003). A focus on credit creation illuminates the dark side of the way monetary authorities address crises by creating more credit. Handling crises this way gives the financial sector reason to believe that authorities will insure them against loss hardly discourages excessive risk-taking behavior.

Rapid and sustained growth of bank credit flows have been repeatedly identified and shown to have great predictive power. This finding can be part of a larger quantitative modeling methodology. One of the pioneers in such an accounting approach, the late Wynne Godley, developed large stock-flow/ sixty and eighty variable models incorporating heterodox behavioral assumptions and institutional relations in which changes in the value of financial stocks, inventories, and household wealth are shown to have power in predicting crises. In Godley's flow-of-funds or financial-balance approach, the money stock is not, as in the mainstream model, treated as exogenous, either in the sense that it is determined outside the model or in the sense that it has no accounting relation to any other variable. It is, as Godley puts it, "as volatile as Tinkerbell" (1996:1). Endorsing and underscoring a comment Joseph Stiglitz made in his Marshall lectures at Cambridge, in which Stiglitz said that the core ISLM core model taught to economics students beyond the elementary level cannot be used for realistic policy guidance because it assumes a constant money stock and has no place for the financial system, Godley goes on to criticize the mainstream penchant for ignoring bank credit.

Godley's work shows that banks functioning in a financial system in historical time can be modeled realistically. His approach can be contrasted with what he suggests is "a crazy aspect of the econometric study of time series that . . . seeks to discover stable parameters where stability is obviously not to be found" (1996:22). In his view, the demand for money is constantly changing with uncertainty and changing expectations with regard to everything from inflation to the political outlook. Milton Friedman's conceit, employing a helicopter when he wants more money in the system, reflects in Godley's view an impoverished and ambiguous role for money and credit in the standard models. His stock-flow approach can be more precise since there are real values that have set relation to each other in the macro economy, and so, by changing values of variables one at a time within a system of equations for which a base solution has been derived, the consequence of various developments can be forecast.

In a 1999 paper Godley forecasts a serious downturn, perhaps a decade away, caused by basic imbalances that have now become manifest to those who ignored them at the time he was writing. The increase in private borrowing put the real economy "at the mercy of the stock market to an unusual extent," and its "crash would probably have a much larger effect on output and employment now than in the past" (Godley 1999:2). At the time mainstream forecasts were predicting continued growth. The difference, as he points out, was due to a profound difference in views of how the economy works. Godley identifies seven unsustainable processes that have become more familiar in the wake of the Great Recession: the fall in private savings, the rise in net lending to the private sector, the rise in the growth rate of the real money stock, the rise in asset prices considerably in excess of growth of profits or GDP, the rise of the current account deficit, the increase in foreign indebtedness, and a last factor that makes sense in his flow accounting, the rise in the budget surplus in the Clinton years. Budget tightening and lower interest rates, he explains (against the consensus view), had led to only a moderate increase in business investment. They had contributed more substantially, however, to borrowing, and that continued expansion of the U.S. economy required that private expenditures continue to rise relative to income, which had its limits. Godley forecasts that within ten or fifteen years "a sensational day of reckoning could then be at hand" (10).

Economists at the Bank for International Settlements tell us that liquidity crises "are not like meteorite strikes," but rather "the endogenous result of the build-up in risk-taking and associated overextensions in balance-sheets over a prolonged period" (Borio 2009:3). Their research focuses on the self-reinforcing process between liquidity and risk-taking, seeing the easing of funding liquidity constraints during the expansion as supporting greater risk taking and increasing risk exposure. When this process goes too far, it sows the seeds of its own destruction, ending in a sudden turnaround—the Minsky Moment. The BIS researchers estimate that although only a minority (20 percent) of credit booms end in a crisis, the longer and greater the boom, the more chance of a bad end. They are optimistic that better empirical models can operationalize early warning indicators for better policy intervention. One hopes their optimism is warranted. Using Godley-style modeling in a Minsky framing suggests that policy makers could become confident enough to take the punch bowl away when the party appears to others to be going well.

Following the Great Recession, examination of long-term data that show that total credit is a good predictor of crises while monetary aggregates and economy-wide inflation rates have not has become more influential. Over the long run, using a developed-country sample, it is clear that whether banks originate lending for productive investment or to fuel consumption and speculation does not matter much (Schularick and Taylor 2009:25). This distinction, or rather lack of a difference based on the purpose of the borrower, becomes important when the credit creation leading to the Great Recession is reconsidered. What is crucial is the rapid increase in credit as a predictor of crisis and the way banks funded this increase. Perhaps economists will develop such a model. Unfortunately, it may be that the ability of the financial sector to contribute outsized amounts to elected officials may offer it significant insurance against the kind of tight control such regulatory aspirations would provide.

The High Cost of Free Financial Markets

With twenty-first-century financial problems, default insurance became more costly for some G7 government financial products than for many blue-chip corporate borrowers. The source of doubts regarding sovereign credit worthiness in the rich countries came not from the fall in tax revenues and expenditures they had undertaken in the face of crisis, but in large measure from the direct and indirect cost of bailing out their banks and the damage done by the crisis they had caused. The absence of effective regulation, along with a secular increase in the expansion of government insurance of the financial sector, had produced this situation. The increased risk the banks took was because the gains were privatized and the losses socialized. Next time, or the time after that, these costs could be much greater. Governments, for their own survival, may have to stand up to the power of finance. The scale of intervention to support the banks in Britain, the United States, and the euro zone—over $14 trillion, almost a quarter of global GDP, "dwarfing" any previous state support for the banking system in the Great Recession (Haldane and Alessandri 2009:1)—is an indicator of the escalating cost. In the twenty-first century the cost of bailing out banks and addressing the damage their excesses produced threatened to bankrupt governments.

Other swings have been described in terms of social structure of accumulation theorizing between periods of regulation and deregulation. After the Great Depression it was realized that the state has to restore the functioning of the financial sector. Following a crisis it can do this by tightly regulating what banks are allowed to do. When the pendulum has swung toward deregulation and neoliberalism, safeguards are cast aside and institutions deemed too important to fail are supported by the taxpayer through extremely large, and increasingly larger, guarantees and other assistance. The fear that public insurance of the financial sector in the absence of strict regulation has created a "doom loop" (Haldane and Alessandri 2009), producing the conditions for the next crisis, has led to a demand both for tighter regulation and, among those who do not believe their effective regulation is possible, for the breakup of "too important to fail" institutions. Such an analysis produces criticism of the Fed and Ben Bernanke, for while another great depression was headed off by turning on the credit spigot, giving free money to the financial sector enabled the next bubble. As Simon Johnson writes, "If any country provides unlimited government support for its financial system, while not implementing orderly bankruptcy-type procedures for insolvent large institutions, and refusing to take on serious governance reform and downsizing for major banks, it would be castigated by the United States and come under pressure from the IMF. Yet this is the approach the U.S. has implemented" (Johnson 2009c).

Washington took the easier route politically of tightening regulations and increasing supervision of financial institutions—easier in the sense that breaking up institutions that were too big and interconnected to be allowed to fail was rejected, and in the sense that the banks basically accepted and, to an extent, helped design reforms. Wynne Godley and the BIS researchers show that it would be possible to do a far better job of anticipating crises through early warning systems of analysis. Whether politicians would allow regulators to take preventative measures in anticipation of possible difficulties is another matter. In the concluding chapter of this book, I describe the data needs required by a better regulatory order, based on the lessons of the current crisis and evaluation of systemic connections promoting fragility. Again, whether the politics of vested interests and the pressure of campaign finance and lobbying would allow even the collection of such data, let alone the use of it to take mature remediating steps, is problematic. The hope that it will not take another or more than another serious crises to move to the type of social regulation of finance is realistically unrealistic. Both the causes of financial crises and the inadequacy of reform remain integral to the normal working of our economic system.

Before describing the causes of the Great Recession meltdown and how it was addressed, it is useful to point out not only that such shocks to the system come as a surprise each time, but that there are hunts for villains, unhappiness that rescues are costly, and assertions that reforms are needed so that "it will never happen again." The new legislation and good intentions are unequal to this promise. While details differ, many of the things that are found to have gone wrong have gone wrong before and were supposedly fixed. The last time, even when it was only a few years earlier, seems ancient history to a present-fixated public and its political leaders. Each time debates over what should be done to restore a well-functioning banking system and then what should or should not be done by government to promote economic growth and employment recycle debates that in their contemporary iteration were crystallized in the Keynesian versus free-market approaches to the Great Depression. There is a *Groundhog Day* repetitiveness that is unlikely to end with this round of financial crisis.

The established response—to throw money at financial institutions to restore them to health—collides with public preference to punish the bankers and their political cronies. Those in charge of policy know that they must restore the banks to health along with other systemically important financial institutions, even if the voters object. If the politicians show or appear to show favoritism toward Wall Street and do too little to help those losing their homes, jobs, and life savings, they have to deal with citizen rage. However, as this chapter has argued, such crises are part of the way our economic system works. Limiting their incidence and depth, and providing better safety-net protections for working families, would seem to be in the government's interest. Yet structural obstacles to such a beneficial outcome are very real. The sad truth is that the inherent rules of capitalism constrain a democracy.

People who in the upswing complained when government tried to impose some controls blame public officials for not restoring growth quickly, and at minimal cost to taxpayers, while complaining that the government is taking away market freedom. This may be an inconsistent attitude toward the state, but in a capitalist economy how much can government intrude on the prerogatives of capital and free enterprise? If crises come from overoptimism feeding on itself until speculative investments finally come to be regarded as too risky and the economy collapses as people pull back, what can policy makers do? Can they know when to step in? Will those seeing their wealth increase so rapidly want the proverbial punch bowl taken away just when the party is going so splendidly? Will their preferences prevail? The answer depends on the power of finance, which in turn depends in significant measure on whether people think there is any alternative to the way things are.

A vast amount of money is made in the financial sector. Less certain are the social value of these obviously incredibly lucrative activities and the impact of innovative financial products traded through regulated, minimally regulated, and unregulated sectors of the industry. The distortion to the economy caused by allowing finance to metastasize and the productive sectors to atrophy could not be easily rectified with debt-driven fiscal policy when the long-running accumulation by financialization faltered.

4

The Shadow of the Financial System

Ever since Jesus in the Temple dealt harshly with the hedge-fund managers of his time, many Christians have been suspicious of finance.

—JOHN MICKLETHWAIT, 2007

Why we are in this situation seems utterly incomprehensible. Who but a Wall Street trader or a professor of economics can say exactly what a "derivative" is, or a "credit-default swap," and why they are responsible for so many people losing their jobs?

—RUSSELL BAKER, 2009

Traditionally, banking was understood as consisting of banks that took deposits and made loans that were held to maturity, when the debt was repaid, with interest payments made along the way. Depositors' savings anchored lending. This system eroded over the decades of the global neoliberal SSA as shadow banking activities became an outlet for capital seeking higher returns, given the lack of investment opportunities with comparable returns in the nonfinancial economy. With profits down in many areas of the real economy in the mature markets of the core, investment banks seeking higher returns put greater amounts of capital at speculative risk by leveraging their own money, borrowing vast sums. What made the situation of the banks and others so fraught with danger was the premise behind the extensive borrowing. As Henry Kaufman (2009a:11) points out, "Traditionally, liquidity was an asset-based concept. But that shifted to the liability side, as liquidity came to be virtually synonymous with easy borrowing." Commercial banks, too, borrowed large sums and relent the money, often to those who speculated with it.

From the start of the global neoliberal era, commercial banks received more and more of their income in fees, guaranteeing commercial paper, on credit cards, and from following investment banks into proprietary trading on their own account through affiliates. The Fed allowed the presumably regulated commercial banks, which had become bank holding companies, to expand into formerly forbidden activities and set up special-purpose vehicles to carry out unregulated activities to get around capital requirements, and so the whole 1930s system was basically gone by the new century. Segmentation of the industry crumbled completely in 1999 when the Gramm-Leach-Bliley Bank Reform Act allowed banks to own all manner of subsidiaries, and the line between investment banks and commercial banks faded. Indeed, the one thing that continued to separate them—federal insurance and support for commercial banks but not for investment banks and finance companies—ended in the crisis as investment banks and finance companies such as GE capital received the same cover and support through fig-leaf formalities in 2008. Earlier in the decade Citigroup, parent of Citibank, earned most of its net revenue from other than interest on loans: from vastly expanded fee income, much of it from alternative investments in private equity, hedge funds, and structured products; and from providing services for fee income to other financial firms. Given the interdependencies generated and other changes in the industry, it does not make sense to see a regulated banking sector and a second or separate shadow banking system.

Increased computer capacity has made low-cost calculations of complex market data possible and liberalized financial markets have widened horizons, contributing to the ratio of global financial assets to world output almost tripling from 109 percent in 1980 to 316 percent in 2005, according to the McKinsey Global Institute. New and unregulated, or minimally regulated, structured financial products became hugely important, profitable, and mainstream. The face value of derivatives, for example, which was under $3.5 trillion in 1990, jumped to over $285 trillion by 2006.

In the neoliberal era other financial institutions have become significant, including investment banks with their important dealer and broker functions, hedge funds, and others. Securities—assets backed by a pool of loans, including, most notoriously, mortgage-backed securities but also other forms of collateralized debt—have become central to the debt market. These securitized assets are classed as derivatives, their value *deriving* from that of the underlying assets.

The nonbank financial firms and the products they buy and sell are widely seen as a second banking system that grew up apart from, but not unconnected to, the older financial system. The shadow banking system includes hedge funds, private equity groups, insurance companies, money market funds, and pension funds, among others, and features funding sources involving the use and reuse of collateral posted with banks and others to finance transactions that show up as non-balance-sheet funding. The Federal Reserve Bank of New York estimates the shadow banking sector in early 2011 to be a $16 trillion entity altogether (it peaked at $20 trillion in 2008) compared to $13 trillion in assets in banking proper (Pozsar et al. 2010). Some of the nonbanks lend money directly to companies; others specialize in trading commodities or other assets. There are nonbanks that borrow short term and make long-term investments. Hedge funds and other institutional investors provided over 50 percent of the half-trillion loans made in the highly leveraged segment of the syndicated loan market (Massoud et al. 2011).

The Federal Reserve's Flow of Funds data do not capture pledged collateral and so considerably underestimate the size of the financial sector (Hördahl and King 2008). Reuse of pledged collateral as collateral in their own name by those to whom it is entrusted (formally called rehypothecation) can prove dangerous to the system when there is a scramble for liquidity. There was a more cautious attitude toward rehypothecation after Lehman Brothers collapsed (see below), leaving hedge funds, among others, trying to get back the assets their prime brokers were holding. During a crisis there is "margin spiral," more collateral needs be put up for the amount of money lent, and so there is a "haircut" on the value of collateral, which is worth less when counterparty risk rises (Singh and Aitken 2010). As assets are sold to raise capital, prices fall further, as happened in 2007–8 (see chapter 5). Globally, gross income earned from securities lending was over $20 billion in 2008, less than $10 billion in 2009, and under $8 billion in 2010 (Data Explorers 2010Q4:4). Since then the market has picked up some, as should be expected in such cyclical markets in which risk appetite grows as confidence returns and falters on unexpected losses. Stock lenders who had reinvested the cash they had taken as collateral in mortgage-backed securities were burned (see next chapter) and after that either put the money in safe money market funds or government bonds.

Gorton (2010:38) defines the shadow banking system as "a combination of the repo market and the necessary collateral, including securitized debt." He declares, "The reality is that the so-called shadow banking system is, in fact, banking" (17). Arvind Krishnamurthy (2010:4) suggests that since a number of different entities behave like banks in debt markets, even though they do not directly take deposits from households, we should simply group insurance companies, hedge funds, and government-sponsored enterprises, brokers, and dealers as "financial institutions." Nonetheless, in what follows I will frequently refer to the shadow banking system as if it were distinct since regulators worried about what was going on in these less transparent financial institutions collected a good deal of useful data that show the extent of their growing importance. Rather than drawing a sharp distinction between traditional banking and the huge, unregulated shadow system that dominates the economy, it would be more appropriate to view only America's smaller community banks as traditional banking and to see the mega commercial and investment banks, hedge funds, and the rest as not a shadow banking system, but perhaps a *shadowy* banking system, more opaque than banking in the postwar SSA and casting a long shadow over the economy.

In 1977 commercial banks in the United States held 56 percent of all financial assets; thirty-two years later, the banks' share had fallen to just 20 percent of the total assets. Within banking two distinct segments evolved: a locally based sector with under $1 billion in assets, accounting for more than nine of ten banks, which continued to receive three-quarters of its income from interest and had virtually no derivative exposure, and a relatively small number of megabanks. Issuance of derivatives by the largest banks, with over a $1 billion in assets, equaled, on average, 2,000 percent of their total assets (Dymski 2010:11, fig. 1). Many community banks disappeared, and large commercial banks increasingly mimicked rapidly growing, highly leveraged nonbank competitors, becoming heavily involved in practices that allowed them to avoid the intent of regulations. They were prompted to do so because they lost much of their traditional business to money market funds, the commercial paper market, and other innovations, which meant that less money flowed through commercial banks in the form of traditional deposits and business loans.

Securitized assets, many originating in the traditional banking system, were important to the explosion of finance. In 2006 banks issued $1.8 trillion in securities backed by mortgages, credit cards, auto loans, and other debt. More than half of the credit card and student loans in the country were securitized. Possible financial reforms, to be discussed in chapter 6, confront the extent to which the older banking system no longer exists. If commercial banks, which in recent years have supplied only 20 percent of net lending out of their own holdings, were unable to sell securitized assets, the economy would be hard pressed to resume a growth trajectory comparable to that experienced in what, in hindsight, is now understood as a bubble economy.

Securitization allowed the banks to increase their asset velocity through leverage and reuse their capital many times over by moving assets off their balance sheets. Banks depended on securitization for a large proportion of their funding and could not replace this source with deposits.

The banks' consumer business model also changed. The financial conglomerates accustomed people through extensive advertising to accept high levels of debt, to use their homes as ATM machines, as the expression goes, and to stay perpetually in debt. While it is frequently said that we are all to blame, and that we all were irresponsible borrowers, the changed cultural attitude toward debt was a result of the extensive campaigns by banks and finance companies pushing their new products, telling us we deserved to consume now and not wait. The commercial banks moved to a strategy of preferring that borrowers not pay back debt but continually pay interest on rising balances. They then securitized these assets as collateralized financial instruments, and they, too, borrowed as much as they could so that liquidity in the system was increased through pyramiding debt. The Fed's economic libertarianism assumed that if the market was buying all of this, it must be all right.

Banks originating or purchasing mortgages and selling them in the form of collateralized debt obligations sponsored special-purpose vehicles (SIVs) that took these assets off of their books, allowing them to do far more transactions with the same capital. What was less understood was that, as the market for these products fell, banks used their sales to these captive entities to hold up seeming demand and thus the prices at which they were able to sell these assets to others. By the end, the SIVs were holding around two-thirds as much in securitized assets as the banks themselves.

As financialization peaked between 2002 and 2008, the amount Wall Street firms put up as collateral for short-term loans (repurchase agreements or repos) tripled from $500 billion to $1.6 trillion as firms saw their assets rise in value, encouraging them to borrow to buy more, using the assets as collateral. Such practices increased the vulnerability and decreased the transparency of the financial system. In 2010 the Financial Crisis Inquiry Commission shed light on the widespread fudging of quarterly books by the large banks, using special-purpose vehicles and hedge funds to obscure their real financial situation and hiding billions in liabilities, a practiced dismissed on Wall Street as "window dressing." Analysis of the data showed such practices were routine, with Bank of America, Deutsche Bank, and Citigroup the most active in such deceptions (Rapaport and McGinty 2010).

The Organization for Economic Cooperation and Development's published total economy balance sheets for 2007 show that in that year the shadow banking system amounted to almost 120 percent of GDP in the United States and more than 60 percent in other OECD economies. This credit proportion was stable elsewhere but had risen rapidly since the mid-1990s in the United States, suggesting that the growth of the shadow banking system was heavily an American phenomenon (Hume and Sentance 2009:9). In the expansion phase of the asset bubble, high-risk strategies made a great deal of money; after the bubble burst, huge losses resulted for many of the highly leveraged hedge funds, buyout groups, and their investors.

The International Monetary Fund (2007:6) warned of the possibility of illiquid market conditions for complex financial instruments, which could amplify a market downturn. The IMF's general assessment in 2006 was that the investment banks, having taken on risks to an unprecedented degree, faced trouble. Central bankers were concerned about the extent of leverage, the surplus of investable funds, and low-cost borrowing conditions. They worried that corporate failures lurked, with consequences for the economies they were appointed to safeguard. But bonuses had never been higher for the bankers, and investors had done quite nicely. Investment bank stock had risen by nearly two-thirds in the previous five years. Academic economists supported the view that free markets allocated resources efficiently, and the Federal Reserve, under the leadership of libertarian Alan Greenspan, whatever doubts he might have as to the frothy irrational exuberance markets displayed, was hardly inclined to interfere.

In September 2009 a joint regulators' report by the Board of Governors of the Federal Reserve System, Federal Deposit Insurance Corporation, Office of the Comptroller of the Currency, and Office of Thrift Supervision found that more than a third of the loans of nonbank financial players such as hedge funds, securitization vehicles, insurance companies, and pension funds were classified as "special mention, substandard, doubtful, or loss." These institutions held 47 percent of problem loans, even though they accounted for only 21 percent of the loan pool.

The next chapter describes the events surrounding the collapse of the financial system from the summer of 2007. The remainder of this chapter continues the discussion of the instruments and institutions that compose the shadow banking system and add to the crisis-prone, high-risk contemporary form of finance. This new industry structure bears little relation to the regime that was established in the New Deal era and was dominant in the national

Keynesian SSA. It depends for its dramatic growth on ability to avoid regulation and the peculiarities of taxation of income, from the deductibility of interest on loans used to leverage asset purchases to the redefinition of personal income as capital gains.

Derivatives

Derivatives have a long history. The earliest records go back to the ancient Greeks. It is known, for example, that the philosopher Thales of Miletus one winter negotiated what today would be a call option—the right, but not the obligation, to buy spring harvest olive pressings. "Time bargains" were made on the Amsterdam stock exchange early in its history, and there were futures trades in rice in seventeenth-century Japan. Modern derivative markets developed in nineteenth-century Chicago for agricultural commodities. The Chicago Board of Trade dates to 1848, and the first recorded futures contract was made in 1851 to allow farmers to sell crops before they were ready for market in order to raise cash and to provide buyers with a fixed and guaranteed priced for delivery at a future date. These contracts were bought and sold by both ultimate purchasers and speculators and were resold many times as perceptions of market conditions and expectations changed. Products such as cotton and orange juice concentrate are joined by derivatives based on weather at some point in the future, and on real estate values. The increased volatility in currency movements after the demise of the Bretton Woods system of fixed exchange rates was a significant impetus to the rapid growth in derivative contracts. They have become a central tool for international business, and the growth in their use has been integral to global neoliberalism.

Derivatives make a major contribution to the working of the economy. They allow purchasing certainty in an uncertain world. An airline can buy an option on aviation fuel, allowing it to buy an essential element of its business at a price agreed upon now for delivery at some date in the future, avoiding the risk that the spot price on the market then will be higher. The company buys certainty over what it will pay at a cost from a seller who is betting that the price will in fact be lower and the option will end up out of the money. If an airline is ordering new planes for delivery two years into the future and will pay in a currency different from that in it earns its income, it may buy a foreign currency forward or an option to buy the amount of currency for delivery at that time. Such options do not have to be exercised, in which case the cost of purchasing such a derivative product is presumably worth the peace of mind. What makes the market is buyers and sellers disagreeing on the likely value of the underlying assets. Airlines and other nonfinancial industries comprise only about 9 percent of the derivative market.

A call option gives its purchaser the right to buy an asset in the future at a prearranged price, usually through a dealer, typically a large bank. The over-the-counter market provides contracts for whatever amount requested to mature on the date desired. A buyer can also go onto the foreign exchange market and contract for the future delivery of a block of currency through a futures contract that matures on one of a number of limited days a year, which might not match the exact date one wants the money. Over-the-counter products are negotiated in a context in which the dealer has the advantage since there is less transparency and no price-seeking process, as there is on an exchange. The more complicated the derivative, the greater the dealer's possible advantage.

Between 1980 and 2007 derivative contracts of all kinds expanded from $1 trillion globally to $600 trillion. Finance theory, discussed in the previous chapter, lends credence to the view that these were safe instruments. The claim that these products enhance market efficiency complemented their income-generating potential and led to growth in the value of the stock of financial assets from six times world GDP in 2001 to thirteen times world GDP by 2007. There are all manner of financial products whose value "derives" from the value of some underlying asset—for example, collateralized debt obligations (CDOs) created from credit card receivables or car loans, as mentioned above. Nothing I say about the problematic use of derivatives below should be understood to suggest that, when used properly, derivatives are not an exceedingly useful class of financial products. Because many CDOs have become so complex that they are not be sold in any existing market or through a bidding process that could establish their value, their price is negotiated and typically based on mathematical models that few understand. Accounting rules require that they be market-to-market every day, and their value is marked to such models. When the value of mortgages undergirding a large but finally unknowable amount of derivatives suddenly fell, different financial institutions set widely different values on their holdings, typically recognizing losses as slowly as they could in relation to their ability to raise new capital. The damage to the economy came from uncertainty as to who was holding how many suddenly "toxic" assets.

Securitization of mortgages, credit cards, and auto loans allows lenders to sell off these assets to obtain funds to make new loans. Because the securities contained are priced to reflect expected income flows, the purchaser's return over the life of a highly rated structured product should generally be assured. The seller of the underlying assets, the bundler of the collateralized debt obligation, and the purchaser of these securities all come out ahead so long as there are no surprises. The sellers of these products managed to go unregulated through the years of the neoliberal ideological hegemony. Securitized assets bundled into collateralized debt obligations could be used as collateral to borrow short term in a repurchase agreement, a loan collateralized by financial securities. Early on this meant safe treasury securities, but as the demand for repos grew, other categories of loans were accepted for repos, including mortgages.

In 2007, according to the Bank for International Settlements, the repo market was about $10 trillion, equal to about 70 percent of U.S. GDP, although the $10 trillion includes double counting of repos and reverse repos taking the other side of the transaction (Hördahl and King 2008:37). The big investment banks—Goldman Sachs, Morgan Stanley, Bear Stearns, and Lehman Brothers (until the latter two failed)—were central to the repo market along with major commercial banks like Citigroup and Bank of America and European-based universal banks like UBS, Credit Suisse, and Deutsche Bank. (The top twenty banks account for 80 percent of activity in this market.) These banks underwrite and trade securities, act as prime brokers (clearing transactions, doing accounting and other services for their customers, and lending significantly to hedge funds), and, as asset managers, sell over-the-counter derivatives. Some do proprietary trading on their own account, something that regulators find troubling since they may be taking market risk with insured depositor monies. The latter practice was brought under some control in 2010 through financial regulation reform legislation (see chapter 6). Some senior executives and board members found it difficult to comprehend the risk-taking activities of their firms. Of course as long as these risks paid off, they were happy to accept the bonuses from such activities. The large broker client accounts are not insured. Clients can be affected, and so when doubts arise as to the health of these institutions, they act quickly to move their assets. Since these banks had high leverage ratios— about thirty times the assets to their equity capital—a run in the repo market could bring them and the financial system crashing down if government did not step in.

The legally mandated disclosure forms for collateralized debt obligations go on and on but are hardly transparent; while they warn against all manner of potential problems, even experts cannot always make good judgments as to their risk. When the safety of such instruments comes into question, tolerance for complex structured instruments fades and markets dry up. No buyers can be found for them, at least not at a price sellers find tolerable. Early in their modern history, complex derivatives were bought and traded by a relatively small number of buyers and sellers who presumably understood them. Many who later entered the market saw only the high returns and did not do due diligence. They accepted assurances of salespeople who encouraged them not to worry. Sellers could point to the triple-A ratings such structured finance carried. This designation conveys (mistakenly in a great many cases, as it turned out) that a financial instrument can withstand Great Depression–like conditions—a 25 percent unemployment rate and an 85 percent fall in the stock market—and still pay its debts.

In January 2008 there were only a dozen triple-A-rated companies in the world, but 64,000 structured financial products carried triple-A scores. Despite such ratings, new products and asset classes involve complex properties, which were not always adequately understood. But they promised high returns, were well promoted, and allowed a rapid rise of debt, leading to serious warnings regarding systemic stability. Although major banks employed presumably sophisticated risk-management tools, a reading of the increasingly agitated *Global Stability Report; A Report by the International Capital Markets Department on Market Developments and Issues*, released by the International Monetary Fund, suggested in the years leading up to the global financial crisis that there was reason for concern.

Gillian Tett (2010) tells of a senior banker, before the global financial crisis, quipping that the International Swaps and Derivatives Association did not need an external lobbyist "since we have Alan Greenspan." The belief of Greenspan and other regulators and policy makers that markets always know best and should not be subject to unwarranted government interference protected the industry from efforts to oversee its behavior. During the Clinton administration Secretary of the Treasury Larry Summers and Fed chair Alan Greenspan were instrumental in pushing through a 262-page rider on an 11,000-page appropriation bill on the last day of a lame duck session of Congress. This rider, the Commodity Futures Modernization Act, removed from all federal regulation what was then an over-the-counter derivative market approaching $100 trillion. There would be no disclosure requirements, capital adequacy rules, or safeguards against fraud. With this reaction by what has been called the party of Wall Street, the Democratic and Republican sponsors of legislation and enforcement measures were supportive of financial unimarket autonomy both on ideological grounds and as a source of political campaign contributions. It also represented the authority of the old boys' club led by Summers, which dismissively humiliated the then head of the Commodity Futures Trading Commission, Brooksley Born, when she attempted to regulate these products.

The proposition that derivatives can reduce risk and lower cost for businesses and consumers is not wrong. It is rather that benefits come with potential for abuse and errors of judgment that can prove extremely costly. For the mostly large banks and other giant financial institutions selling them, derivatives are a major source of profitability. Diversifying their own risk, such institutions are able to provide a range of valuable services to the risk adverse and punters alike. By rearranging who holds risk to those more willing to bear it and more widely distributing risk, derivatives presumably increase market efficiency. This is the theory. The problem is that they can be, and are, abused and need to be carefully regulated, like much else in finance. In practice, by spreading risk, derivatives can become potential conduits for contagion.

While there are limits to the amount of goods and services produced, and the amount of equity in the firms that produces them, derivative trading is limited only by imagination and willingness to speculate. Because derivative assets can be used as collateral for short-term borrowing, their underlying transparency becomes important for creditors in such arrangements. Transactions using derivatives cost a tenth as much, or even less, compared to those in underlying markets. Because it is possible to increase leverage to the point that the risks taken by 1920s investors seem tame by comparison, they offer a low-cost way to diversify portfolios and to trade at a fraction of the cost of buying and selling the underlying assets, allowing a small capital base to support a huge amount of ownership with borrowed money. This means that small movements in an unexpected direction can wipe out a position. Because the financial order is globalized, data on transactions proprietary, regulation minimal, and coordination inadequate, systemic risk can easily grow. The worry is not only that those taking on risk do not know what they are doing—although as in all businesses there are the less skilled and error prone—but that sensible decisions based on the historical range of likely outcomes can come upon unique dramatically different conditions and disastrous losses suffered with implications for the health of the entire system.

Wall Street, being Wall Street, found that small-town civil servants who represent public pension funds and managers of other pools of investable money could be sold all manner of derivatives that they did not understand. Salespeople from the likes of Goldman Sachs and JPMorgan Chase (which between them collected over $1.25 billion from state and local governments in the United States and elsewhere) promised high returns for struggling school systems and underfunded retirement funds. Many jurisdictions were bankrupted when such deals blew up, forcing draconian service cuts. As became well known, and as described in the next chapter, there is evidence that those selling the products knew what they were doing. Fabrice Tourre, a Goldman vice president who described himself in e-mails as "the fabulous Fab," said that "the entire system is about to crumble at any moment." In Tourre's e-mails, publicly revealed when the SEC filed fraud charges against him, he wrote of his "Frankenstein" creations, "a product of pure intellectual masturbation, the type of thing which you invent telling yourself: 'Well, what if we create a "thing," which has no purpose, which is absolutely conceptual and highly theoretical and which nobody knows how to price?'" He noted that "the poor little subprime borrowers will not last so long," and that he did "not intend to wait for the complete explosion of the industry and the beginning of distressed trading" but saw "more interesting things to do in Europe." When Senator Carl Levin read these comments to him when Tourre appeared before Levin's investigating committee, Tourre said he was sorry he wrote those e-mails—not because they reflected on the immorality of the way he was getting rich, but because "they reflect badly on the firm and on myself." He said the SEC probe had been hard on him and his family and criticized the "unfounded attack" (Swanson and Heflin 2010).

In 2010 Goldman Sachs paid a fine to the SEC and promised to change its practices regarding what it would reveal to investors as a result of being found to have created a derivatives portfolio so that a hedge fund could bet against the instrument that it had a major role in creating. In general, though, the firm, like the rest of Wall Street, chose to obscure what it had done, and continues to do, from investigators. Goldman obstructed the investigation of such dealings by the Financial Crisis Inquiry Commission (FCIC) by delivering five terabytes or two and a half billion pages of mostly meaningless material in response to requests for information. FCIC chair Phil Angelides, whose task it was to explain the factors that had created the financial collapse, responded, "We did not ask them to pull up a dump truck to our offices and dump a bunch of rubbish."

Derivatives can pay dividends in some questionable uses. The Internal Revenue Service believes their use enables Wall Street banks to avoid collecting billions of dollars in withholding taxes on stock dividends. Equity swaps can give investors, such as hedge funds, the benefit of stock ownership (receiving the equivalent amount of dividends) without actually owning the shares. This allowed avoiding the tax that is normally levied on stock trades. This is especially lucrative to offshore hedge funds and foreign investors in what is a vast, unregulated market. The details of swaps need not concern us here, any more than the specifics of Enron's Raptor vehicles, but the ways in which derivatives can be used are hardly all benign. High-tech money laundering robs the state not only of revenue but of legitimacy.

Enron, at the start of the new century the sixth most valuable corporation in America, spectacularly crashed when it could no longer juggle its accounts. Among its transgressions, it raised cash using derivatives, including credit swaps with Citigroup, to move debt off its books. Citi paid Enron, and Enron promised to repay Citi over five years; by its pushing the obligation to repay into the future, Enron appeared to have more money than it did. These prepaid swaps, technically derivative transactions, were really disguised loans. The banks hedged against loss if Enron did not pay, shifting their risk to unsuspecting others. While Enron's collapse in 2001 should have been a wake-up call followed by significant regulatory changes, the needed steps were not taken, setting the expectation of future, even more dramatic abuses, which were not long in coming.

Internationally, banks push the envelop of legality by offering derivatives designed to arbitrage earning over time and space in order to move money to jurisdictions or forms of payment that face lower taxation. In 1999 Japan's Financial Supervisory Agency found that Credit Suisse First Boston had long marketed plans to help Japanese companies conceal losses by investing in derivatives trades. Banks have designed derivative trades to help customers avoid credit controls. Derivatives are used to move the date at which income is booked to periods where such gains are offset by losses, minimizing taxes. Such structured finance is a huge business and affects the fiscal viability of governments, as the incoming socialist administration in Greece found when the use of derivatives sold by Goldman Sachs to hide the extent of the government deficit under the outgoing conservative party was discovered, setting off a panic in euroland. Local governments in the United States and Europe learned that the presumably safe derivatives they had purchased to lower their cost of borrowing instead led their payment burdens to balloon. Much to their consternation and taxpayer outrage, they had been locked into complicated arrangements for as much as thirty years with high termination penalties. Such deals threatened to bankrupt local governments, their pension funds, and public finances in many jurisdictions. Local officials had trusted swap advisers (who would get paid only if the officials agreed to these dangerous transactions). The officials were never told what the maximum losses could be from these swaps. The Italian Treasury investigating such deals found that some were structured so that local authorities would lose money in almost any economic environment.

Collateralized Debt Products

The collateralized debt obligation was invented in 1983 by a First Boston team to attract investors to Freddie Mac mortgage pass-through securities that were generally not triple-A investments, and so not of interest to conservative investors, nor high enough yielding to draw investors looking for better returns. The cutting up of mortgage bundles into risk segments or tranches, so that presumed supersafe assets could be sold to one type of investor and the riskier ones bundled for separate sale to those willing to take on greater risk for potentially higher return, satisfied different constituencies and expanded the market for these assets. Higher risk tranches would take all the loss first but promised higher returns. Mortgage brokers made commissions by originating and servicing collection from homeowners (who were able to get lower-cost mortgages thanks to widespread securitization). Since there was so much money to be made selling CDOs or collateralized loan obligations (CLOs), there was pressure to produce more "raw material," spurring loan originators (for whom fees to be earned provided incentive) to push loans on potential borrowers.

CLOs were a great success, and their use expanded dramatically as markets accepted the idea that investors holding the bottom tranches absorb possible losses, and those at the top are protected, since the loss is unlikely to be total even in the case of failure of the enterprise. The size of the CLO market grew dramatically, turning them into a danger to the economy. David Henry (2006:90–1) explains the significance of the scale of corporate collateralized debt obligations:

In fact, unbeknownst to many, CLOs are pumping up the entire economy. Because their loans are secured by the assets of the borrowing companies, which means they'll retain more of their value in bankruptcy than unsecured bonds like those wiped out in 2001 and 2002 during the wave of defaults. By refinancing existing corporate debt on better terms and by supplying money for companies to heal and grow again after the last recession, CLOs have helped drive default rates down to 20-year lows. Hedge funds added to the enthusiasm by loading up on junk loans. And the economy has grown, allowing companies to pay down debt and adding to the confidence of CLO investors. It's a virtuous circle.

But, as Henry was aware, the availability of such huge amounts of money was driving what were more and more questionable deals. Risk analysts at the Federal Reserve warned that many who were piling into CLOs or CDOs did not understand the risk they were taking since in a downturn losses could be significant.

There have been many unflattering characterizations. To Martin Mayer (2009), the CDO is "a single instrument expressing a garbage pail of loans and notes and bonds. It is all but impossible to value because it mixes together many disparate risks. Most people who think about it at all come to the conclusion that its not very useful for trading or for investing. In short, it is an excrescence that ought not to exist." This harsh judgment stems from the way these instruments have been used to pass often heavily disguised risk on to the unsuspecting. A properly functioning market, in which originators of CDOs exercised due diligence, would allow loan-originator specialists to sell off packages of loans to obtain capital for more loans while purchasers who had no expertise (if they could trust the sellers) could benefit from the return to their investment. Unfortunately, the incentives and regulatory mechanisms did not provide reason for such confidence; hence this sort of scathing judgment.

The inventiveness of the financial sector met the demand for more collateralized assets by taking the junior tranches (the riskier parts) and creating new products on the crucial assumption that the risks of the highly risky components were not correlated. The new CDOs, called CDO squared or CDO^2, do not finance new mortgages or other loans but serve to expand the repo market. Of course if these new structured products are heavily composed of subprime mortgages, purchasers may be surprised to find that the price they paid grossly underestimated the riskiness of the product. Since so many CDOs had subprime mortgages as their underlying asset (Coval, Jurek, and Stafford 2009:15, table 3), the damage was substantial (see chapter 5).

The models on which the CDOs' value was based, however, treated them as liquid, presumed to be salable without significant loss at a moment's notice. As the crisis deepened, it was clear that most CDOs were grossly overvalued and unsalable, except at deep discount. In 2003 investment guru Warren Buffett had made his famous weapons-of-mass-destruction statement, warning, "Large amounts of risk, particularly credit risk, have become concentrated in the hands of relatively few derivatives dealers. Derivatives are financial weapons of mass destruction, carrying dangers that, while now latent, are potentially lethal." While the statement raised some eyebrows when first made and was widely quoted after the debacle, the presumed sophistication of the pricing models (that no one seemed to really understand) seemed adequate. However, as discussed in the previous chapter, outcomes that the models said could occur only once every ten thousand years became common; events at an almost impossible twenty-five standard deviation were frequent occurrences. The catastrophic drop in real-world valuations discredited the assumption of financial economists' dynamic hedging (the continuous buying and selling of securities to adjust their prices in a smooth fashion).

Credit Default Swaps and AIG

Credit default swaps (CDSs) were sold to protect investors from risk they might be taking by holding CDOs. Fear of serious asset valuation loss led to spectacular growth in these credit derivatives, allowing investors to presumably buy protection against downside risks. The existence of such contracts produces moral hazard. Greater risk is undertaken because the investor is insured by such reputable firms as the American Insurance Group (AIG). Credit default swaps can be used to speculate against possible occurrences in markets without actually owning any of the assets in question. Selling guarantees seemed safe bets by companies that were later unable to meet their obligations when there was widespread need for them to be honored. Earlier, in 1999, the President's Working Group on Financial Markets had foreseen no systematic risk from CDSs since "private counterparty discipline" would, it was convinced, ensure that the market worked efficiently. Such conclusions by industry experts and legislators were typical of the belief structure of the period: faith in unregulated markets. When one considers that CDS spreads for major banks had fallen steadily for four years into the early summer of 2007, giving no warning whatsoever of the impending financial crisis, one must doubt the ability of the financial market to judge risk ahead of doom; hence the panic that always characterizes the collapse of bubbles, as Minskyan analysis suggests will occur.

The growth of credit default swaps was rapid. First created in the mid-1990s, by 1998 they were a small market, a mere $180 billion, but then rose to $6 trillion in 2004 and $57 trillion by the summer of 2008, falling to $41 trillion by the end of that year, according to the Bank for International Settlements (on the nature and size of this market, see Stulz 2010). The use of credit default swaps gave those who purchased them incentive to see businesses fail. By buying CDSs, a creditor could be assured of a payoff, and so the failure of the company was preferable to a workout in which a creditor would take a write-down that would keep the company alive. Lawyers made a great deal of money contesting which creditors had first claims to the carcass of firms destroyed. The market is interconnected, as the major CDS dealers guarantee each other. In 2009, after all the damage done worldwide, five banks accounted for half of the CDS market, a greater concentration than before the crisis since several major players disappeared. This does not transfer risk but concentrates it within this small circle with potential systemic consequences (European Central Bank 2009). Little changed even after the collapse of the American Insurance Group showed the dangers that uncontrolled usage of CDSs could bring to the financial system.

The buying and selling of CDOs and CDSs produced a complex interdependent pattern of obligations, which meant that if one large financial firm got into serious trouble it affected the entire sector. Merrill Lynch, which had barely any presence in the CDO market in 2002, was the world's largest underwriter of these products by 2007. It bought CDS protection from AIG in vast volume until AIG refused to sell protection on even the highest-quality portions of Merrill's CDO positions. Unable to find a replacement, Merrill self-insured. Its unhedged mortgages continued their dramatic growth. It made a fortune—until it did not. The firm collapsed and was bought by Bank of America, which was understood at the time to have vastly overpaid, bringing Bank of America itself to the verge of disaster. AIG had sold guarantees to banks and others all over the world, and so its possible failure would have wide impact.

The American Insurance Group is an international financial services holding company with $1 trillion in assets at its peak, 116,000 employees in 130 countries, and 74 million customers. The company's small office in London, AIG Financial Products, with fewer than 400 employees, earned over $2 billion in 2005 in pretax profits by selling insurance on a half trillion dollars of securities, mostly credit default swaps. AIG was one of a dozen firms in the United States that enjoyed a triple-A rating and so not only could borrow at low cost but was a credible source of CDS protection. AIG sold most of the over $500 billion in such insurance to European banks. Buying these products was a legal way for banks to make more loans with their same capital base, overcoming the intent of regulations by creating, as observers pointed out, "money out of nothing." Under the Basel Accords, the banks could appear to reduce risk on their loan portfolios. The ploy was called "freeing up regulatory capital." It allowed them to bring the 8 percent capital set aside under the Basel rules to below 2 percent. AIG sold a product called 2a-7 puts, which allowed money market funds to invest in high-risk bonds because AIG promised to buy the bonds back if they went bad. Thus money market funds, which were supposed to hold only the safest commercial paper, were endangered and their depositors threatened if AIG failed to make good.

By selling CDSs, AIG was in effect renting its triple-A rating to the CDOs that it was insuring. CDSs were not categorized as an insurance product, although that is what they were, and so AIG did not put any capital aside in the event of defaults. To increase its profits, AIG offered "collateralized triggers" or "pay as you go" type swaps for which they promised to provide collateral if the underlying debt fell in value. AIG would have to post collateral if its own rating were to go down. Both of these things happened, costing AIG tens of billions of dollars it did not have. When the holders of AIG's CDSs, led by Goldman Sachs, demanded more collateral, the firm could not provide it and would have collapsed without government aid. The federal government bailed out AIG, first with $85 billion and then with a series of four additional grants, each using tens of billions of taxpayer dollars, totaling over $170 billion by early 2009, with other subsidy mechanisms amounting to over $200 billion. This federal bailout of AIG was in effect a rescue of the Western banking system, for it was not only AIG that was being rescued but those on the other end of AIG's derivatives deals—Goldman Sachs, Merrill Lynch, and others, including twenty foreign-owned financial giants that engaged in deals on which AIG could not make good.

Sorting through the structure and holdings of a large financial institution is very difficult. Regulatory arbitrage and tax concerns as well as a penchant for secrecy as to operations means competitors, customers, and governments do not always know what they are dealing with in evaluating finance industry players. AIG booked many of its credit derivatives through its London-based French banking subsidiary. To protect itself from embarrassing questions, in

1999 it had purchased a tiny Delaware savings and loan so that it would be regulated by the toothless Office of Thrift Supervision, totally unqualified to understand what AIG was doing. AIG's savings and loan operations represented one-thousandth of the balance sheet of its financial services unit. Almost nonexistent capital requirements allowed it to insure risks it could not support.

What the public came to understand about the AIG bailout—and what angered it most—was that seventy-three of AIG's employees each received over a million dollars in bonuses effectively out of taxpayer monies after the firm collapsed. These were variously described as performance and retention bonuses. AIG refused to disclose details, saying they were proprietary. Obama senior adviser Lawrence Summers explained that the government could do nothing to stop the bonuses. Legally, he said, they had been paid. None of this was satisfactory to an angry citizenry. Congresswoman Carol Maloney said of the proprietary secrecy argument, "But we are the proprietors now. Taxpayers own the store, and we should see the books." Barney Frank, chairman of the House Financial Services Committee, argued that the government should "exercise its ownership rights" over the group (it was an 80 percent shareholder) to renegotiate the contracts. He declared, "I think we should look at it from the standpoint of us as the owner" and say, "No I am not paying you the bonus. You didn't perform. You didn't live up to this contract." Many receiving retention bonuses had left the company or were scheduled to be laid off. AIG claimed that it would never have paid the bonuses without approval from the Treasury and the Federal Reserve. One of Treasury Secretary Timothy Geithner's top bank supervisors when he was at the New York Fed, Sarah Dahlgren, was the lead overseer of AIG. She sat in on the board meetings and participated in compensation committee meetings. Geithner said he knew nothing about the bonuses until days before they were paid. While the bonuses were a tiny fraction of the cost to the taxpayers of the bailouts, the public understood them as a measure of the contempt shown by Wall Street and Washington for working people's money. Many who were not used to Wall Street's ways wondered for whom Summers and Geithner were working.

Bailing out AIG was a way of giving even more money to the financial institutions that Washington was already bailing out directly and through various other indirect means. As Eliot Spitzer blogged, "It all appears, once again, to be the same insiders protecting themselves against sharing the pain and risk of their own bad adventures. AIG was nothing more than a conduit for huge capital flows to the same old suspects, with no reason or explanation." Geithner, Summers, and company were bent on saving the financial structure, at taxpayer expense, pretty much as it had existed, no matter what it cost.

Hedge Funds

Hedge funds lack precise definition, although they have been characterized by the extent to which the SEC does not regulate them (Paredes 2006:1–2). Hedge funds are secretive by nature since their strategy is to seek out inefficiencies in markets and take positions based on expectations of market movements, information they are obviously loathe to share. They are businesses that speculate in financial assets, using different strategies, employing leverage, and promising high returns. Their major asset is trading acumen and techniques that cannot be patented and could quickly be copied if known to competitors. "With the freedom to trade as much or as little as they like on any given day, to go long or short on any number of securities and with varying degrees of leverage, and to change investment strategies at a moment's notice, hedge fund managers enjoy enormous flexibility and discretion in pursuing investment returns" (Chan et al. 2006). These investments can be highly illiquid given that closing out positions as a result of an unlikely adverse occurrence results in sharp market movements against them. They must wait out the market until a correction presumably will move prices back in the direction they expect.

Management fees for hedge funds are high—typically 20 percent of trading profits plus 2 percent of assets under management. Top hedge-fund managers do quite well. In 2007 the ten best-compensated together received $14 billion, according to the magazine *Trader Monthly*. LCH Investments estimates that the top ten hedge-fund managers have earned over $150 billion for their investors since they were founded. George Soros, to choose one of the most successful, has made $32 billion for his clients since 1973. He and three hundred employees earned more than Apple, which employs more than thirty-four thousand employees. John Paulson netted more than $5 billion in 2010, the largest known compensation in the industry's history (his bets on gold were a significant factor). This payout exceeded the previous record, the nearly $4 billion Paulson made shorting subprime mortgages in 2007. The amount made by the top ten hedge funds is, remarkably, a third of the returns to the entire hedge-fund industry; the largest hundred made more than three-quarters of the total amount earned by the seven thousand or so firms in the industry (Mackintosh 2008), a point to bear in mind when the average profitability of the hedge-fund industry is discussed.

Structured as limited partnership or limited liability companies, hedge funds designate investors as limited partners to minimize regulation. They are exempt from registration requirements under U.S. securities laws, are usually registered overseas in some friendly island jurisdiction, and are exempt from supervision in the major markets where their investors live. One percent of the hedge funds were registered in New York. The most popular place for them to register was the Cayman Islands. Only very high income "accredited investors" can put their money in hedge funds. Since they are considered sophisticated players, the hedge funds are exempt from the 1933 Securities Act and other investor protection legislation. Because they limit themselves to qualified investors—persons and companies with at least $5 million in overall investments and institutional investors with at least $25 million in assets—they are exempt from the Investment Company Act of 1940, which prescribes the structure and reduces the leverage of investment companies and the investments they are allowed to make. At the height of their activity, hedge funds accounted for more than half of the credit derivative trading volume, and half of the New York Stock Exchange trading. As a major force in the less transparent debt markets (which in 2006 were 1.5 times larger than the stock market), hedge funds accounted for about 60 percent of all trades in the CDO securities market and held the riskiest classes of CDOs.

Observers see some hedge funds as trading on nonpubic information and moving markets in violation of insider trading rules. Critics such as Joseph Stiglitz (2010:10) see a good deal of "financial alchemy" at work. Paul Woolley (2010:135) suggests that hedge funds "display all the features that contribute to a higher level of rent extraction." The negative implications of hedge funds' creativity in a number of areas are discussed in the literature. Massoud et al. (2011) find evidence consistent with short-selling of the equity of hedge-fund borrowers prior to the public announcement of loan originations and loan amendments. It simply means that hedge-fund lenders as quasi-insiders have access to information others in the market do not have and create a conflict of interest given that they are more likely to lend to highly leveraged, lower-credit-quality firms. This access to private information is potentially most valuable.

Because hedge funds in the mid-2000s generated a huge volume of commissions, perhaps more than half of the total revenues of major brokerage houses, securities firms constantly fed the hedge funds ideas and information as a way of drumming up business for themselves. This was seen as a normal business practice and suggested at best unfair trading advantages for hedge funds, and at worst insider trading. Hedge-fund borrowers were an important source of bank revenues. As Morris Goldstein (2005:8) writes, "In an environment where flows into hedge funds are strong, where banks face strong competition from other suppliers of services to hedge funds, and where hedge funds are very important clients to banks, how heavily can we count on a regulatory model where banks are the agents primarily responsible for exercising oversight over the risk-management practices of hedge funds?" While reform limited bank investment in such funds, what might prove excessive lending to them was not considered in legislation adopted. In this regard it should be noted that the Financial Crisis Inquiry Commission reported that hedge funds pulled $86 billion in assets from investment banks in the week following the bankruptcy of Lehman (see chapter 5), creating serious liquidity problems for banks (Mollenkamp, Lucchetti, and Ng, 2011).

According to the SEC, such funds (perhaps ten thousand at the peak) controlled $2.4 trillion in assets in 2006. Successful hedge funds attracted entry by less skilled, opportunistic players and less sophisticated customers. Hopes for high returns eventually did not match the amounts being thrown onto the market. It was not only highly leveraged players who then faced the prospect of serious losses when hedge financing, in Minsky's use of the term, turned into Ponzi financing. In a world where banks mimic hedge funds in their trading activities and no longer retain the credit risk on the bulk of the loans they originate, or where banks are bypassed entirely in credit markets where loans are resold, those who originate the creation of credit worry less about risk. The incentive is to increase the volume of credit without worrying about loan quality.

Hedge funds bought CDOs and then used them as collateral to borrow to buy more, leveraging up their positions. The repo market creates vast amounts of credit in financial markets. This liquidity can dry up quickly, given that repos are very short term; most are overnight. If the value of the underlying assets diminishes, less can be borrowed on the given collateral's face value. This reduction, the haircut, eventually increased effectively to 100 percent as the default rate on subprime mortgages rose. The size of the haircut depends on the expected value of the collateral in secondary markets, and of course the probability of default. When such an episode strikes, deleveraging is rapid and extreme as there is a flight into cash and to hold only the safest assets (mostly U.S. treasuries). It is not just lenders who must worry: the hedge funds, which put their assets up as collateral, may not get them back if their counterparty itself has used them to borrow. Rehypothecation of securities owned by prime broker clients is a sizable source of a bank's financing, so this is no small matter. When the economy falls into recession, the collateral declines in value and haircuts increase. Fewer new loans are made. Liquidity dries up. The repo market closes down.

The early hedge funds depended on individual skill in seeking arbitrage opportunities. They were able to find them often enough to make a great deal of money doing so. But when the number of funds increased and the amount of money invested in the industry grew astronomically, the funds had to accept greater risk to similar strategies in the face of falling returns. The amounts of borrowing meant that when the market turned, many could not survive. U.S., U.K., and European regulators meeting with bankers asked for details of how they were using portfolio netting (a practice that allowed the hedge funds to use illiquid assets, such as credit default swaps and other instruments, as collateral to reduce the overall margin requirement held against their loans). They feared, correctly as it turned out, that in the event of a big market dislocation, at least some hedge funds would be unable to sell securities and meet their obligations. While hedge funds did not need to be bailed out in the Great Recession years, they may need to be in future crises, suggesting that greater regulation is a reasonable precautionary measure. Their lack of transparency, combined with their large impact on financial markets, made such arrangements problematic given the huge amounts of money at their command.

In June 2006 the European Central Bank warned that hedge funds had created a "major risk" to global financial stability, but it saw no obvious remedies. It likened the risk to that of bird flu. In early 2007 the International Organization of Securities Commissions (IOSCO) declared that hedge funds have a basic conflict in the way they value assets and that many put the interests of their managers ahead of investors. Valuations of less liquid assets are inherently difficult, but there seemed to be a systematic bias in the way they were done so as to favor management in some hedge funds.

In mid-February 2007 the Group of Seven finance ministers reached agreement on more closely monitoring the then $1.5 trillion hedge-fund industry. Angela Merkel, Germany's chancellor, held the G7 presidency that year. She took the lead in making clear that her government saw hedge funds and the compensation of their executives as matters of great concern. Her preference for strong regulation was met by resistance from the United States and Britain and thus came to nothing. The Americans and British agreed only to voluntary self-regulation. Germany was forced to soften its stance even though the hedge funds and the commercial banks, which are regulated, had grown similar in their operations, were now closely entwined, and were systematically dangerous. In the French election Nicolas Sarkozy promised to tax "speculative movements of capital" by hedge funds if he were to become president. This demand, to reject, as Sarkozy put it, "capitalism without ethics or morals," resonated with voters but proved illusive. It was not long before the Group of Twenty (G20) took up these issues, but that expanded group of systemically significant countries focused on the liquidity and capital requirements of banks and did not give the same attention to hedge funds.

The rationale for regulation of finance, with its strong externalities and social impact, came up against the hedge-fund threat to move to a domicile on some exotic island from which they would be even less influenced by the desires of regulators. In a neoliberal climate, such threats seem to have stopped politicians rather than spurring them to take the bull by the horns and face the need for reregulation at the global level, forbidding inflow and outflow to and from under- or unregulated jurisdictions as necessary. Coordination was made difficult by the reality that Anglo-American policy makers found nothing wrong with hedge funds retaining their freedom. As has been noted, in the United States regulators saw hedge funds as contributing to the better functioning of financial markets. Alan Greenspan, speaking in May 2006, said, "Hedge funds are a plus for the financial system. They increase the efficiency of the markets by taking advantage of mispriced securities and other market inefficiencies." By the end of 2007 fund of funds that held assets in many separate hedge funds accounted for 43 percent of the hedge-fund industry. Brokers had encouraged wealthy customers to finance their fund of funds purchases on credit—shades of the 1920s. These investments added another level of leverage to the hedge funds' own high leverage. At their peak period of 2008, hedge funds had $1.9 trillion under management. By the end of that year, the amount dropped to $1.4 trillion. More significantly, at the peak leverage allowed them to have more than $6.5 trillion in total assets. By the end of that year, the McKinsey Global Institute estimates their gross assets had fallen by nearly two-thirds to $2.4 trillion (Roxburgh et al. 2009). During 2008, as hedge-fund clients increased redemptions, the consequence of accepting such an assumption was made clear.

The collapse of two Bear Stearns hedge funds in June 2007 signaled that the high-leverage game was up. Bear's balance sheet was loaded with extremely risky assets, and the firm had made the conscious decision to not hold capital against possible losses. (The firm chose to borrow cheaply in the overnight market, which meant that lenders could decide each day to withdraw these loans.) They were extremely vulnerable to a loss of faith in the soundness of their holdings. When credit became tight—and in 2008 when Bernard Madoff was revealed as a Ponzi schemer who had stolen, by one estimate, $65 billion in investor funds, people began to wonder what the story was in other secretive hedge funds whose strategies and perhaps honesty became suspect. This put further downward pressure on asset valuations. The average hedge fund lost 22 percent in 2008, according to the Morningstar 1000 Index, better than the 38 percent drop in the stock market that year as measured by the S&P 500. Worried investors, seeing that the hedge-fund game was paying lower returns and often needing cash to meet other commitments, pulled their money out. The ten thousand hedge funds, with their more than $1.7 trillion in assets, were facing a major cash squeeze. The size of the industry was halved by the end of 2008, but it shrank even further. In 2009 many hedge funds stopped allowing redemptions. Others were forced to sell off many of their better assets to meet client demands for cash. But for the year as a whole, the top funds turned in strong performances. Indeed, in 2009 hedge-fund pay roared back, with the top twenty-five managers averaging a billion dollars each, more than they had before the crash. As noted above, the most successful of them did even better the following year.

One would not want to tar all hedge funds and the people who work for hedge funds as dishonest and socially irresponsible. Hedge funds hire very smart people to track down every possible bit of information that offers insight into expected price movements in financial markets. Their employees maintain wide contacts, and the firms explore all the avenues they can think of to gain the edge. They hire meteorologists to anticipate future crop results—for example the likely price of orange juice concentrate, based on expectations of rain and sun in Florida in coming months. This is not unethical, let alone illegal. Of course, getting illicit access to a government crop report ahead of public release (the premise of the movie *Trading Places* starring Dan Ackroyd and Eddie Murphy) would be a crime punishable by jail time. Where a direct payment of cash for information can be proven, insider-trading laws are deemed to have been broken. However, there are many interactions in which gossip is exchanged, mutual favors are carried out, and information is pried out of sources without a provable intent to collude.

There are also the "idea dinners" at which hedge-fund managers discuss particular stocks as well as market trends and other matters of mutual interest. There is steady use of instant messaging, e-mails, and private chats. Such activities are not illegal unless the government can prove that such sharing leads to artificially influencing market price, a tough hurdle in a courtroom where "fraudulent intent" is the standard for proving guilt. At the same time, it is hard to avoid the observation, as a *Wall Street Journal* headline characterized the issue, that "Hedge Funds' Pack Behavior Magnifies Swings in Market" (Strasburg and Pulliam 2011).

There remain all manner of questions that arise from the technology-driven innovations used, allowing hedge funds and other traders' servers to be colocated at exchanges, which gives them a fraction of a second lead to facilitate flash orders, which one might think of as an unfair advantage. SEC rules allow trading of New York Stock Exchange–listed shares on other platforms and so permit computer programs to break up orders and execute multiple slices at the speed of light over different trading venues. The minuscule gains posted per share add up to serious money, given the total volumes involved. Hedge-fund arms races with more and more expensive equipment allow for making money by arbitraging among trading platforms. Nothing much of social value is created, although high volume increases market liquidity and lots of money can be made.

A host of issues are involved in information availability and generation. Popular economic models assume that information is available to all at no cost. If some had information and withheld it, or supplied it only at a price to insiders, financial markets would not be efficient, and so such models suppress the possibility that information is a commodity that can be bought and sold like other commodities. A major hedge fund such as the Galleon Group carried out a thousand trades a day, based on discovery of possible price movements to come, and received perhaps a thousand calls a week from people pitching ideas and information, according to its head, the billionaire Raj Rajaratnam. Rajaratnam, one of the richest men in America, had a web of contacts in a host of industries from technology to health care that included people who were investors in his fund and in a position to offer tips. In the fall of 2009 the Securities and Exchange Commission accused him of trading on inside information, claiming it was able to connect the dots between insider information, which led to large Galleon trading profits and quid pro quo payoffs. Galleon and its head were accused of trading nonpublic information involving Google, Hilton, and IBM, among other companies. Twenty-two people were arrested as part of this case in the fall of 2009, and more in subsequent years as the case developed further. Other hedge funds tried to figure out what stocks Galleon held, anticipating it would have to liquidate positions to satisfy expected redemptions as college endowments, public employee pension funds, and others withdrew from the tainted hedge fund, pushing the price of these stocks lower. There is nothing illegal or wrong about this—just smart hedge-fund thinking.

Hedge funds, like other companies, spin their results as favorably as they can. When does spinning become misrepresentation and an individual or firm become punishable for misleading its clients? A study of 444 due-diligence reports carried out between 2003 and 2008 finds that one in five hedge-fund managers misrepresented their fund and its performance to investigators, and, more broadly, 42 percent of "misrepresentations" and "inconsistencies" were classified as "verification problems." Fifteen percent told some category of lies to due-diligence companies when they knew the company was hired to verify what they were telling them. Rule bending, it turns out, was a leading indicator of fund collapse (Brown et al. 2008). Peter Morris (2010) concludes that realized returns are lower than advertised even for the top quartile fund managers, and that returns fall when risk is adjusted.

Since reporting is voluntary and the firms choose whether and how to report, there are a number of biases in the data, and it is difficult to tell how profitable hedge funds are as an industry. Certainly some have done very well, and others have failed spectacularly. Burton G. Malkiel and Atanu Saha (2005), using data from 1996 to 2003 and correcting for problems as best they can, find that returns are reduced from a reported 13.5 percent to 9.7 percent after fees, which is almost 3 percentage points below the return on the S&P 500 stock index over these years. They find a wide divergence in performance between the best and worst performers and little persistence from year to year in which firms performed well and which poorly. The chance of a firm that produced in the top 50 percent doing so again the following year was no better than 50–50. For 2010 the average hedge fund is understood to have gained 10.49 percent, well below the 15 percent gain in the S&P 500 stock index, as the market came back (Zuckerman 2011). Later studies show a disconnect between the long-term returns of hedge funds, which do not seem to be any better than a passive investment in the S&P 500 index (Ibbotson, Chen, and Zhu 2010; Bird, Liam, and Thorp 2010), and the assumption that the hedge funds earn superior returns. Indeed, while the people who run hedge runs often do well, the return to investors based on a sample of nearly eleven thousand hedge funds between 1980 and 2008 is only 6 percent, lower than the S&P 10.9 percent return over the same period (Dichev and Yu 2011:249). Despite such findings on average returns, there is the reality that the most successful hedge funds do well, earning their principals and their clients' fortunes. For example, the top ten hedge funds made $28 billion for their clients in the second half of 2010, $2 billion more than the net profits of Goldman Sachs, JPMorgan, Citigroup, Morgan Stanley, Barclays, and HSBC combined. Those who have led these hedge funds and done well over time have themselves become rich beyond the imaginings of most mere mortals. George Soros made $35 billion for clients (after fees) since he established his Quantum Fund in 1973. John Paulson is closing in. His Paulson & Co. made $5.8 billion for his investors after fees in the second half of 2010, compared to the Quantum Fund's $3 billion.

Private Equity

The decline of growth in many sectors of the American economy, described in chapter 2, was accelerated by these firms. While merger movements at the turn of the twentieth century and in the 1920s took place in periods of an expanding economy by bringing together smaller firms to form powerful industrial giants or took the form of conglomerate mergers and acquisitions in the 1960s, the most recent wave of buyouts was quite different. Companies were bought, not for empire building, but to be restructured and spun off again. Under the regime of maximizing stockholder value, their workers were forced to make concessions, and the companies loaded up with debt. Others, it should be said, performed valuable services in restructuring firms, injecting capital, and helping them grow more effectively. The industry stresses the ways its members make a valuable contribution. Critics focus on the frequent destruction of viable firms, the losses to workers, and the tax law that allows profit taking at a heavy social cost.

The growth of private equity was a significant factor in reducing the corporate share of taxes paid in terms of the total amount the government collected. This was part of a larger trend. At the end of World War II, American corporations had contributed 50 percent of the total; in 2006, only 7 percent. To many governments, especially in Europe, the tax loss from the use of borrowed money to do these deals and the social costs of weakening or destroying going concerns have led some political leaders to see corporations as "locusts." Such asset stripping is perfectly legal and is considered to be a means of increasing the efficiency of the economy. In a dynamic economy, new firms are always coming into being, others grow in new directions, some properly pass from the scene, and others are destroyed unnecessarily because of financial manipulation. It is difficult to distinguish between a reasonable euthanasia and a murder-for-profit of a viable entity. If a firm can be profitably destroyed, it may well suffer such a fate. Corporate raiders and private equity groups work at dismantling companies, downsizing, and extracting stockholder value. In many cases private equity improves efficiency and operating performance of the firms it buys, justifying its takeover and receiving generous compensation. At the height of the buyout fever, just about any company in the United States could be seen as a takeover target, given the willingness of banks to lend. The buyout firms used huge amounts of leverage and the taxpayer to foot the bill through the tax code, which allows deductibility of interest on debt.

Private equity after the turn of the twenty-first century was a more refined version of the corporate raiders who used junk bonds in the 1980s to take over companies, using mostly borrowed money in that earlier period of low interest rates. The market was strongly influenced by the prospect of such takeover bids, high premiums helping to propel a bull market (to the stock market crash in 1987), and was surely a factor in the later financial bubble. Michael Jensen argued that such buyouts increase market efficiency since entrenched management of public companies was not maximizing stockholder equity. He saw "the eclipse of the public corporation" at the hands of private equity (Jensen 1989). Jensen's timing was poor as the junk bond market crashed, resulting in defaults and bankruptcies in the early 1990s, and these transactions dropped. They revived in a new wave in the new century, with buyout firms paying significant premiums on current stock prices of 15 to 50 percent, financed with 60 to 90 percent borrowed money. Interestingly, a popular exit strategy was a sale to another private equity fund, a route that has increased considerably over time, while the chances that a company returns to a public listing have decreased significantly (Kaplan and Strömberg 2009:129).

Private equity firms usually looked for companies in mature industries with a steady cash flow. Retail goods producers, utilities, and department store chains made good targets. The group borrowed money to buy a company with strong balance sheets, using the target's own capital to repay the debt. Investors in such funds might include university endowments and pension funds. Private partnerships classify their profits as "carried interest," a term of art that allows them to be taxed as capital gains at less than half the rate of earned income. (When private equity firms buy a company, its profits are also treated as capital gains for tax purposes). The new owners often borrowed even more money and used it to pay themselves dividends (innocently called dividend recapitalization or "recaps"), frequently bankrupting the company. This is of minor consequence to the buyout firm, which has appropriated as much "owner equity" and outsized management fees as it can. CEOs of target firms are often given (or in effect take for themselves) "unscheduled" stock option grants while takeover discussions have started but not yet been made public; in such cases the price paid for the company is less—that is, the takeover premium is smaller. In effect the option is a last-minute extraction by the CEO from the present owners of the company. A sample of 110 published deals between 1999 and 2006 shows that CEOs received an extra $5.7 million on average this way (Fich, Cai, and Tran 2009). It is yet another instance of "springloading," as the practice of granting options ahead of announcements that will raise the value of a company's stock is called. Existing managers are often given generous new contracts to stay on and manage the company after a leveraged buyout, giving them an incentive to help the private equity group get control on advantageous terms. In hostile takeovers, new managers are typically brought in to squeeze cash out of the company to meet profit expectations.

In total there were 110 megadeals (those with a value of more than $5 billion) for a combined $3.5 trillion in 2006, the year before the Great Recession started. That year saw Kohlberg Kravis Roberts (KKR) raise $5 billion for a new buyout fund, triple the amount it had targeted. KKR, which had pioneered the buyout business, certainly knew how to make money at the trade. It did the first leveraged buyout of a publicly traded company, Houdaille Industries, in 1979 for what would later look like a paltry sum of $355 million before going on to the biggest deal to that point, the $25 billion RJR Nabisco buyout in 1988, and then breaking its own record with the 2006 $33 billion buyout of the hospital group HCA. By 2007 KKR controlled thirty-five corporations with nearly a hundred billion in annual revenues and over half a million employees. When it started out, the money was all raised domestically. By 2006 half was coming from outside the United States. Similarly, the firm was hunting deals globally. KKR, while a pioneer, was hardly alone. Other big players included Bain Capital, which was formed in 1984, Black-

stone (1985), Carlyle (1987), and Texas Pacific (1993). These firms saw themselves as cleaning up and turning around companies that had been poorly
managed. Their ruthless cost cutting and movement of jobs to cheaper locations was "making better operating decisions," as Henry Kravis explained
(Sender 2007:C1). Others were more critical.

Some private equity firms were, as a matter of strategy, driving companies
into bankruptcy to get control, a practice called innocently "loan to own,"
making a secured loan that a firm could not pay back and whose failure to do
so gave the private equity firm control of its assets as first lien holder. While
earlier private equity firms might be seen as deploying assets of declining
companies, freeing them up for better uses, making companies more efficient
by pressuring executives to increase returns, and adding a discipline to businesses where it was lacking, as more players moved into the game with short-
term time horizons, the cost to American capitalism grew. Credit ratings of
the companies spun public were far lower, and fees extracted ate up more of
the companies' reserves, pushing them into weakened positions from which
some never recovered. Warren Buffett as a value investor warned his shareholders that the private equity firms are "deal flippers" whose financial engineering extracts value but does damage to companies in the long run. As
has been noted, such efficiencies involved layoffs, concessions, and speedups.
Private equity owners can evade collective bargaining processes and escape
the application of key parts of industrial relations legislation. To many workers, the characterization of what these firms do as "rip, strip, and flip" rings
painfully true, as the International Trade Union Confederation claimed.

The deals done between 2005 and mid-2007, which were half of the private equity invested in all of history, allowed founders of leading private equity groups to take their companies public. Just eleven men took away $6
billion in cash in this process. Since lobbyists hired by the hedge-fund and
private equity industries fought back against efforts to have their individual
winnings taxed as income after large donations to key politicians, they got to
keep much more of it than many considered just. Not long after insiders sold
ownership shares, revenues and earnings of the firms dropped precipitously.
Wags on Wall Street pointed out that at the low share prices of their companies, the same men could take their companies private again, paying stockholders a 100 percent premium, and still walk away with a huge amount of
change in their pockets. Going public ahead of the crash was private equity's
ultimate buyout, confirming the view that what Wall Street is about is smart
guys thinking about ways to make money from dumb ones. Private equity

firms, rather than creating value, can merely reallocate value. Older workers would not easily find new jobs, certainly not with the same wages and benefits. In this way the buyout firms put downward pressure on the prospects of all workers. One trick used was to have loans made in the form of derivatives, which had senior claim to assets.

From 2002 to 2008 as much as half of the increase in net corporate debt in the United States came from leveraged buyouts. Global buyout deals were $580 billion in 2007 but $150 billion in 2008, with smaller deals more common as financing takeovers became more difficult. Companies acquired through buyouts were 2.7 times as leveraged as the average listed company in 2002 and four times as leveraged at the peak of the buyout bubble in 2005. Over $400 billion of these loans would mature between 2009 and 2014, which would have represented more of a refinancing challenge if the Fed had not kept interest rates as close to zero as it could, igniting new buyouts. The extent of the downturn meant that the companies that had been bought were generally doing worse than expected and so having a hard time meeting the large debt obligations with which the private equity groups burdened them. By pledging more company assets to creditors to obtain loans (and so minimize the amount of their own capital put at risk in a buyout) the private equity firms made it more likely that creditors would force the breakup of companies unable to pay their debt, rather than allowing them to survive in a Chapter 11 bankruptcy proceeding (an alternative that would save jobs and allow rehabilitation of the business). Thus the calculation to load targets with maximal debt contributed to job loss, undercut prospects of secure retirement, and ended health plans of these workers.

In 2006, at their peak, private equity firms acquired 667 companies worth $372 billion, companies taken private in such "de-equitization" public-to-private transactions. These deals depended on the availability of funds that could be borrowed at low cost and the deductibility of the interest cost of borrowing the money to buy with very little, relative to the total cost of the buyout, of the private equity firm's own capital. How much value was added depended on the likelihood the market gave to possible default on the large debt. Since default rates were historically low, banks were ready to lend to finance these undertakings. So were pension funds and insurance companies. Lenders were relaxed about terms and offered low-cost loans since they had funds needing to be placed. Private equity was able to raise huge amounts of money for these activities. They joined together in "club deals" to share risk. Buyouts were good for the stock market since the private equity firms paid a premium on the market valuation, which drove up the stock price of potential takeover targets. As discussed in chapter 2, it did not make sense for a corporation to keep a lot of cash as a safety measure or for future expansion since to do so made the company a potential takeover target. Companies had to adopt a shorter time horizon owing to the threat of private equity groups' strategies.

By the end of 2008 investors were selling their private equity shares at less than thirty cents on the dollar, fearing financial Armageddon and seeing the events of the early fall of 2008 (the failure of Bear Stearns, Lehman, Fannie, and Freddie) as the equivalent of the 1929 crash for debt markets. By early 2009 most of the $100 billion or so in leveraged buyouts since 2005 had been wiped out. The groups had leveraged their equity investment with borrowing of roughly $1 trillion. Perhaps a third of that had defaulted. The calculations behind these deals were based on what were in fact the unusual circumstances of a bubble economy, macroeconomic conditions that were different from the less upbeat, longer-term historical experience. It was all based on a gamble that the bubble would continue. While people might be impressed by, envious of, and maybe in awe of people who are smart enough to become fabulously wealthy in the context of global crisis, bankers, hedge-fund managers, and private equity mavens came to be seen in a new and less flattering light by an angry public focusing on the bankruptcies, unemployment, pension losses, and huge debt the federal government was taking on in an effort to address the damage the financial sector had wrought. Yet by late 2009 banks were again extending loans to hedge funds and private equity firms at precrisis levels. For Citigroup, Bank of America, JPMorgan Chase, and Morgan Stanley, offering loans and cranking up leverage were the routes to higher profits at a time when commercial real estate loans and mortgages continued to sour and credit card losses mounted (given a 10 percent or so unemployment rate). In general, lending to businesses and consumers was less profitable and was perceived as riskier than lending to hedge funds and buyout groups, which were profiting from restructuring deals in the wake of the economic crisis. Indeed, the hedge funds and buyout groups were reporting that banks were calling them up offering loans.

The diversity of experiences makes generalizing hazardous, but one wonders what social gains can flow from the reality that companies have been bought and sold many times by different private equity groups after being owned for a short time by each. Simmons, the bedding company, went through six rounds of buyouts over a two-decade period, beginning as a healthy company with $164 million in debt in 1991 and ending in bankruptcy in 2009 with $1.3 billion in debt. Its last owner pocketed $77 million in profit through all manner of fee income, declared dividends, and other tactics. Altogether the buyout firms took away three-quarters of a billion dollars before abandoning the corpse of a once more than viable, respected firm. One needs to wonder about such secondary buyouts when a company like Simmons is sold from one private equity firm to another and is typically profitable each time for a new buyer. (About 25 percent of all private equity deals in 2010 were secondary buyouts, according to Thompson Reuters.) When equity groups take control, they direct the firm to take out large loans that can be used to make a dividend payment to the new owners, sometimes returning all the money they paid for the company, and of course they maintain control of the firm. These dividend recaps load the company up with still more debt.

From 2005 through the third quarter of 2008, private equity groups added $741 billion in debt to the companies they had bought. It was therefore not surprising that of the 105 big companies filing for bankruptcy in 2008, 66 were owned by these buyout outfits. Loans made on the deals were trading at a third of their face value. Like Simmons, half of all firms defaulting on debt in 2009 were owned or had been owned by private equity groups. As in the case of Simmons, employees were left without jobs or pensions (Creswell 2009). Since these deals were done with an average of 60 percent debt and 40 percent equity, the drop in the market (by more than 40 percent) made many buyout firm positions essentially worthless. It is a cyclical industry.

There is irony in the involvement of pension funds desperate for higher returns to meet mushrooming commitments to retired workers in underfunded plans investing in buyout funds, and these funds buying control of companies and putting the screws to workers to reduce wages and pension costs to pay off the loans taken out to gain control of the firm. Such activities put pressure on competitors to do the same; hence the wider phenomenon of a sea change in the status of pensions. Coinciding with the rise of leveraged buyouts was acceleration in the number of companies "freezing" their pension plans (so that members stop accruing benefits). By 2007 around a quarter of pension plans in the United States had been frozen, with the expectation that the number would more than double in the next five years. In Britain, where financialization dominated the economy to even a greater extent than in the United States, about 70 percent of pension plans had been frozen or simply terminated. A similar development is evident in the provision of health care by employers, where companies rid themselves of such obligations and unions are forced to accept special-purpose vehicles that take over benefit obligations for a lump-sum payment by the company. Should that vehicle fail to meet health and retirement liabilities in years to come promised to retirees, the company is not liable.

Deal flipping could be quite profitable for the principals. For example, when Burger King was taken private in 2002, the chain, which at the time was unprofitable, started paying its new owners (Texas Pacific, Bain Capital, and the buyout arm of Goldman Sachs, in the sort of club deal that made the antitrust staff at the Justice Department uncomfortable) tens of millions in unspecified "professional fees" as well as quarterly management fees for monitoring the business, serving on the board, and such, and paid generous dividends, borrowing to make the payment before the company was taken public again (after a $30 million fee for termination of management was paid). Together the buyout firms collected as much as they had invested (before revenues) from taking the firm public, while they retained three-quarters of the ownership. After considerable turnover in 2010, Burger King was once again up for sale.

Such stories catch the imagination of investors and assure huge sums flow into leveraged buyout firms. There are clearly a number that have done very well. However, taken as a whole, leveraged buyout firms' returns to its investors (net of fees paid) between 1980 and 2001 were less than those of the S&P 500 index. There are, to be sure, questions of the data. These firms can use unusual rules on how they book profit. When risk adjustments are made, a basket of listed companies in an index fund does substantially better; indeed, it does better when compared even to the best-performing private equity firms as a group (Phalippou and Gottschalg 2009). At the height of the buyout fever, banks were competing to lend money to these firms as underwriting standards dropped. With lots of cheap credit available, this went on until there was no more low-cost credit available for the private equity groups and they had to shelve plans for new takeovers and scramble to finance the debt of companies they owned. After the bottom fell out, lending terms became more stringent if money could be found for such purposes at all. The period of "strip and flip" came to a halt. It would come alive again as the economy recovered.

While researchers find that operating performance increases after a private equity firm takes over, because of data limitations there are conflicting judgments of the impact of survivor bias and sample composition. There are also issues regarding the great leverage involved: returns not adjusted for the risk this leverage carries can bias findings. With adjustments for such factors and subtracting the generous compensation going to private equity managers, one can find outstanding performance in only some of the larger, more mature firms in the industry (Acharya, Hahn, and Kehoe 2010). Studies also cover different time periods. These things may explain the conflicting findings. Cyclical patterns in private equity mean that success crowds more money into such investments, returns fall, and there is a decline in activity until the next upsurge.

The most successful firms appear to maintain higher returns than the industry as a whole, which may not beat a stock market index after fees; this persistence must be put up against the credibility one gives to the social cost of dismemberment of enterprises that could have remained viable if not subject to buyouts and selloffs. If one sees capitalism as a system of creative destruction in which the laggards need to get culled from the herd as a matter of system maintenance, private equity is a powerful agent for this necessary process. If, on the other hand, one stresses a social cost/benefit approach, there is reason to limit current incentives favoring private equity, including the tax deduction of interest costs in takeovers and the special tax treatment of carried interest, the name that income management receives that allows it to be treated as capital gains for tax purposes instead of as income to be taxed at a considerably higher rate.

President Obama suggested that he might follow up on a campaign promise to make carried interest be taxed as regular income, and so at 35 percent rather than 15 percent. This led Stephen Schwartzman, CEO of Blackstone, with a net worth of $8 billion and paying fewer taxes as a proportion of his income than his chauffeurs and secretaries do, to liken Obama's suggestion to "Hitler's invasion of Poland," an obscenity that was received with raised eyebrows even on Wall Street. Amid 10 percent unemployment and troubling growth of the national debt, Wall Street honchos scorned a more equitable treatment of their income for tax purposes. Some insisted that President Obama was antibusiness, a charge widely echoed when the administration made any move to address what many saw as inequities in the system.

Private equity groups, their managers, and investors have made a huge amount of money. The judgment one makes of these firms, as for so much else in the financialized economy, comes down to an evaluation of their societal impact. Do they serve the interests of the society in reorganizing and in some cases liquidating dysfunctional companies, weeding out inefficiency, or are they more generally characterized by destroying companies, as in the Simmons case described earlier, profiting at the expense of workers and taxpayers?

Financialization's Growing Shadow

The continued low cost of borrowing in the years after the 2000–2001 bubble collapse had not led to much real investment in the United States but to more borrowing to fund stock buybacks that would prevent being takeover targets or for use by private equity in takeovers, as well as increased debt levels rather than an increased investment in corporate growth. The leveraged buyout firms were what Mohamed El-Erian (2007:13) called the new liquidity factories, which create money by vastly increasing leverage and so liquidity in the system. Central bankers and certainly monetary theorists have yet to come to grips with the power of private players to endogenously create money—something that has always been the case but was happening on a far larger scale than ever before. On the downside, leverage works to contract liquidity in a reverse of the way it works in the expansion. Monetary authorities became prisoners to the financialized economy they do not control or effectively regulate but have to protect in a period of crisis.

Discussing hedge funds, private equity groups, and investment banks as different types of financial institutions is helpful in understanding what each does, but it should not obscure the interconnections among these and other financial institutions, nor the reality that the same large players are active in each of these areas. The world's largest private equity group is the investment bank Goldman Sachs. Goldman Sachs Asset Management is one of the world's largest hedge funds, and as the most powerful broker-dealer on Wall Street (if it overcomes supposed "Chinese Walls" between divisions) it has information access allowing its different arms to benefit from information generated elsewhere in its conglomerate structure, all the while having access to Treasury and Federal Reserve support if it oversteps. Tens of billions of its debt are backed by the FDIC. It is involved in all significant segments of the shadow financial system. Goldman played both sides in a number of transactions. Its brilliance extended to profiting ahead of and against its own clients and betting against the products it sold. None of this is to say Goldman is not terrifically good at what it does, more profitable, and perhaps less likely to fail than its rivals. It is both a big fee payer and an aggressive buyout player while it arranges such deals for its customers. In its activities and advice to clients, it, like other parts of the new financial order, shapes what is still thought of as a separate real economy. Since pension and mutual funds hold 80 percent of Goldman Sachs stock, it is too important to too many people to be allowed to fail, even as it routinely pays half its profits to employees who have incentive to enter risky endeavors.

Defenders of hedge funds and private equity firms point out that it was the banks whose problems produced the system's difficulties. Yet the hedge funds were big buyers and traders of CDOs. By 1985 hedge funds had over $1 trillion under management and were trading half of the plain vanilla over-the-counter options contracts in the United States, 70 percent of the value of exchange traded funds, and a third of all future contracts, junk bonds, and credit derivatives. They played a dominant role in trading distressed debt (accounting for over 80 percent of the volume) and were influential in less liquid, more exotic instruments. Private equity funds financed real estate development companies and mortgage lenders. In 2006 a third of the $1.5 trillion in U.S. mergers and acquisitions was carried out by private equity firms—triple the share of the previous year. Private equity firms paid investment banks $11 billion in fees for arranging loans, merger and acquisition advice, and stock and bond underwriting that year. Equity underwriting was the second biggest source of fees for JP Morgan in 2006. In expansions hedge funds, banks, and buyout firms increase their liabilities. In the expansion phase of a business cycle, the assets they hold rise in value, strengthening balance sheets and lowering their leverage, encouraging them to take on more leverage. They borrow more to maintain the same ratio of assets to liabilities. They borrow to buy more assets, which pushes asset prices higher still. This continues as the feedback of higher asset prices leads to lower leverage, encouraging more borrowing to purchase more assets.

Another way to look at this is that rather than the demand curve sloping downward, as well-behaved textbook demand curves do, the demand curve for assets is upward sloping. As the cycle peaks, the first, more skeptical players wonder about the possibility of asset prices rising further and become cautious, reducing their leverage by selling some assets. As assets are sold, their price stops going up and more players sell. As price falls, there is an increased supply of these assets thrown on the market. (The supply curve, instead of sloping upward, slopes downward.) This process too is cumulative. In downturns their assets fall, but they reduce their liabilities even more. As more assets are forced onto the market, prices plunge, confirming the Minskyan understanding of financial crisis. The procyclicality of speculation is difficult to control in a capitalist economy in which successful risk taking is so amply rewarded and innovation stays ahead of regulation. The cost of this structural reality can be great.

While hedge funds and private equity groups did not cause the crisis, their activities increased the severity of the downturn, and the next crisis could well originate in their overreaching, as in the collapse of the hedge fund Long Term Capital Management in 1998, which required a rescue coordinated by the New York Fed to save the financial system. The pyramiding of leverage to create liquidity on a base of high-risk assets can affect the entire highly indebted financial system with damaging spillover effects, as will be discussed in the next chapter.

What should the monetary authorities do in the expansion phase of the bubble? Here the problem is that they have traditionally been watching the money supply for signs of trouble, but, unlike in the simple bank model where the liabilities of the institutions were primarily depositor money, banks (and the shadow banking system of hedge funds and others) buy assets and use those assets as collateral to borrow more funds. This increases the money-creation multiplier of the financial sector considerably. As noted in chapter 3, the conventionally measured money supply does not capture this expansion of credit. From the beginning of the neoliberal SSA, money has not been a good measure of liquidity even as bubbles have become more common. The use of asset-backed securities and other nondeposit-based funds has changed the game, leading to the question, how is liquidity best measured? The best indicator of the availability of credit seems to be the growth of collateralized borrowing, and in particular the stock of outstanding repurchase agreements (Adrian and Shin 2008). This suggests that if there were political will, regulators could do a better job of moderating financial crises. It is unlikely given the power of Wall Street that such structural initiative by the government is possible without a major change in the balance of social forces in the country.

Among the perceived inadequacies of financial reform (see chapter 6) was that in limiting proprietary trading by banks. The 2010 Frank-Dodd Act pushed risky activities toward the hedge funds and other lightly supervised shadow banking sector entities. The logic was to separate banks—which, because of the central role they play in the economy, are regulated by the government, have depositors protected by the FDIC, and are assisted by the Fed when they get in trouble—from financial companies that are free to speculate with investors' money and left to take losses when they fail. This is an unlikely outcome. As the shadow banking system grows so large that its importance looms over the economy, and despite regulatory reform regulated banks continue to engage in high-risk activities, this approach by lawmakers seems questionable. Really existing capitalism is not so easily controlled.

5

The Coming Apart

No one can read the chronicles of those earlier crashes without sensing—with a chill—that history is repeating itself. The story of the modern capitalist economy is a rhythmic repetition of cycles, syncopated by eerily similar crises. These crises, while their details differ, are but variations on the same theme. Easy money, geared up by leverage, floods the financial system through innovative products. This simultaneously pumps up asset prices and obscures their speculative nature, with euphoria usurping the place of analysis. Until, one day, something triggers a loss of confidence in the continued rise of prices, and the whole leveraged edifice crumbles.

— Financial Times, EDITORIAL, 2009

We have a sorry history of the banking industry driving statutory and regulatory changes. Now banks want accounting fixes to mask their reckless-ness. Meanwhile, there has been no acknowledgment of culpability in what top management in these financial institutions did—despite warnings—to help bring about the crisis. Theirs is a record of lax risk management, flawed models, reckless lending, and excessively leveraged investment strategies. In the worst instances, they acted with moral indifference, knowing that what they were doing was flawed, but still willing to pocket the fees and accompanying bonuses.

—JAMES S. CHANOS, 2009

The global financial crisis, or the Great Recession, had its trigger in the collapse of the housing market and the impact of unpaid sub-prime mortgages on securitized debt in the United States. It was the third business cycle in a row rooted in an asset bubble and was far worse than one might have thought from the dollar amount of underlying mort-gages involved. In the era of national Keynesianism, home owners unable to meet their mortgage obligations would not have produced anywhere near the same damage; it was the extent of financialization and the interconnect-edness of segments of finance in an antiregulation climate of high leverage and confidence in efficient financial markets.

Some economists (Dooley and Garber 2009) are so adamant that the cri-sis was caused by insufficient supervision and regulation of financial markets that they suggest that other leading candidates are "misconceptions." They dismiss the net inflow of saving from emerging markets to the United States, easy money policy in the United States, and financial innovation in their focus on regulatory errors. Each of these causes, as well as others including the failure of regulation, is an aspect of financialization. The supporting norms of neoliberal financialization were important enabling features, encouraging dangerous behavior, thanks to financial product innovation that mushroomed in the new millennium, producing a different trade-off between risk and reward. The originate-and-distribute model, the use of CDOs and over-the-counter selling of derivatives to speculate on market movements, and the compensation system, which strongly favored immediate high returns, all had rationales in modern finance theory. Economists have played a substantial role in giving credibility to such illusions.

The ideas that ordinary people somehow had a correct model of the economy in their heads when economists so obviously had wrong ones, that financial markets were efficient and to be trusted, and that asset prices always reveal accurate valuations seemed strange indeed amid the meltdown of Wall Street. Basic models had come to accept that all relevant information was indeed known and so markets were efficient. What the actual workings of financial markets leading to the crisis showed was that asymmetrical information characterizes these markets and it is quite possible to take advantage of counterparties who lack accurate knowledge.

The value of mortgages was known to originators and willfully unquestioned by the megabanks packaging collateralized debt obligations but was not available to the buyers of financial products who were misled on a consistent basis. Those who sold dodgy products as fast as they could, even as buyers became more concerned, at least strongly suspected (and often well understood) the real risks. They raised the prospect of an "extreme market event"—in effect "fattening the tail." Monetary authorities played a role not only in their unwillingness to question questionable activities of participants in financial markets, but in their understanding of the role of monetary policy in what others saw as serial bubble blowing.

The collapse of the New Economy bubble in 2000–2001 led the Federal Reserve to dramatically lower interest rates and keep them low for a long time in an effort to stimulate the economy. One of the most important consequences was to significantly reduce the monthly cost of a mortgage. Home sales boomed. In 1995 home prices in the United States rose by 1.7 percent, and then doubled over the next decade. In 2005 alone they increased by 15.7 percent. Housing prices, which had historically tracked inflation, rose between 2001 and mid-2005 at a rate 50 percent faster the overall rate of inflation; thus economic growth over these years heavily depended on housing. The price of owning a home compared to renting grew. This ratio, which historically had been fifteen to one, increased to twenty to one and more. By 2006 those looking at the situation from a Minskyian perspective saw a highly fragile state of affairs with low cushions of safety and inadequate provision for liquidity. The economy could avoid a descent into instability only as long as house prices kept rising, interest rates did not go up, and new mortgages came into the pipeline and were bundled into CDOs and sold to buyers who were confident that they were paying reasonable prices for structured products.

As housing became more expensive (the ratio of the median house price to median household income increased from three to one in 2000 to five to one in 2006), the industry developed ways to hold down the (at least initial) cost of a mortgage, feeding the housing bubble. While new mortgages peaked in 2003, the expansion was extended by opening up, on a huge scale, an essentially new market of low-income, first-time home buyers who in the past had not qualified for mortgages. This subprime market offered low initial rates to buyers, many of whom did not have the money to sustain their payments when the rates were reset. Close to three-quarters of securitized subprime loan payments from 2004 and 2005 ballooned after two or three years, a ticking time bomb. Brokers made more money by talking borrowers into subprime mortgages even if they qualified for lower-interest regular mortgages. In 2006, 61 percent of subprime borrowers had credit scores high enough to qualify for lower-cost conventional loans.

The volume of credit rose exponentially because mortgage originators and other players lowered their standards, irresponsibly leveraging to the maximum extent in search of larger capital gains. Many real estate investors used rental income to finance mortgages, assuming that rents and property values would continue to rise. The assumption that the market, no matter how high it rose, could only continue to rise, or that they would be smart enough to get out before the collapse, is at the heart of all bubbles. Loan to value of homes reached 100 percent in 2006, meaning that these new homeowners had zero equity in their property. At this point a quarter of buyers put down nothing. They were in fact under water the minute they bought since the cost of reselling is a positive number (Haughwout 2011). The financial sector, from mortgage originators through bundlers and sellers of CDOs to purchasers of these products, was moving from a speculative to Ponzi financing and the economy becoming, in Minsky's terminology, a "deviation-amplifying" system.

Without excessive subprime borrowing, the real estate market would still have deflated and affected owners of collateralized mortgages, but this would have happened sooner and done less damage. The details of systemic corruption, discussed below, may seem secondary to the basic economics of the situation. However, it was the incentives faced by market participants and an unwillingness of the government ex ante to restrain what are seen as market forces that caused unnecessary suffering and crippled the lives of many millions of Americans (a useful, detailed, stage-by-stage critical evaluation is found in National Commission on the Causes of the Financial and Economic Crisis in the United States, 2011).

Triggering the Crisis

To understand what went so wrong, it is important to comprehend the incentives of decision makers. In the case of housing finance, mortgage originators' fees are paid upfront; thus their goal was to come up with many mortgages regardless of the interests of home buyers and what they are able to pay over the full term of the mortgage, or the interests of whomever the mortgage's eventual owner turns out to be. A 2007 report from Credit Suisse found that roughly half of all subprime borrowers in 2005 and 2006, peak years of the market explosion, provided little or no documentation of their income. Originators bundled mortgages and sold them to investment banks, which sliced and diced securities into collatoralized debt obligations and sold them to investors. The rating agencies gave most of these CDOs triple-A grades.

The Senate Permanent Subcommittee on Investigations bipartisan report (2011:6), commenting on the issuer pays model, concluded, "When sound credit ratings conflicted with collecting profitable fees, credit rating agencies chose the fees." The fees were generous, ranging up to $135,000 to rate a mortgage-backed security and up to three-quarters of a million dollars for a collateralized debt obligation. As evidence gathered by the subcommittee shows, the credit rating agencies "were aware of problems in the mortgage market, including an unsustainable rise in housing prices, the high-risk nature of the loans being issued, lax lending standards, and rampant mortgage fraud. Instead of using this information to temper their ratings, the firms continued to issue a high volume of investment grade ratings for mortgage backed securities" (Senate Permanent Subcommittee on Investigations 2011:7).

In the euphoria of the period, loans were made to people with little or no chance of ever paying them off. The presumption that anyone who could not pay could resell their home for more than they paid for it, or the lender could take possession and sell it for more than the debt owed, meant that the ever-rising value of the home was seen as adequate collateral for the debt. (Standard & Poor's used a rating model that did not accept a negative change in housing prices.) Hence "NINJA" loans flourished (No Income, No Job or Assets). The overall size of the prime mortgage market had peaked in 2003 at about $4 billion worth and fell to only $2.5 billion in 2004. The subprime market rapidly expanded to fill the vacuum. Subprime mortgages were 70 percent of the total mortgage market in 2006, up from 10 percent in 2001. Collaborative circles of deceit gamed the system by inflating appraised values and the credit worthiness of borrowers. That many loans were unethical, violated industry standards (such as they were), and were illegally drawn up resulted from an incentive structure that rewarded such behavior. Pressure from the banks to obtain more mortgages to bundle into profitable CDOs almost demanded such lax practices. The Federal Reserve had authority to investigate and regulate much of this, but through the period of the most extreme abuse, Fed chair Alan Greenspan consciously chose to not do so.

The high return promised by collateralized debt obligations constructed by bundling mortgages, increasingly subprime and Alternative-A (Alt-A, a step above the subprime category), could be composed of thousands of individual mortgages and mixed with other credit instruments, such as credit default swaps, as their underlying collateral. It was impossible for a buyer to do due diligence on such products, which were nonetheless in demand thanks to their promised payments and high ratings. To keep up with demand, synthetic CDOs were created to mimic the performance and return of other CDOs. CDO-squared products combined other CDO segments in instruments that were constructed to shadow returns of CDOs and could not be priced except by highly complex computer models. CDO-cubed instruments were even more preposterous in their construction. They had nothing to do with providing liquidity to the housing market but were purely gambling vehicles. They had no social value. They contained no actual mortgages. What purpose did they serve except as pure gambling instruments like a roulette wheel or an office betting pool on sports events?

Derivatives could be sold with confidence, thanks to the ratings agencies Fitch, Moody's, and Standard & Poor's, which gave almost all of them triple-A ratings. As has been previously noted, they did this based on recent performance in an economic upswing. It also turned out they were actively advising clients—the issuers of CDOs—on how to achieve high ratings when they bundled noninvestment-grade assets. The rating agencies said that they were basing them on what the issuers shared, and they were not obliged to check to see if what they were being told was true or not. This hardly seems to be what regulators had in mind when they mandated that the rating agencies safeguard the investing public. Covenants that might ask for information and place constraints on cash-flow coverage, earnings before interest, tax, depreciation, and amortization (ebitda), or the ratio of ebitda to net debt as against some target level offered some measure of how safe repayment was likely to be. Most derivatives were cov-lite instruments: they asked little in the way of restrictive covenants to protect the interests of lenders.

By the end of 2009 Moody's, Standard & Poor's, and Fitch were being sued by, among others, the attorney general of Ohio, who claimed they had cost the state's retirement funds close to half a billion dollars by approving high-risk securities. The charge was that they were in league with the banks that sold these unsafe products, aiding and abetting the misconduct of the issuers, allowing the securities sector to grow nearly a hundredfold between 1980 and 2008. In terms of systemic risk, the U.S. comptroller of the currency reported that in 2004 five commercial banks accounted for 96 percent of the total national value of derivatives. It was in the interests of these firms to sell customized, complicated products and not allow derivatives to become commodified and pricing transparent. Standardized contracts that could be sold on exchanges would impart a significant measure of safety to derivative trading since the exchange would impose margin requirements on counterparties. It would also open up pricing for derivatives so that banks could not hide both losing positions (but, like other participants, put up money when prices went against them). This would make markets more competitive and reduce profitability for the banks.

The Fed continued to willfully misunderstand what was happening in this sector, relying as a matter of ideological commitment on the market to promote efficient allocation of the housing stock and monitor mortgage contracts. The assumption that housing prices would continue to rise was essential to the logic of pushing subprime and Alt-A loans. (Alternative-A loans required little documentation and were called in the business "liar loans." They had a low or no down payment. These buyers too would have trouble meeting their obligations.) The acceptance that prices would keep rising lent plausibility to a strategy that was intended to fill the pipeline and satisfy the strong demand for collateralized debt obligations from investors looking for higher returns than could be found in traditional investments in the real economy. By spring 2010, 93 percent of subprime mortgage–backed securities issued in 2006 were downgraded to junk status.

In 2006, while the subprime market was beginning to collapse, Secretary of the Treasury Henry Paulson explained that the housing market was experiencing "a correction," a "repricing of risk" that would work out without doing much harm to the rest of the economy. He urged banks to take their bad loans and bundle them into off-balance-sheet holdings. Indeed, he said the real problem facing Wall Street was excessive regulation. Toward the end of 2006, he said that while he was not in favor of lifting all regulation, "excessive regulation slows innovation, imposes needless costs on investors and stifles competitiveness and job creation." Fed chair Ben Bernanke assured the markets on May 17, 2007, that "we do not expect significant spillovers from the subprime market to the rest of the economy or the financial system." Within three months of the statement a global credit crunch sent all financial markets dramatically lower.

The gross liability of the U.S. financial sector was 21 percent of GDP in 1980 but 116 percent of GDP in 2007. In significant part, this was because of lending in the subprime market and the pyramiding of derivative products constructed on the base of loans. Because of the way collateralized debt obligations were constructed, the same mortgage might be part of many products and pieces owned by many investors to the point where untangling ownership was nearly impossible. Collusion between auditors and mortgage originators allowed questionable accounting strategies to flourish. Court-appointed investigators found professional dereliction and negligent misrepresentation that enabled the country's biggest mortgage originators to provide loans to people with poor credit histories, feeding "a brazen obsession with increasing loan originations, without due regard to the risks associated with the business strategy," as the examiner in the New Century bankruptcy's final report stated with regard to the events that led to the company's downfall. This evaluation had some impact in the industry (Missal and Richmond 2008).

Payoffs to those who might have raised questions about what was going on included U.S. senators and Senate employees, to whom thirty "VIP loans" were extended by Countrywide, which also gave similar bargains to 170 employees of the then privately owned Fannie Mae and Freddie Mac. In the company's view, these were business costs to help Countrywide continue practices that fed its growth, (The records revealing these dealings were subpoenaed by Darrell Issa, ranking Republican on the House Oversight and Government Reform Committee, after the collapse of Countrywide and the subprime pyramid scheme.)

The banks had incentive not to turn bad loans back to the likes of Countrywide, which would simply peddle them elsewhere and cost the banks business. It was widely suspected that such giant Wall Street institutions sold loans they knew were bad. There is evidence that they did do due diligence followed by demanding lower prices when they bought them, but that they sold the CDOs to investors as high-quality loan pools, another way to increase their own profits on such transactions. Companies like Bank of America and Citigroup were fined—money that came from stockholders—while the executives who lied to the stockholders kept their bonuses. In companies like Wachovia, where there was evidence of illegalities, whistle-blowers had repeatedly called attention to the firm's funneling of drug money, but no one was indicted for criminal wrongdoing.

While it was the mortgage originators such as Countrywide and Ameriquest that got the most initial attention, the most prominent mega financial institutions were involved in misleading investors at a much higher level of fraudulent behavior. The Financial Industries Regulatory Authority accused Deutsche Bank of misleading investors about how many delinquent loans went into six mortgage securities worth over $2 billion that the firm underwrote. Even after the "error" of understating delinquency rates was discovered, the bank continued to report the misstatements on its Web site, checked by investors. It paid a paltry $7.5 million fine without having to admit or deny the allegations, saying it had cooperated fully and was pleased to have the matter behind it. The Securities and Exchange Commission fined Citigroup's chief financial officer $100,000 to settle allegations that he misrepresented Citi's subprime holdings. He said they amounted to $13 billion, somehow leaving out another $40 billion in subprime mortgages, which if publicly known would have led investors to take an even more jaundiced view of the megabank. Under the law, he and Citi's CEO had to sign off on the accuracy of their quarterly financial statements. The year he was alleged to have done this, he took home $19.4 million. The fine amounted to one-half of 1 percent of what he received from Citi for, among other things, hiding this information. He did not have to acknowledge wrongdoing. The SEC said he knew the real extent of the subprime holdings. Phil Angelides and the Financial Crisis Inquiry Commission revealed that even Citi board members, including Robert Rubin, knew the real situation.

There was also criticism of the remaining Big Four accounting firms, but it was unlikely that even serial offenders would be shut down after Arthur Andersen, Enron's auditor, was forced out of business. The shrinking universe of large accounting firms assured their immunity. And despite assurances of reform and "never again," after Enron there is evidence of accommodation by the large accounting firms to shoddy and illegal practices to maintain income flow. Like the rating reports based on what the evaluators were told by issuers, the accounting firms said they could hardly be expected to investigate numbers they were given and used in good faith. However, when companies collapsed, it seems the accounting firms were involved in facilitating fraudulent practices even if the Justice Department was not about to prosecute them and jeopardize the private auditing system as it exists.

There were those, including European central bankers, who warned of potential dangers. Financial markets are liable to overshoot, they said. But on Wall Street bonuses had never been higher, and, as Charles Prince, then the head of Citigroup, famously told the *Financial Times* in July 2007, as long as the music was playing, his bank would be out there dancing. A year later he was gone. Citigroup took the largest write-offs of any investment bank in history, and the leviathan was on its way to bankruptcy, necessitating a major government rescue. This now famous "keep dancing" comment is often cited to suggest how stupid Citi was to keep playing as the market turned. But Prince could ill afford to stop dancing too soon. That was the point. To do so would have meant lower earnings over what might be an extended period, a sure ticket to investor dissatisfaction, and a falling stock price. Even in a bubble situation, the smart money keeps dancing until (they hoped) just before the stroke of midnight. As Warren Buffett wrote in a 2001 letter to his stockholders, the "giddy participants all planned to leave just seconds before midnight. There's a problem, though: they're dancing in a room in which the clocks have no hands." A few years later, after the damage was done, Federal Reserve reviews of how Citi got into so much trouble were turned over to the bipartisan Financial Crisis Inquiry Commission. They revealed the inadequate oversight of Citigroup by the New York Federal Reserve, whose president from 2003 to 2008 was Timothy Geithner. The commission heard from a former Citi mortgage lending officer how decisions on poorly written loans were changed from "turned down" to "approved," and 80 percent or so of these defective loans were sold to Fannie Mae, Freddie Mac, and other investors. The largest banks, including Citi, were left with illiquid, highly risky assets on their own books, which they could not sell, and were unable to borrow or roll over short-term debt.

The Institutional Risk Analyst (2009) declared, "For the world's largest banks, the OTC derivatives markets are the last remaining source of supranormal profits—and also perhaps the single largest source of systemic risk in the global financial markets. Without OTC derivatives, Bear Stearns, Lehman Brothers and AIG would not have failed, but without the excessive rents earned by JPMorgan Chase . . . and the remaining legacy OTC dealers, the largest banks cannot survive." From such a perspective, AIG should be in bankruptcy and all its creditors treated "fairly." "Fairly" meant that using public funds to honor AIG's debt was "ridiculous, even criminal." Fair meant they should have been paid off at steep discount and not made whole by the Fed.

While the administration and the Fed were trying to save the banking system, free-market-oriented pundits were damning government intervention. The lesson of AIG, Gerald Seib (2009) wrote, was that the "government by and large has no business owning and running businesses—and it is the majority owner of AIG. The cultures of the public and the private sectors are simply too different." Further, he declared, "Nationalization would distort markets, create unfair advantages and introduce either political considerations or suspicions of political considerations into business decisions." However, allowing AIG to go bankrupt would have adversely affected those who bought its CDS protection. They, in turn, would suffer punishing, perhaps fatal, losses given their already threatened position. If government took Seib's advice, a Great Depression would likely have followed. Government "interfered" to restore market confidence as best it could. This is not to say that what it did was the right approach. As I shall argue, the better approach would have been a far larger dose of government, a state-controlled bankruptcy procedure of nationalization, and making stockholders and irresponsible lenders take losses for business decisions gone wrong followed by a government reorganization of failed financial firms. The United States was not ready for such a solution (in keeping with market principles that failure should not be rewarded) and, as a result, invited a new crisis.

The Obama administration and the Fed were, if anything, more afraid of nationalization than the *Wall Street Journal* was. They were terrified at the prospect of having to manage and take responsibility for major financial enterprises and were prepared to pay seemingly any price to avoid this. Nor was the culture of private finance quite what Seib seemed to think it was. More realistically, the Treasury and the Fed are effectively captured by, or at least protective of, the institutions they regulated and whose continued profitability or return to profitability is seen as their primary task. It was ironic, then, that in late 2009, when the special inspector general for the Troubled Asset Relief Program (TARP) looked into why the Geithner-headed Federal Reserve Bank of New York had "caved in, " as a *Wall Street Journal* article put it, to demands by AIG's trading partners that they be paid in full just two days after UBS had offered to accept ninety-eight cents on the dollar and there seemed to be room to negotiate, it turned out that the Fed had considered itself a creditor to AIG rather than a regulator that could impose its will. In sharp contrast to the settlement the government later imposed on the automobile industry, when GM and Chrysler faced bankruptcy and the government drove a hard bargain, the Fed approached the banks with a request for "voluntary" concessions. The banks naturally declined.

The once big-five Wall Street investment banks at first found needed capital from sovereign wealth funds and other foreign investors but were soon forced to reorganize themselves. If a strict market test was applied and assets held were marked to market, most, if not all, were insolvent. As the bubble inflated, they had tripled their earnings from 2002 to 2006 (to more than $30 billion), averaging 22 percent return on equity—largely by borrowing many more times their capital, reaching leverage ratios of 30–35 to one, that is, borrowing ninety-seven cents for every three cents of their own money (multiply by billions please). They reined in the practices that had made them so much money as best they could, but when creditors became worried and wanted their money back, not only did Bear Stearns and Lehman Brothers collapse, throwing global financial markets into a panic, but Merrill Lynch sold itself to Bank of America, and Morgan Stanley and Goldman Sachs changed legal status to became commercial banks to qualify for huge infusions of public capital. Lehman had been in talks with Bank of America and Barclays for the company's possible sale, but unlike in the case of Bear Stearns, regulators refused to put in money for a purchase, and the largest bankruptcy in history took place. Ben Bernanke said that the Fed could not legally lend to Lehman since it would not be extending liquidity but transferring funds to an essentially bankrupt institution that had liabilities in great excess of its assets. The Fed seemed to have reasoned that letting Lehman fail would serve as a warning to others taking excessive risks. Lehman's vulnerability was well known, and it provided a "natural test case," as Frederick Mishkin (2010:6), a member of the Fed's Board of Governors at the time of the decision, writes, "an object lesson to market participants that they should take measures to protect themselves." This may have been true, but the September 15, 2008, failure of Lehman produced panic in financial markets not seen since 1929.

In response, the government and the Federal Reserve extended enormous amounts of money to the financial system without much of an overall plan, fingers-in-the-dike style, creatively finding new functional fingers and strong-ly backing them with the support of generous funding. In a financial ver-sion of the military Powell Doctrine, overwhelming amounts of money were poured into loan facilities and outright purchase of assets to restore confi-dence to the markets. Three days after Lehman failed, the Asset-Backed Com-mercial Paper Money Market Mutual Fund Liquidity Facility was announced (the acronym shortened to AMLF from the possible ABCPMMMFLF). A day later the Treasury announced it would temporarily guarantee assets of money market funds since Lehman's defaulting on obligations to one of the largest and oldest money market funds had caused losses that led to a run on other funds. Within weeks, the Fed announced the Commercial Paper Funding Facility (CPFF), to purchase commercial paper from eligible issu-ers, and a complementary program, the Money Market Investor Funding Fa-cility (MMIFF), to provide further loans (Schnabl and Kacperczyk 2010). In all, the Federal Reserve created seven emergency liquidity facilities to provide liquidity to the segments of the financial industry that had previously not enjoyed such coverage, from the commercial paper market to money market funds and primary dealers, as well as arranging foreign-exchange swaps with other central banks. The claim that while the banks needed to be bailed out by Congress with the Troubled Asset Relief Program the foreign exchange derivatives and hedge funds did not is therefore highly misleading. This is important in the discussion of whether there should be tighter regulation of these markets.

If the agenda was to restore the health of the financial system, the alpha-bet soup of rescue vehicles should be seen as a creative set of interventions, and the generous terms for the banks and others a correct approach. By 2010, as most beneficiaries appeared to have returned to health, and even the most abused of the vehicles, the TARP, had paid back almost all of the money the government had invested (and, as assets of AIG and the auto companies were sold, might even turn a profit for taxpayers), it should have been clear that, within the framework that the government and the Fed had approached the crisis, they had been quite successful. This was hardly a con-clusion most Americans were about to accept. Indeed, in the election that year those in Congress who had voted for TARP, a program created by the

Bush administration and supported by about half the Republicans in Congress, were pilloried.

There were other important issues besides whether all the TARP money would be paid back to the taxpayers by the banks. Much more was at stake. For one thing, the TARP loans did not impose costs on existing bank equity holders. The government could have demanded significantly more for its purchase of bank equity and its debt guarantees. If the government had secured the same terms as Warren Buffett received for helping Goldman Sachs, for example, taxpayers would have gained between $39 and $55 billion instead of losing between $29 and $44 billion, according to one calculation. Estimates for other bailout payments suggest the government could have captured 50–80 percent of the benefits of the plans that went to equity holders (both estimates from Veronesi and Zingales 2010). The way the bailout was carried out, it was not simply a matter of whether money borrowed was paid back, but of to what extent the government intervention redistributed value from taxpayers to those owning bank stock. Second, and related to this, was the extent to which "huge taxpayer costs for non-TARP programs that directly and indirectly enabled many of the large banks to repay their TARP funds" should be credited, and not the banks themselves with the repayment. (Atkins, McWatters, and Troske 2011). Compared to the hundreds of billions in new potential liabilities the government-sponsored entities—the Federal National Mortgage Association, Fannie Mae, the Federal Home Loan Mortgage Corporation, and Freddie Mac—took on from the banks, and the issue of whether the trillions of mortgages they supported should be left to the private sector, TARP was small potatoes.

The Extent of What Had Happened and Allocating Responsibility

For the United States, in the relevant years of our story, George W. Bush's ownership society philosophy set the federal agenda. As Jo Becker, Sheryl Gay Stolberg, and Stephen Labaton write:

> From his earliest days in office, Mr. Bush paired his belief that Americans do best when they own their own home with his conviction that markets do best when left alone. He pushed hard to expand home ownership, especially among minorities, an initiative that dovetailed with his ambition to

expand the Republican tent—and with the business interests of some of his biggest donors. But his housing policies and hands-off approach to regulation encouraged lax lending standards.

For years Bush ignored warnings from experts that these policies would lead to massive defaults. Much of the problem, as Lawrence Lindsay, his top economic adviser, had warned (before Lindsay was fired for another warning, his public estimate on the cost of the war in Iraq) that no one wanted to stop the bubble, especially a bubble created by policies the president wanted and which were profitable for so many.

A change in policy would not have been appreciated. This was especially true for major campaign contributors from the mortgage industry. Among them was Roland Arnall, founder of Ameriquest, then the nation's largest supplier of subprime loans. He and his company had invested more than $20 million in political donations in Washington. (The top twenty-five subprime mortgage originators spent $380 million lobbying and in campaign contributions in the decade to the point that their troubles finally brought the game to a halt, according to the Center for Public Integrity.) At the state level, from east to west, north to south, Ameriquest's money was spread around to convince legislators in states as different as New Jersey and Georgia to relax laws controlling mortgage originating. The tactics Ameriquest used to move mortgages have been described by former employees who worked in a boiler-room cheesiness where loan officers used a brightly lit beverage machine as a tracing board to copy borrower's signatures onto blank documents (Muolo and Padola 2008). The company was forced to settle allegations in thirty states that it had preyed on borrowers with balloon-payment mortgages and hidden fees. Bush appointed Ameriquest CEO Arnall his ambassador to the Netherlands. Neither man wanted an investigation of subprime loans. Ameriquest failed soon thereafter and was sold to Citigroup. Between 2003 and 2005 Citigroup had tripled its issues of CDOs and appreciated its control of Ameriquest, an important source of subprime mortgages. It was itself at the time close to an Ameriquest writ large.

Earlier, Democrats had been the big boosters of home ownership. President Clinton and his HUD secretary, Henry Cisneros, cut minimum down payments and raised the size of mortgages the FHA would guarantee as part of a program to "rekindle the dream of home ownership for America's working families." Following George W. Bush's "Ownership Society," the Obama administration supported home ownership during the housing crisis to put a floor under home prices as it attempted to revive the economy, putting huge amounts of taxpayer dollars at risk, insuring trillions of dollars of questionable loans. While free-market ideologues have spun this history as a series of bad decisions by the government, the entities that got in the most trouble were at the time privately owned. They chose short-term income-maximization strategies built on lawbreaking, which brought failure and forced takeover of their firms. This was the case for mortgage originators such as Countrywide and Ameriquest and also Fannie Mae (after it was privatized and before the government had to take over 79.9 percent ownership), with its $11 billion in accounting fraud and other abuses, as a privatized entity was, as an eighteen-month-long Treasury Department investigation determined, "motivated by a desire to show stable earnings growth, achieve forecasted earnings and avoid income statement volatility" (Hughes and Swann 2006:1) It was the "earnings at all cost" to maximize executive bonuses, not "orders from government," that caused excesses for which taxpayers would be responsible. The FBI had its hands full investigating mortgage fraud and especially the rings of speculators, appraisers, brokers, and housing professionals who ran these games. By 2008 it had opened investigations into at least twenty-five large companies, including Lehman Brothers, the world's largest bankruptcy, the privatized Fannie Mae, and of course Washington Mutual, the biggest retail bank to go under in U.S. history.

Researchers find, not surprisingly, that brokers, since they do not bear the ultimate cost of mortgage defaults, "may have a lower incentive to screen applications carefully" (Mayer, Pence, and Sherlund 2009:29; also see Keys et al. 2008). These economists may possibly be correct in this not very startling judgment since it is widely recognized that the pressure to churn out mortgages was intense. Investigative journalists interviewing employees heard that "At WaMu [Washington Mutual] it wasn't about the quality of the loans; it was about the numbers. They didn't care if we were giving loans to people who didn't qualify. Instead it was how many loans did you guys close?" Investors in WaMu soon found their stock worthless. The federal government in September 2008 organized a sale of what had been the sixth largest bank in the United States to JPMorgan Chase in which that company was relieved of the burden of potentially tens of billions of WaMu's losses, thanks to the generosity of the U.S. taxpayer.

In 2006 a senior Countrywide Financial executive explained that the company's algorithms made it so successful, "We understand the data and can price that risk" (Farzad 2007:38). Countrywide CEO Angelo Mozilo made

$46 million that year. He made another $100 million by selling stock before the company collapsed. He had the distinction of being the first prominent head of a subprime lender to be charged by the SEC with deceiving his investors. He was also charged with inside trading. If one wanted to anticipate the subprime meltdown, one could do worse than note that Mozilo, who led Countrywide to the best stock performance of any financial service company over the bull market, a 23,000 percent rise, was among the most celebrated CEOs. *Forbes* in 2005 put Countrywide on its "Most Admired Companies" list. *Barron's* named Mozilo one of the thirty best CEOs in the world. In 2006, when *American Banker* presented him with a lifetime achievement award, it was surely time to dump Countrywide stock. The company collapsed the next year.

The Securities and Exchange Commission investigation of Mozilo under the Obama administration turned up e-mails like one from April 2006 in which the former chief executive of Countrywide had written, "In all my years in the business I have never seen a more toxic product," referring to loans allowed to borrowers with poor credit who were allowed to buy homes without putting any money down. It was clear from the e-mail trail that he understood the dangers of adjustable rate mortgages and the serious lack of compliance in his firm. He was aware that Countrywide was selling "poison." He settled with the SEC, agreeing to pay $67.5 million in the civil fraud case brought against him. (He kept the $656 million he made between 1998 and 2007 and the $77 million buyout bonus he was given when the game was up, and he left the company.)

Michael Lewis (2008) interviewed one industry professional who offered the judgment that while he knew subprime lenders could be scumbags, "what he underestimated was the total unabashed complicity of the upper class of American capitalism." It was the case, or appeared to be the case, that the whole of the financial industry was complicit. The top ten investment banks that bought the mortgages, including Merrill Lynch, Lehman Brothers, and Bear Stearns, sold $245 million in mortgage-backed securities in 2000. They sold $1.5 billion worth in 2006. Later it would be said that bonus seekers ignored the interests of stockholders, but at Bear and Lehman employees held somewhere around 30 percent of company stock. It was not only bonus incentives that led traders to take and their supervisors to allow such risk, but as owners there was a desire for the firm to engage in successful risk taking.

After the Lehman Brothers bankruptcy on September 15, 2008, it turned out that the firm, like its peers, in a pattern not so different from that pursued by Enron, used regulatory arbitrage strategies not only to avoid taxes but to find the most forgiving legal environment for what proved to be dishonest dealings. Its Lehman Brothers Treasury unit in Amsterdam, for example, sold $35 billion worth of what *BusinessWeek* called "dubious bonds . . . baroque in their complexity." Few investors read the six hundred pages in documentation that came with these bafflingly complex instruments sold in four thousand or so variations. The risks were well buried. The bonds sold to unsuspecting individuals as risk-free savings tools soon lost almost all of their alleged value. Since national regulators did not, and seemingly cannot, keep track of what is being sold abroad, by whom and to whom, those who believed they had been cheated had a hard time finding effective legal redress despite more than seventy-five insolvency proceedings in fifteen countries against Lehman. Each country has its own rules, inviting conflicting judgments sure to enrich lawyers for decades to come.

Tens of thousands of foreign companies were officially located in mailboxes in Amsterdam to take advantage of lenient tax laws. Lehman's Amsterdam subsidiary was run out of a London office, which itself was set up as a subsidiary of Lehman Brothers Holdings in New York. This was one instance of the thousands of overseas subsidiaries Wall Street firms set up. When Lehman collapsed it had 433 subsidiaries. Citigroup in 2009 had more than 2,400. In 2009 the General Accounting Office released a study finding that eighty-three of the nation's hundred largest corporations, including Bank of America and Citigroup, had subsidiaries in offshore tax havens in 2007. Citigroup had 91 subsidiaries in Luxembourg and 90 in the Cayman Islands. A Brookings study finds that 30 percent of the profits earned by U.S. companies abroad come from the Netherlands, Ireland, and Bermuda. Few transnational corporations have many employees or real business in these places. The banks help nonfinancial companies by facilitating loans from tax havens like the Cayman Islands at high interest to subsidiaries in high-tax areas where they are deductible expenses.

Firms taking government bailouts and major government contractors were among those who maintained subsidiaries in fifty tax havens identified by the GAO. Strapped for revenues, governments began to take more serious action. Findings such as these led to OECD meetings of tax authorities. At one of these in Paris in 2009, Pravin Gordhan, the South African finance minister, explained that "aggressive tax avoidance is a serious cancer eating into the fiscal base of many countries." Within the United States, state governments found they were losing large amounts of potential corporate taxes from companies registered in the onshore tax haven called Delaware where shell companies similar to those found abroad deprived other states of taxes they would otherwise be able to collect. The line between legal avoidance and criminal fraud, and governments looking the other way and keeping their regulators a few steps behind, are interesting matters that are exposed in time of economic crisis and instances of corporate collapse. The iceberg out of view is immense.

The Collapse

Dating the beginning of the end is a matter of judgment. One good candidate is August 3, 2007, when the two Bear Stearns hedge funds collapsed as the underlying assets they held were found to be nearly worthless. It was a shock. Bear itself had made large mortgage loans to scam artists who recruited borrowers with good credit to apply for large loans, using false income and asset statements and finding appraisers to inflate the value of the homes in question. The homes would then go into foreclosure, and the ring would split the loot. Bear provided for the purchase, bundling, and sale of the product. Many lenders were defrauded this way. The banks, competing for market shares, accepted "stated-income" or "liar's loans." Estimates for 2006 put such losses from fraud at $4.5 billion. By 2006 it is estimated that 70 percent of new home loans in California were purchased with low or no document loans, something that evidently did not overly worry regulators. Such scams were easy to pull off. The investment banks buying the mortgages to bundle into CDOs and quickly sell them off did not ask questions. Nationally, by the end of 2007, a quarter of subprime loans that were transformed into securities by Barclays Bank, Deutsche Bank, and Morgan Stanley in 2006 were in default, according to Bloomberg.

Once such assets were questioned, the extent to which Bear itself was heavily leveraged meant that it would quickly have folded without access to new capital. At the end of February 2008, public disclosure of its 10-Q filings (the report companies must file quarterly with the Securities and Exchange Commission disclosing relevant information to investors) showed that it then had only $12 billion in assets. Had it been allowed to go into sudden bankruptcy, with its $14 trillion of derivative contracts, the notional value of futures, options, and swaps with thousands of counterparties, a great web of complexly interconnected financial arrangements, would have painfully come apart (Cecchetti 2009:69). It was understood at the time on Wall Street and in The City in London that no matter what irresponsibility was involved, the Federal Reserve could not let Bear go bankrupt. Indeed, this was no extension of needed liquidity but an act to prevent systemic collapse. As Michael Lewitt (2008) writes, "The failure of a firm of the size and stature of Bear Stearns would be as close to an Extinction Level Event as the world's financial markets have ever seen." Given such potential, the commitment that the New York Federal Reserve, under its president Timothy Geithner, made to get JPMorgan Chase to purchase Bear, while hardly a routine operation at the discount window, a loan on good paper, was understood to be necessary to avoid a collapse (or an "Extinction Level Event").

From the traditional allowable pattern of Fed activity, as Stephen Cecchetti (2009:70) writes, "The subsidy implicit in the loan to Bear Stearns is clearly a fiscal, not a monetary operation." As he notes, the Fed was effectively acting as the fiscal agent of the Treasury and ran the risk of compromising central bank independence if such rescues were to become accepted as normal procedure. This may have been a factor in the refusal to provide resources on a scale needed to prevent the collapse of Lehman Brothers. Looking forward, financial reform has not fundamentally changed reliance on the repo market for leveraged short-term loans to purchase assets, which may prove to be mispriced. If the pattern of asset bubbles continues, bailouts will continue to be expensive, and failure to bailout seriously overextended institutions will have dramatic costs. While the next crisis is unlikely to be a replay of the last one, if there is faith that financial markets are efficient, it will be hard to avoid.

In the most recent instance, many of the presumed quality mortgages (not the subprime and Alt-A ones) could be seen to be dangerous and would soon default as people lost their jobs and housing values fell precipitously, putting many of these underwater, the mortgage payable exceeding the realistic selling price of the home. However, as long as the demand for CDOs was growing rapidly, the industry came out with new products—CDO^2, which were created using other CDO tranches, and CDO^3, using tranches from CDOs and CDO^2 and collateralized by credit default swaps. The risk associated with complex CDOs was impossible to value since they were priced by abstruse mathematical models. Each might have valuations of a thousand, and complex CDOs tens of thousands, mortgages backing them. Because banks could keep CDOs off their balance sheets with no required capital and kept a significant stake (to convey to potential investors that they were safe, and had a large volume of product in the pipeline), when the music stopped they were left facing huge loss exposure. By some estimates, the SIVs had assets that in total exceeded well over 50 percent of the assets of the banks that were held directly on their own books. Some were smarter than others. Goldman Sachs continued to sell such derivatives, even after it decided that it was unwise for the firm to hold them on their own account.

Goldman had figured things out ahead of the pack, before the bubble reached its peak. As early as 2005 some Goldman people saw the crash coming, and in 2006 the firm as a whole adopted a position based on the expectation of disaster in the collateralized debt market. Many banks had bought protection against such an eventuality from Goldman; Goldman then bought protection to cover itself from AIG in the form of credit default swaps. It made a profit on these transactions as it was paid more than it paid AIG. After a while, the banks figured this out and went directly to AIG. Goldman at the same time was a big originator of collateralized debt obligations in which these banks, pension funds, and others invested (it underwrote $23 billion of the $89 billion in CDOs that AIG insured). Goldman's products included subprime mortgages from Countrywide and New Century, which were to be among the biggest flameouts in the mortgage-origination business, leading some to wonder if Goldman knew how bad the assets it was bundling were (Ng and Mollenkamp 2010).

The seller of a credit default swap promises to pay the buyer a set amount if a specified event happens, such as a financial instrument not paying as specified or a company defaulting on a loan. The buyer pays a set amount each quarter to the swap seller and receives the promise of a large payment if there is a default on the contract specified. Buyers and sellers of CDSs include banks, insurance companies, and hedge funds. Such protection was sold in large amounts by firms that thought the risk of ever having to make good on the insurance was slight—until markets collapsed and they were on the hook for amounts so huge they could not possibly pay and faced bankruptcy themselves. It was not only AIG "which went from being a high-quality AA-rated insurer to near-bankruptcy in one week" (Krishnamurthy 2010:13), but companies nobody had paid much attention to, such as ACA Financial Guarantee, that were significant in inflating the mortgage bubble.

Bear Stearns had made a sizable investment in ACA, seeing the potential in insuring CDOs against loss by selling CDSs, and installed its own person to push the company into this product big time. By 2007 insuring CDOs was 90 percent of ACA's portfolio. The tiny company played a big role in this insurance market. Its "guarantee" proved worthless even though its "insurance" emboldened investors. This was because, by having insurance, the investors were allowed to book profits on CDOs immediately (since the profit was guaranteed) even if it turned out that they never received the income. The insured later settled on partial restitution. When Securities Capital Assurance (SCA), a Bermuda-based bond insurer, settled after the subprime mortgage market collapsed, companies like Merrill Lynch received fourteen cents on the dollar on the insurance they had bought. This was better than the nothing Merrill feared it would get if the firm collapsed without a settlement.

AIG had insured far more than these smaller companies had and was essentially in the same boat. The Fed claimed that, because it feared a meltdown of the entire financial system, it had no choice and no legal authority to do anything else but rescue AIG (and the banks to which it owed huge amounts of money and which otherwise would have sustained tens of billions in losses). The Fed initially kept secret the information about which creditors were bailed out and planned not to divulge information regarding the deal it had made until 2018. It declared that this was essential to ensure it would be able to sell the CDOs that it took onto its books at face value. There was controversy regarding the way regulators rescued AIG with rationales such as "respect for the sanctity of the contract" and "there was no way they could force the banks to take haircuts," even though at least one major bank had agreed to negotiate with AIG a reduction in what was owed the bank. The Fed assured the banks that they would be paid in full at the start of negotiations. Judgments by investigators suggested that had the Fed merely guaranteed AIG's debt (forcing Goldman and others to return AIG's collateral based on its increased shaky position, which they did not want to do), it might have cost less than buying the stuff at face value. Congress wanted to know what Tim Geithner knew and when he knew it, and why banks were told that negotiating was voluntary.

Citigroup kept creating loan pools for a year after the housing market started to sour. One of the last, launched on July 27, 2007, was named Bonifacius, after a general immortalized by the historian Edward Gibbon as the last of the Romans because he died as the empire was collapsing. Even such products, rushed to the market as it was collapsing, received top grades from Standard & Poor's and the other rating agencies. By the early fall the new Bonifacius, along with the rest of the mortgage industry, was collapsing. Citigroup lost more in total securitized debt after it dropped in value than it had made selling such products in the bubble years. In 2008, after the collapse, an SEC investigation of the rating industry found that analysts had expressed doubt about the ratings their companies were giving bonds backed by subprime mortgages. An April 2007 e-mail declared that the firm's model did not capture half of a deal's risk, but "it could be structured by cows and we would rate it." Another e-mail later that year criticized CDOs and said, "Let's hope we are all wealthy and retired by the time this house of cards falters."

Pyramiding the Underlying Mortgages and Collapse

Paul Tucker, head of markets at the Bank of England, speaks of the age of "vehicular finance." Banks sold their CDOs to a host of new "vehicles," many of which they themselves created to buy the CDOs and move ownership off their own books (to avoid regulation requiring capital to be set aside to cover exposure). Banks guaranteed such borrowing so that, when trouble arose, it was they who had to support these special investment vehicles that they either created or backed by extending to them lines for liquidity when and if they needed them. The beauty of SIVs was that as self-standing investment funds that issue asset-backed securities (typically three-month commercial paper) and buy long-term securities (heavily CDOs), they pay less in short-term interest than they earn on these long-term investments—so long as they have access to short-term credit and the long-term assets hold their value. They operated essentially as hedge funds. At their peak in 2006–7, they held $1.4 trillion in assets.

It was only when problems developed for the SIVs, as their basic business model collapsed with the subprime mess, that even banks not legally bound to do so felt obligated for reputational reasons to take the losses on what were often esoteric, complex, and, as it turned out, "junk" assets back onto their own books. The relationship between banks and SIVs was one from which the banks could not walk away. By the end, the SIVs still had some $400 billion in assets that did not show up on bank books. That of course was the purpose of SIVs. They were designed to allow banks to reduce the capital they had to set aside as security against risk and to obscure the risks they were taking from regulators. The lack of transparency was the point. The instruments they bought and sold likewise were complex and opaque. While each looked new, and in important ways was new, the same "mistakes" by the same players are evident. The SIVs, it turned out, were BRVs—"bankruptcy remote vehicles" that the banks did not have fiduciary duty to disclose. The damage to the banks in their collapse was, however, painful.

The banks had been able to get themselves into so much trouble thanks in part to the Securities and Exchange Commission, which, at an April 28, 2004, meeting, granted them exemption from their brokerage unit limit of the amount of debt they could carry, freeing reserves against potential loss that they had been previously required to maintain. Regulators allowed the investment banks to increase their credit risk by giving them permission to invest in mortgage-backed securities, credit derivatives, and other exotica. What became uncomfortably clear was that a giant, collectively built financial structure was in essence a pyramid scheme with such interdependencies that no part of it was safe when the bubble lost hot air.

When Bear Stearns collapsed as the garbage nature of the securities it was selling (all dutifully given AA or AAA ratings) was revealed, there were wide reverberations. Bear was a big broker/dealer in the mortgage market, buying and selling securitized mortgages and related products, functioning with borrowed money highly leveraged. The failure of Bear funds sent the Dow down 279 points, a large drop at the time and prefiguring more dramatic declines to come, prompting an SEC investigation. The SEC inspector general found that the agency had failed its mission. The staff had been aware of Bear Stearns's overextension but made no effort to limit Bear's mortgage securities concentration. He said that the SEC had failed to carry out its mission. Because of Bear's extensive relationships with all sorts of banks, hedge funds, and other financial institutions, its collapse would have had strong knock-on effects. After the funds collapsed, Citigroup and Bank of America wrote down $10 billion on an arrangement that only a short time before was seen by the big banks as a smart source of immense fees.

Rather than continuing to bail everybody out, three months after Bear Stearns's collapse the Bush administration let Lehman Brothers go bust. In retrospect this was widely seen as a mistake. By seeming to say "let the market handle it," the Treasury Department made a bad judgment about how the financial market operated. The day after Lehman went under, the $62 billion Reserve Primary Fund, the oldest money market firm in the country, "broke the buck." Each dollar someone had in the money market fund was suddenly worth less than a dollar because Reserve had a large exposure to Lehman's debt and suffered serious losses. Money markets a day earlier had been thought just about as secure as FDIC-guaranteed accounts. To prevent a run on all money market funds, the government had to insure all their accounts. Lehman, as the world's biggest ever corporate bankruptcy, had other impacts as well. The most important was to spread fear through the markets. Hedge funds took losses when Lehman collapsed. Given their need for low-cost borrowing to support their high leverage and the prospect of lower future earnings, people pulled money out of the hedge funds.

The Bush Administration and the Banks

The bankers worked to avoid governmental regulation. They hoped the widely held ideological conviction that government was to blame would direct attention away from them. In April 2008 a plea from the head of the world's bankers' industry association, the Institute of International Finance's Josef Ackermann (also head of Deutsche Bank, a major seller of subprime mortgages and CDOs), asked for less government interference. "We are resolved to do our utmost to clean our houses first and not leave it to the regulators to do that for us." He warned against "premature regulatory measures." His was only one of numerous warnings by the industry, their political friends, and a host of financial pundits that the government "not go too far." The American Bankers Association's (ABA) chief executive, Ed Yingling, arranged fly-ins for delegations from around the country to prevent the U.S. Congress from "overreacting." The ABA spent millions to lobby and in campaign contributions, a powerful industry watching over its interests in the traditional manner. Yingling lobbied Senator Christopher Dodd, the chairman of the Senate Banking Committee, in much the same way his father did when he held the same position and lobbied Thomas Dodd, the senator's father.

The Fed and the Treasury supported the priority of financial innovation and the broad approach of George W. Bush's ownership society premised on free choice in the marketplace. The Bush campaign to privatize Social Security and make people's future retirement prospects dependent on the stock market rather than being guaranteed by government is perhaps the most famous manifestation of this philosophy. Had it succeeded, Wall Street would have had even more control over workers' retirement funds, and uncertainty, in what is better called the "risk society," would have furthered the goals of a radical individualism and the undermining of the fragile residual norms of social solidarity. President Bush praised Christopher Cox when Cox took over as head of the SEC in June 2005 as "a champion of the free enterprise system" who understood that it was "built on trust." Others held to a different perspective. Cox had been called, "the single most destructive regulatory appointee" (Kuttner 2005:13), as shown by his background. As a member of the House Commerce and Finance Committee, which was defending Wall Street, he had been a leading sponsor of what was called the Private Securities Litigation Reform Act, which made it harder for equity investors who were cheated by lies and misrepresentation to sue. The commission, Cox said, was a small agency, and so it had made sense to rely heavily on self-regulation by stock exchanges, corporations, mutual funds, and the rest. In hindsight this was unwise, he concluded.

In 2008, following the SEC inspector general's report, Cox strongly criticized the agency's monitoring of Bear Stearns and acknowledged the SEC's program "was fundamentally flawed" because "investment banks could opt in or out of supervision voluntarily," and this weakened the effectiveness of SEC. Cox did not ask why the SEC had been systematically underfunded so it could not carry out its legal mandate effectively. Nor did he comment on how the investment banks, including Goldman Sachs when headed by Henry Paulson, had lobbied hard for the SEC as the umbrella regulator as a way of avoiding stricter regulation and in favor of the voluntary program that the SEC adopted. Cox will be remembered most for his admission, after Bernard Madoff revealed he had engaged in systematically defrauding investors of, he said, $50 billion in what was the largest Ponzi scheme in history, that the SEC had received "credible and specific allegations regarding Mr. Madoff's wrong doings" and that the agency had "apparent multiple failures over at least a decade." At the time of the Madoff case, federal officials were bringing in the fewest prosecutions for security fraud since at least 1991, despite an apparent upsurge in such criminality in the industry.

In the months leading up to the 2008 election, a lame duck George W. Bush repeatedly tried to reassure markets. "In the long run," he said, "I'm confident our economy will continue to grow, because the foundations are solid." It was also the case, as Keynes had fatuously said in response to similar assertions, that "in the long run, we are all dead." Secretary Paulson eventually asked for more authority, lots of it, which he hoped he would not have to use. As he said to the Senate Banking Committee on July 15, 2008, "If you have a bazooka in your pocket and people know it, you probably won't have to use it." The markets saw matters differently. Paulson was doing little to address a deepening crisis, and it turned out that neither did he have a bazooka nor did his talents in the use of the weapons at his disposal impress financial markets. Both the Fed and Treasury wanted to address the crisis by building confidence and hoped that flooding the market with liquidity and guarantees would be enough. They were not.

Paulson met each new collapse as a one-off event and refused to offer a systemic analysis or solution to a deepening crisis. Finally, in September 2008, he gave Congress a two-and-a-half-page "plan." This proposed legislation included this statement: "Decisions by the Secretary pursuant to the authority of this Act are non-reviewable and committed to agency discretion, and may not be reviewed by any court of law or any administrative agency." He wanted $700 billion dollars to be spent any way he wanted without oversight or legal review. He did say his plan was to use the money to buy the most toxic assets of the banks at prices higher than the distressed current market price, at close to their hold-to-maturity price. He said the government could be expected to receive the full amount promised even though this was far in excess of what the assets would fetch in the market at the time. Following a public outcry that this would be a tremendous reward to those who had caused the crisis, officials insisted the Treasury would not "overpay" for toxic assets. With great reservations, but under threat of a market meltdown, Congress passed the Troubled Asset Relief Program and gave Paulson the $700 billion in early October.

While $700 billion was authorized, only $250 billion was committed to banks. It was paid back. The Treasury made a significant profit on the taxpayers' investment in interest payment and the sale of warrants with interest and saved the system from a meltdown, a very real prospect. Nonetheless, even in the rearview mirror most Americans thought TARP a costly waste and unnecessary—fewer than three in ten said they believed it was necessary "to prevent the financial industry from failing and drastically hurting the U.S. economy," according to a Bloomberg poll in July 2010. Tea party candidates and others used an incumbent's vote for TARP to challenge him or her in primaries and the general election in 2010. While the Treasury shut down the program in October 2010, politicians were still running against spending money on TARP a month later, demanding that "we get our money back from the banks," which of course had already mostly happened.

A week after Bank of America received $15 billion from TARP, it announced that it was spending $7 billion to increase its stake in the China Construction Bank. Such expenditures were good business for banks, which saw growth prospects in China but not in the United States. Banks receiving TARP funds also used them to buy smaller competitors to position themselves for after recovery. They returned to their penchant for paying themselves outsized bonuses but were less willing to increase lending in the real American economy. While widely criticized for taking public funds and not helping to rekindle domestic growth, they were showing sound business judgment. In the absence of federal guidelines to the contrary, they were building reserves against further bad loan problems and not extending many new domestic loans even to seemingly creditworthy borrowers. They were taking essentially free money from the government and buying government bonds with it, and the largest banks were engaged in proprietary trading in a rising market that was exceedingly profitable.

The strategy of large banks was to become larger still. Bank of America had for a long time grown through acquisition of other financial institutions. It had begun as a small lender, which grew as NationsBank in North Carolina (changing its name when it swallowed Bank of America). It had bought Fleet Boston Financial, the credit card giant MNBA, US Trust, LaSalle Bank of Chicago, and Countrywide. In late 2008 it overstepped when it purchased Merrill Lynch, the nation's largest brokerage firm, for $50 billion in stock. It became the country's largest bank but at a cost of near self-destruction. Merrill had itself between 2005 and early 2007 made twelve major real estate company acquisitions to get its hands on more subprime and other mortgages. Bank of America paid a premium on all its acquisitions, including Merrill, a purchase that proved costly, given the outsized losses Merrill suffered. Within days of consummating the merger, the two companies together were worth only $40 billion. Investors were outraged; lawsuits ensued. Fortunately the Treasury was ready with more taxpayer money to pump up Bank of America. Merrill had already received $25 billion from the Treasury. Just before the merger, John Thain, Merrill's CEO, gave out early bonuses of $4 billion. After the deal he asked for a $35 million bonus for himself. Instead, he was fired for allegedly misleading his new boss, Kenneth Lewis, who only a few months earlier had been toasted as "Banker of the Year" by the magazine *American Banker,* which praised him as being "a critical force for stability in tumultuous economic times." Watching who *American Banker* chose to celebrate fits our sense of an early warning sign. In 2001 it chose Kerry Killinger of Washington Mutual as its honoree; in 2005, Ken Thompson, former chief of Wachovia. Both ran their institutions into bankruptcy.

Two-thirds of TARP money went to eight institutions. Almost three hundred others received the rest. The Treasury itself did not track the money. That task was given to Bank of New York Mellon, one of the nine big recipients, which was paid a fee of $20 million to oversee a process from which it directly benefited. The Office of Financial Stability paid tens of millions more to law firms, management consultants, and others. Except in the cases of Citigroup and AIG, the Treasury did not look at what the banks did with the money. While Secretary Paulson said that for every hundred dollars invested the Treasury would receive stock and warrants valued at a hundred dollars, the Congressional Oversight Panel found that it had overpaid considerably, getting sixty-six cents on the dollar. Such estimates and public discussion considered the TARP program in isolation from the many other ways the Fed and government agencies extended credit to the financial sector, which amounted to an estimated $14 trillion. (There have been higher and lower estimates, as this is a difficult calculation to make.)

Intervention by the Fed and Treasury providing loans, loan guarantees, purchase of illiquid financial assets of questionable worth, and government stimulus avoided an Irving Fisher–type debt deflation of the sort the United States had experienced in the past, but such a victory comes at a potentially substantial cost. The solution to the crisis continued a pattern evident and growing since the end of the national Keynesian SSA, the progressive increase in risk taking and expansion of government safety nets for the financial sector, indeed a ratcheting up of taxpayer-sponsored insurance of private finance. Not just in the United States, but globally, the coverage of bank risk by governments increased substantially over this extended period (Laeven and Valencia 2008), with expectations of taxpayer assistance increasing greatly as a result of the ways policy makers addressed the Great Recession. Bank of England economists estimated the support given to U.S. and U.K. banks as equal to two-thirds of annual output. Expanding implicit and explicit rescue commitments promised a widening gyre, which, as noted earlier, they called "a doom loop" (Haldane and Alessandri 2009).

Misdirected Blame

Free-market conservatives have offered a narrative of why the financial crisis had taken place. They blame government regulation aimed at redistribution to favor the poor. They excoriate a Democratic Congress for imposing the goal of increasing home ownership for the poor on Fannie Mae and Freddie Mac and passing the Community Reinvestment Act (CRA). While it is true that liberals favored increasing home ownership for low-income Americans, it was after Congress had given these government-sponsored enterprises (GSEs) freer reign as for-profit companies beholden to their stockholders that they took on heavily toxic portfolios. That Freddie and Fannie got most heavily in trouble after they were privatized and went all-out taking risks they should not have taken is omitted from this narrative of blaming the government. Even when these GSEs were public, they did the bidding of the private interests that counted on them for support. Elected officials promoting greater home ownership did not prefer it this way, but when under direct government control the standards were far higher.

Fannie Mae, more formally known as the Federal National Mortgage Association, was created as a public entity to help stabilize the housing market in the Great Depression. It became a publicly traded company in 1989. Because of the implicit government guarantees that Fannie enjoyed, it continued to operate with even less capital than the banks did. As a private, for-profit entity, it was scandal prone, offering early warning signs of what was to come. Between 1998 and 2003 Fannie's top five executives received $199 million, much of it thanks to inflated reported earnings. In 2003–4 Fannie Mae and Freddie Mac (the Federal Home Loan Mortgage Corporation, created in 1970 to expand the secondary market for mortgages, Fannie's "brother" government-sponsored enterprise) had to restate their earnings by over $11 billion in one of the worst accounting scandals of those scandal-ridden years. They were accused of fraud in concealing expenses to increase stated profits. The then head of Fannie left with a $90 million retirement package based on business practices that had raised the company's stock but later led to its collapse. This too should have been a warning of things to come.

Politicians encouraged home ownership as a matter of government policy to be sure, but as important, if not more so, was the pressure on investor-owned Fannie and Freddie as profit-driven companies. The continued close relations with government are shown in the revolving-door phenomenon. When Democrats controlled the White House, Fannie's chair and chief executive had been director of the Office of Management and Budget. The company's vice chair had been deputy attorney general under Bill Clinton before she and the chair assumed their positions of leadership at Fannie Mae. During the successor Bush administration, Fannie's regulator, the Office of Federal Housing Enterprise Oversight, was headed by a friend of the president from his days at Andover. It was on his watch that the companies he regulated moved decisively into subprime mortgages. He was charged with allowing the companies to cover up their insolvency through dubious accounting schemes and even of "pimping for the stock prices of the undercapitalized firms he regulates" (Becker, Stolberg, and Labaton 2008). In the

2008 presidential season, John McCain's campaign manager was a lobbyist for expansion of Freddie and Fannie mortgages. The head of his vice presidential vetting panel was a lobbyist for Fannie Mae, as were fund raisers and at least one longtime aide. Top Obama backers, consultants, and contributors lobbied for the GSEs as well.

These companies were major Washington players. Fannie and Freddie spent $200 million in the decade before their collapse lobbying and in campaign contributions, according to the Federal Election Commission. Among their achievements was keeping their regulator, the Office of Federal Housing Enterprise Oversight, weak, underfunded, and dependent on Congress, which enjoyed the lavish payoffs from Fannie and Freddie. In the aftermath of their failure, they were seized by the government on September 8, 2008. Congressional hearings revealed that senior officials at both companies had ignored repeated warnings from their own staff regarding the extreme danger of their exposure to the increasing volume of subprime mortgages. The House Oversight and Government Reform Committee found they held one in three subprime mortgages when they collapsed, presumably valued at $1.6 trillion. Their chief executives, faced with focused questions, stonewalled, refusing to answer simple questions—the answers to which would perhaps have been self-incriminating. The twins had long asserted they had minimal subprime and Alt-A mortgage exposure. "Minimal," it turned out, was a bit of a stretch. The total obligations of the two, which the government has taken on, were $5 trillion, give or take some billions. The entire national debt of the U.S. government in 2008 was $9 trillion.

Some lawmakers objected to these takeovers: they did not want the government involved in the mortgage business. This, of course, was to ignore the reality in these and other cases that when a private company (and both Fannie and Freddie, I must emphasize again, were privately held companies) loses so much money that it cannot survive and yet is deemed too big to fail, the government has little choice. The government takeover was accompanied by policies to keep the mortgage guarantees flowing to support the housing market. Freddie and Fannie continued to buy most of the mortgages written and were modifying loans to keep people in their homes. The Treasury committed another $400 billion to keep them solvent, on top of the $110 billion it had used to save them earlier.

Few of these lawmakers remembered the 1995 report by the nonpartisan Congressional Budget Office that valued the subsidy to these companies at $6.5 billion and estimated that fully a third of this subsidy was appropriated by the managers and stockholders who kept it for themselves, instead of passing it on to low-income home owners. This is not to say that the public takeover and vast contingent liabilities that the taxpayer was assuming in order to hold up the housing market were a small matter.

In early 2010 Fannie and Freddie owned or guaranteed $5 trillion in U.S. residential debt, having originated three-quarters of new mortgages in 2009, and the default rate on the mortgages they held was rising. Stuck with $300 billion in loans to borrowers at least ninety days overdue, the companies undertook a large number of audits in 2010, looking for, and frequently finding, irregularities in underwriting that allowed them to force banks to repurchase mortgages that were found to contain improper documentation and outright lies. They said the taxpayer should not bear the cost. The amounts were hardly trivial, threatening to wipe out the loan originators' profits even though the repurchases represented only a very tiny proportion of all defaulted loans. Given the huge increase in taxpayer exposure (since Freddie and Fannie, in the interest of aiding the housing market, had agreed to absorb unlimited losses for the next three years), the issue of what to do about these giants became politically charged. Since they had been effectively nationalized, it could be argued that their debt should be counted as part of the ballooning national debt, something the Treasury Department was loathe to do. Freddie and Fannie required what could turn out to be about $1 trillion from the government.

The problem loans in these institutions continued to mount as the housing market was essentially nationalized. The Treasury took the cap off the $400 billion credit line it had extended to Freddie and Fannie. Investors had been nervous despite the fact that they had until then used "only" $112 billion of the monies. The blank check was written to assuage their worries. It created a huge potential liability for taxpayers, who may not have noticed since the Obama administration chose to announce the change on Christmas Eve 2009 while people's attention was elsewhere, and since December 24 fell before the year-end deadline for action, under existing legislation, to make changes without going back to Congress for permission. The difficulty that the Obama administration had in deciding what to do with Fannie and Freddie was understandable. Without government underwriting of the housing market, the economy would have likely fallen into depression, yet how long and at what cost to taxpayers could the government subsidize this market waiting for relief from falling home prices? Removing government support and allowing the market to find a new (far lower) equilibrium would have dramatically increased the number of mortgage payers who would simply walk away from their homes, given the equity they held at the lower property value, pushing real estate still lower and increasing fear and panic in the market. To subsidize the market was proving exceedingly costly for taxpayers. It would be interesting to see the extent to which Fannie and Freddie under government ownership would go after the banks that had knowingly sold them nonconforming mortgages.

To try to refloat the housing market, the federal government in 2009 relied on tax incentives for new home buyers and on the Federal Housing Administration (FHA), part of the U.S. Department of Housing and Urban Development. This government agency had been brushed aside in the heated years of the housing bubble since quicker, better terms and higher profits for private housing sector affiliates did not require its insurance. In the face of the collapse of the private mortgage market, the FHA filled the void by taking on responsibility for most mortgages issued. In 2007 and 2008 politicians pushed it to insure huge numbers of loans to unqualified buyers so that by late 2009 nearly one in five of the loans it had insured in 2007 fell into the category of "seriously delinquent," and its own finances were endangered. If it stopped lending before the housing market recovered, that would not be good for the economy, given its role. In 2008 the FHA had guaranteed four times the dollar value of the mortgages it had guaranteed in 2007. Perhaps 20 to 25 percent of loans it insured after housing prices had fallen dramatically faced serious problems. Many were in default with expectation of large future losses, which would require the need for a government bailout of the FHA. By 2010 it had insured over five million single-family home mortgages with a presumed value in the neighborhood of $7 billion. It was insuring around 40 percent of new loan originations on very generous terms, leading to worries that it would be left holding many billions in defaulted mortgages. Despite a slight toughening of terms, it would continue to support home buying at about the same rate. Around 90 percent of newly granted home loans by the start of 2010 were backed by Fannie, Freddie, the FHA, or other government-related institutions. The likely losses from insuring these mortgages, taking them off the books of private companies, may be so huge as to dwarf other government direct crisis-related expenditures. But this comes after these companies failed as private entities.

Politically, many Republicans opposed this seemingly reckless expansion of its obligations while some Democrats insisted that the housing market

would be "dead" without this step, transferring risk from mortgage originators to the taxpayer. Both were probably right. On the one hand, such intervention can be seen as crowding out private competitors from the market
for mortgage securities; on the other, the government-related share of the
market increased with the failure of private players, as has been described.
It might be better if private financial institutions allocated credit without
government, but, if government were not involved, the secondary mortgage
market in a time of crisis for the housing sector would simply dry up.

As to the CRA, the Cato's Institute's former chairman, William Niskansen
(2008:42), understands it, as "the first lesson" one needs to learn from the
global financial meltdown. This is scarcely a defendable proposition even if
it is the case that bankers and ideological free marketers have always hated
the law. The logic behind CRA was that some part of residents' deposits in
local banks should be reinvested in the neighborhood. The CRA came about
as a result of the redlining of certain communities. Some banks literally or
figuratively drew red lines around low-income neighborhoods and refused
to make loans there. They took the money of depositors who lived in these
locations and used it to grant mortgages in suburban areas and other places.
Senator Phil Gramm of Texas and others denounced proponents of the CRA
as "extortionists," likening it to the Mafia and claiming that it was "an evil
like slavery in the pre–Civil War era." Such hyperbole, so characteristic of the
senator, was ridiculous. By the time of the subprime crisis, this 1977 legislation was thirty years old. Its requirements had been less and less followed
by banks or enforced by regulators. Most important, the CRA made little or
no difference in mortgage practices in the years in which the subprime crisis
came to a head. Because the overwhelming majority of subprime mortgages
were written by finance companies not subject to the law at all, the charge
that helping the poor caused the financial meltdown is a flimsy, ideologically
driven argument with little or no basis in fact.

A related argument that is also often made is that it was poor people getting loans they did not deserve and could not pay that caused the problems
in the mortgage market, and it was government pressure that led to them
get these mortgages. It is more accurate to say that these loans were pushed
on low-income and heavily minority communities by profit-hungry mortgage originators. The government should not have let this happen. While in
some tellings no one had foreseen the subprime crisis, in fact among those
who called attention to what was going on were advocates for the poor. For
example, William Brennan, director of the Home Defense Program at the At-

lanta Legal Aid Society, who worked in inner-city Atlanta, testified before the Senate Special Committee on Aging in 1998, a decade before the subprime loan collapse, that subprime loan originators had been earning enormous profits, arranging mortgages that poor people clearly could not afford. Brennan told the committee, "I think this house of cards may tumble some day, and it will mean great losses for the investors who own stock in those companies" (Aaron 2009:1). Others, including Jodie Bernstein, director of the Bureau of Consumer Protection of the Federal Trade Commission from 1995 to 2001, offered similar testimony on the way subprime mortgages were being bundled with nobody having responsibility for assessing their real value and then being sold. In a climate of neoliberalism, neither Bernstein nor the members of Congress holding hearings got much attention.

Over the next decade, state-level antipredatory lending laws were preempted by federal regulators. In effect, the Office of Thrift Supervision and the Office of the Comptroller of the Currency, at the urging of the banks, declared that banks did not have to comply with state laws protecting consumers. As has been discussed, the Fed had no interest in using its authority under the 1994 Home Ownership and Equal Protection Act to limit fees and interest charges or prohibit practices that harmed borrowers. Rather than seeing this as the federal government forcing lenders to give mortgages to the undeserving, the reality is that market-friendly political policies condemned many poor people to become victims of rapacious and dishonest lenders.

A key element in the 2007–9 subprime crisis was a broad transformation from "racial exclusion in US mortgage markets to access to housing credit under terms far more adverse than were offered to non-minority borrowers" (Dymski 2009). Racial exclusion was replaced by extortionist racial inclusion. Many of those targeted for such loans were lured to refinance mortgages that were near being paid off with large equity in their homes. Many of the new mortgages at low teaser rates were taken by people who did not understand that rates could go up by enough that they could lose their homes, as many later did. While foreclosures hit all manner of neighborhoods and higher unemployment rates brought large numbers of presumed safe mortgages into default, an analysis using federal mortgage data, completed in 2009, on foreclosures filed since 2005 shows a pattern playing out across the nation of counties with black and Hispanic majorities heavily hit. A study of New York City showed defaults occurring three times as often in mostly minority census tracts as in mostly white ones. Eighty-five percent of the most affected neighborhoods (where the default rate was at least double the regional average) had majority black and Hispanic home owners (Powell and Roberts 2009).

When the subprime mortgage crisis first hit, the Bush administration backed the Hope Now Alliance, a government-sponsored private sector organization that did little to stop foreclosures. The program was widely seen as a public relations effort. As Brian Grow, Keith Epstein, and Robert Berner (2009) write, "One reason foreclosures are so rampant is that banks and their advocates in Washington have delayed, diluted, and obstructed attempts to address the problem. Industry lobbyists are still at it today, working overtime to whittle down legislation backed by President Obama." The outcome was, as *BusinessWeek* headlined with reference to a March 2, 2009, story, "A Mortgage Rescue Banks Can Love." The following month 340,000 more mortgages went into default, adding to the millions of Americans who had already lost their homes. The Obama administration's plan offered to fund loan modification and cover more losses of the mortgage issuers. Its orientation was to use incentives for private, voluntary modification of mortgages, lengthening them, and reducing interest rates. The plan did not call for writing down the principal. This was a problem since so many mortgages were underwater. The Obama mortgage relief plan did not put mortgage holders under any compulsion to participate, and rental assistance to keep people in their homes was very limited. The government helped banks, but foreclosures continued apace. The help fell far short of what was needed.

In early 2010 one in ten mortgages was a month late. Combining those in foreclosure as well as those delinquent amounted to one in seven mortgage holders. Where the problem had initially been in subprime and Alt-A loans, sustained high levels of unemployment were making it difficult for millions of home owners to meet their obligations. High-quality mortgages were the largest category of problem mortgages. Five or six million mortgages were in the foreclosure process. As banks failed, the FDIC had become a large landowner from the inventory of 150 failed banks, with more to come. The agencies that the government had taken over, Fannie Mae and Freddie Mac, along with the Federal Housing Administration, were by the end of 2009 providing 90 percent of all new mortgages in the U.S. housing market. Many of these would default.

The government sponsored enterprises are a Rorschach test in American politics. To some they represent the unwarranted intrusion of government into the housing market. To others they represent the use of government to encourage a socially desirable goal—increasing home ownership in the society. To help support the housing market these government sponsored enterprises took on more dud loans. Their inventory of foreclosed residential properties quadrupled in the three years to early 2011. The number of properties they owned increased fivefold to a total of nearly a quarter of a million units, about a third of all repossessed homes in the country. When Congressional Republicans wanted to scale back government backing mortgages to let the free market allocate housing resources they were visited by groups of large contributors, the Financial Services Roundtable, the Mortgage Bankers Association and others in the industry who explained that privatization would mean a smaller and considerably more expensive mortgage market. Would they really want to kick the industry already on the ropes? Free market economists might go on about how government guarantee eliminates essential market discipline, but were elected officials really ready to let the country suffer the consequences of removing these distorting subsidies? It can be argued that they should, and for good measure withdraw the interest deductibility of mortgages, but any sudden move in these free market directions would likely send the economy into a deep downturn given the importance of the housing sector.

An area that received little or no attention from Washington was justice for the vast numbers facing foreclosure who were victims of illegal deceptive and predatory lending practices but were too poor to get legal help (Clark with Barron 2009). In theory, the Legal Services Corporation would be an avenue of assistance, but it has been so underfunded since the days of Newt Gingrich's Contract with America, when its budget was drastically cut and it was forbidden to take on class-action suits (which would have been a powerful tool against criminal lending practices by banks), that it could not begin to take on these time-consuming cases. While large law firms do a good deal of pro bono work, they do not take on such cases. They get so much revenue from banks that they have both expertise in this area and incentive not to anger the banks from which they get business. As a result, large numbers of home owners who have valid claims against lenders do not get their day in court and suffer foreclosure.

The bookend to the fraud in mortgage origination was the illegalities in repossessing homes by the banks. In the fall of 2010 Bank of America, the country's largest bank, along with others, suspended foreclosures in a scandal over fraudulent practices. As discussed earlier, Bank of America had acquired Countrywide, the number one originator of mortgages and also the number one server. The fraudulent practices it and similar firms had engaged in came back to haunt the megabanks as case after case of loans that were given to people who had no prayer of paying down the mortgages was uncovered. Buyers of collateralized mortgage obligations, including investment firm giants BlackRock and Pimco, as well as the New York Federal Reserve Bank, wanted their money back from the country's largest bank holding companies for losses suffered on these gamed securities. Hedge funds (bottom-feeding vulture funds paying a nickel on the dollar) bought up devalued CDOs, intending to go after the banks to get 100 percent of the original security's price. Since the Federal Reserve had bought $1 trillion or so of mortgage-backed securities from banks, for it to ask for serious amounts of money back on them would cut substantially into bank profits and require another bailout. Freddie and Fannie had huge holdings as well. The government would have to decide whether it would save taxpayers' money and make the banks disgorge some or even all of their profits. These profits had been "earned" in significant measure because Fannie and Freddie had taken the potential losses on these toxic products. Wanting the housing market to recover, the Obama administration was in an awkward position.

At the same time that the banks were rushing to foreclose on home owners, they could not show courts they actually had the right to take possession of the properties. The slapdash work in setting up the mortgages was matched by the slipshod, blatantly illegal foreclosure process. Documents were forged. People who were signing affidavits claiming that they had personal knowledge of the facts involved were signing hundreds of such documents a day without in fact looking at backup paper, which in many cases did not exist. Those doing this work were poorly paid and untrained bank employees who had been hired as production line workers to throw people out of their homes. Robo-signers executed paperwork vouching for details of contracts they had not seen. Backdating, forging of signatures, and other violations of law were grounds for people to fight eviction and for bond holders to demand their money back from banks.

Given the sheer volume of properties involved, the industry had come up with the Mortgage Electronic Registration System, a database that "owned" mortgages no matter how many times the mortgage was transferred from lenders, loan servicers, underwriters of mortgage backed securities, and others. The original promissory notes, the only legally accepted proof that a mortgage exists, were lost or destroyed in the electronic process, making a large number of foreclosures of dubious legality.

The mess was a fitting continuation of the subprime fiasco. The outcome would matter for the more than six million homes on which foreclose filings had been made and the millions more in the pipeline. There were scandals involving multiple banks foreclosing on the same borrower, banks seizing homes from people who did not have mortgages, and other horror stories, but the larger issue was one of false affidavits—whether claimants had the legal right to foreclose. The Lender Processing Services, a company that is middleman for more than half the foreclosures in the United States, listed in its price list for services it provides what was clear to lawyers and other knowledgeable observers as an offer to create a "collateral file" that contained documents allowing a foreclosure to proceed. That is, it would create various documents the bank should have had on file but did not.

These were not matters of a mistake or carelessness, but purposeful violations of laws that govern secured transactions that involve property with loans against them. They were gross violations of traditional property rights. Documents were fabricated in taking away people's homes just as they were in granting mortgages. With foreclosed properties accounting for one in every four homes sold in the United States, real estate deals in progress and many consummated were brought into question. Congress was inclined to wave its magic wand and declare these forecloses valid, but the travesty involving property law was hardly clear. Obama White House senior advisor David Axelrod expressed concern that problems in establishing a chain of title might hurt the banks, could delay economic recovery, and were probably minor. It is useful to look at this inability to bring the housing market back to health since it was a drag on the prospects of economic recovery and continued to have painful consequences for millions of women, men, and children in families that were losing their homes.

It is useful to go back to the goals of the Emergency Economic Stabilization Act (enacted on October 3, 2008), which set up TARP. For the Treasury Department, this law was about saving the banks. For Congress, which on the first attempt by the Bush administration to rush the legislation through rejected it, the concern was that banks that had caused the crisis were being rewarded. Congress demanded as a condition for passage that a second goal be fostered—preserving home ownership, giving aid to endangered home owners. The act instructed the Treasury to modify mortgages so people could stay in their homes. After the law was passed, Treasury extended help to the banks without directing or requiring them to extent credit to home owners even though President Bush had agreed that billions of dollars were to go to preventing foreclosures. The Treasury did not ask the banks what they were doing with the money. The Obama administration essentially followed the Bush priority of helping the banks by not forcing mortgage servers to help homeowners. The ineffective voluntary programs of both administrations were failures. The thinking at the Treasury was that the banks remained weak and a requirement to modify mortgages could push them over the edge. The government under Bush and then Obama promoted voluntary reduction of interest and extended repayment terms that did not address the deep drop in housing values that left many millions of families owing far more on their mortgages than their homes were worth. In February 2009 the Obama administration announced the Home Affordability Modification Program (HAMP) along with a promise to help up to four million families with mortgage modification; as much as $75 billion, it was said, would be needed for HAMP. Two years later only about $1 billion had been spent, and the program had helped only 680,000 families with permanent modification out of the 2.7 million who had sought to participate (Zibel and Radnofsky 2011). Almost 6.7 million U.S. homes were foreclosed between 2000 and 2010, and 3.6 million more could go through foreclosure by 2013, according to Moody's Analytics. Millions of families losing their homes had been saddled with mortgages they could not be expected to be able to pay off given their incomes, and many lost jobs in the downturn.

The reason for the government failure to help many of those seeking aid was that mortgage servers preferred to foreclose than to modify mortgages. Investigations of the situations of home owner applicants revealed a pattern of banks denying many whose incomes and credit scores appeared to qualify them for mortgage modification and who had done all the paper work and paid legal fees but still faced foreclosure. Banks lost paperwork and made many embarrassing errors, foreclosing on people who in fact did not have mortgages, and on others where the bank had no proof it held the mortgage. The Treasury refused to discipline the banks. It was more concerned with their viability than with the rights of homeowners. The Republican-controlled House of Representatives, saying the foreclosure relief program was a failure, voted to kill it. Liberal Democrats in Congress pointed out the banks had fought the government in ways that had made the program ineffective.

State attorney generals demanded compensation for the widespread violations of state laws in bank foreclosures, suggesting penalties of $20 billion to recover some of the ill-gotten gains and to add pressure to fix a dysfunctional system. Their proposed new procedures would prevent the industry from foreclosing until homeowners had formally been denied a loan modification in writing. This was in response to the robo signing of thousands of mortgages without due process. Banks had been stringing people along, collecting payments and all manner of fees and then foreclosing. Among other rules, the state attorney generals wanted homeowners to be able to have a single contact at a bank handling their case, to avoid the runaround many desperate homeowners had been getting.

Then, as mentioned, there is the matter of the MERS Corporation, a computerized central system few had heard of, set up by the industry, which claimed to hold title to half of all home mortgages in the country—some sixty million loans. The Mortgage Electronic Registration System (MERS) does not actually make loans. Courts in many states found that banks using this system violated property rights and legal requirements. The Federal Reserve and the Treasury Department defended the banks. When Elizabeth Warren, whose role in establishing a consumer protection agency is discussed in the next chapter, was asked by the attorney generals for advice, senior Republicans accused the Obama administration of a "regulatory shakedown" and demanded a halt to a proposed $20 billion fine on the industry (Braithwaite and Kapner 2011).

As a candidate, Barack Obama had suggested that bankruptcy judges be able to reduce the principal on a first home. (If one declares bankruptcy, the judge can reduce the principal owed on a second home and even a yacht, but not on the home people live in and are in danger of losing, thanks to bank influence on Washington lawmakers.) Banks resisted writing down principal even though in most cases they would be better off to do this than to foreclose and have to resell the house. The banks worry that more homeowners with mortgages would threaten not to pay so they also would get writedowns. Furthermore, mortgage servers, as opposed to the holders or insurers of the actual mortgages, had no incentive to avoid foreclosures. The situation is complicated by the huge amount of second liens on homes. These are high-interest loans, including home-equity loans, that can come to 15–20 percent of the value of the home. Well over 90 percent of first liens are owned by the government (through its ownership of Freddie and Fannie). Hundreds of billions in second liens are held by the banks, which carry them on their books at full value when their market value is perhaps 40 to 60 percent of their face value. A number of large banks would suffer losses large enough to push them under if the principal on mortgages were written down to realistic levels. This is why Bank of America, the nation's largest mortgage servicer, with well over a hundred billion in second liens on its books, was so resistant to pressure to write off tens of billions of dollars in mortgage debt.

Household equity in the United States in 2010 fell to the point that homeowners held only 38.5 percent of equity in real estate, down from 60 percent in 2005. Almost everyone who bought between 2005 and 2007 had negative equity. Ten percent were estimated to have a negative equity of 25 percent or more (Haughwout 2011). Those with negative equity were in effect renters. The official drop in home ownership did not begin to reflect the actual decline. The gap between official ownership and those who had any equity in their homes was 44 percent in Las Vegas, a city particularly hard hit by the crash of the real estate bubble, and well above 20 percent in places like Phoenix and Detroit. By such a realistic measure, as a result of the Great Recession home ownership fell by 20 percent nationally (Haughwout, Peach, and Tracy 2010).

Helping the Banks Recover

Under Bush and Obama, the executive branch tried two approaches to dealing with the banks' capital ratios. The original TARP proposal was to lower the denominator by buying toxic assets. These, as discussed earlier, were hard to value. Henry Paulson moved to increase the numerator, the bank's capital, by buying preferred stock. This, however, made it difficult for banks to raise private capital since government ownership diluted the value of the holdings of other owners. Toward the end of Bush's presidency and in consultation with the incoming Obama administration, the government went back to helping out on the denominator, reducing the banks' risk-weighted assets, by insuring them against losses above a certain level. This meant that banks did not have to sell assets at the deep discount at which they were valued by the market. It was a tactic that created great potential liability for taxpayers but successfully lessened uncertainty.

In the effort to restore the financial sector to health, other officials found any number of creative ways to feed money back into the financial sector. More than 40 percent of the monies made available came from the Federal Reserve (over $8 trillion estimated in mid-2009), followed by the Treasury (over a third of the total), and a smaller amount from the FDIC (over $2 trillion) and other agencies such as the FHA in residential mortgage guarantees and a host of joint agency programs. More than 90 percent of the money was earmarked for Wall Street or for Fannie Mae and Freddie Mac to take questionable mortgage-backed assets from the banks and other holders. In 2009 financial institutions borrowed $300 billion at extraordinary low rates under the FDIC's Temporary Liquidity Guarantee Program. The Fed's commitment of up to $1.25 trillion in the Term Asset-Backed Securities Loan Facility allowed them to sell mortgage-backed securities. The Fed bought more than 70 percent of all the mortgage-backed securities conforming to Fannie Mae and Freddie Mac standards. To focus only on TARP, as officials and members of Congress people did, was misleading. Of course to see TARP as a money-losing investment, however much one might condemn undeserving recipients, is also a mistake. The government lost very little money and might even end up turning a profit as it was paid back by AIG and from sale of GM shares. Politically this did not register with voters, much to the discomfort of almost half of the House Republicans who voted for TARP and were on the defensive in primary challenges on this issue from tea party activists. A large number of voters presumed TARP was created by President Obama and not, as in fact it had been, under President Bush.

In opening the public spigot in such a fashion, the goal was to get back to the old normal (with some safeguards in place). The strategy was to throw an excessive amount of money at the financial sector on the theory that confidence would return when investors and institutions knew the government would spend whatever it took to help them. Within a year of the darkest days of fall 2008, many large banks had returned to profitability and looked forward to what was presumed would be recovery and a return to normalcy. In an ironic echo, citizens were again told "there is no alternative," as they had been told with regard to the liberalization of financial markets. The government took responsibility for the survival of the banks. Public anger mounted through the summer of 2009. President Obama, in addressing the bankers, said, "If you have presided over an enormous meltdown that has resulted in about $10 trillion worth of wealth being lost, you might want to be a little self-reflective and perhaps change your business goals. And when I see Wall Street not doing that, it tells me not only that they have forgotten the recent past, but they are putting the country's economic future at risk." No doubt. But the actions the government took would do little to force different behavior.

The president's comment that financiers might be more self-reflective put some in mind of Franklin D. Roosevelt's 1936 comparison of bankers to a drowning man who is saved by a lifeguard and after four years returns to angrily ask the lifeguard, "Where is my silk hat? You lost my silk hat!" Only the bankers in 2009 did not wait four years but only four months. Government, Wall Street seemed to say, was at fault. It had failed to set and enforce proper rules; or, as John Kay (2009) puts it, "Widely expressed among financial market participants is the view that we would never have trashed the house if our parents had supervised us properly." It is up to the state to prevent aggressive behavior that is deemed socially harmful. The crisis Q.E.D. is the fault of government. Given government failure, it is the responsibility of taxpayers to provide a new silk hat.

Of course, the relationship between the financial players and the government is quite different from that of parent to child. Even when the public wants banks to act differently, the electorate does not have the final word. The structural and instrumental power of finance capital is such that government is more dictated to than commanding. The parent-child analogy also fails in that Wall Street provides the brain power and personnel to staff the key policy-making and regulatory positions that make the rules. It is not surprising, then, that attempting to restore the status quo ante in a more sustainable form is always the first impulse of government when faced with a crisis. Despite public anger, the political influence of the financial sector was felt not only through its deep-pocketed generosity to campaign funding and its extensive lobbying, but in the backgrounds of the mutually shared culture and attitude of the close-knit community that trafficked between Washington and Wall Street and in the strong neoclassical dominance among academic economists, opinion molders, and policy players. How little changed was impressive against the background of all that had happened. Household wealth fell by 17 percent between December 2007 and December 2008. This was more than five times the decline in 1929, and the shock to the system was far greater than at the start of the Great Depression.

From 2002 to 2007 American households extracted $2.3 trillion from their homes and increased their consumption spending on the presumed value of their homes. This spending stimulated economic growth. When home prices fell, this wealth effect operated in reverse as the debts came due. Unlike the drop in asset valuations in the Great Depression, monetary and fiscal policy responded quickly, preventing a continued downward cycling. This did not, however, bring about recovery, significant employment creation, or robust investment. The demand for austerity measures in the face of the rising federal deficit, even given dramatic loss of public services, especially at the state and local levels where governments were forced to balance budgets with painful cutbacks, layoffs, and other unpopular measures, threatened to make the situation worse. In chapter 8 more will be said about this sharp division over how best to address the ongoing crisis. The immediate issue was what government should do to revive the financial system and then what regulatory measures were needed so that such crises would be less likely and less severe in the future.

6

Rescue and the Limits of Regulation

Today, with a huge global financial crisis and a synchronized slump in economic activity, the world is changing again. The financial system is the brain of the market economy. If it needs so expensive a rescue, what is left of Reagan's dismissal of government? If the financial system has failed, what remains of confidence in markets? It is impossible at such a turning point to know where we are going.

—MARTIN WOLF (2009A)

It is easy to speak of new rules. But less easy to identify rules which could avert crises such as the one we are experiencing and, even more so, could prevent different types of future crises.

—ANTONIO MUTTI, 2010

It is unlikely that anything government can do in a capitalist economy can prevent economic crises. Nonetheless, rapid growth of credit should be a signal for regulatory measures. Policies are available to lean against the wind and take the punch bowl away to keep the party from getting out of hand. This will not prevent cycles but can moderate both damage from overexpansion and then the extent of the collapse—if there is effective government intervention. For this, however, the government must be free of the control of those they presumably regulate and be able and willing to take steps that powerful interests will not like. This is asking quite a lot in our system of democratic capitalism.

There are reform measures that can reduce the severity and perhaps the incidence of financial crises. Some of these are at the level of what responsibilities key regulators such as the Federal Reserve are willing to accept. Alan Greenspan took the position that the Fed could not predict bubbles and needed to wait until after they collapsed and then take action to repair the damage. He did not believe the Fed should investigate possible fraud, believing that the market would deal with that. If top regulators come from libertarian backgrounds and do not believe in regulation, they will, like Greenspan, see their job as guardians of the financial system only insofar as they prevent inflation. If regulators are appointed who, ex ante, pay attention to asset bubbles, demand more capital reserves (and, importantly, higher-quality capital) since they know failures can occur and taxpayer cost should be minimized, and permit less leverage, along with limiting the extent of pure speculative plays by any institution or group of institutions that separately or together potentiality can trigger a systemic crisis, these guardians may operate quite differently.

Saving the Banks

The Obama administration, in addressing the situation it inherited, adopted the view that the banks' troubled assets were undervalued by temporary panic and illiquidity and would rise in value once normalcy returned. The government's task was to restore the health of the large financial institutions by extending as much assistance to the banks as it could. President Obama's role in this was to try to persuade Americans that by helping the banks the government would be helping the economy, and that the interests of Wall Street and Main Street were the same. When public anger grew too intense, he struck a populist note now and again, but few thought his heart was into a Teddy Roosevelt posture. More typical was a speech at Georgetown University on April 14, 2009, in which the president told his audience, "Although there are a lot of Americans who understandably think that government money would be better spent going directly to families and businesses instead of banks— 'Where's our bailout?' they ask—the truth is that $1 of capital in a bank can actually result in $8 or $10 of loans to families and businesses, a multiplier effect that can ultimately lead to a faster pace of economic growth." The operative word is "can" ultimately lead to growth. This could be the case if banks did actually increase lending to families and businesses. In the fifteen months to the end of 2009, the banking industry, despite trillions of dollars of assistance, drained more than $3 trillion of credit from the economy. A year later (April 24, 2010), the president, speaking at Syracuse University, said, "Ultimately there is no dividing line between Main Street and Wall Street. We rise and fall together as one nation." This view was not widely shared on Main Street.

Not only had bank profits and bonuses moved to precrisis levels, but corporate America was experiencing precrisis profitability—not because the demand for its products had grown, although there was some restocking of inventory and some companies were seeing sales return, but mostly from productivity increases from laying off large numbers of workers, cutting pay, and speedups. Banks were not lending. They held extensive toxic assets on their balance sheets, including commercial real estate. A game of extend and pretend was keeping losses from being recognized. In the summer of 2010, two-thirds of commercial real estate loans were underwater and maturing in the next three years. Real estate values were over 40 percent below their October 2007 peak. Importantly, the market for securitization had slowed dramatically. It was proving hard going for policy makers to repair a financial order and growth strategy based on real estate and a securitization, which had collapsed. The Fed and Treasury were not willing to focus on the importance of the failure of the repo market, which had become so central to the banking system. They continued to treat the situation as a liquidity problem, not an insolvency problem that required accepting write-downs of inflated values. These devalued assets weighed heavily, preventing new lending, and led to a hoarding of liquidity given an uncertain future.

While small businesses desired to borrow, the Federal Reserve reported that America's five hundred largest companies were sitting on $2 trillion in cash, choosing not to invest, the highest percent of liquid assets held idle in fifty years. It was said this was because the Obama administration was antibusiness. But it was more reasonably the result of skepticism on the part of firms that were having trouble increasing sales and saw no reason to expand production. In the face of continued high unemployment and uncertainty, American consumers were not spending. American households together had $8 trillion in low-yield liquid accounts. Given continued uncertainty, banks, nonfinancial companies, and consumers were not creating the demand that could generate satisfactory growth. The federal government stepped in with transfer payments to those without jobs and some stimulus spending, but hard-hit state and local jurisdictions cut spending and laid off large numbers of teachers and other public workers. While people feared the growing deficit, it was difficult to see how government immediately spending less in such a situation would not make the situation worse. Yet that is what many demanded.

Because of public anger, much of the assistance extended to Wall Street was in forms that did not need congressional approval. It was given either by the Fed or executive branch agencies. A consistent element of the aid was seeing that the banks got more for their assets when public entities purchased or insured them than the market thought they were worth. In this basic strategy, the Obama team continued the approach of the previous administration. The rescue represented a minimum of a $1 trillion cost to government and likely far more, depending on the exposure of taxpayers to the future obligations from loan guarantees, especially Freddie and Fannie mortgage portfolios.

Deception as to the state of the banks involved obscuring large numbers. Such lowballing of the situation made it easier for Secretary Geithner's public-private partnership (PPIP) approach to get legacy assets, called by most others toxic assets, off the banks' books. Under his early plan, investors could buy such assets, with taxpayers responsible for 95 percent or so of the purchase price, a procedure Geithner said would establish their market price. Few thought such a subsidy could produce fair market value. In a real market sale, the IMF calculated that banks would be forced to take write-downs, which would wipe them out since losses would vastly exceed their equity. If investors overpaid with taxpayer dollars and the assets proved of little value, there would be a massive redistribution of wealth from citizens to the banks. Should the purchases prove profitable, the investors would get dramatically high returns on their limited-risk capital. The Treasury strategy offering maximal support was premised on the idea that without such aid the financial sector would not recover, and there would be prolonged crisis. If the strategy succeeded, financial markets would come back, returning the monies the government had put at risk. The Treasury Department reported in the fall of 2010 that the government would likely get back $21.5 billion of the $22 billion that it had committed under PPIP.

Before the collapse, the banks had competed with lower interest rates and offered covenant-lite loans, often made to private equity groups and hedge funds with little to no collateral. Two-thirds of corporate loans were bundled into collateralized loan obligations. Banks made what were called "toggle-PIK" loans, which allowed the borrower to pay interest on loans with new borrowing. Such temporizing helped the banks hold on. They allowed borrowers to formally avoid default by delaying payments along the lines of pay-option mortgage loans, which permitted home buyers to pay only a fraction of the interest, adding the rest to the mortgage. Such arrangements kept defaults down and bank profits up. Between 2003 and the 2007, peak financial stocks doubled in market value to reach 22 percent of the S&P 500 index total value, in part thanks to such practices. After the economy went into formal recovery in 2009, banks delayed reckoning and spread out defaults, waiting for the economy to fully recover and raise the value of the dud assets that they continued to hold. The government and the Fed sought new ways to channel money to the banks in the belief that their recovery was the necessary and perhaps the sufficient condition to restore economic growth.

In late 2009 the office of Neil Barofsky, the special inspector general for the Troubled Asset Relief Program, released its report on the government bailout of the American Insurance Group. AIG had received $182 billion in what the report described as a "backdoor bailout" of its counterparties. Barofsky was critical of the Fed for not forcing the banks to accept a deep discount on what they claimed due from AIG, which was "far above the market value at the time." One of Geithner's faults was his exceedingly trusting attitude toward what bankers told him. He seemed incapable of seeing anything done by the pillars of Wall Street as possibly matters for regulator skepticism—and certainly not for law enforcement action. Barofsky's report dismissed the conclusion offered by Goldman Sachs that an AIG bankruptcy would not have materially effected the firm. Geithner, who, as head of the New York Fed had arranged for the AIG bailout in cooperation with Secretary Paulson, said at the time that Goldman would not have been affected by an AIG collapse. Barofsky explained that Geithner had not actually studied Goldman's positions but simply taken its chief financial officer's word for this.

Goldman was AIG's largest trading partner and would in fact have been seriously affected had AIG not been bailed out. While the popular discussion featured suspicion that the government was favoring Goldman in the context of a decision to do all that was possible to restore the financial system, such a backdoor bailout of the major banks was a positive step from the Fed's perspective. Given public opposition to the Fed's strategy, it made sense to obscure to the greatest extent possible the many channels through which policy was pumping money into these institutions.

The special inspector's report was critical of the Fed's claim that making the AIG counterparties publicly known would have "undermined A.I.G.'s stability, the privacy and business interests of the counter-parties, and the stability of the markets." When the Fed was forced to divulge this information, none of that happened. (The privacy of the banks receiving government largesse was eventually violated, quite reasonably in the minds of most observers.) Yet if one is focused on the Fed's overarching strategy, the poor quality of some of its ruses is almost beside the point. The effort is to obscure the extent to which financial institutions were being helped and, as quietly as possible, to channel huge amounts to them to restore their health, while avoiding a popular backlash.

The Congressional Oversight Panel in an August 2010 report notes that the lack of data on where the money committed to AIG went made it difficult for Congress or anyone else to ask whether foreign governments should have contributed to the financial rescue. Much of the initial $70 billion of TARP money went immediately from AIG to banks in France and Germany. The cash going to AIG equaled twice what France spent on its total injection program and half of what Germany spent. From the Fed's perspective these were quibbles. To critics of the way it handled the crisis by shoveling public monies at the banks that had been responsible for the crisis, there were important questions regarding where other monies went and why the United States should bail out foreign banks with taxpayer money. For the Fed, the global financial system was a single unit that it was protecting.

As for the specific episodes of corrupt practices by financial institutions that voters wanted punished, Barofsky opened up sixty-five cases investigating potential fraud in various bailout programs. Regulators who saw their job as supporting these institutions were less interested in looking into such matters. "When I first took office, I can't tell you how many times I'd be having a sit-down and warning about potential fraud in the program and would hear a response basically saying, 'Oh, they're bankers, and they wouldn't put their reputation at risk by committing fraud,' " Barofsky told the *New York Times* (Morgenson 2009). It was also said that rating agencies and investors do due diligence, so market prices are realistic and should be accepted without question by government regulators. Barofsky continually ran up against the insider culture of Wall Street, which stretched the truth and pushed the line of legality. When he pointed this out, he said, it was "trying to shame the shameless." He fought the Treasury when he sought to obtain statements under oath from bankers to find out how they used government funds; his report found that some had gone to purposes directly contradictory to congressional intent. He insisted on his independence when the Treasury Department pushed to have him report only to it. Under such a restrictive scenario it is unlikely that Barofsky's critical findings on Paulson and the questions his work raised with regard to Geithner would have seen the light of day.

In May 2010 the House Committee on Oversight and Government Reform released a quarter of a million pages of previously undisclosed documents. They revealed that the Treasury Department had gone against the recommendations of those it had hired to advise it on dealing with AIG's obligations. These firms, Morgan Stanley, BlackRock and Ernst & Young, offered a number of options that called for deep concessions from the banks.

Instead the documents showed that Treasury officials deferred to the banks. The Fed asked no concessions and kept the negotiations secret as long as it could. "During the A.I.G. bailout, New York Fed officials prepared a script for its employees to use in negotiations with the banks, and it was anything but tough; it advised Fed negotiators to solicit suggestions from bankers about what financial and institutional support they wanted from the Fed" (Story and Morgenson 2010).The script reminded government negotiators that bank participation was "entirely voluntary." The thread running through all this is the close relationship between the Treasury Department and Wall Street. Treasury was committed to protecting the banks, treating them as generously as possible and granting them monies in such overwhelming amounts that there should be no question in reassuring markets as to their viability. Channeling the maximum it could to the banks through AIG was consistent with this purpose.

Inner Circles and Revolving Doors

Looking at the commanding heights of financial capitalism, it is really a very small club. More than half of all the debt of households, nonfinancial companies, and government in the United States is held by the top fifteen institutions, and among them there is a tremendous concentration of assets in the top five and even the top three megabanks. Among current and former members of the board of the New York Federal Reserve Bank are former president E. Gerald Corrigan, managing director of Goldman Sachs; Chairman Stephen Friedman, retired chair of Goldman Sachs who was forced to step down as New York Fed chair when his purchases of Goldman stock while a board member became public knowledge; and Sanford Weill, the former CEO of Citigroup whom we encountered earlier in the story. Others close to Tim Geithner include his mentor Robert Rubin, who went to Citigroup and for whom Geithner worked in the Clinton Treasury Department; and Lloyd Blankfein, head of Goldman, whom he frequently consulted. Secretary Geithner's chief of staff was Mark Patterson, who cashed in his long experience on Capitol Hill as a key staffer for the Senate majority leader to become a federally registered lobbyist for Goldman Sachs. Until April 2008, according to federal forms, he lobbied on issues of bank regulation and other areas central to the work of the Treasury Department before becoming Geithner's chief of staff.

The relationship between an instrumentalism that draws key Wall Street representatives to high-level positions as policy makers in Washington and the structural role that finance plays was evident when, as president-elect, Barack Obama presented his economic team, drawing approval from Wall Street and dismay from people who expected "change we can believe in." The appointees, heavily Clinton administration retreads, were people who had introduced deregulation policies and had actively prevented regulation of derivative contracts, hedge funds, and the high leverage used by private equity firms. The Obama administration economists had intimate relations with Wall Street. The individuals working out the plans for the government listened to the preferences of those who would benefit from the way the government chose to restore the system. Not only were the working relations in devising the plans very close, but the people entrusted with the public interest were part of the culture and had long experience and connections to the top circles of the American financial elite.

Citibank contributed its former chief financial officer at its Alternative Investments unit to be deputy assistant to the president with responsibilities for international economic affairs. And so it went. One can understand that knowledgeable people come from the industry and after public service return to it, but this means they arrive in and leave Washington with the industry mindset, interests, and values. As with other Obama appointments, the issue was not whether such people were smart and experienced; it was, what would their bias be in guiding policy? One does not expect people with populist ideas of the sort that might be endorsed by a majority of Americans to end up in such positions. The function of this community can be understood as promoting and perpetuating the hegemony of international finance capital. And why not? There is no conspiracy involved. Members of the financial epistemic community speak the same language and share an overlapping world view, a conventional wisdom that is the normal discourse for people entrusted with such work, who move easily from academia to key positions in government to consulting for hedge funds.

Bradford DeLong, a former Clinton official, told an interviewer, "Hank Paulson is a man who grew up in American finance and cannot imagine a world in which America does well and its financial sector does badly" (Luce 2009). DeLong thought Paulson's successor, Timothy Geithner, a different sort of person because he had never pulled down a multibillion-dollar bonus. However, Geithner had long lived in the Wall Street culture. (In most discussions and even media reports it was assumed that he had come from Goldman

Sachs even though he had not. He had, however, been offered the top slot at Citigroup.) In his job at the Fed, as late as 2007 he advocated measures to allow banks to lower their reserves, which made them more vulnerable in the event of problems and made rescue by the Fed more expensive. The rescue that then followed was surely in sympathy with the interests of the bankers. If Bear Stearns was given to JPMorgan Chase on incredibly favorable terms and Washington Mutual was brokered to JPMorgan Chase, one might ask, could it have anything to do with insider discussions with Jamie Dimon, JP Morgan Chase's CEO, who sits on the board of directors of the Federal Reserve Board of New York where he worked closely with Geithner? As Jo Becker and Gretchen Morgenson (2009) write of the New York Fed, it is "by custom and design, clubby and opaque."

> An examination of Mr. Geithner's five years as president of the New York Fed, an era of unbridled and ultimately disastrous risk-taking by the financial industry, shows that he forged unusually close relationships with executives of Wall Street's giant financial institutions. . . . His actions, as a regulator and later a bailout king, often aligned with the industry's interests and desires, according to interviews with financiers, regulators and analysts and a review of Federal Reserve records.

Geithner's calendar as secretary of the treasury, obtained by the Associated Press under the Freedom of Information Act, revealed that through the busy crisis days and in the formulation of a government response he was in touch most frequently with three men: Lloyd Blankfein, Goldman's CEO; Jamie Dimon, Blankfein's counterpart at JPMorgan Chase; and Barack Obama. He was on the phone several times a day to all three. Hank Paulson, before him, had the same sort of short-list contact circle, with concentrated dialogue with Goldman people at the firm he had led before taking over the Treasury Department. Such advice presumably shares a number of characteristics. It is well informed, up-to-date, and unlikely to provide information or offer suggestions that are not in the interest of their institutions. Many observers saw these relationships and contacts as evidence of the incestuous relation between regulators and regulated, a case of regulatory capture. For the officials involved, the working relationship was productive, allowing them to do their job better—a job they saw as protecting the health of the financial system.

Perhaps the key player in the Obama administration, deciding on how to deal with hedge funds, was Larry Summers, a managing director of D. E.

Shaw. From late 2006 he advised the company on risk strategy. In April 2009 the White House released information from his financial disclosure statement, showing that in the previous year he had received over $5 million in compensation from the $40 billion private equity and hedge fund, as well as $2.77 million in speaking fees for two appearances for Goldman Sachs, which netted over $200,000. Citigroup, Lehman, and JPMorgan Chase were other generous payers for the privilege of discussions with Summers. As adviser to the president, he actively supported deregulation and counted on market forces to promote efficient allocation of resources. As he said to a Senate subcommittee in July 1998, "The parties to these kinds of contracts are largely sophisticated financial institutions that would appear to be eminently capable of protecting themselves from fraud and counter-party insolvencies." One severe critic, Robert Scheer (2009), wrote of Summers, "No one has been more persistently effective in paving the way for the financial swindles that enriched the titans of finance while impoverishing the rest of the world than the man who is now the top adviser to President Obama."

These close relations seem inevitable, given the experience needed to do the job. It makes the incumbents easy targets for criticism from all sides and open to questioning of their motives. Such criticism can be unfair to people who take difficult jobs for low or no pay. Their "payoff" is rarely that they directly benefit financially in any simple sense from decisions they make. However, they come from, and typically go back to, work in the industry. They come with the culture of Wall Street, which influences their decisions, and go back with a deep knowledge of government, which benefits their private-sector employers.

The government carried out extensive efforts to influence perception of the health of the financial sector, including the very sensible idea that the government would carry out stress tests to separate solvent banks from insolvent ones, protecting the debt of the former but not the latter. The initial presumption was that the risk of the insolvent banks would fall on their owners and unsecured creditors while depositors would be protected if the banks could not raise needed capital. The idea was that by letting the banks that were found insolvent fail, the government would return discipline to the industry and end the moral hazard of banks deemed too large to fail taking on excessive risk in the belief that the state would protect them from their own errors. But the test set up was not rigorous. As H. Peyton Young, Oxford economist and senior fellow at the Brookings Institution, politely said, "It's a highly game-able system." Still the banks argued that the government's stress test had been too stringent and in a number of cases got the Treasury to change findings. By first quarter 2009, banks were claiming a return to profitability, assertions greeted in the financial press with stories headlined: "Bank Profits Appear Out of Thin Air" and "Sharp Pencil Lets Citigroup Declare Profit." Citigroup was able to talk the Treasury stress testers down from their needing $35 billion in new capital to only $5.5 billion.

Many wondered at the way the goal posts were so easily moved. Bank of America increased its profits by $2.2 billion simply by revaluing upward Merrill Lynch assets it acquired, leading one management professor to comment that although perfectly legal, this is also perfectly delusional. All of this was after the Fed had plowed more money into Citigroup and Bank of America than their entire market value in exchange for restricted ownership stakes, paying 120 percent of their value initially for minimal ownership claims. Goldman Sachs struck out the terrible results of the month of December through the expedient of changing its reporting calendar and erased the $1.5 billion it lost by omitting to report on that month at all. All this was true, but if the goal was to prevent bank failures and having to nationalize banks, this strategy was sensible—and it worked. One can disagree with the strategy and suggest that nationalization would have been better, even in the case— perhaps especially in the case—of one or two megabanks, in order to send a signal that excessive risk taking would not merit bailouts in the future either. But, given the strategy chosen, many of the criticisms on tactical decisions are misplaced. This is not to say that working people did not have every reason to complain bitterly, given their own situations.

The Geithner–Wall Street approach could work because confidence is so important to markets and finance. The Fed kept interest rates near zero to give the banks essentially free money used to earn their way back to stability. Some of these funds were used to expand proprietary trading, earning high returns at a time when individual investors remained cautious while the markets soared. The largest financial institutions employed funds available at zero or one quarter of 1 percent interest prevailing from December 2008 to make money trading derivatives, stocks, and bonds in a rising market, not by making loans. Unemployment remained at disastrously high levels.

Unfortunately for Main Street, the relative autonomy of the financial sector from the work-a-day lives of ordinary Americans made it possible for the substantial assistance to Wall Street to have little spillover impact for the rest of the country. The government was in a sense choosing its primary social partner, to use the European term for class interest and hegemonic bloc formation. Small and medium-sized banks were not helped the same way and failed in significant numbers. Many were bought by bigger banks at bargain prices with subsidies from the FDIC. As it ran out of money, the FDIC borrowed from the big banks it had saved. Increasingly, the market power that accrued to the largest banks meant they were able to borrow at lower cost since they were perceived as safer than smaller banks. This too-big-to-fail advantage is estimated to be equal to almost half the 2009 projected profits of the eighteen largest financial institutions (Baker and McArthur 2009). Implicitly or explicitly, the decision had been made to encourage the biggest banks to get bigger still, making it far more difficult to think of ever winding them down in case of subsequent failure. This was hardly a deterrent to their greater risk taking in the future.

The Road Not Traveled—Nationalization

Prominent economists expressed skepticism over the bailouts, including Joseph Stiglitz, a former chair of President Clinton's Council of Economic Advisers; Paul Krugman, Princeton professor and *New York Times* columnist and, like Stiglitz, a Nobel Prize winner in economics; and Simon Johnson, MIT professor and former chief economist at the International Monetary Fund. In an essay titled "The Quiet Coup," Johnson (2009a) suggested that the finance industry has captured the government of the United States and continues to guide its rescue efforts in its own interests and not those of the country. From an international regulator's perspective, it all looked familiar. He describes what he calls "a classic Kremlin bailout technique," the assumption of private debt obligations by the government, which acts to squeeze ordinary citizens and make taxpayers and service recipients bear the cost of financial-sector debt. That is to say, the ruling class of the United States and its dominant fraction, finance capital, manipulates government policy in much the same way the Kremlin or a rent-capturing elite of any global South debtor country might. In this view American crony capitalism reflects the collusive relation of the financiers, their regulators, and elected officials. Johnson writes, "If you hide the name of the country and just show the numbers, there is no doubt what old IMF hands would say: nationalize troubled banks and break them up as necessary."

As an alternative to bailing out the banks, there was early in the financial meltdown much talk of the Swedish way of resolution, which wiped out stockholders, put toxic assets in a "bad bank," sold them off over time, and reprivatized the good banks following their reorganization. Rather than strengthening the banks as they had existed, the Swedish fix nationalized banks and restructured them. This was carried out by the conservative center-right coalition in power in Sweden at the time, market-oriented officials who nationalized the banks to save the taxpayers money. The government imposed strict guidelines on companies receiving public assistance, including risk management and cost cutting. Swedish regulators hired qualified real estate people to sell off the assets and maximize taxpayer returns on their investment. The Swedes early offered blanket guarantees to any investor holding bank liabilities (except, importantly, stock and subordinate debt holders). They did not take a piecemeal approach but were decisive and clear in their actions. Of course they had only five large banks to worry about. Still, the lesson, as explained by the Swedish finance minister responsible for bank restructuring, Arne Berggren, was that the government was a commercial investor: "We were a no-bullshit investor—we were very brutal." The authorities took control. "You take command. If you put in equity, you have to get into management of the business, [otherwise] management is focused on saving the skins of the [remaining private] shareholders" (Larsen and Giles 2009:7). They ran the banks with transparency to keep the trust of the public and markets. They refused to buy assets from privately owned banks because officials said it would have been impossible to agree on a price, and they were not in the business of giving privately held banks subsidies. Real capitalists, the message seemed to be, nationalized.

Interestingly, respected elders of an earlier Republican Party (as opposed to the "just say no to anything the Democrats propose" party), from an era in which some form of bipartisan statesmanship was possible, endorsed the general outline of the Swedish solution. James A. Baker III, chief of staff and treasury secretary for President Reagan, and former Fed chair Alan Greenspan, among others, proposed nationalization of failed banks. Baker pointed to Japan's lost decade (1991–2002) when it held up its zombie banks, postponing recovery. While he "abhorred" the idea of government ownership and invoked the sainted memory of Ronald Reagan to this effect, he urged consideration of something akin to the Resolution Trust Corporation to liquidate the bad assets of the banks (as the RTC created in 1989 did for the failed Savings and Loans). Baker, Greenspan, and others did not see a good outcome from reinflating a finance-driven bubble economy. Experience in a multitude of other countries suggests that providing massive liquidity and open-ended guarantees to insolvent institutions (and in effect resurrecting a number, perhaps a very large number, of them) distorts risk-taking incentives and, by undermining market discipline, promotes future crises (Calomiris, Klingebiel, and Laeven 2005). Such research finds even the short-run benefits of bailouts oversold. They increase the cost of resolving the crisis and prolong it (Honohan and Klingebiel 2003).

American banks could have been divided into three groups: the healthy, the hopeless, and the needy. The first group was left alone, the second closed down quickly, and the third was reorganized and recapitalized, preferably through debt-to-equity swaps, but if necessary through equity investment at the market price of the stock. Shareholders would lose their investment and bondholders would take a haircut (partial losses). Such a program would give banks in the future incentive not to risk such a fate. Barack Obama commented favorably on the success of the Swedish nationalization, but he quickly followed this evaluation with a remark about the different cultures of the two countries, making it clear that such a solution, in his view, was simply not possible in the American context.

The White House, whether under the management of Republicans or Democrats, was never ready for such a business-like approach. Ironically the abuse the administration would take for being "socialist" would keep any chief executive from considering a protaxpayer, hardheaded business approach to banking. In its defense, the U.S. banking system was so much larger than Sweden's and the interconnections such that it would have been a substantially more complex operation, leading to a "radical overhaul" of the global financial system, as Vikram Pandit, Citigroup's CEO, said (Guerrera 2009:17). Pandit preferred more taxpayer money and, at a point at which Citigroup's stock was selling at less than a dollar a share, asked that the government buy 40 percent of the bank (with of course no more interference than when the government owned half as much of the company).

Despite shows of populist rhetoric on occasion from the White House, the country was not ready for the scale of government takeover that would have been necessary to nationalize banks as the Swedes and others had done. In 2010 the Democrats were to lose control of the House of Representatives, badly bruised by voter sentiment that the Obama administration had done too much and that liberals had led a Big Government takeover, even though the president had actually interfered in the market as little as he could have without failing to meet minimal obligations to return the economy to some semblance of normality. The White House, in responding to the crisis, faced a series of decisions in which there were not good choices, only less bad ones. The president and his advisers may not have always been right, but the public anger at not quickly repairing the economy and reducing joblessness was understandable, even if it was unreasonable. After a major financial crash there is usually a long period of slow growth and high unemployment unless the government intervenes on a scale the public is generally unwilling to contemplate. Had the president come in, as FDR did, after three terrible years of greater recession/depression, he would have had more room to maneuver. As it was, the president was criticized both for doing too much and for doing too little, often by the same angry people.

By late 2009 the three largest American banks—Bank of America, JPMorgan Chase, and Wells Fargo—had become the overwhelmingly dominant providers of financial services of all sorts. The three together controlled a third of the nation's deposits. Two years earlier, the top three banks had only 20 percent of the industry total. The thought that the survival of Bank of America (16 percent of GDP) or Citigroup (13 percent of GDP), which had not so long ago been in serious question, had been restored and strengthened through government action could be seen as a reward for the damage they had caused. Because larger banks had absorbed weaker and failing ones, the industry had become more concentrated. In 1997 the six dominant banks had assets equal to 20 percent of the country's GDP; in 2009, an amount equal to about two-thirds of the nation's GDP. They were too big to be allowed to fail, making any living will that they developed unlikely to be implemented.

The size of the burden of rescuing the financial sector would not be known for some time. One of the major worries was the nonperforming loans held by Fannie Mae and Freddie Mac. From September 2008, when the government seized the companies, to September 2010, the cost of keeping them functioning rose by over $150 billion as Washington took responsibility for homes in foreclosure that had once been the responsibility of the private financial sector. It was paying $1 billion a year to mow the lawns on these properties and for other maintenance. Some of the same real estate firms that had initially sold the foreclosed properties were hired by the agencies to resell them. Since prices had fallen so much, Fannie and Freddie were recouping less than 60 percent of the money borrowers had failed to repay. Their contingent liabilities were huge. According to the Congressional Budget Office, likely losses in the summer of 2010 amounted to $1 trillion out of the $5.5 trillion in mortgages and loan guarantees Fannie and Freddie had acquired. The eventual total was likely to go higher. Rahm Emanuel, the White House chief of staff (and a former investment banker and Freddie Mac board member), said that the resolution of these institutions would have to wait. (When Emanuel resigned his post to run for mayor of Chicago, he was replaced by William Daley, vice chairman of JPMorgan Chase.) Confronting the extent of Fannie and Freddie's losses would dramatically increase the federal deficit. The Obama administration did not want to fully nationalize them, nor could they be sold, given their debt. Treasury Secretary Geithner would only say that some day in the future the companies "will not exist in the same form as they did in the past." Meanwhile they would go on bailing out the banks and offering life support to the housing market. Without the buying by them and the FHA of 95 percent of all new mortgages, the housing market would be dead in the water.

While Washington's focus was on what to do about Freddie and Fannie, the extent of bank malfeasance exposed grew. As the first decade of the twenty-first century wound down, there were a number of court cases against the large international banks. The Guardia di Finanza, the Italian financial police, took over the real estate property, accounts, and stockholding of JPMorgan Chase, UBS, Deutsche Bank, and others in a case involving issues of local government bonds over the decade (about $46 billion worth) and the losses sustained by following the bankers' advice on derivatives. The deals were complicated, but the failed promise of a safe way to reduce the cost of long-term debt is familiar enough. The investment bankers, it appeared, had taken advantage of unsophisticated local officials, and local taxpayers suffered great losses as a result. J.P. Morgan Securities forfeited hundreds of millions of dollars in derivative contract fees in a settlement with an Alabama county (with, as usual in such cases, neither admitting nor denying any of the government's accusations). It seems its employees had bribed county commissioners to win the business, which turned out poorly for the county when absolutely safe investments turned into unbearable losses, burdening taxpayers. Calpers, the California Public Employees Retirement System, was embarrassed by a former board member who made $50 million in "fees" for arranging investments that could cost the already strapped state hundreds of millions of dollars.

Hapless Citigroup was caught by the Financial Industry Regulatory Authority (which oversees broker-dealers) and fined $600,000 for using complex derivatives to help offshore clients avoid billions of dollars in taxes. Its imaginative products included total return swaps, which involved customers selling stockholdings to the bank during periods when dividends were paid (for which they would receive income from the bank equal to the dividend and any appreciation in the value of the stock). Citi, again as usual, was allowed to neither admit nor deny wrongdoing. A year later, in the summer of 2010, Citigroup agreed to pay $75 million to settle SEC charges that it failed to disclose more than $40 billion in exposure to subprime mortgages to its investors. Its former chief investment officer and former investor relations director agreed to pay personal fines of $100,000 and $80,000, respectively, for drafting and approving misleading statements at a time when investors were hanging on every word from the bank as to what the losses might be from toxic bank holdings. When these were later revealed, they cost former CEO Charles Prince his job in November 2007. Citi eventually lost $30 billion on the assets and required more government support than any other bank. It was not alone in obscuring its holdings to investors. Such instances touch the sort of morally questionable and illegal practices of the period, which, for the most part, governments were not interested in delving into too deeply while they were rescuing these same firms from their own mistakes and dishonest dealings. Critics considered the SEC charge of unintentional fraud to be relatively minor given what Citigroup and others had done.

The Debate Over Domestic Financial Reforms

In November 2008 the nine biggest participants in the derivatives market created the CDS Dealers Consortium lobby in pursuit of their interests. In chapter 4 the victory of these institutions in preventing the regulation of derivatives was described. They were no more interested in disclosure and transparency when efforts were made once again to regulate their very profitable business. Nor were the hedge funds. Their chief lobbyist for the Managed Funds Association, Darcy Bradbury, a former assistant treasury secretary and senior vice president of D. E. Shaw, the group that paid Larry Summers so well when he was no longer secretary of the treasury and before he was Obama's top economic adviser, lobbied to convince the administration that hedge funds did not present systemic risk to the economy and so should not be included in legislation. Other segments of the financial sector had their lobbyists at work to kill, stall, and water down proposed legislation. Securities and investment firms gave over $150 million in political contributions in 2007 and 2008, according to Federal Election Commission data. The top five, which had been treated so generously by the government—Goldman Sachs, Citigroup, Bank of America, JPMorgan Chase, and Credit Suisse—gave away or spent in lobbying over $50 million. Over the previous decade, financial interests contributed more than $77 million to members of the House Financial Services Committee alone according to the Center for Responsive Politics.

Close supervision lowers potential profits for major players, who logically resist such constraint. In one form or another, this contradiction is always at the center of conflicts over financial regulation. It echoes through the history of the nation. It is never resolved and reflects conflict of interest, which is the central contradiction of the organization of finance in a capitalist economy. Within our system the question is always where the line is drawn to favor freedom for financial institutions and restraints on that freedom in the interest of stability and consumer-friendly rules. The Obama administration's initial strategy can best be described as an accommodationist minimalism. It preferred to use market incentives to give the financial institutions a push in the right direction. Whether such nudge strategies (Thaler and Sunstein 2009) would work remained to be seen, since in a Minsky perspective the buildup to the next crisis comes in a period of overconfidence and so a new overextension that is not conventionally visible is not nudged away. The desire was to confine reform to "market-oriented" solutions in contradistinction to restructuring the industry and criminal prosecutions of those who had broken the law to discourage potential criminals stepping so blatantly over the line in the future.

President Obama explained his philosophy to those who worried that government was taking on too much and controlling too much, which should be left to the market: "I think the irony . . . is that I actually would like to see a relatively light touch when it comes to government. . . . You set up some rules of the road, ensure transparency and openness, guard against huge systemic risk that will lead . . . government potentially having to step in, to avoid a depression, and then let entrepreneurs and individual businesses compete and do what they do." The administration was doing more because it inherited a mess. It would, the president said, clean it up, lay down "rules of the road," and step back. He insisted he did not want to run any bank (or automobile company). The question, though, was whether the light touch would work. Could a set of reforms that would have prevented the last crisis be expected? By such an essential criterion it turned out there was reason for pessimism.

In terms of the mainstream discussions, there were three positions on financial crisis resolution that carried over to the regulatory reform discussion.

Two of these have been described by Charles Wyplosz (2008) as the "Larry Summers 'don't scare off the investors' view" and the "Willem Buiter 'they-ran-into-a-wall-with-their eyes-open' anti-bailout view." The logic of the Summers perspective is to not intrude too seriously on bank profitability by imposing demanding structural reform on banks' size, structure, and ability to make money. The logic of the position attributed to Buiter is there must be serious controls and industry reorganization. The third approach to reform is the argument that intrusive government and its regulatory handcuffs were responsible for the crisis. It was expressed by Richard Shelby, the ranking Republican on the Senate Banking Committee, when he offered his view of the Dodd-Frank Act: "This bill promises more government, more costs, slower economic growth and fewer jobs" (Politi 2010).

The first approach is the Wall Street–friendly stance of the Obama "propeller head" economic advisers. The second reflects much of the angry public. The third is the conservative, free-market approach characteristic of the Republicans, "blue dog" Democrats, and supported by many conservative neoclassical economists. All three are found in the legislative approach that attempts to put in safeguards to protect against a future breakdown of the financial system without overly discommoding the banks and the investor class, and not overly regulating finance. While regulators are given power to take over and wind down financial firms, it is not clear how, or if, they could use it; that would depend on the political mood and the conditions of a future financial crisis. Whether the FDIC, which was given authority, would have the competence to run such a megabank in resolution is itself an open question. Dodd-Frank, which affected almost every aspect of the U.S. financial services industry, was over 2,300 pages. It was both complicated and vague in its provisions, which would be interpreted by regulators charged to enforce it. The law, passed the Senate on July 15, 2010, and sent to the president, who celebrated its signing the next week, left hundreds of specific rules to be decided by regulators and dozens of important issues to be studied before further action was taken.

By the end of the summer, the SEC was announcing some of the hundred rules for derivative trading, hedge funds, and credit rating firms it had plans for, while the Commodity Futures Trading Commission would be writing about sixty rules, the Fed fifty or so, down through the alphabet of agencies involved in financial regulation. What the legislation would mean in practice depended on the outcome of these processes, the influence of lobbyists who would continue to negotiate with the regulators as they formulated the rules, and importantly the funding for the enforcement to follow. By that early date, banks had already developed ways around restrictions placed on their ability to extract fees from credit card holders that Congress had just mandated. For example, they pushed so-called professional cards to a classification that does not require the twenty-one days after a billing statement before a payment is due and allows them to raise rates on existing balances if late payment is made to another creditor and to change credit agreements without giving advanced notice—things banned under the Credit Card Accountability and Responsibility Disclosure Act of 2009. In pushing these cards to small businesses, banks obviously did not mention such matters in the large type of the come-ons.

Dodd-Frank created a Consumer Financial Protection Bureau that the law stated was to ensure that consumers had timely and understandable information with which to make responsible decisions in financial transactions and to protect them against unfair, deceptive, and abusive practices while promoting fair competition in the financial services industry. A number of Republican House members found this another instance of government takeover of the marketplace. Representative Blaine Luetkemeyer of Missouri said the agency was "the last thing our lenders need," Robert Dolt of Illinois ridiculed the "theoretical protection" the agency would provide, and Sean Duffy from Wisconsin complained that the agency "could trump safety and soundness" (Milbank 2011). Elizabeth Warren, the Harvard law professor and consumer advocate who was the driving force behind the creation of the new agency, explained that Americans "are looking for an honest marketplace." They want to know the real cost of financial products and the consequences of their decisions "and not be blindsided by expensive hidden fees, interest rate changes, or payment shocks." As things stood, she said, "the lender that wins a customer's business isn't always the one that offers the product that best matches the consumer's needs and preferences" (Warren 2011).

On the larger issues of the degree of freedom of finance—the conflict between private interests and societal security—the strategy of the Obama team was to undertake broad discussion among significant players and recommend what it considered consensus rules consistent with its own preferences, but, as the president said, rules that do not "tilt at windmills." The administration would choose its fights and not use its limited power on what it saw as secondary issues. However, many of these presumably secondary issues were quite important. The administration did not go after important legal loopholes when this would inflame opposition, nor did it forbid practices or propose strict regulation of financial instruments that special interests would expend significant fire power to defend.

Paul Volker, who had opposed repeal of the Glass-Steagall separation of investment and commercial banking legislation, had not been reappointed by President Reagan, who replaced him as Fed chairman with Alan Greenspan as chair of the Federal Reserve System. Volker supported Barack Obama in 2008, giving him some needed credibility in the financial community. The new president appointed Volker to head an Economic Recovery Advisory Board. From this position Volker proposed forbidding commercial banks to engage in proprietary trading, taking a far stronger stand on regulating Wall Street than Geithner and Summers did. He was critical of the banks using internal units as hedge funds and sponsoring and capitalizing other hedge funds and private equity firms. The idea was to wall off investment banks, which would be free to buy and sell securities on their own account with investor money but not be bailed out by taxpayers if they ran into trouble, from commercial banks, which would not be allowed to speculate with depositor monies. In Volker's view, if the government allowed these large, multifunction entities to exist, sooner or later, no matter what regulatory attempts to restrict them were made, they would get in trouble again. "The banks are there to serve the public. These other activities create conflict of interest," he said. The Obama White House did not like this proposal but eventually was forced to back it since the president's advisers had such little credibility with the public and their mild, Wall Street–friendly reform proposals were costing Obama support.

Unlike Geithner and Summers, Volker was closer to those critics who understood that there had been a crisis of "an entire architecture of financial dysfunctionalities." (The term is from Dymski 2010.) The administration avoided larger questions concerning the purpose of the financial system and the distance between the existing regime and a socially optimal one. Volker (2010:12) suggests four questions that are of social importance but were not part of the public conversation reflecting the administration's deliberations: Has the contribution of the modern world of finance to economic growth become so critical as to support remuneration to its participants beyond any earlier experience and expectation? Does the past profitability of and the value added by the financial industry really now justify profits amounting to as much as 40 percent of profits by all U.S. corporations? Can the enormous rise in the use of derivatives, complicated options, and highly structured financial instruments really have made a parallel contribution to economic efficiency? If so, does analysis of economic growth and productivity over the past decade or so indicate visible acceleration of benefits flowing down to the average American worker, who even before the crisis had enjoyed no increase in real income?

Volker was skeptical regarding the ability of the limited financial reform proposals (and the law as it emerged from Congress) to adequately answer these questions. He was convinced of the importance of ending too-big-to-fail, requiring the breakup of megabanks, and moving the most aggressive strategies to firms that play with their investors' money and would not be bailed out in the event of failure. Another benefit of making publicly insured institutions smaller and limiting their activities would be that their political influence over the writing of laws that set the terms of what they are allowed to do and how regulations are administered would be reduced.

As for the "Volker Rule," due in significant measure to White House lobbying, the Dodd-Frank bill, instead of forbidding banks from investing in hedge funds and private equity funds, allows them to invest up to 3 percent of their capital in such funds so long as this is done by separate subsidiaries. The way the law is written, there is some uncertainty as to how restrictive the rules will prove to be. The Dodd-Frank legislation did mandate that most derivatives be traded through clearinghouses. But it is not clear that this would not exacerbate financial crises. Exchanges could be one more too-big-to-fail institution requiring a bailout since it is in the nature of a failure of derivatives that there is a discontinuity—a jump-to-default when a company (say, Lehman) suddenly goes bust. A huge amount of money would be needed to make good on contracts. As Mark Roe (2010) writes, "Regulators worried that an interconnected Bear or AIG could drag down the economy. Imagine what an interconnected clearinghouse's failure could do."

Regulators will decide which derivatives must go through clearinghouses and how long traders have to disclose pricing information. There is exemption for nonfinancial companies using derivatives to hedge business risk. How extensively banks would have to spin off derivative operations was up to regulators. There was a sense that the Volker Rule had been so diluted that observers such as Nouriel Roubini thought restrictions on derivative trading are not meaningful. Others were cheered that the restrictions were stronger than had been expected a year earlier when the jockeying began. Indeed, judgments as to the success of regulatory efforts are made on two grounds: what seems politically possible at a certain point in time, and what is needed. The two criteria usually produce different conclusions.

The Obama administration saw higher capital requirements for systemically significant financial institutions as preferable to making the effort to impose structural reform on the size and composition of the industry. It was this weapon that made it into the legislation. The problem with this is, as Raghuram Rajan (2009:9) writes, "A number of banks went directly from being well capitalized to default. Part of the problem lies with the accounting, which allows banks to hide various losses. But the bulk of the problem lies with the sheer magnitude of the losses in a systemic crisis. . . . The levels of capital required to protect banks fully from failure would be extraordinary."

Some hedge funds might be included among companies that regulators designate as "systematically important" and so would face, along with other such institutions, stricter leverage, liquidity, and capital requirements and be required to draw up a living will for their dismemberment in the case that regulators seize them to prevent contagion, which could threaten the economy with a collapse. Other hedge and private equity funds would also face some degree of SEC scrutiny. That federal regulators for the first time would have the clear responsibility to break up big firms that pose a grave risk to the financial system (via the Kanjorski Amendment) is potentially exceedingly important, depending on whether regulators in the next crisis use it and are effective in their actions.

While breaking up banks that were thought too big to be allowed to fail was a widely applauded reform measure, the Obama economists wanted to preserve what was seen as the comparative advantage of the giant American financial institutions, believing they could impose better, stricter regulation. This argument is not supported by the evidence. There is a need to stop allowing banks to be too big to fail. The Kanjorski Amendment included in the Dodd-Frank legislation gives federal regulators the right (and the responsibility) to break up the megabanks when they pose a "grave risk" to financial stability. Whether regulators actually would take such steps will be seen.

One would expect when times are good and the future looks bright that the banks would not only find new ways around capital restrictions but prevail on regulators to relax standards and once again set up shadow vehicles. Shifting to unregulated arm's-length subsidiaries and finding new routes to regulatory arbitrage is standard practice and would intensify as soon as capital requirements were binding on profit opportunities. The better alternative was to downsize the banks that were insured by the government and to narrow the risks they would be allowed to take. This would make banks less profitable. On the one hand it might be better if banks were downsized and there was less investor interest in what could become once again a rather dull business. However, finance will seek ways to peel off the most profitable aspects and embed them in nonbank, or at least less regulated or unregulated structures. Policy makers face an unpleasant decision: either make banks that enjoy public protection safer and face the prospect of the most speculative aspects of finance moving to less transparent and less regulated or even unregulated institutions, or permit the banks to continue to engage in such activities and try and regulate them in ways that protect the public more but are not intrusive to the point of driving activities away from the regulatory purview. The third alternative—serious regulation of all financial activity that exposes the economy to systemic problems—is the best choice but demands a far greater control footprint for government. It is politically the most difficult.

There was debate over which financial institutions would be deemed systemically significant and so subject to greater restrictions and oversight. The FDIC, charged with taking over and winding down such financial firms, wanted a far larger number of banks, hedge funds, and insurance companies to be monitored and restrained. The Fed and Treasury saw the need to watch only a handful of megabank holding companies. It was widely suspected they would act to save these pillars of Wall Street, which would be seen as too important and interconnected to be closed down. At Basel there was agreement to make those declared systemically important financial institutions (SIFIs) hold an extra 1–2.5 percent equity above Basel III's 7 percent core capital on risk-weighted assets.

Simon Johnson and James Kwak (2010) suggest that the United States limit commercial banks to no more than the equivalent of 4 percent of GDP and investment banks to 2 percent of GDP, which would force the largest six banks to substantially downsize. Haldane (2010), reviewing the literature, concludes that the maximum efficient scale of banking "could be relatively modest. Perhaps it lies below $100 billion. Experience suggests there is at least a possibility of diseconomies lying beyond that point." The 145 banks whose assets in 2008 together totaled more than $100 billion accounted for 85 percent of the assets of the world's top 1,000 banks (ranked by Tier I capital). These 145 banks received over 90 percent of the support extended by the government during the global financial crisis. Breaking them up would increase competition in the industry, which would lower the economic rents the banks currently receive and reduce the cost of any future bailout for taxpayers.

The law also instructs the SEC to order all companies to adopt claw-back policies to recoup as many as three years of ill-gotten pay from current and former employees after a material restatement, even if the individual was not to blame but only passively benefited. Companies are to adopt and enforce such claw-back policies. Again, it remains to be seen whether companies in fact are active in this regard. It is possible that such awards will escape reconsideration and that deferred bonuses may continue to be made on generous assumptions favorable to executives. A review by the Fed in the summer of 2010 found that many banks had "deficient" pay procedures that did not discourage "imprudent risk." Kenneth Feinberg, the Obama administration's special master for executive compensation, found that in late 2008 the major financial companies paid out more than $2 billion in bonuses and other payments to their most important employees; nearly 80 percent of the sum, in his view, was unmerited. One company handed out bonuses equal to a quarter of its bailout. Feinberg had no authority to claw back the money.

Finding effective ways to change incentives is not easy. It is partly a matter of regulatory courage and in some measure the reluctance of legislators and other elected official and advisers to actually adopt and enforce measures that would make a difference. An approach not adopted, for example, is to require banks to automatically convert debt to equity in the event of serious repayment problems. This would dilute the value of existing ownership claims and concentrate the mind of owners to limit overly risky strategies. Such a step would be triggered by objective measures such as the bank's capital ratio falling below some benchmark and would encourage banks to stay better capitalized.

It made sense to establish procyclical regulation of banks, forcing them to hold more capital in expansionary periods for protection in the downturn (Hart and Zingales 2010). This did not make it into the legislation, but, if it had, it is not clear that regulators would confidently recognize the need for decisive action or be willing to stand up to those who would benefit from continued ability to hold lower capital and leverage it to excess. The Minskyan policy logic of such policies is in tune with an understanding that regulators must pay attention when it looks like "a great moderation" and "this time it is different."

The Obama administration suggested that the Federal Reserve be charged with being the watchdog on the lookout for "systemic risk." Many questioned continued reliance on the Fed as the centrally important regulator, pointing to its past practice and ties to the banks it regulated. Ben Bernanke had been wrong fairly consistently in his forecasts. In late March 2007 he told the Joint Economic Committee of Congress that the subprime crisis would be contained and have no impact on other sectors of the economy, and he continued to make optimistic forecasts that missed what was happening. Two years later, when asked when the recession would end, he said, "My forecasting ability on this recession has been about as good as the win-loss percentage of the Washington Nationals." (They had finished in last place the previous season.)

Bernanke, an outstanding mainstream economist with access to any opinions he might seek and backed by a talented team of researchers at the Federal Reserve, could hardly promise accurate forecasting. Given the Fed's past record, it would seem better to limit risk taking than presume the Fed would detect problems and be able to effectively address them only on an ad hoc basis. Congress had its doubts. While in the final legislation the Fed's power increased, Congress set up a council of regulators to give others a voice in policy deliberations. Critics of giving the Fed more responsibility pointed out that in the past its failure to foresee systemic problems did not make it a good candidate for the job. Simon Johnson (2009) writes, "[I]n principle the Fed had exactly this kind of leadership role before—and under both Alan Greenspan and Ben Bernanke it was a reckless cheerleader and facilitator for the unsustainable real estate boom." As he argues, "If the Fed had been stronger before, the crisis now would be worse."

The New Deal creation of the Federal Deposit Insurance Corporation and the Fed's adoption of too-big-to-fail protection of big depositors at large banks put an end to the runs on banks so often experienced in the nineteenth-century United States. Yet in 2007–8 there were the functional equivalents of bank runs. These took place in the repurchase agreement market where overnight there were demands for repayment that could not be met. The banks borrowed heavily in the short-term repo market by putting their securitized bonds up as collateral. Data from the New York Federal Reserve district tell us that the primary dealers in Treasury securities (which included four of the five then independent investment banks and several of the investment bank divisions that were part of financial conglomerates) had less than a half trillion dollars in such assets in 1994 but $1.5 trillion in 2000 and about $4.5 trillion in 2008; about half of these were issued by the primary dealers overnight from the 1990s through 2003 and almost two-thirds by mid-2008. Moreover, as the boom built, they used private mortgage-backed securities for up to two-thirds of their collateral just before the crash. The New York Fed Flow of Funds data show that total investment bank liabilities doubled between 2003 and 2007. Without strong enough regulation and regulators who were determined and empowered to limit the extent to which the financial sector could in effect "make money" by financial asset creation, there is no reason to think another financial bubble will not sooner or later occur. Financial reregulation should limit the capacity of the private financial system to make money. The Dodd-Frank financial reform bill does not do this.

When financial products declined in value with the start of the subprime crisis, the banks, which packaged, sold, and held securitized debt obligations, could no longer count on repurchase agreements as their main source of funds. Selling dicey assets on the market to raise money pushed CDO values downward. Rather than acknowledge the state of things, the banks preferred to hold on to them, hope for a future rise in value, and access central bank and government funds. To avoid the promiscuous use of this source of credit, it was proposed that lenders be forced to take a haircut, a write-down in the value of such debt as part of a resolution mechanism, rather than rescue efforts pricing these assets at unrealistically high values.

Alternatively, there were proposals that the government insure all such assets to return confidence to the market. Imposing a tax on their use would increase the cost of using repos, which would act as a disincentive. The banks, of course, do not like the thought of their major source of funds becoming less viable for them, and purchasers of derivatives complained that even a small penalty for their use would kill the market, which existed on slim margins. The social risk/private reward trade-off is evident in almost all such reform proposals, as is the power of Wall Street in forestalling their implementation.

Beyond Dodd-Frank, there were other initiatives that could have a significant impact. All too aware that financial statements were not reflecting actual asset and liabilities of the megabanks and other corporations, both regulators and investors found it difficult to assess risks. Markets not functioning properly produce unease and fear. A coalition of businesses, accountants, regulators, and not-for-profit groups (including such heavy weights as HSBC, Tata, the big four accounting firms, top corporate financial directors, and senior business school professors) under the name of the International Integrated Reporting Committee sought agreement on overhauling international company reporting. The endeavor, supported by the International Accounting Standards Board, the US Financial Accounting Standards Board, and the International Organization of Securities Commissions, was one of a number of efforts to restore trust by established players.

Dodd-Frank has little to say about hedge funds and private equity, which, while they did not cause the crisis, did do a great deal of damage, as argued in chapter 4, imposing short-term criteria and debt burdens on productive corporations, forcing them into debt, and depriving them of their ability to invest in long-term growth. As major players in the financialization that characterizes the SSA, they escaped with only minimal reporting requirements. The megabanks, such as JPMorgan Chase, which runs the largest hedge fund in the world (as measured by assets managed), can accommodate to changes mandated by Dodd-Frank. As Nomi Prins (2010:A12) notes, "since private-equity funds can both invest in hedge funds and do anything a hedge fund does . . . hedge funds could just change their name to avoid registration or information sharing." Neither hedge funds nor private equity need change the way they do business.

The import of the interconnectedness of markets, in which wholesale funding came in the form of overnight loans that provided the perception of liquidity yet could break down forcing the Federal Reserve and other agencies to step in when panic strikes, creates a reality that such separation is untenable. Certainly the decision to draw a line between the regulated banking system, which the government stood ready to rescue, and the shadow banking sector, which would not be given access to official credit and liquidity and rescued, crumbled with the Great Recession. Such a separation is difficult, if not impossible, to maintain because of the way financial markets are now structured. As Sandra Krieger explains,

> The search for yield by investors without proper regard or pricing for the risk inherent in the underlying collateral is a common theme in shadow banking. The long intermediation chains inherent in shadow banking lend themselves to this—they obscure information to investors about the underlying creditworthiness of collateral. Like a game of telephone where information is destroyed in every step, the transformation of loans into securities, securities into repo contracts, and repo contracts into private money makes it quite difficult for investors to understand the ultimate risk of their exposure. (2011:6)

As a result, too much risk is taken on by market participants, including banks, which often backstop such credit creation. Since so much credit is created outside of the regulated banking system, officials have lost control and end up having to extend protection well beyond those institutions they formally oversee.

When regulators impose greater restrictions on the institutions they do regulate, this only gives shadow institutions greater comparative cost advantages and still more credit is created beyond the regulated sector, but tied to it. This is the reason the TARP funding of bank rescues was only a small part of the total funding the Fed felt needed for the rescue effort. The procyclical volatility of credit creation is the problem that is not yet being realistically addressed. Unless investors face real losses and governments accept the consequences in economic dislocation, allowing widespread losses as a way to discipline players, crises may grow beyond the capacities of governments to rescue economies in financial crises.

Reforms under Dodd-Frank tried to establish procedures whereby large financial firms, whether called banks or not, that are "systematically important financial institutions" (inevitably SIFs) are identified and subject to closer cross-border supervision. It was left to the regulators to identify such institutions requiring intense scrutiny. The law allows them to be put out of business and their boards of directors fired, and the shareholders to lose everything. The government would pay some of the debt to prevent contagion to the rest of the system. It remains to be seen how, or even whether, this will work.

Barney Frank declared that he would give the bill that bore his name an A-minus "when you consider that six months ago people were saying the Volker rule had no chance." This sort of political grading reflected the congressman's assessment of how difficult achieving reform had been. President Obama celebrated the legislation as the toughest since the 1930s, asserting that the reform will foster innovation and improve stability without sapping the vitality of the American financial system. Those who had hoped for more serious control of Wall Street saw the legislation as a fig leaf. It did not address too-big-to-fail and would only marginally change the incentives that had led to the financial meltdown. It had significantly watered down the original concept that Volker had proposed to totally separate banks, which would be eligible for government protection, and speculative activities, which would be separated off and not protected with public guarantees, although it was not clear how the new rules would work and what regulators would decide should count as capital and proprietary trading.

The Republicans had almost all rejected the reform bill in its totality as unwarranted government interference and control of financial markets. Senator Richard Shelby, ranking Republican on the Finance Committee, declared the bill would create "vast new bureaucracies with little accountability" and "undermines the competitiveness of the American economy." Other criticisms included that it would raise the cost of borrowing, discourage innovation, make lots of work for lawyers, and throttle the industry. Because of near unanimous Republican opposition and the fact that the Senate continues to operate under self-chosen rules that allow forty-one members to thwart the will of the majority by declaring they will filibuster legislation, the Democratic leadership was forced to make concessions to muster the sixty votes needed to pass Dodd-Frank. These included removing provisions that would have affected Boston-based asset-management companies and mutual funds and taxation of the financial sector, to get the vote of Massachusetts' junior senator Scott Brown. Other concessions were adopted to win the two Maine Republican senators, together the three Republicans voting for the bill.

The Democratic leadership also had to remove provisions favored by a majority of senators from their own party, such as Byron Dorgan's amendment to outlaw naked credit default swaps (buying such protection against loss without owning the reference entity on which the swap is written and understood by those supporting the measure as a usage akin to buying fire insurance on your neighbor's house and then lighting the match). CDSs invite the sort of plays that Goldman Sachs was shown to have sponsored, assembling portfolio products so that its savvy customers could buy protection against their likely failure. Senator Sheldon Whitehouse's amendment, which the Democratic leadership jettisoned, would have repealed federal preemption and allowed states to set their own limits on consumer interest rates charged by banks, limiting usurious charges. Many economists favored Senator Sherrod Brown's amendment to break up too-big-to-fail institutions, but it also failed in the effort to get a bill passed with some needed conservative support.

At the same time as legislators were making proposals for future reform, both parties were holding dozens of fund-raisers on Wall Street. Wall Street was the second leading source of funds for all candidates for Congress during this period when financial reform was being debated (behind the health care industry, which was giving even more as legislators considered health care reform). In the early part of the 2010 election cycle, in 2009, the securities and investment industry gave $34 million: 62 percent went to Democrats and 37 percent to Republicans, according to the Center for Responsive Politics. As many on Wall Street grew upset at the regulations being discussed by the Democrats, giving shifted. In January and February 2010 the political action committees run by Goldman Sachs, J. P. Morgan, Morgan Stanley, and Citigroup donated twice as much money to the Republicans, sending a strong message.

The reform debate had been particularly lucrative for the fourteen freshmen who served on the House Financial Services Committee and who raised funds more than 50 percent greater than others in the congressional freshman class did and so were more competitive in their reelection campaigns. They tended to be the more vulnerable and so received help from their party's strategists. The five largest banks together had 130 lobbyists, including key former staffers for Senate and House committee chairs and key members who crafted the legislation. In the three months leading to the final bill, the banks spent over $6 million on lobbying. Over the longer haul, the large Wall Street firms were dominant contributors. Goldman Sachs from 1989 through 2009, political action committees and employees were the number one source of contributions to the Democratic Party (over $20 million) and the fourth largest source for Republicans ($11 million), again according to the Center for Responsive Politics. Weak regulation is perhaps not unrelated to the investments of Wall Street firms in politics and politicians.

When the House-Senate conference committee agreed upon the final bill, bank stock prices rose because, as the *Wall Street Journal* headline put it, "Biggest Banks Manage to Dodge Some Bullets." Peter Eavis's analysis and commentary in the *Journal* was headlined "A Bank Overhaul Too Weak to Hail." There was, of course, as described above, a broader range of opinion. The legislation was indeed the toughest reform legislation since the 1930s, but this was because there had been little legislation to strengthen regulation in the intervening period. Indeed, for the previous three decades banking reform had all been deregulatory, deregulating finance. The key provision of the law, the so-called Volker Rule, which forbids banks from investing in hedge funds or engaging in proprietary trading, had been watered down, as had the Lincoln amendment to force banks to bundle their derivative operations onto separate entities. Much of what the law did deal with were "distractions: they do little to rein in systemic risk" (*Financial Times* 2010b:6). Completing financial regulatory reform, the editorial writers thought, "is less a final victory than an opening shot in a long struggle." The political power of financial players should not be underestimated.

Can Economists Do Better?

The divisions within the economics profession continue. Some continue to hold what may seem to many as naïve faith in free financial markets. Others work pragmatically to develop better forecasting models of when crises can be expected and proposals as to what actions might be taken. Once the importance of the credit cycle is acknowledged, as Borio and Lowe (2002:22) write, "the central bank might opt for higher interest rates than are justified simply on the basis of the short-term inflation outlook if there is clear sign of financial imbalances, such as if credit growth is rapid and asset prices are rising quickly." Rapid credit growth has been found to be a leading indicator of a coming crisis (Eichengreen and Arteta 2002).

What may look like a period of great moderation, healthy growth, and the absence of inflation may be the prologue to a financial crisis. The Minskyan idea that beyond a certain threshold productive growth in finance becomes speculative excess and then Ponzi financing is useful to economists looking at this cumulative process for signals intimating an impending crisis (Kaminsky and Reinhart 1999). Data sets on equity prices and property values in a sample of industrial countries compiled by economists at the Bank for International Settlements (Borio and Lowe 2002) capture this cumulative impact of rapid asset price growth, producing bubbles and crises in a manner consistent with Minsky's model. McKinsey & Company researchers (Buehler, Mazingo, and Samandari 2010) find that the ratio of tangible common equity—that portion of equity which is neither preferred equity nor intangible assets—to risk-weighted assets outperforms all other measures as a predictor of future bank distress. Better forecasting and greater safeguards built into the system can reduce the cost of crises.

Regulators are aware they need effective ways to track the cross-jurisdictional movement of funds and risk. Such data demands are a logical outcome of concern with macroprudential regulation (Crockett 2000; Bernanke 2008). They require expanded access to more real-time data. Regulators cannot simply look at individual bank activities in single jurisdictions but must consider consolidated global balance sheets and have access to off-balance-sheet information. Tracing connections should be expanded from systemically important banks to institutional interconnections with hedge funds and private equity, currency positions, and rollover risks in repo markets. The movement of financial activities from regulated to shadow banking institutions requires expanding the realm of regulation to all potentially dangerous financial practices by firms, whatever they are called. It is encouraging that members of the Financial Stability Board created to deal with such global issues understand what is at stake. The board is charged with developing and implementing strong regulatory and supervisory policies. As the group's chair, Mario Draghi (2010) states, "The systemically important institutions will need enhanced supervision—supervision which is broader, more effective and more intrusive." Such awareness of the interconnectedness of financial markets, extending from the provision of household credit to international capital flows, requires attention to the correlations among disparate markets and the need to prevent concentrated power and to limit leverage. It also raises the contradiction between democratic decision making and financial market imperatives, as well as, at a deeper level, the acceptability of electoral outcomes so heavily dependent on money politics.

Academic experts have explored the requirements of more effective regulation, explaining why detailed data need to be gathered on specific categories of financial products, and not only from regulated banks (Hanson, Kashyap, and Stein 2010). Key regulators need more extensive data to understand the complex interconnections between financial firms and markets, the makeup of liabilities as well as assets, and the currency composition of instruments traded (Hannoun 2010). There is remarkable consensus among more far-sighted regulators that they need to consider the entire financial system. Globalization of finance means that regulators must assess the worldwide balance sheets of sectors of finance such as pension funds and insurance companies along with off-balance-sheet entities. Experts can design better intelligence-gathering systems and build models highlighting credit conditions to anticipate potential crisis situations. Regulators can develop a better understanding of what they should do nationally and globally, but without governmental support their success will be limited when they take on powerful financial institutions.

In the United States the omnibus financial reform enacted in the summer of 2010 established an Office of Financial Research (OFR) with authority to force financial firms, including banks, hedge funds, brokerage firms, and private equity, to turn over confidential information under the wide definition "all data necessary"—and even to tell these firms how they must report data. With the power to scrutinize the entire system, the OFR has the potential to see dangerous financial trends, allowing preemptive action to be taken. Whether it would dare use its power is to be seen. The OFR will be part of a regulatory order controlled by the Treasury and the Fed, which can both be expected to remain under Wall Street's sway. Moreover, politics will limit the extent to which stricter regulation will be possible.

Leading up to the election, the financial sector dramatically shifted its contributions to the Republicans. The election of a Republican majority in the House a few months after the passage of Dodd-Frank brought Spencer Bachus of Alabama to the chair of the Financial Services Committee. Bachus described Dodd-Frank as "a massive intrusion of federal government into the lives of every American" (Gapper 2010). He made clear his desire to repeal important parts of the law. Bachus opposed the provisions that empowered the government to seize and liquidate large, troubled financial institutions, favored controlling the power of the Consumer Financial Protection Bureau, and urged reconsideration of the limits on credit card fees approved in the previous session of congress. He warned he would use his power to restrict the budget of the SEC and the Commodity Trading Commission. Scott Garrett, the new chair of the subcommittee overseeing the SEC, made clear he did not favor increasing the regulator's budget when "everybody is being asked to cut back" (Braithwaite and Scannell 2011). Mary Schapiro, SEC chair, said she needed eight hundred more staff to write and police new rules, including investor protection and risk management. She would not get the funding. Instead, among other impacts, enforcement officials had to postpone taking testimony in investigating alleged Ponzi schemes of the Madoff sort because the budget constrained their travel. The financial industry expected there to be a "breather from all the excess regulation and Congressional legislation," as one industry spokesperson stated. "Our members are ready for common sense to reappear" (Schwartz 2010). The big banks asserted that tighter regulation reduces the availability of credit and promotes unnecessarily slow growth. Academic research finds "these arguments either fallacious or irrelevant, or else . . . unsupported by empirical experience or by adequate theory" (Admati et al. 2010:1). But it is not academic judgments that count most.

The power relations in our capitalist democracy are such that adequate regulation is difficult to legislate because it limits profit-making opportunities, and, if put into law, is hard to enforce effectively. It is a depressing thought that effective financial regulation at both the national and international levels will have to await a worsening situation. More substantial reform will in all likelihood accompany broader shifts in public philosophy and interpretations of financial market operations. For a start, this requires ending the extreme financialization and speculation that are at the heart of how the economic surplus is appropriated. The expectation from the perspective of a social structure of accumulation is that such a new financial regime will be accompanied by the coming into being of a new political coalition, new state market understandings, and other significant changes. With years of suboptimal economic performance possibly ahead, it seems relevant and necessary to discuss what might be done of a more radical sort to promote growth. One of the tasks of the final chapter is to look at this important question from a social structure of accumulation perspective.

7

Nations, Globalization, and Financialization

In a society in which the money-maker has no serious rival for repute and honor, the word "practical" comes to mean useful for private gain, and "common sense," the sense to get ahead financially. The pursuit of the moneyed life is the commanding value of the relation to which the influence of other values has declined. So men easily become morally ruthless in the pursuit of money and fast estate-building.

— C. WRIGHT MILLS, 1956

Although I have made a fortune in the financial markets, I now fear that untrammeled intensification of laissez-faire capitalism and the spread of market values to all areas of life is endangering our open and democratic society.

— GEORGE SOROS, 1997

America's problems at first produced widespread *schadenfreude* from those who had long been lectured by Washington. In his opening remarks to the UN General Assembly in September 2008, Secretary General Ban Ki-Moon spoke for many when he declared there was a need for "less uncritical faith in the 'magic' of markets," an obvious riposte to Ronald Reagan's announcement three decades earlier at the dawn of the neoliberal ascendancy. President Reagan told the General Assembly that the United States would not make redistributive concessions to poor countries. Instead of looking for paternalistic handouts, they should put their faith in "the magic of the marketplace." The secretary general was signaling that the world crisis was due to undeserved faith in deregulation and free markets. About the same time the German finance minister told his parliament, "The US will lose its status as the superpower of the world financial system. . . . When we look back 10 years from now, we will see 2008 as a fundamental rupture." He praised German financial sobriety.

It was soon clear that even if the crisis was born in the USA the world economy was too integrated and financial practices too similar elsewhere to avoid a broader reading of the situation. Much to the distaste of many Germans, their government was soon contributing serious money to save the "spendthrift" Greeks from budgetary disaster. What many angry taxpayers did not understand was that it was German and other foreign banks that had lent so heavily to Greece and were now being bailed out. The reality that the five most heavily indebted euro zone members owed German banks on the order of 900 billion euros was a sobering thought. Germany's policy makers saw a need to protect the weaker debtor countries as a matter of European solidarity (and less publicly to save their own banks). Taxpayers were inclined to vote out politicians ready to give their hard-earned money to wastrels. The cost of insuring against the risk of default by European governments by early 2010 was higher than for the top investment-grade private corporations for the first time, if one compared the combined risk default of the fifteen developed European nations and Markit's iTraxx Europe index of Europe's top 125 investment grade companies.

Once the crisis broke, the issue was who would pay. Different groups saw their own interests as reflecting the correct and necessary policy response. The mantra of the German government, the European Central Bank, and others was "no default, no bailout, no exit," which Arvind Subramanian (2010) explains meant "European private-sector holders of Greek debt would be spared any pain (no default). The European taxpayer would be protected (no bail-out). And European companies would be sheltered because Greece could not devalue its currency (no exit)." The Greeks were to accept a punishing austerity because they had made their own bed and would have to lie in it. It was a Greek problem, and they were told to do what Americans were soon to be told: cut social spending, fire government workers, cut promised benefits, and accept the rest of a familiar package that places adjustment on working people.

To many Greeks things were seen as more complicated. When the new socialist government came into office, it found that the previous conservative party regime had created a public deficit two to three times what was publicly acknowledged. The conservatives were able to hide this with dishonest bookkeeping in significant measure thanks to Goldman Sachs, which had sold them derivatives that essentially mortgaged the country's airports and highways to raise money to reduce the debt, and other expedients that hid loans and provided off-market swaps to put more money into the government's hands. If one viewed only half the transaction, the government's position looked fairly good. This was because, as structured by clever folks at Goldman, the other half was hidden and not acknowledged in official deficit and debt calculations. When the new government revealed this, Greece, as part of the euro zone, could not devalue its monetary unit, the traditional means of adjusting an external imbalance, and so was forced into a punishing austerity.

As the new government looked for sources of tax revenues, it sent inspectors to visit crowded marinas near Athens to see who owned huge power boats and compared their ability to pay for them with the income taxes they declared. It turned out that thousands of wealthy Greeks "forgot" to declare ownership of yachts, swimming pools, and luxury cars, as required on their annual tax forms. The marina registry turned up owners whose declared income would have barely paid for the fuel the boats used. People were declaring incomes that could neither heat their luxury homes nor put gas into their fancy cars. In one wealthy suburb, only 324 residents checked the box on their taxes affirming they owned a swimming pool. The tax authorities, consulting a satellite photo, found 16,974 pools, many behind high gates. For 2009 the Federation of Greek Industries estimated that the government lost perhaps $30 billion to tax evasion. If collected, this would go a long way toward helping address the fiscal crisis. Of course, it was not only the well-to-do who cheated; so did shopkeepers, and the tax collectors were known to take bribes. But those who ran the system were so corrupt, and the wealthy ship owners and lawyers evaded taxes on such a gigantic scale, that they set the tone and made reform difficult.

European Central Bank president Jean-Claude Trichet made clear that help would be extended to the Greeks only after "vigorous steps" were taken to reduce the deficit and "under close and constant EU supervision," raising sovereignty issues. In Athens students and farmers protested and clashed with police. The farmers blockaded the main roads and attempted to drive hundreds of tractors and other farm vehicles to the parliament. Large protest marches demanded that the rich, not the working people, pay. The new prime minister denounced the corruption that pervaded the state and attempted a root-and-branch set of reforms.

The complicated interconnectedness of countries and international banking was dramatized when Iceland, in a sudden spasm of collapsing banks, became overnight a near basket case. The government had privatized banks in 2003 (before that they had been run like government departments in a low-key, unexciting manner), leaving decision making to the free market. By 2007 Iceland's three biggest banks had made loans equal to nine times the size of the country's total economy. Some of these, it turned out, were described as "strange" loans given to government ministers. All three of the large banks counted their owners as their biggest borrowers. One of these leading tycoons borrowed from Kaupthing's Luxembourg unit to acquire a chalet and land in the French Alps. The loan was a fraction of the billions of euros the banks lent their biggest shareholders.

One of the banks, Landsbanki, took in billions in deposits over the Internet from some 400,000 depositors in Britain and Holland alone. At their peak the country's banks had obligations of $250,000 for each of its 300,000 citizens. The Islandic banks had grown twentyfold between 2001 and 2008 until they dwarfed the ability of the country to bail them out. When the three main Icelandic banks failed, they made Moody's list of the eleven biggest bankruptcies in history. The country's average income fell from 160 percent to 80 percent that of the United States. After the collapse, a half a million savers in northern European countries who had been attracted by the high interest rates paid by the Icelandic bank branches in their countries faced losses. London, using antiterrorist legislation, froze the assets of Landsbanki and pushed Iceland "into the abyss," as outraged Icelanders saw it.

Voters in Iceland decisively repudiated the eighteen-year rule of the conservative Independence Party and put into office the interim alliance of the Social Democrat and Left-Green parties. Of course the new government could not do miracles or undo what had happened. The country owed "reparations" larger than the payments demanded of Germany by the French and British after World War I. After Iceland's financial collapse, the market priced the risk of default far higher in countries ranging from the Ukraine to Pakistan and Argentina. The question was asked: What is the difference between Iceland and Ireland? The wags answered, "One letter in six months."

The collapse of the property bubble in Ireland, the former "Celtic Tiger," was indeed painful. Housing prices dropped by over 50 percent, and from its peak in 2007 to the beginning of 2010 Ireland's annualized nominal GDP fell by 26 percent. Irish bankers were to blame as their net liabilities went from 20 percent of GDP in 2003 to over 70 percent by 2008. In September 2008 the government, cronies of the bankers and the large property tycoons, had the taxpayer assume the liabilities of the banks rather than letting senior creditors take their losses. This not only was unfair but put an impossible burden on citizens for generations to come. Young people once again (as they had during the great potato famine) saw no future in the land of their birth and left for Australia and Canada in search of work and new lives. Britain was hardly immune to the pattern of overextended banks and unsustainable borrowing. There was talk of "Reykjavik-on-Thames," and the incoming coalition government, which displaced the discredited

Labour Party in 2010, was soon imposing austerity measures that shocked the country. Some saw the country's own "Iceland problem" best dealt with by shrinking the size of its own financial sector, which had become too big and costly to bail out.

Latvia (formerly the "Baltic Tiger") suffered extreme budget cuts in health and education spending and just about everything else as its gross domestic product declined by a quarter. Loans and cheap credit quadrupled between 2004 and 2008 to nearly equal the country's GDP. Foreign borrowing went, as it did in so many other places, into a real estate bubble of booming construction of homes and commercial buildings, rather than raising export capacity, which would have contributed to debt repayment. Mortgages on properties that had lost easily half their value could exceed incomes, which had dropped precipitously. Debt from excessive foreign currency borrowing prompted antigovernment rioting of dramatic proportions. Latvian protests in the past had involved standing around, singing, and going home. They graduated to rock throwing and Molotov cocktails. A contracting Latvian economy was not good news for Swedish banks, which had lent heavily to the Baltic nations and experienced falling stock values of their own as a result. There was fear expressed in Europe of repercussions if the Lat, the country's currency, was devalued since this could spread panic regarding the possibility of similar devaluations in other weak currencies. Eighty-seven percent of Latvia's debt was in euros and other foreign currencies. It was unpayable, as was the case for many other debtors, and so the question was: Would the good citizens of countries in such predicaments accept the garnishing of their wages for the rest of their lives? Next door in Lithuania, public spending was reduced by 30 percent and public-sector wages by about that. Pensioners' benefits were cut, flooding soup kitchens.

The extent of unpayable debt and the extreme austerity demanded of citizens varied from country to country but pointed to a continuation of severe recession/depression conditions well after recovery from the Great Recession. The generalized debt crisis required major structural transformation of economies and produced political challenges for governments as the contradictory interests of debt holders demanding payment and citizens being told they had to accept a lower standard of living to pay off debts produced wide social unrest. Demonstrators carrying signs reading "We won't pay for your crisis" and suggested that the alternative to saving the banks' top executives and stockholders was nationalization of failed banks and greater taxation of the rich, including serious repatriation of income hidden in tax havens.

What happened to the PIGS—the derisive shorthand for Portugal, Ireland, Greece, and Spain—or the PIIGS, if one included Italy, impacted the euro and the global economy. The dominant explanation, that these countries had been fiscally irresponsible, was hardly universally accurate and tended to ignore that some governments had been able to spend because of asset bubbles that economists and others mistook for solid growth. Countries such as Ireland and Spain to an even greater extent in proportion to the size of their economies had property bubbles larger than the United States had. The property boom had spread prosperity, which gave their governments false confidence in continued economic growth. When the bubble collapsed, so did their economies, and the fiscal position of their governments. The prosperity of the period allowed the export champions, Germany and the Netherlands, to build up large surpluses, which were lent without much due diligence to the likes of Greece and Portugal. The private sector too misjudged what was sustainable. Rather than tending toward equilibrium, markets had overshot. The animal spirits of the herd, encouraged by successful expansion, had gone too far and collapsed. These events called attention to the destabilizing impacts of large capital inflows, loss of competitiveness, and inability to repay debt, factors that have long created financial crises. In the era of heightened globalization, financial product innovation allowed dangerously high leverage, and employment of derivatives obscured the actual debt levels of a number of banks and national governments.

Italy, with the help of JPMorgan, used derivatives to bring its budget seemingly into line, committing future payments that were not booked as liabilities. Perhaps other countries have as well. European banks proved adept at using derivatives too, in their case to avoid capital requirements for buying triple-A-rated structured products that could be counted against Basel II capital requirements, foiling the intent of regulators. These opaque and finally dangerous products were widely funded through repurchase agreements with U.S. money market mutual funds. Such regulatory avoidance came back to haunt large European financial institutions, which needed government bailouts in the wake of the collapse of the value of these securitized obligations. European banks in both current account surplus and deficit countries created large amounts of asset-backed commercial paper and used off-balance-sheet vehicles, funded with short-term debt, to purchase long-term assets. Like the American banks engaging in these practices, they retained credit risk associated with these special investment vehicle assets.

As to Germany's own "sound regulatory system," a parliamentary probe found that the giant financial firm Hypo Real Estate Holdings needed to be nationalized and rescued to the tune of more than 100 billion euros (at the time $143 billion). The Finance Ministry claimed that the fall of U.S.-based Lehman Brothers Holding had dragged Hypo down. Actually a report by Bafin, the German finance regulator, had warned before Lehman fell that Hypo's Dublin-based Depfa Bank was funding Hypo's short-term capital needs using dangerously risky strategies. Hypo's compliance with banking regulations and its skill in managing liquidity and other risks, the regulator's report said, "must be seen as nonexistent." Germany's *Landesbanken*, public banks under the direction of politicians, were sitting on tons of toxic assets. As it turned out, the first banks to collapse and be bailed out by their government were not in the United States but in Germany. IKB Deutsche Industriebank and Sachsen Landesbank, having provided credit guarantees of more than three times their equity capital, failed, revealing serious lack of German "financial sobriety." In the summer of 2009 Gunter Verheugen, the German vice president of the European Commission, declared that his country had shown itself to be "the world champion in risky banking transactions." This was surely a claim too far. There were many plausible competitors for the title of the world champion in risky banking. The Icelandic economy collapsed courtesy of its bankers. The damage Irish Anglo Bank did to Ireland is momentous.

The UN secretary general expressed alarm at the millions of people in poorer countries falling into poverty and asked for more emergency aid from the richer countries, although without much response. Martin Ravallon, director of the Development Research Group at the World Bank, calculated that if it were not for the crisis, the number of impoverished people in the world would have been fifty million lower. Food and Agricultural Organization data showed hunger rates up in every region of the world. Oxfam International reported on the harsh impact of falling trade flows, declining investment, and shrinking remittances. South African finance minister Trevor Manuel warned that such crowding out left emerging markets in a state of "decoupling, derailment, and abandonment." As matters developed, speculative capital continued to enter his economy, but the development needed to put a dent in South Africa's high levels of unemployment and poverty was not forthcoming.

Bond markets demanded that all but a few small advanced economies adopt fiscal tightening, which was expected to go on for at least five years, and for some countries the best part of a decade. Citibank's chief economist warned that "we are getting close to the position where there may no longer be a risk free security (in the sense of free of default risk and with a safe rate of return) anywhere in the world. . . . Triple-A sovereign ratings may in the not too distant future be found only in the history books. . . . The sovereign debt of some leading emerging market economies could be safer than that of any of the G7 countries" (Buiter 2010:10). How many European countries might have to reschedule debt in the same manner as poor Third World economies would be interesting to see.

Surplus-holding nations demanded that debtors be more responsible and live within their means. Debtor nations urged surplus nations to consume more domestically and import more. Looking at financial difficulties arising from imbalances in capital flows and problems with counterparties domiciled elsewhere, there is reason to want international regulation and harmonization of financial regimes across nation states. Yet there is obvious hesitance to give up sovereignty and a natural inclination to privilege the interests, institutions, and norms of one's own country. Given the problems in finding mutual accommodations, it is tempting to seek protection from external dangers behind national walls, but the internationalization of finance makes this difficult. At the same time initiatives to create jobs and promote growth will happen primarily at the level of each national economy acting within a competitive global economy.

While the United States was not directly exposed to European difficulties, serious problems anywhere in the world economy spread ill effects, and American financial institutions were intertwined with European banks in many ways. For example, through money market funds Americans provided more than half a trillion dollars to European banks for their day-to-day operations. Still, the U.S. situation looked significantly less serious. Outstanding American debt was lower relative to GDP (although a large absolute number) than the debt of euro zone nations and Britain and had grown more slowly.

The highly complicated and extensive interconnectedness of countries and financial institutions meant that consequences were felt widely. The Great Recession was dealt with in the United States and elsewhere as a crisis of the financial system, and actions taken focused on restoring the viability of major financial institutions, guaranteeing debt, and stimulating growth. Built-in stabilizers and decreased tax collection sent government deficits soaring. The dominant reactions to the aftermath of the crisis were regulatory reform, which did not change the basic structure of the financialization of economies and demand for austerity measures in the face of engorged national debt levels. Economists and policy makers faced with lack of needed jobs were called upon to help those affected to find work and to maintain transfer payments to those who remained unemployed. Fear that continued growth of deficits would lead to higher borrowing costs and affect currencies created tension between addressing social pain and the demand for fiscal probity. Ignored in this debate was the larger context of these discussions: the inability to reproduce capitalist accumulation on an expanding basis in what had been the core of the world system. Debt-driven growth had provided a fragile basis and one that did not reverse declining labor shares in national income, rising inequality, international imbalances, and sovereign debt-produced tensions in economies of the traditional core of the world system.

Globalization of Financialization

From 1980 to 2008 the world's financial assets nearly quadrupled relative to the size of global GDP. In 2007 the total value of financial assets peaked at $194 trillion (Roxburgh et al. 2009:8). As a group, emerging market economies had become significant creditors to the richer nations. Most of the global borrowing (which rose by 70 percent between 2000 and 2009) was by the United States, Britain and the euro zone countries. This borrowing was increasing significantly more rapidly than their rate of economic growth. Borrowing also increased in the developing world, but more in line with their better economic performance.

What is often missing from these discussions is more fundamental consideration of whether the financialization of the previous decades had been good for society and whether there was a way to promote more balanced growth that was considerably less reliant on debt. Financial markets were disciplining democracy and narrowing the prospects of societies. Many economists viewed this as a good thing. It forced responsible behavior even as it allocated capital more efficiently. Stanley Fisher, the IMF chief economist at the time, made the case to the 1997 annual meeting of the organization for amending its articles of purpose to enable the IMF to actively promote financial liberalization. The a priori case for doing so based on received theory seemed unimpeachable. However, not only have IMF researchers not been able to find empirical evidence for such benefits (Kose et al. 2006:8); there was in fact little support for the view that there would be benefits from financial liberalization, except at the level of a priori theorizing. The history of financial crises suggests that, on the contrary, the price of liberalizing finance in the neoliberal era for many countries has been high indeed.

Findings that financial integration is essentially uncorrelated with real investment in productive capacity and short-term capital flows, not long before celebrated as increasing efficiency, in practice proved dangerously destabilizing. As Schularick (2010:4) concludes, "Globalization during the past decade was diversification finance, not development finance in the form of net transfer of capital." This led him to write, "It could finally be time to ask how we can make financial globalization safe for the world instead of trying to make the world safe for financial globalization." What has become clear is that volatile inflow of capital in the form of portfolio investment, seeking to benefit from short-term differences in rates of return on assets in different currencies, produced asset bubbles; created inflationary pressures leading to higher interest rates, which hurt local businesses in the nonfinancial economy while increasing the incentive for more carry trade speculation; made a country's exports less competitive as the value of its country rose; and ended in falling asset prices, tightening of lending standards, and, too frequently, recession.

The more financially integrated a country is and the more extensive its financialization, the greater its need for foreign reserves. Once reserves are taken into account, the usual measures of potential difficulty—current account balances and short-term debt levels—are not statistically significant predictors of a coming depreciation of its currency (Obstfeld, Shambaugh and Taylor 2008). Developing countries have been right to build up reserves to protect themselves from speculative attack on their currencies.

Empirical evidence does show that in the first modern era of globalization (1880–1914), opening up to the international capital market correlated with higher domestic investment. However, in the current period, changes in identical measures for financial integration are essentially uncorrelated with changes in domestic investment (Schularick and Steger 2007). The different patterns in these two periods of financial globalization are consistent with our analysis of the role financialization plays in the contemporary global neoliberal social structure of accumulation. In the recent period, what we see are high gross flows but limited net capital transfers uncorrelated with higher aggregate investment in receiving countries. For the most part, what was happening was speculative movements of money and diversification finance

(Obstfeld and Taylor 2004). A great deal of this was asset swapping among wealthy countries, and increasingly by the newly rich elsewhere into core financial markets. These are not the sort of one-way transfers that neoclassical economics suggests would dominate international finance and allow poorer countries to draw on global savings for long-term development. The financial speculation that dominates contemporary world capital movements leads to misalignment of currencies and affects trade balances and relative costs, invalidating the simplistic application of the theory of comparative advantage.

In the current period, capital flows to emerging market economies that are invested in speculative assets, equities and property. Nor does conventional theory describe the essentially vendor finance, so important in the twenty-first century, which China extends to the United States and Germany provides to its European neighbors. The inflow and outflow of foreign capital has not followed the patterns that mainstream theory predicts; instead, it is significant that such vendor finance and short-term speculation result in highly volatile exchange rates, violations of purchasing-power parity, trade imbalances, and more internationally correlated business cycles generated by repeated financial crises (Blecker 2005).There is a great deal of borrowing in one currency to invest/speculate in assets in another. Adair Turner, UK Finance Services Authority chairman, argues that we are seeing a large carry trade that is "economically valueless." Lord Turner notes that, while lucrative returns have been available from short-term positions held using currencies borrowed in low-interest-rate economies and invested in other financial markets in speculative punting, if he could "wave a wand" and greatly reduce the carry trade, "I'm pretty certain the world would be a better place" (Sorkin 2010).

The Bank for International Settlements' 2010 triennial survey shows that currency trading volume had reached $4 trillion a day, a 20 percent increase over 2007 and nearly 70 percent more than in 2004. Low interest rates in the United States were encouraging a huge carry trade for speculative investment. Much of this money flowed to emerging market economies to buy stocks, bonds, and property. This drove asset inflation in these rapidly growing economies, producing inflation, and encouraging a rapid growth of imports. Little of it went to investment in plant and equipment or other productive capacity. The impact was to push the currencies of these countries up, which made their exports less competitive, something their governments attempted in various ways to prevent. They also feared that rapid inflow could even more suddenly be followed by rapid exit, as had happened so many times in the past to countries, either because investors became spooked or problems in their own economies forced them to bring capital back home.

Large short-term speculative flows can be fickle. The estimated carry trade–related deals account for 15 to 20 percent of market activity in the global foreign exchange market, a market in which London alone turns over more than $1.5 trillion a day. Haruhiko Kuroda, president of the Asian Development Bank, estimates that the size of the yen carry trade at its peak was around a $1 trillion, and Zhu Min, deputy governor of the People's Bank of China, puts the 2010 dollar carry trade at $1.5 trillion, although hard figures are not available. For many countries, rapid movement of speculative capital in and out of their economies represents clear and present danger. A major reason for central bankers' caution in announcing interest-rate changes well in advance is not unrelated to fears that a sudden need to unwind positions can be disastrous. Some countries have responded by imposing capital controls; some intervene in currency markets to drive their currencies down by buying dollars (added to their already outsized reserves) and earning low returns in U.S. Treasury securities. For the euro borrowers, no currency adjustment is possible, so long as they continue to use the same monetary unit. In the efforts to get national economies growing again, there was little acceptance on the part of surplus countries of the notion that they should do much to address imbalances. Indeed, especially the Germans strongly advocated more austerity for their domestic economy and urged similar austerity for their neighbors.

As for the banking sector in poorer countries, it has become clearer that aping the more advanced financialized economies has not been a positive strategy (Rodrik and Subramanian 2009). Justin Lin (2009:76), the World Bank's chief economist, argues that those sorts of financial markets and institutions in the developed world are inappropriate for low-income countries and that if the goal is to provide services to enterprises and households, small local banks are best. He cites the examples of the successful development trajectories of Japan, South Korea, and China, which adhered to simple banking systems, did not integrate their finances with global markets, and did not build up stock markets until late in the development process. Asian banks "have, in effect, been treated as capital-providing utilities" (Bisson, Kirkland, and Stephenson 2010:7). Much of the Western literature has seen Asian banking systems as inefficient, part of crony capitalism, and in need of becoming more like the Anglo-Saxon banking ideal.

A heterodox literature sees Asian industrial policy and state direction of banking as a plus for economic growth in these countries. It is unlikely, given the financial meltdown and discrediting of the Anglo-American model of banking, that there will be convergence to this tarnished "ideal." It is likely that we shall hear less of Asian authorities' need to adopt more sophisticated capital market structures and allow unfettered capital movement. At the same time, as these economies grow, their bankers and financiers look for greater gain in riskier Western-style financial products. (Problems did develop later as these countries experienced broader financialization.)

Many smaller developing nations were forced to liberalize early and ran into difficulties. To avoid destabilizing currency movements, countries must hold large foreign reserves, overwhelmingly in U.S. dollar–denominated government securities, in order to have a buffer against foreign exchange crises and speculative attacks on their currencies. Failure to replace the Bretton Woods fixed exchange rate system with a currency and financial regime capable of providing stability has effectively allowed, indeed encouraged, these imbalances.

Economies that pegged their currencies or put up substantial barriers to foreign capital movements, resisting financial liberalization, experienced manageable growth of financial assets in a context of greater stability. The compound growth rate of financial assets in India was 19 percent and in China 24 percent between 1990 and 2008, faster than overall growth but not out of line with the need to expand their financial sectors. They did not allow foreign financial institutions free entry but maintained tight control. However, as their rapid growth rates continue to substantially exceed those of the wealthier countries, "financial depth" is expected to increase significantly faster in emerging markets than the countries of the core for the foreseeable future (Roxburgh et al. 2009) even as their ratio of financial assets to GDP is significantly lower than the countries of the core and GDP growth significantly faster. Officials from the International Monetary Fund have taken all of this onboard and note that "partly in response to buoyant demand conditions, the financial system developed new structures and created new instruments that seemed to offer higher risk-adjusted yields, but were in fact more risky than they appeared." They see the buildup of systemic risk in the period as a result of deficient regulation and conclude that, "given that regulation is likely to always remain imperfect, the crisis points again to the dangers of large capital inflows. Large capital inflows can lead to excessive risk taking and expose domestic financial institutions, households, and firms to exchange rate risk" (IMF

2009b:4). They recommend constraints on the foreign exchange exposure of domestic financial institutions and other borrowers.

For everybody's good, a new international currency regime is badly needed. Keynes at the end of World War II proposed that both surplus and debtor nations adjust to imbalances with rules for when and how governments adjust the value of currency. Then the United States, as the largest creditor nation, had different ideas, as well as the power to impose its will. Now the United States is the world's largest debtor, and, while it retains a strong political and military position, it now must negotiate on a different basis as a global power shift continues (Hoge 2004).

Spreading Financialization

In Europe even before the crisis, there had been "slow and fragile accumulation" accompanied by a substantial decline in wage shares in national income (Stockhammer 2008). In Germany, the homeland of the "coordinated market economy" (Hall and Gingerich 2004), financial value orientation grew at the expense of physical investment in a process that looked very much like convergence with the Anglo-American model and away from its traditional one (von Treeck 2009b). Owing to the memory of the country's financial crisis of 1931, Germany had banned share buybacks, but after 1998 they were allowed again. In 1991 the tax on stock exchange dealings was removed. In 2002 taxation of capital gains changed to favor investors and hedge funds were legalized. Deregulation of labor markets and partial privatization of pension funds in Germany are other indications of this trajectory. Weak domestic consumer and industrial demand for loans from the late 1990s led Germany's financial sector to look for opportunities abroad. One place they were found was in American-originated securitized loans, much to investors' later regret. In the continent's second largest economy, France, the ratio of dividend payments to net operating surplus rose dramatically from the end of the 1980s (Dallery 2009:501). Duménil and Lévy (2005:38) find that while in the early 1980s the profit rate for financial corporations was well below that for nonfinancial corporations, by the late 1990s profits for the financial corporations greatly exceeded those for nonfinancial corporations. Epstein and Jayadev (2005: Table 3.1) report a higher rate of labor exploitation and transfer to rentier income for most OECD countries.

Even in Japan, Ashby Monk (2009:59) tells us that Japanese corporate managers are primarily concerned with their stock price as a measure of performance, and defined benefit pension plans are undergoing serious erosion similar to that in the United States. Similar patterns are observed in middle-income countries generally, where strong foreign bank entry and growing financialization are moving in the same direction. In Latin America financial liberalization was one of the outcomes of the response to the debt crisis of the early 1980s and led to a large increase in foreign ownership of banks and expanded consumer lending (Malinowitz 2009). In Mexico 80 percent of bank assets came into foreign ownership (Lapavitsas 2009:123). This was a global trend. Governments succumbing to the pressure for financial liberalization ended up financializing their domestic economies, with significant control of the process in the hands of foreign-owned institutions. By the early 1990s Korea had responded to political pressure not only from foreign interests but from its own large companies to escape state control and to borrow abroad for financial liberalization (Epstein 2005:14). The levels of such borrowing grew and proved costly in the wake of the Asian financial crisis later in that decade.

Turkey's experience in the financial crisis from 2001 was very much like that of other emerging market economies, which relied on capital inflows to finance a growing external deficit and fund domestic investment that produced more external debt and capital abandoning the economy on fears of exchange rate deterioration. Repeated crises did not discourage reliance on foreign capital inflows, which in Turkey, as in many emerging markets, led to greater foreign control of the local financial sector. Finance absorbed almost 60 percent of its incoming foreign direct investment as foreign bank presence in the economy grew (Akyüz and Boratav 2005).

There were varying ideas on how blame should be allocated and corresponding competing conclusions as to desirable policy, with clashes among regulatory authorities as to rules best adopted to make international financial markets safer. In Canada, where the country's small number of very large banks did not run into trouble as their U.S. counterparts did (due to a very different regulatory environments), the government saw no reason to accept taxation of its banks to fund future bank bailouts as the United States, Britain, and Germany proposed. The British wanted foreign banks with extensive operations in London to provide more capital reserves to these operations. Foreign banks do not wish to do so. The British authorities complained bitterly when the Germans moved to regulate foreign hedge funds and private equity groups (which were heavily located in London) and banned some forms of short selling, which they said was not healthy for German financial markets. French officials lobbied against international reforms that would force their banks to divest themselves of insurance subsidiaries. Each country negotiates from the particulars of its national financial regimes and unique circumstances. Global agreements that involve even the appearance of national concessions or movement toward "world government" provoke outrage from segments of most electorates and are likely to await an intra-elite consensus. In the United States, where once there was substantial bipartisan elite agreement on foreign policy, fear of the future translated into extensive opposition to a lesser role for the "leader of the free world" implied in multilateral negotiations. Competing interests plus a natural resistance to ceding sovereignty to any supranational regulatory agency make negotiations at the international level slow going.

While the United States has lost relative economic clout, it remains the one country with veto power in the major global state economic governance institutions, the IMF and the World Bank, created at the end of the Second World War through extended discussions between the declining hegemon, no longer so great Britain, represented by John Maynard Keynes, and the Americans, represented by Harry Dexter White. The institutions they created allocated voting rights based on the economic strength of nations at the time. As a result, in the International Monetary Fund at the start of the twenty-first century, Belgium had 103 votes for every billion dollars of its much smaller GDP, compared to China's 25 votes for every billion dollars of its far larger GDP.

Countries of the global South had been invited to G7 meetings, though the Brazilian foreign minister suggested that developing nations had been asked "only to take part in coffee breaks." This changed with the formation of the G20, which brings together the main developing and developed economies that together produce 85 percent of global GDP, account for 80 percent of world trade, and contain two-thirds of the world's population. When it met for the first time in Washington in November 2008, the G20 got off to a slow start. It was warned by President George W. Bush not to go down the road of overregulation and "abandoning free markets." Its September 2009 Pittsburgh meeting marked something of a coming of age for the G20, but behind the inevitable resolutions endorsing cooperation lay conflicting national interests and changing clout of members. The balance of power in such negotiations will shift still further as the GDPs of the so-called E7 (China, India, Brazil, Russia, Indonesia, Turkey, and Mexico) are growing significantly faster than those of the G7 countries.

The 2008 U.S. National Intelligence Council's quadrennial report, "Global Trends 2025: A Transformed World," a summary of the thinking of U.S. intelligence agencies prepared for the incoming administration, projected an end to U.S. dominance and suggested that the country would in the future be one among many global actors. The report was consistent with the reality that American military dominance did not automatically translate into victory in Iraq or Afghanistan, for example, and that costly wars of choice and efforts to remake the world through shock and awe might not be the best U.S. foreign policy. As the report foresaw the situation, "Although the United States is likely to remain the single most powerful actor," its "relative strength—even in the military realm—will decline and US leverage will become more constrained." It recognized that the United States would be forced to share power with other key players, such as China, India, and Russia, and that there would be less room "for the US to call the shots without the support of strong partnerships." National security, even as traditionally understood, was being redefined in practice in a globalized world.

In early February 2009 Director of National Intelligence Dennis Blair told Congress that the global crisis and the instability it could ignite was a more severe threat to the United States than terrorism was. It was a matter of both the impacts of the crisis and the loss of American reputational capital. The "increased questioning of U.S. stewardship of the global economy" was, Blair thought, a very serious problem for the country. Issues of nuclear proliferation and terrorism were further down his list. Increasingly there is a question of what the United States can afford to do in the world in budgetary terms as well. Such a global perspective suggests that much of the discussion of the financial crisis in the United States is too narrowly focused. The inability of the country to offer leadership in addressing the financial crisis, the rise of new centers of economic power not ready to take the initiative, and the global mobility of finance mean that market forces continue to dominate. Governments respond to what they think financial markets demand. This is a willful abrogation of responsibility based on the acceptance of the primacy of the market.

Coordinating Issues and Criminal Behavior

In addition to global financial crises, there are areas of concern governments need to pay attention to on an international level: procedures to address the cross-border impacts of failure of individual transnational financial institutions; controlling capital movements that are agreed to be inappropriate; and monetary imbalances among countries, which have potential to cause crises of the international payments system. For example, after the 2008 crash of a Lehman subsidiary in the Netherlands, it turned out the company had issued four thousand or so notes drawn up by company officials in London that held a third of the firm's prebankruptcy assets. Resolving such complicated responsibilities for repayment claims needs to be made as straightforward and unambiguous a process as possible or else we get a mess, as in this case, in which Lehman's UK arm rejected plans of administrators for Lehman U.S. regarding an international framework coordinating bankruptcy proceedings among subsidiaries. Lehman's organizational chart showed eighty subsidiaries worldwide in more than a dozen countries. But as Mike Atkin, head of the Enterprise Management Council (a group of banks, regulators, and information technology companies), said, "Wait a minute, . . . what is Lehman? Lehman isn't one entity—it's 10,000 entities. We don't know what our exposure is because we're not sure *what* Lehman is" (Braithwaite 2011). Progress on international coordination and adjudication in such cases remains confused since national legal systems differ. Coordinated cross-border bankruptcy requires working out of provisions for such financial institutions.

The need for better global-level regulation should have been learned in 1991 when the Bank of Credit and Commerce International collapsed, taking with it its depositors' money. BCCI was chartered in Luxembourg by a Pakistani businessman with Saudi Arabian backing and operated in seventy countries from headquarters in London. Its secret account holders ranged from the American CIA funding the contras in Nicaragua, to the Abu Nidal terrorists. It specialized in the accounts of narcotics trafficker, money launderers, and tax evaders. Well over a decade after BCCI collapsed, the Bank of England was still defending itself from depositor suits for "knowingly and recklessly" failing to supervise it properly. While there may not be a large number of criminal banks out there today, we do not really know. International regulation has hardly made needed progress since BCCI collapsed.

The ease of international capital mobility has encouraged tax avoidance, tax cheating, and illegal capital flight, overlapping and hard-to-detect practices. Serious disclosure and regulation of money flows could address the vast extent of criminality and tax cheating by corporations and wealthy citizens that drain the public fisc. Financial firms have found ways to move tax losses across borders so that, for example, Merrill Lynch was unlikely to pay taxes in Britain for several decades after charging its U.S. losses to a London subsidiary. Even if it made record profits for the next sixty years, it would pay no taxes, a benefit that would accrue to its new owner, Bank of America.

Banks are major facilitators of illicit capital movements. In 2008 a federal grand jury indictment of UBS offshore banking activities for its rich American clients read in part: "The executives involved occupied positions at the highest levels of management within the bank, including positions on the committees that oversaw legal, regulatory issues, tax, risk assessment and the specifics of cross-border transacting." In August 2009 UBS agreed to pay a fine of $780 million and disclose the names of 4,450 wealthy Americans suspected of evading taxes. In exchange Washington dropped proceedings that could have led to the withdrawal of the bank's license to do business in the United States. Swiss courts said the deal violated that country's law, leading the Swiss government to quickly change the law (since UBS's takeover of PaineWebber in 2000 meant well over a third of its employees were to be in the United States). Not to make the concession demanded by Washington would have been a pyrrhic victory for sovereignty. At the same time, Swiss lawyers, it is understood, continue to advise American clients on how to fund accounts from Cayman banks in order to set up foundations in Liechtenstein to serve as an umbrella over a Panamanian or Hong Kong corporation—providing those little extra layers of privacy for which their bankers are renowned. When UBS had to turn over records of American clients to Washington, Swiss bankers moved operations to Singapore to avoid revealing them.

Of course it is not only Swiss banks that are engaged in money laundering. The largest U.S. banks have been integral to tax avoidance and especially helpful to Third World tyrants and other well-connected criminals in laundering money. Nigerian dictator Sani Abacha, who stole a reported $4 billion from that poverty-stricken but oil-rich country, relied on London bankers as conduits for getting funds to Switzerland. While the kleptocrats from former British colonies prefer London, Latin Americans typically favor U.S. banks, most significantly (at least in the past) Citibank, which has been the conduit for much money laundering over the years. It was Citi that assisted Raul Salinas, brother of Mexico's president, in moving $100 million or so out of Mexico. Gabon's tyrant, El Hadj Omar Bongo, was among other high-profile Citi customers. Chase, Bank of America, and others were also found by a Senate probe to be active in moving huge amounts of money in what was called "an atmosphere of complacency, with lax due diligence, weak controls and inadequate response to troubling information," a very generous formulation of banker greed and criminality. The report also finds banks "fully aware" in a host of instances of what was going on. Indeed, it describes the bankers' role in soliciting such business. These practices did not stop. Jason Sharman, a respected money-laundering specialist, makes the "educated guess" that "there's more corrupt money in the United States than in any other country in the world" and "the gap between U.S. rhetoric on this issue and follow-through is huge" (Shenon 2011:19).

Western corporations and financial institutions have developed techniques for mispricing, false documentation, dummy corporations, shell banks, numbered accounts, and a host of other techniques to avoid detection. The scale of such activities is so large that what amounts to a conspiracy of mutual interest and officials looking the other way is a major factor in reducing tax collections globally and in aiding and abetting criminal activity. The movement of alleged terrorist monies is a tiny fraction of the total illegal money laundering, which the IMF puts at $1 trillion a year, a figure that dwarfs most of the world's economies and makes it perhaps the largest "business" in the global political economy and a major profit center for the international financial institutions. It can be prevented by denying offshore noncompliant jurisdictions access to the larger economy banking systems and by closer supervision of banks and multinational corporations. Some progress has been made to change all this, but hardly enough. Much of the poverty in many Third World countries could be alleviated if the wealth produced was not being systematically looted by local elites and removed from the countries with the help of Western banks. A good deal of the austerity demanded in developed countries with large fiscal problems could be lightened substantially if transnational capital was not allowed to escape taxation.

European Sovereign Debt and Bank Exposure

Financialization in Europe was a general phenomenon, but it was most advanced in Great Britain, which, like previous hegemons, had followed the path from being the world's dominant producer nation to becoming dependent on finance. The City of London had a long time ago become the leading center of world finance, eclipsing other parts of the British economy. A look at the country's business assets by major sector in 2000 shows banking assets equal to 40 percent of GDP, well above other sectors; in 2007 they were equal to 130 percent of GDP, dwarfing the other parts of the economy

(Haldane 2010:18). Financialization had increased elsewhere in Europe as well. The kind of property bubble experienced in the United States was seen in such countries as Spain and Ireland, which had very different institutional arrangements, suggesting that corruption of subprime mortgages in the American case was not necessary to produce a housing bubble and collapse.

Government debt in the euro zone was not a general problem before the global financial crisis. Overall it had gone down from 72 percent of GDP in 1999 to 67 percent in 2007, before the crisis struck and drove it up again. Nor was it countries with high taxes and larger welfare-state spending that got in trouble when the financial crisis occurred, but those who had greater inequality, more tax avoidance, more corruption, and too much borrowing. The strong welfare states, especially the Scandinavians (thought by free marketeers to be hopelessly insensitive to market realities), were not the countries in trouble. Those with the strongest and most extensive programs, again the Scandinavian countries, but also the Dutch, French, and Germans, have much healthier economies. The problems the latter three nations have are with their banks. Efforts to blame greedy workers rather than reckless financiers fit preconceived, ideologically driven understandings but are factually inaccurate. Other governments competing to please financial markets imposed austerity, accepting that the problem was government debt. But many of these countries before the crisis had run government surpluses and had low debt-to-GDP ratios. Some that had higher debt ratios than they liked had accrued the higher debt due to too generous tax cuts. Socialization of bank debt and the cost of the deep downturn resulting from the financial crisis drove up public debt.

As the crisis deepened, imbalances internal to Europe loomed large. In early summer 2010 the Bank for International Settlements made public a study revealing that French and German banks had lent nearly a trillion dollars to the countries of Europe's periphery that were experiencing severe fiscal problems. French banks had lent $493 billion to Spain, Ireland, Greece, and Portugal. German banks lent them $465 billion. A study by Royal Bank of Scotland economists about the same time showed that the total amount of debt issued by the public and private sectors in Greece, Portugal, and Spain and held by financial institutions outside these countries was about $2 trillion, which was over 20 percent of the entire euro zone GDP. A sovereign default by these countries would devastate the European financial system and be the reason for the EU and European Central Bank (ECB) rescue of Greece, Ireland, and Portugal.

A number of interrelated issues were involved. One was how the pain would be distributed among banks, taxpayers, workers, and public-service recipients as a result of unpayable sovereign debt. A second was how banks would be regulated in the future to minimize chances of a new financial crisis. A third was the crisis of the euro and the continued viability of a common currency for nations with different growth prospects. A host of other concerns, from the role of the ECB to government accounts transparency, were also issues.

The longer-run issue is the extent to which the power of finance will prevail and the financialization of society will continue to be the dominant moment of the accumulation process. This larger issue was eclipsed in the immediate concern that taxpayers would take on their liabilities. The most visible redistributions were taking place in Europe, where the budget problems of euro zone countries and the lack of centralized control mechanisms for the EU over the fiscal choices of members had consequences for the risk exposure of citizens of other EU countries. Debt repayment would require punishing austerity, limited only by the capacities of governments to enforce painful cutbacks against the opposition of their citizens. If the adjustments proved unobtainable, or if austerity measures slowed growth so that in budgetary terms they became counterproductive, could the European Union come up with sensible workout procedures to share the burden between creditors and debtors in a longer term perspective? Would there be a vetting in the future of national budgets by the European Commission, an obvious and dramatic intrusion on national sovereignty? Would the extent of cross-border lending by banks become a policy issue? The global financial crisis raised a host of such issues that Europeans were not ready to address. As in the United States, a better answer would be to crack down on tax evasion and make tax avoidance more difficult. There is discussion of EU-wide harmonization, which, if successful, could be a source of substantial revenue.

The ECB acted in dramatic fashion, purchasing the bonds of governments whose finances were in crisis, accepting bonds no matter that rating agencies might have downgraded them. Like the Federal Reserve purchase of banks' questionable assets, the ECB provided liquidity to the Greek government and stood ready to do the same for other governments in need. In taking such action, ECB president Jean-Claude Trichet created a precedent over the objection of other European central bankers who feared he was creating a "transfer union." Axel Weber, the Bundesbank president, publicly warned of possible inflationary consequences. The activism was seen as going beyond the remit of the ECB into fiscal policy. The ECB's action followed the EU and IMF rescue programs and were seen by Trichet as supportive of the preservation of the European Union and the euro.

Toward this end the seventeen euro zone states created a temporary bailout fund in June 2010 with a 250-billion-euro lending capacity, with contributions ranging from 3.5 percent of the total from Belgium to 27 percent from the Germans and agreement in principle to increase the amount to 440 billion euros. To satisfy Germany and Finland, one of the six euro zone countries with a triple-A rating, where the True Finns Party showed a sudden electoral surge with a promise to block future bailouts, the European Financial Stability Facility (EFSF) had to limit its activities. Importantly, the EFSF could not buy sovereign bonds on the primary or secondary market. This constraint was a problem, and a European Stability Mechanism (ESM), agreed to in 2011 after extensive discussion, was scheduled to replace the EFSF in mid-2013 with 500 billion euros in lending capacity (only 80 billion in cash and 620 billion euros in guarantees and callable capital), which would be used to buy bonds, if necessary, in the primary market when the country in question agreed to a bailout and an austerity program. Cynics, perhaps not inaccurately, suggested that Greece, Ireland, and Portugal would remain under the safety umbrella for a long time as program followed program, loan followed loan, and repayment was put off again and again. Whether eventually funds would be used to buy sovereign bonds on the secondary market at a discount, as a partial default was recognized as necessary, might be a likely eventual outcome. A complete bailout by the ESM would be a bitter pill for taxpayers, especially if a larger European economy were to require assistance. The national polities in the euro zone are unlikely to accept what would be asked of either the taxpayers in the stronger economies, who would be called upon to come up with huge amounts to bail out creditors, or the people of the debtor nations forced into deeper austerity. Logically these measures would need to be followed by a rethinking of the macroeconomic and financial regimes in place at the level of the union and the global banking system.

The Basel Committee on Banking Supervision, made up of central bankers and regulators from twenty-seven countries, had to decide on how strictly it would constrain banks and the specifics of how this would be done. These are innately difficult issues to resolve, and negotiators are under pressure from home banks and political leaders to moderate reforms. National regulators had different preferences. Some wanted tough liquidity rules and a straightforward leverage ratio. Others wanted more freedom for individual nation-based criteria. In its meetings during the panic period, the Basel Committee was serious about ending the gaming of the system by limiting such bank tactics as counting deferred tax assets (DTA) as part of capital. DTA is money the bank says it will save when it earns profits in the future. But this "capital" has zero value in a crisis when the bank is losing money. A compromise agreement was reached, leaving some important issues only partially addressed. Some of the provisions that the negotiators could agree on would not take effect for many years. Others would be studied and delayed until agreement could be reached.

From what we understand about the causes of the crisis, it seemed eminently sensible to require banks to hold more long-term funding (or, as it is termed, "the net stable funding ratio"). But this would, the banks said, cost them trillions of dollars. Their profits were tied to access to the very short-term repo market, and that had been their downfall when those markets froze. There was resistance by the banks and sympathy from their governments, preventing strict liquidity requirements. It was agreed that banks should be given an extended period before having to comply. The new capital requirements, while better than the old ones, represent the same sort of compromises that led to the obvious deficiencies of Basel I and II. Industry spokespeople called the increased Basel III mandates too high, although researchers suggest they seriously overestimate their cost (Admati et al. 2010). Economists at the international regulatory institutions completed studies showing effects one-eighth the size of those asserted by the banking industry association (Basel Committee on Banking Supervision 2010; Macroeconomic Assessment Group 2010 [established by the Financial Stability Board and the Basel Committee on Banking Supervision]).

While Basel III was an improvement, it is unlikely to be enough to stop the next crisis. Even if the new stricter capital rules had been in effect, they would not have prevented the last crisis. In mid-2008 Lehman Brothers held more capital than is required under Basel III. The Basel III higher capital requirements are lower than those already being held by the large U.S. banks and others. More substantial restrictions are necessary—perhaps three or four times as high. Banks will not hold more quality capital on their own. Many whose capital exceeded the new requirements were under pressure form stockholders to pay higher dividends or buy back their own stock with the money rather than keep it as a precautionary cushion.

On the questions of macroeconomic recovery measures, there was a wide consensus in European establishment circles that the increase in government debt resulting from rescue efforts and stimulus had become a serious problem. The Bank for International Settlements' 2010 Annual Report, while acknowledging the "still fragile and uneven recovery," said that a number of countries had reached the limits of fiscal stimulus and declared that greater austerity measures are needed. BIS general manager Jaime Caruana's speech to the annual meeting emphasized that "without substantial fiscal reform bouts of volatility in financial markets become more intense and interact strongly with the fragilities in the financial system. This could disrupt markets, tighten funding conditions and sharply increase risk aversion" (Bank for International Settlements 2010) The people in the effected countries would just have to make do with less, or they would be punished by financial markets, or, as Caruana said, "in the current unsettled times, the alternative of having to cope with the financial and macroeconomic disruption that a sudden loss of market confidence could cause would be far worse." Workers and taxpayers might not like it, and they asked whether not pleasing the markets could be more painful. Still, there are limits to how far people can be pushed. Prioritizing feeding the bankers and acknowledging that this would require destabilizing the growth prospects of the economies involved, with consequences of continued stagnation and suffering, are not attractive. The political and mainstream media efforts to win acceptance of such policies, the social priorities of its logic, and the impacts of the austerity being demanded have hardly rebuilt confidence in the existing system.

Countries of the European periphery faced four alternatives: a continuation of austerity and neoliberalism; a radical enlargement of the euro zone budget and fiscal transfers from the rich countries to the poorer ones; exit from the euro, which would provide a devaluation option; or accepting restructuring of the debt with losses to creditors. This last would not be easy since major banks would be in serious trouble; leaving the euro would throw economies into chaos and force a vastly more activist role for governments, which might find they would have to take over their banks and perhaps nationalize strategic industries so they can adjust to the shock. Yet there are limits to austerity and opposition to a transfer union. Muddling through promises a painful period of temporizing and adjustment that in fact would socialize the debt over time by EU taxpayers. It would seem that if the euro is to function for its member users, there will have to be greater political integration and centralization in economic policy making. Different economic institutions could come from the social impacts and political mobilizations they engendered that are hard to predict.

The United States and China

The most prominent surplus/debtor relation in the world system is the U.S.-China balance-of-payments situation. How it is addressed depends partly on how it is understood. Ben Bernanke promulgated an influential analysis of the U.S. balance of payments problem, which sees the United States as the passive recipient of the world's surplus savings, or "saving glut" as he characterized it (Bernanke 2005). In what may be thought of as the Fed story (endorsed by Bernanke's predecessor Alan Greenspan), the Federal Reserve could not do much in the face of global savings surpluses that found their way to the United States and held down U.S. interest rates. This view has been challenged by those who point out that Fed interest-rate decisions fell well below what historical experience suggested they should have been, and that the Fed was guilty of monetary excesses in the period leading up to and during the housing boom and so is responsible for the bust that followed. John Taylor (2007), in a paper presented before the market collapsed, estimates a model simulating the counterfactual impact of a more restrained monetary policy impact based on his 1992 Taylor Rule for optimal monetary policy. He demonstrates that the actual monetary policy the Fed chose was a key cause of the boom and bust that was soon to become evident. In Europe too, the ECB allowed an expansionary monetary policy that was widely understood as a response to the Fed policy. Both held down interest rates, encouraging those chasing yield to take on more risk. It was excessive risk that led to bank insolvency and to the costly bailouts. Allocating blame is, as usual, complicated. In this matter there are three contributing factors: Federal Reserve policy, funds coming into America from abroad (especially China), and lack of productive investment in the United States, diverting funds to financialization activities. Of the three, the second is the most popular, especially for politicians seeking an external blame answer.

Timing of the Chinese "savings glut" suggests that it was not the source of U.S. difficulties. The United States has been running a trade deficit since 1976, when China's current account surplus was negligible. Until 2000 the largest creditor was Japan. Since then, China has been the major exporter, although to a significant extent it finished products using Japanese and other East Asian parts suppliers so that its export figures to the United States would need to be adjusted for the large imports it requires to produce goods for export. Looking only its own value added reduces this figure very substantially.

However, the share of an ever-growing Chinese GDP that is exported rose from 10 percent in 1979 to over 24 percent in 2009 and became the world's largest exporter. China's rise may not be so different from Japan's or South Korea's in its mercantilist policies, but the scale of the country is of a different dimension. It is able to use up-to-date technology (while restricting the importation of the high-tech products that it wishes to produce domestically) with a lower-wage workforce to produce the same products that the countries of the core had not long before exported to China, shifting the axis of the global production system. This creates a split between the interests of U.S.-based transnational corporations and American workers. The former see less reason to invest in the United States. It is to be hoped that the Chinese import market will create jobs in the United States and elsewhere to match its exports, which have grown so remarkably. It is possible that in time the Chinese market will create jobs in the United States, but with global excess capacity and austerity measures in so many countries, Chinese production looms large.

By 2006 the United States ran a $235 billion deficit with China (U.S. exports to China amounted to $52 billion while imports from China were $287 billion). These were goods that Walmart, Mattel, and others once sourced at home. U.S. multinationals relied on China for a very considerable part of their profitability and were powerful forces preventing any action by Washington to reduce this flow. It should be pointed out that in 2007, when China's current account surplus reached $372 billion, the combined current account surplus of Japan and Germany was $464 billion. Yet only China was seen as the problem. As Terry McKinley (2009:3) writes, "The main difference between these advanced economies and China seems to be that China is realigning the global balance of economic and political power while Germany and Japan are not." Isolation of China as the problem was to a considerable extent motivated by fear concerning the future of U.S. hegemony in a context of loss of competitiveness. It was a loss of competitiveness that preceded the rise of China. Today, however, China is the fulcrum on which the global economy shifts. In 2009 it was the second largest importer in the world and contributed, by some estimates, 50 percent of global growth.

The role of U.S.-based transnationals and the trend away from investment in the territorial United States, described earlier as closely related to financialization and changing corporate governance and labor relations norms of the global neoliberal SSA, come into play here. This can be seen in the timing of U.S.-China imbalances, which is important before one accepts a too easy and too exclusive blame on China politics. From 1997 to 2004, while China's surplus doubled, the U.S. deficit increased by four and a half times. China's surplus was $29 billion in these years, during which the U.S. deficit rose by $490 billion. After that, China's surplus rose at a rate comparable to that of the U.S. deficit. The timing of these developments suggests that it was financialization in the United States, the growth of debt, and a loss of competitiveness that initiated the imbalance. The extremely low interest-rate policy of the Federal Reserve, after the 2000–2001 New Economy boom deflated, led to private capital outflows on a substantial scale that forced other countries, which did not want to see their currencies appreciate against the U.S. dollar, to take offsetting actions. They sold bonds domestically and recycled dollars into the purchase of U.S. government assets.

China saves approximately half of its GDP and in 2009 produced 28 percent of global savings. Chinese household income is 60 percent of China's GDP, but consumption is 35 to 40 percent. In the United States between the late 1990s and the first half of 2007, personal consumption rose from 67 percent of GDP to 72 percent, funded by unsustainable borrowing. There will have to be a new balance, with America adding export capacity and China increasing domestic spending. The Chinese should over time adopt welfare-state mechanisms for old age and health care and U.S. consumers should continue to pay off debt and save more. This is generally agreed. Over time the Chinese should free their currency to float and the United States needs to increase exports substantially or watch the value of the dollar drop and faith in its currency diminish. The Chinese government says that increasing domestic consumption is a major priority. In this it is responding to domestic and foreign pressures. Domestically, while Chinese wages recently have been rising by double-digit amounts, for a long time productivity has substantially outpaced wages, with the surplus funding rapid accumulation and industrial growth. The United States says it takes seriously the need to become more competitive and fiscally responsible. But these are painful adjustments.

China's becoming the workshop of the world has seriously affected domestic U.S. manufacturing even as it has been a boon to retailers and transnational consumer goods manufacturers sourcing from China. Causation is more complex, however. The discussion of financialization of the U.S. economy in chapters 2 and 6 and in other parts of this book indicates the extent to which the dominance of maximization of shareholder value in the short run, the imposition of private equity firms' targets, and loading them up with debt and depriving them of capital to invest have undermined America's capacity to produce competitively. Germany, with a different set of institutional arrangements, has done considerably better in maintaining its industrial base, although, as noted, financialization has increasingly transformed basic features of that economy. The United States has rejected industrial policy in the past (except in its stealth industrial policy, which for some goes by the name of the military-industrial complex). In the twenty-first century's globalized economy, government interventions elsewhere are setting a pattern that calls for a U.S. response. It is not at all clear that less government and appealing to a freeing of the American entrepreneurial spirit are a basis for a more internationally competitive job-creating and living standard–enhancing outcome. American dislike of an interventionist state, the underinvesting in infrastructure and human capital, and the attitude that industrial policy is anathema do not promise a successful response to the challenges of globalization. While elites in Asia have pursued a state-led industrial policy strategy to build an indigenous capitalism, capital in the United States has long had a globalization outlook and taken the surplus produced by American workers (thanks to the low-cost raw materials coming from the global South) to invest in new production sites in emerging market economies.

Economics students are taught that an increase in savings leads to a fall in interest rates and produces an increase in real investment. But growth in the production of goods and nonfinancial services has lagged savings, which have found their outlet in property and other asset speculation, much of it in new structured financial products. What Bernanke described as the global savings glut did lower interest rates but was not matched by a growth in real investment. A good deal of the money went to further debt creation, allowing U.S. consumers to continue to increase spending well beyond their income. Thanks to the low cost of borrowing and the attractive cost of imports, America's current account deficit grew. This contributed to loss of sales for domestic producers, job loss, and downward pressure on wages (Bibow 2010). The inability of the United States to use low-cost capital productively is central to explaining what has happened to the American economy in the global neoliberal SSA.

In the context of weak global demand, with many governments cutting spending despite huge GDP gaps between their potential and actual output, each looked for ways to increase exports in a disturbing echo of the "beggar thy neighbor" strategies of the Great Depression years. In the fall of 2010 Brazil's finance minister, Guido Mantega, spoke of "an international currency war" having broken out. His remarks followed interventions by the central banks of Japan, Switzerland, South Korea, and Taiwan to prevent their currencies from rising. Thailand introduced a tax on foreign holdings of bonds. Brazil also took action to slow capital inflows, moving to make companies pay more tax on money raised abroad through loans or bond sales. Europe worried that such actions were forcing up the euro.

The dollar exchange rate reflects a number of choices, including U.S. military spending around the world, overseas investment by U.S.-based speculators, and of course Americans' use of debt to consume in the face of stagnant or falling real wages. Fed policies of easy credit do not and cannot address these matters, and their relative ineffectiveness should not be surprising. In a really free market global economy, the Chinese would not be limited to relending their earnings to Americans via purchase of government securities but would be buying American companies. But, like the OPEC governments before them, Washington has made clear that any effort to use their surplus to buy important American corporations is not acceptable.

Though under political pressure "to do something about China," governments in the West hesitated to do so because of the interests of their own transnationals who produce there and fear of retaliation against their own exports to China. They also do not want to see interruption in their profitable sourcing from that country. In 2009 foreign-funded enterprises in China accounted for most of that country's exports (56 percent according to the Chinese). It is estimated that a Chinese-made Barbie doll that sells for $10 in the United States leaves the Chinese manufacturer with only thirty-five cents (Liu 2010). Chinese workers may get the jobs, but the foreign companies capture the value added when the products are marketed. It is also the case that China's export surplus has been falling, and, as Chinese leaders point out, it remains a poor country, with GDP a fifth that of the United States (measured in purchasing power parity terms). If growth slowed down, it could face serious unrest.

Wages in China are rising at a double-digit rate because its vast reserves of rural, low-cost labor are being incorporated into its modernization, and labor shortages in many places have become a reality. The country's population is aging fast. In a few years its working-age population under sixty-five will begin to shrink, and the proportion of the population that is over sixty-five will double in twenty-five years. The Chinese will be older on average than Americans within a generation, and China could become an old, poor country instead of the young, poor country it has been through its decades of remarkable growth. It has not put resources toward meeting the needs of its older people, putting its surplus into investment instead. Indeed, in shutting its state-owned factories it reduced expenditures such employers had made on benefits for their workers and retirees. Young Chinese do not get much in the way of benefits in the new plants producing for foreign transnationals or other businesses run by Chinese entrepreneurs. It is presumed they will return to poverty in the countryside or to marginalized zones on the periphery of cities when they are worked out, joining tens of millions of older former workers. For all the talk of increasing domestic consumption, it is likely that China is going to grow its exports as much as it can until then in the hope of addressing the needs of the retirees as far in the future as it can out of a much larger GDP. However, China faces labor shortages and is experiencing widespread, if localized and uncoordinated, work stoppages and other protests, and with labor supply and demand conditions now favoring workers, the government is being forced to make a virtue out of a necessity and approve rising wages.

In 2011 China moved beyond its targeting of new yuan bank loans, recognizing that while a decade earlier almost all loan funds were raised from banks, not only were companies selling stocks and bonds to raise huge sums, but banks had learned to use off-balance-sheet lending to evade government-imposed lending limits. They used a variety of ruses such as bank acceptance notes to guarantee off-the-books loans. Inflation is a serious problem resulting from such credit creation. Property speculation in many places may be creating property booms. Whether China can avoid real estate bubbles and a growing propensity of wealthy and not even so wealthy Chinese to turn to financial speculation remains to be seen. In 2009 the Shanghai, Shenzhen, and Hong Kong stock exchanges attracted $60 billion from initial public offerings, more than twice the amount raised by IPOs in the United States. Whether animal spirits lead to overleveraged speculative excesses even in rapidly growing China will be interesting to see. The Chinese monetary authorities certainly want to guard against the possibility. However, Chinese banks are increasingly engaging in complex arrangements to hide the size and nature of their lending in amounts in the hundreds of billions of dollars, which suggests that bad real estate and infrastructure loans may come back to plague these banks as off-balance-sheet dealings come home to roost. The Chinese government, despite its authoritarian powers, is finding prudential regulation of its financial markets a difficult task. Not only in China but in other growing emerging market economies, asset speculation looks to many observers as the next bubble.

The Global Economy as a Context for Reregulation

The *World Economic Outlook*'s update (IMF 2011) offers perspective on differential rates of growth. For the United States, setting 2005 as a base year at 100, GDP was 105 in 2010; it was 104 in the euro zone and 102 for Japan and the United Kingdom. For Brazil in 2010 it was 125, India 147, and China 169. These are truly impressive differences. For the United States and other countries of the traditional core with slow growth, high unemployment, large public-sector deficits, and pressure to reduce government spending, it will be a class-biased, uneven sort of affair as budget-reducing measures continue to reduce the social wage. This seems inevitable as long as financial markets are allowed the power to discipline governments an effective taxation is not imposed at the global level and tax avoidance is not significantly reduced.

The IMF sees general net debt for the G7 countries rising from 52 percent of GDP to 90 percent in 2015. Current policies promise austerity measures that will hurt working-class living standards, hold overall growth in check, and allow continued trends of growing inequality with distributional impacts from working people to the top 1 percent of the pyramid. While the decline of the traditional core of the world system—the United States, Europe, and Japan—is expected by many people who see the rise of China and other emerging powers, some thought should be given to the sustainability of adequate demand to absorb all the surplus being created, which finds no outlet except in financial activities.

Economists' endorsement of free trade and free capital markets was based on models that make assumptions that are not good approximations of contemporary realities. As the world increasingly functions as a single unit rather than an international economy, a megaeconomic analysis is badly needed. Any new SSA for the United States will have to take into account the changed position of the territorial U.S. economy and the bubble growth and income inequality stemming from financialization. McKinsey & Company researchers (Bisson, Kirkland, and Stephenson 2010:1) suggest that "this decade will mark the tipping point in a fundamental long-term economic rebalancing that will likely leave the traditional Western economies with a lower share of global GDP in 2050 than they had in 1700." Earlier reference was made to world-systems theorists' (Arrighi and Silver 1999) suggestion that hegemonic powers, losing their leadership position in production, move to finance as an accumulation strategy.

As emerging market economies (surely a new name for these now system-ically important powers is needed) move up from being suppliers of low-cost goods and services to become large-scale providers of capital, talent, and in-novation, they are the new growth centers of the twenty-first-century world system. The relation between China and the United States is part of a larger phenomenon of rapid development in emerging markets and slow growth in the countries of the traditional core of the world system. From 1980, as has been noted, there has been a decline in labor share of national income in the United States and other richer countries of the core. There has been as well an increased degree of inequality among workers, with those at the upper end doing far better. Huge literatures exist of the relative contribution of global-ization, technological change, and other factors in creating these trends. Fi-nancialization, in the era of global neoliberalism, was a capital logic response to the world's export-weighted global labor force quadrupling between 1980 and 2005 (IMF 2007:5). Just as economics has a lot to reconsider when it comes to macroeconomics and financial economics, its confident faith in free trade and factor endowment–determined international specialization and di-vision of labor in trade theory must come to terms with a global economy in which poorer countries become richer by producing what the rich coun-tries produce—a world in which industrial policy has been shown capable of producing rapid development and, unlike Anglo-American conventional wisdom, stresses productionist government policy (Rodrik 2010). There is an extensive literature that conjures with the issue of how to increase the per-meability of underdeveloped countries to ideas and technologies that could increase their rate of development. Such models of development model the gap between the world stock of technology and organizational knowledge and the stock in a poor country. The rules influencing the rate at which ideas from the rest of the world enter the poor country and can be used provide a measure of catch-up in such models. Romer (2010:98) writes: "Innovation in meta-rules, the rules for changing rules, would be particularly valuable if they made it easier for groups of people to transition from an existing set of rules to better ones that have been shown to work elsewhere."

One wonders if there is an application closer to home than the poor in un-derdeveloped countries. As the twenty-first century grows older, the question seems relevant whether, after decades of denying that economic development models used by Japan, in its high-growth period, Taiwan, Korea, and China can work (a conviction held against evidence that they have done so [Ams-den 2001; Wade 2004]), this assertion must now be more realistically studied.

Could some tinkering with metarules conventionally embraced in slow-growing advanced economies be in order? Could this make "it easier for groups of people to transition from an existing set of rules to better ones that have been shown to work elsewhere"? Might it be useful for development economists to study the American political system and the dominant economic ideology and model the removal of impediments to growth? It may be time for nation building at home and a transition from a financialization-anchored regime of accumulation to a new investment strategy to promote employment and growth. It will be difficult to come to an equitable, workable global regime reform unless the people of the major powers are comfortable with their domestic situation to the point where they are ready to risk moving to broader agreements calling for compromise and solidarity at a higher level. Concluding this chapter, and before returning to an agenda for the United States, it is useful to say something more about global financial regime reform.

An international perspective confirms that it was possible for countries such as Spain and Ireland to have property bubbles without institutions such as Fannie Mae and Freddie Mac; under different institutional arrangements, for immorality in Icelandic banking to bring a deep national crisis; and for outsized sovereign debt to threaten the value of an important currency. The cross-border obligations of banks and the weak collateral they offered in a context of a lack of a global lender of last resort put pressure on limited political commitment to the existing international financial regime. Without a replacement for the Bretton Woods fixed exchange-rate system, global imbalances will continue to build up, financial markets can become unstable, and national governments can be trapped in circumstances requiring painful austerity measures citizens oppose.

As the manifestation of extreme anger and frustration turns to finding targets upon which to vent rage, the world faces what Dani Rodrik (2011:xix) describes as the fundamental political trilemma of the world economy:

> We cannot simultaneously pursue democracy, national determination, and economic globalization. If we want to push globalization further, we have to give up either the nation state or democratic politics. If we want to maintain and deepen democracy, we have to choose between the nation state and international economic integration. And if we want to keep the nation state and self-determination, we have to choose between deepening democracy and deepening globalization. Our troubles have their roots in our reluctance to face up to these ineluctable choices.

Deepening democracy would mean a flowering of economic democracy so that the money politics that now dominates our governance systems at the national level (Bartels 2008) would be superseded by a fuller democracy in which ordinary citizens would have a greater role in the decisions that affect their lives. We could maintain a significant degree of national determination within a framework of global governance that could go well beyond the current remit of existing global governance state institutional regimes (Tabb 2004). Constructively addressing the global trilemma could be possible. The most important change would be effective economic democracy within nation-states. It would also be highly contested. As discussed in the next chapter, the country is deeply divided between advocates of "freedom from"—freedom from Big Government, individual liberty, and space for people to make choices in the marketplace—and "freedom to"—government support of basic needs, quality education, and job creation so that people could have freedom to live better lives, since as individuals they cannot control the larger economic forces that shape their lives. The former stresses the right to become rich, seen as the incentive that drives personal effort. The latter sees the power of the rich over the economic and political processes of society as the problem. With basic divisions over first principles in macroeconomics and the role of government in a democratic society, the United States and the world face a long period of a malfunctioning SSA and deep disunion before a new hegemonic alliance emerges capable of bringing about institutional change and a set of stable social, political, and economic relations. For Europe, how stronger economies can support weaker ones is only one aspect of distributional questions. The other is how the asssets that have gone into hiding to avoid risk and the tax collector can be mobilized for productive use. Debate over the class dimension of the economy cannot be avoided.

8

The Present in History

*Our economy is badly weakened, a consequence of greed and irresponsibility
on the part of some, but also our collective failure to make hard choices and
prepare the nation for a new age. Homes have been lost, jobs shed, businesses
shuttered. Our health care is too costly, our schools fail too many—and each day
brings further evidence that the ways we use energy strengthen our adversaries
and threaten our planet. These are the indicators of crisis, subject to data and
statistics. Less measurable, but no less profound, is a sapping of confidence across
our land; a nagging fear that America's decline is inevitable, that the next
generation must lower its sights. . . . We remain the most prosperous, powerful nation on Earth. Our workers are no less productive than when this crisis
began. Our minds are no less inventive, our goods and services no less needed
than they were last week, or last month, or last year. Our capacity remains un-
diminished. But our time of standing pat, of protecting narrow interests and
putting off unpleasant decisions—that time has surely passed.*

—BARACK OBAMA, INAUGURAL ADDRESS, 2009

*It's as if 2008 never happened. Once again the world's investors are pumping
up bubbles that will probably explode in their faces. After the popping of a real
estate bubble led to the first global recession since the 1930s, world markets are
frothing like shaken Champagne.*

—PETER COY AND ROBEN FARZAD, 2011

By early 2011 the stock market had recovered most of its losses, and
Wall Street executives were enjoying record bonuses. The new financial sector regulations were unlikely to do much to prevent the next
crisis, even as the increased moral hazard—based on the extensive subsidies
that governments responding to the global financial crisis had provided—
raise expectations of similar bailouts for irresponsible risk taking gone wrong
in the future. Simon Johnson (2011) warned that "the big banks have won
completely this round of boom-bust-bailout. The risk inherent to our financial system is now higher than it was in the early/mid 2000s. We are set up
for another illusory expansion and another debilitating crisis." Summarizing
the way this crisis had been handled in the United States, he concluded that
the top bankers "pulled off a complete snow job." But banks cannot long
prosper while the rest of the economy stagnates.

At the level of macroeconomic policy, the large federal deficit made further economic fiscal stimulus politically unacceptable. The Federal Reserve,

fearing the prospect of deflation if the economy did not grow faster, stepped into the breach by increasing the money supply through quantitative easing ($1.7 trillion in debt purchases over fifteen months to March 2010). A second round of $600 billion in quantitative easing—QE2, as it was called—was announced by the Fed just after the November 2010 election was intended to make regular purchases through June 2011. Money was injected into the system at preannounced intervals to generate inflationary expectations with the goal of preventing deflation of the sort that plagued Japan during a decade of stagnation. The argument for quantitative easing is that when the Federal Reserve buys treasury securities, it lowers their returns and raises their price, causing investors to increase the demand for other assets, particularly stock purchases, raising equity prices, increasing household wealth, and generating more household spending (Bernanke and Reinhart 2004).

Quantitative easing was intended to encourage investment and job creation. The financial accelerator worked as Bernanke expected (Bernanke and Gertler 1996), although the domestic impact was not what he may have hoped for. Rather than creating jobs in the United States, with the dollar falling in value, investors looked to make long-term investments in countries with strong currencies. Cheap credit led to speculative investment in commodities (where prices rose, considerably affecting household food and energy costs) and to increased carry trade, with speculators pouring funds into faster-growing emerging market economies (bidding up their currencies, imparting inflationary pressure, and reducing their exports). There was suspicion that the United States was encouraging the decline in the dollar to reduce the burden of its debt obligations.

The opening chapters of this book described the ways financialization and globalization transformed the American economy in the neoliberal SSA. This final chapter focuses on the lesson learned from the financial crisis and turns to the issue of a possible successor SSA. I argue that a long-range vision requires redefining the role of finance and disallowing speculative strategies that risk the necessity of continuous costly bailouts. There is need for deleveraging, securing government revenues to promote sustainable growth, and avoiding an unnecessary default on basic public functions. While these issues hold public attention, the concern of this book has primarily been the lack of appreciation of how finance works and does not work in the current SSA.

The actual practices of American megabanks have major impacts on the economy yet are by and large ignored by economists who teach and write about money and banking. It has been argued that financial economists and macroeconomists need to move beyond the policy discussions that have dominated for decades and undertake more empirical study of financial institutions and their capacity to destabilize the economy as well as the redistribution of income and wealth that come from market power and asymmetric information among participants in financial markets. This requires jettisoning long-held orthodoxies concerning the efficiency of such markets and employing concepts of an evolutionary political economy, analyzing how banks and finance have changed into entities quite different from what mainstream finance theory understands them to be, as well as how interconnected the global financial system has become, requiring costly and complicated rescue efforts in times of crisis. The economic system has evolved into a form of financialized capitalism to such an extent that quantitative changes reflect a qualitatively different stage of capitalist development. From this perspective one may readily endorse José Gabriel Palma's observation that the economics profession has been looking at financial markets "mostly like creationists look at evolution" (2009:866).

There are, of course, those who will have none of this. Forced to recognize that financial markets may not be efficient in the way they once insisted, they claim that efforts to interfere with markets through ill-conceived government regulation will be rued. Government failure, it is said, is worse than market failure. Alan Greenspan (2011), in an important intervention in which he effectively recants his former recantation and reframes the issue to be the flawed understanding the Dodd-Frank Wall Street Reform and Consumer Protection Act has of financial markets and the hubris of those who think they can successfully regulate financial markets, writes that "in pressing forward, the regulators are being entrusted with forecasting, and presumably preventing, all undesirable repercussions that might happen to a market when its regulatory conditions are importantly altered. No one has such skills . . . the overwhelming set of interactions is never visible." The still powerful view among financial economists, influential participants, and even some regulators is of self-stabilizing properties of financial markets. Hence the demand to see regulation as the problem, and the viewpoint expressed by the powerful chair of the House Banking Committee, Alabama Republican Spencer Bachus, that "In Washington, the view is that the banks are to be regulated, and my view is that Washington and the regulators are there to serve the banks" (Orndorff 2010). When this remark, made to a local paper in his district, the *Birmingham News*, was widely picked up by the national media, the senator tried to explain his incendiary statement, but his stance was clear, setting up a context for refighting the battle over tighter regulation of the financial system.

I have suggested that central bank researchers and other economists are making important strides in conceptualizing how bubbles can be understood and detected, and what can be done to make financial markets safer. It is possible as well to look at Greenspan's examples of "unanticipated adverse outcomes" and see ways to address such outcomes. The job of the regulator is to make the financial system safer even though, or rather because, the incentives in the system make it less so. Participants will seek work-arounds and there will be unanticipated impacts. Such problems do not make regulation counterproductive and certainly do not suggest that government would best not meddle with markets. Greenspan is correct that it is impossible to remove all risk. This is not the goal, however. The task is keeping systemically dangerous risks manageable so that losses can be absorbed by those knowingly taking them, and ensuring that they are not shifted onto the unsuspecting client or the taxpayer. It is difficult to disentangle the need for more effective financial regulation from the structural need to downsize the harmful, system-molding power of finance in the U.S. and global economies.

The continued dominance of global neoliberalism and financialization raises politically potent issues, ranging from their impact on income inequality and insecurity to employment and the fiscal crisis of the state, international competitiveness, and uneven development in the world system. Most central is the question: who shall pay for the exceedingly large losses? If economies are producing at a lower level, fewer goods and services are available, and if debt taken on by the public sector must be paid down, what will be the policy decisions as to who will pay more in taxes and for services formerly provided by the state? Such questions reflect the change in conversation that took place after the Great Recession formally ended. Attention was redirected from the culpability of Wall Street in creating the financial crisis (and the vast fortunes with which many walked away) to large public deficits and the need to drastically cut them. This chapter thus has a double burden of discussing the lessons that have and have not been learned with regard to financialization and connecting this question to the discussion of federal budgets and taxation policies that arose in the wake of continued crisis.

Of Lessons Learned, Not Learned, and Unlearned

There were, and are, economists and regulators who find no problem in a fiftyfold growth of securitized debt in the United States between 1980 and

2000—before it really took off. Few in positions of influence asked whether it was a good thing that investment banks doubled their leverage between 2004 and 2007, why it was that by 2007 Wall Street accounted for two-thirds of all private debt, why the productive sectors of the economy were surrendering capital to feed financial speculation, or why domestic demand was increasingly met through imports paid for with borrowed money. When the liabilities in the financial sector grew from 64 percent of U.S. GDP to 114 percent over the decade from 1997 to 2007, economists generally thought that, since markets knew best, this massive borrowing was not a problem, even though it was overwhelmingly short term and collateralized by assets subject to repricing. In this book I have argued that the assumptions they made, the models they used, and the conclusions they reached were remarkably inaccurate. After the collapse, over 90 percent of the triple-A-rated securities backed by subprime mortgages issued in 2006 and 2007 were downgraded to junk. In the Great Recession, subprime lending of $400 billion wiped out about $40 trillion in aggregate global financial assets (Greenspan 2010). Such numbers suggest the extent of leverage, capital market imbalances, and, in short, the corrupting dominance of financialization that had come from the transformation of banks with short-time, quick-profit horizons, a much increased appetite for risk, and a very different relation to their clients. As has been discussed, traditional theories of financial intermediation, which presume that banks take deposits mainly from households and make loans that are held to maturity, are out of date. In the new model,

> when banks participate in financial markets, they cater to investor sentiment. Banks use their scarce capital to co-invest in newly securitized loans when asset prices are high, and to buy or hold on to distressed securities when asset prices are low. Expanding the balance sheet to securitize is so profitable in good times, however, that banks borrow short term and accept the risk of having to liquidate their portfolio holdings at below fundamental values in bad times. (Shleifer and Vishny 2010:307)

With the SSA transition, investment banks also transformed in essential ways. Goldman Sachs, "a name once synonymous with professionalism and integrity," which had maintained a public position that its business depended on "trust and integrity and putting client interest first," betrayed that trust, leading to a "surreal situation" in which dealing honestly with clients was no longer to be counted upon (Stewart 2010). The collapse of Lehman reflected the same developments. That company had financed many of the great industrial enterprises of twentieth-century America, had a grand tradition of investment banking with long-term relationships that went out the window, replaced by a short-termism that, as for Goldman and others, represented a capitalism that "makes money by betting on failure rather than success" (Chapman 2010).

In its 2011 report, the Senate Permanent Subcommittee on Investigations described a variety of "troubling and sometimes abusive practices" at mega-banks such as Goldman Sachs, Deutsche Bank, and JPMorgan Chase. Goldman settled for what was a tiny penalty (given its earnings) on allegations of defrauding investors in Abacus. It was also in negotiation with the SEC over another CDO, called Hudson, in which Goldman held 100 percent of the short side (betting the asset would fall in value), which the company told clients was "sourced from the street" when in fact Goldman had selected and priced the assets without third-party involvement—and of course benefited when it failed to perform. The subcommittee found that Deutsche traders privately referred to the securities they enthusiastically sold as "crap." Deutsche's billion-dollar-plus Gemstone 7 was one of the "pigs" traders rushed to sell "before the market fell off a cliff." JPMorgan Chase placed half a billion dollars of pension funds and other client money in Sigma, an investment it issued. Court documents reveal that top bank officials were told it was not a safe vehicle, information not shared with clients. The bank collected nearly $2 billion on Sigma's collapse (Story 2011). JPMorgan Chase faced further allegations with regard to another billion-dollar-plus investment vehicle called Squared (Eaglesham 2011).

While there would continue to be efforts to prosecute financial-sector players believed to have violated the law, institutions remained immune, and no high-ranking figure from a large financial institution, no matter how culpable, went to jail. The SEC settlements were generous to the banks, allegedly because "the agency was concerned about taxpayer money in effect being used to pay for settlements" (Morgenson and Story 2011). While the fifty state attorney generals moved toward more severe penalties and more substantive reform in the way banks handled mortgages and foreclosures, the country's top bank regulator went "back to its old tricks." Federal regulators hurried to settle with the megabanks whose mortgage servicers were found to engage in widespread corrupt and illegal foreclosure practices. As Joe Nocera (2011) wrote, "to be honest to call the Office of the Comptroller of the Currency a 'regulator' is almost laughable. . . . The O.C.C. is a coddler, a protector, an outright enabler of the institutions it oversees."

The Fed brought major U.S. banks back from the dead. Rather than Walter Bagehot's canonical criteria of lending only at a penalty rate against sound collateral, it accepted a great deal of questionable collateral on generous terms. In the case of Citigroup, the Fed accepted $156 million in triple-C collateral and even lower-graded securities, assets with high probabilities of default—not at all what had been considered acceptable for backing bank loans in the past. Such standards meant that the Fed was not supplying liquidity based on secure collateral; rather, it was offering major subsidies in violation of previously understood rules governing the extension of credit by the central bank. Tens of billions in loans were made to hedge funds through the Term Asset-Backed Securities Loan Facility. Some used their loans to short the U.S. housing market, intensifying the real estate debacle. The Fed permitted them to use illiquid asset-backed securities as collateral, thus expediting huge profits and averting possible collapse. Loans were also made to foreign banks, some with small operations in the United States.

In late 2010, two years after Congress ordered the Federal Reserve to release details of its rescue transactions, both those on the Right, who saw a government takeover, and those on the Left, who saw a government dominated by Wall Street, had their suspicions confirmed. The data showed the extent to which the Fed had saved leading financial institutions and nonfinancial corporations in danger of collapse. It dispensed $3.3 trillion in liquidity and more than $9 trillion in short-term loans and other financial arrangements to banks and companies. Because of the global interdependence of these institutions, much of this went to foreign banks. The Fed lent $181 billion to the Bank of Scotland, $123 billion to Germany's Dresden Bank, and $105 billion to Belgian-French Dexia. The biggest seller to the Fed's Commercial Paper Funding Facility was UBS of Switzerland (the insurer of the American Insurance Group). Barclay was among the largest borrowers (allowing it to absorb Lehman Brothers). The interconnections of global banking, to say nothing of these foreign banks' extensive operations in the United States, meant that, in the Fed's view, these measures were as necessary as the monies it used to prop up Citigroup, Bank of America, and companies such as Harley-Davidson, Verizon, and Toyota. The Federal Reserve acted as the lender of last resort to inject needed liquidity into the global economy.

There are two issues here. The first is the need to consider the global financial system as a whole. As a leading historian of financial crises, recounting how the Dutch came to rescue the Bank of England in 1695, tells us, "The reigning center at a given time presumably has a responsibility to act as lender of last resort to other countries in financial crisis when trouble threatens to spill over national boundaries" (Kindleberger 1993:275). The second issue is how such rescues are carried out and whether in the contemporary case the Federal Reserve placed conditions on its assistance that were best from the perspective of encouraging a healthy recovery and discouraging the need for future loans of this kind.

With regard to the second matter, Senator Bernie Sanders of Vermont complained that the American people got little in return because "the Fed failed to require loan recipients to invest in rebuilding our economy and protect the needs of ordinary Americans." He labeled the loans "corporate welfare" (Nichols 2010). The *Wall Street Journal* praised Sanders for insisting that the Fed disclose the recipients (in a provision he initiated that was added to the Dodd-Frank Act) and offered "kudos to our favorite Socialist for demanding it." While libertarians at the *Journal*'s editorial page decried interference in the free market, what upset the senator and many other Americans was that the Fed had asked for so little in return for saving these corporations. The Fed may have saved American, and indeed world, finance capital, but many citizens saw little recovery in their own lives.

What the decision-makers at the Fed and Treasury appear not to have learned is the most important lesson of all: that the financial sector has grown too large, too dangerous, and too parasitic. To prevent new and even more costly financial crises, it needs to be shrunk and restructured to fulfill its central purpose of mediating between savers and those who can use capital to increase the productive capacity of the economy. They did not learn that the unregulated reliance by major financial institutions on the short-term repo markets is too dangerous to be tolerated. Their failures stem from the difficulty of relinquishing the core of mainstream financial economic theories that have reigned for the previous three or four decades.

Some lessons have been learned. For one thing, we are less naïve concerning systemic safety and the benefits of presumed portfolio diversification. It has become clear that if asset holdings are diversified similarly, the system as a whole lacks diversification, and that financial institutions following similar strategies take on similar risk and render the entire system vulnerable. Second, as Minsky leads us to expect, the system is subject to tipping points where there is a sudden discontinuity and reversal in Keynes's animal spirits. Third, focusing on the importance of financialization to the global neoliberal SSA makes clear the role of credit overextension in causing such crises.

Fourth, the complex networks of counterparty exposure are better understood, as is the recognition that reregulation requires a global perspective.

The global financial crisis should force a reassessment of misguided certainties central to neoliberalism: that self-regulation provided by the discipline of the market guarantees efficient allocation of financial resources; that modest capital requirements provide protection against random shocks from outside the financial system; that bankers have every incentive to preserve their institutions and so will not act in ways to endanger them; that government intervention in financial markets, however well intentioned, impedes the innovation and risk taking that promote economic growth; and that mathematical models can accurately predict risk in the face of uncertainty. All these assumptions came to be widely questioned with the Great Recession.

Financial markets turned out to be neither efficient in allocating capital nor self-correcting. As the discussion of the Minsky-Keynes financial approaches in chapter 3 argues, a period of low default rates, strong bank profitability, and seeming stability (or "great moderation") should not be taken as evidence that all is well. Increased leverage rationalized by the rising value of collateral-backed loans can instead indicate growing financial fragility. Unless regulators understand these things and are willing to take the punch bowl away even though everyone is happily enjoying the party—and to face the dissatisfaction earned by their preemptive actions —we are looking at a future of continuing asset bubbles and financial collapses. Moreover, the impacts of the global financial crisis, despite official optimism, are hardly behind us, as is made clear by continuing painful austerity measures imposed by governments.

Emerging market economies, as discussed in the previous chapter, had learned to build up foreign currency reserves as protection against sudden capital outflows harming their economies. Following the global financial crisis, they have performed far better than the economies of the core. This has brought new inflows of speculative capital, forcing up their exchange rates, hurting their export competitiveness, and bringing inflation. They learned, against IMF teachings—and because of their strong economies they were free of IMF leverage—to use capital controls to protect against unwelcome capital flows. After decades of the organization preaching the virtues of free capital markets, IMF researchers were forced to review the evidence and conclude that "empirically, there does appear to be a negative association between capital controls that were in place prior to the global financial crisis and the output declines suffered during the crisis. . . . Although causation is far from established, the empirical evidence suggests that the use of capital controls was associated with avoiding some of the worst growth outcomes associated with financial fragility" (Ostry et al. 2010). There never was much evidence that liberalization was always the best policy, as the Washington Consensus had taught when neoliberalism was riding high (Tabb 2004: chaps, 7, 8).

The governments of money-center banks continue to favor liberalized capital movements despite the global imbalances that do so much harm. As regulators realized they needed to rein in some practices of mobile finance capital, efforts to tighten regulation beyond what powerful players found acceptable led to threats to abandon the jurisdiction. In an autumn 2010 speech, Lloyd Blankfein warned that Goldman Sachs could shift its operations around the world if regulatory demands became too strict in certain states (Jenkins and Murphy 2010:13). Each government is afraid to be stricter than jurisdictions that might become attractive to these firms and their job-creating operations. Unless the perceived cost of doing so becomes intolerably high, one can expect governments to support the preferences of financial institutions, much as Britain did in the 1920s by returning the pound to the gold standard to please its financiers and rentiers despite resulting domestic austerity and widespread economic damage. Some governments, believing that they cannot fund another major bailout, nonetheless insist on tougher standards and attempt to strengthen international accords. It will be a struggle. If governments do not move forward to establish global rules that are encompassing and enforced, financial markets will continue to erode their sovereignty and make it more difficult to effectively regulate in the future, possibly after a deeper crisis.

The historical experience of debtors unable to pay international creditors was shaped by the power relations between the militarily powerful governments of money-center nations and the governments of poorer, weaker peripheral states. The strong imposed collection procedures on the weak, often sending in the marines to set up tax collection in harbors on incoming goods, tariffs being the major source of government revenue in the nineteenth and early twentieth centuries. Debt payments were also extended, giving debtors more time to pay when imposition of harsh austerity measures was not enough to force earlier repayment. The goal was to avoid the creditors having to write off bad debt and themselves take losses.

Today for the debtor nations of the euro zone, military occupation is neither likely nor necessary given the power of financial markets to isolate those who do not pay debt and the demands of creditors for austerity. These governments do not want to see their credit status so diminished as to raise the cost of future borrowing or risk having capital markets closed to them. Nonetheless there are limits to the austerity citizens in democratic societies will accept. Moreover, when there is no choice but to default, consequences may turn out not to be as terrible as predicted. Argentina, which had followed IMF's strictures, tied its currency tightly to the dollar, liberalized its economy—only to see it collapse under its foreign debt burden—then defaulted against IMF advice, suffering far less than predicted, and indeed recovering much faster by defaulting than if it had accepted prolonged austerity to pay creditors. Icelandic voters in referenda refused to accept payment plans premised on endless deep austerity. The threat by Iceland's major creditors, the United Kingdom and the Netherlands, to prevent Iceland's entry into the euro zone looked less credible given the euro's problems and the straitjacket less competitive peripheral members experience by not being able to devalue, an option Iceland took advantage of and which helped its economic fundamentals.

A Classical Take on Finance

Serious research is only beginning to understand how the financial crisis is a result of economic inequality, overaccumulation, and overexpansion of credit. Most mainstream discussions allot no role to distributional considerations, but this may be a serious mistake (Atkinson and Morelli 2010). It may be that there was

> an increase in inequalities which depressed aggregate demand and prompted monetary policy to react by maintaining a low level of interest which itself allowed private debt to increase beyond sustainable levels. On the other hand the search for high-return investment by those who benefited from the increase in inequalities led to the emergence of bubbles. Net wealth became overvalued, and high asset prices gave the false impression that high levels of debt were sustainable. The crisis revealed itself when the bubbles exploded, and net wealth returned to normal level. So although the crisis may have emerged in the financial sector, its roots are much deeper and lie in a structural change in income distribution that had been going on for twenty-five years. (Fitoussi and Saraceno 2010)

If changes in income distribution can be seen as to some extent responsible for the financial crisis, financialization can also be understood as contributing to greater inequality. David Zalewski and Charles Whalen (2011) correlate changes in financial structure and income inequality for a sample of developed nations using the IMF's Financial Index, which measures the character of a nation's financial transactions, and OECD figures on income inequality. Their analysis suggests that in almost all the countries in their sample, both financialization and income inequality increased over the decade beginning in the mid-1990s. While there is a correlation between the growth of money market capitalism, financial instability, and economic inequality, policy choices of individual governments can make a big difference in the distribution of gains and losses, as the consistently more egalitarian outcomes in the Nordic countries demonstrate. It is possible to be internationally competitive on the technology frontiers and demonstrate the same influence of financialization but use progressive taxation and an extensive welfare state to promote a more inclusive economic development. It is a matter of the power of contending social forces (Andersen et al. 2007; Zalewski and Whalen 2011).

Alan Greenspan (2011) has applauded the contribution of financial services to economic activity. His data interestingly indicate that the contribution of financial services to U.S. GDP rose sharply between 2008 and 2009. Andrew Haldane notes that the largest increase ever recorded in financial services output was in the fourth quarter of 2008, during the Lehman bankruptcy and the collapse of major banks. What is wrong with this picture? The problem is the conventions of national income accounting that show the remarkable contribution of finance to economic growth when financial collapse brings on serious economic downturn. As John Kay (2011) writes, "accounting systems are not well adapted either to measuring the cost of risk-bearing or the rewards to it. There is frequent asymmetry between the treatment of gains and the treatment of losses. Returns to leverage tend to show up simply as an increase in output." As financial services increase their leverage, this is an increase in inputs that by convention shows up as an increase in GDP.

Duncan Foley (2011) examines how the U.S. economy in the neoliberal era increased real output measured as value added but employed fewer workers than one would expect from the previously dependable Okun's Law (the rule of thumb that a 1 percent change in aggregate demand leads to a half percent change in employment). To explain this outcome he draws on classical economic understanding of production and how it should be measured.

In modern economies with rapid growth of the service sector, measuring output relies on an important proxy value. In manufacturing there is an independent measure of value added (the difference between sales revenues and the cost of purchased inputs). However, in the FIRE sector, which has been the fastest growing part of the economy, and in similar industries such as education, health, and government, there is no independent measure of value added and so value is imputed to make it equal to the incomes generated. When wages and profits go up, value added is presumed to go up by the same amount. This may be the best national income assessment accountants can make, but it means that when "Apple Computer or General Electric pay a bonus to their executives GDP does not change (since value added does not change—the bonus increases compensation of employees but decreases retained earnings), but when Goldman Sachs pays a bonus to its executives, GDP increases by the same amount" (Foley 2011:3). The finance industry employs very few people in relation to the total compensation employees receive. For this reason finance can contribute hugely to GDP but far less to employment, suggesting an answer to why Okun's Law does not predict as well as it had during the national Keynesian SSA and FIRE's contribution to GDP as conventionally measured grew. Finance has become increasingly important (as previously noted, at the height of the bubble it was receiving over 40 percent of domestic corporate profits) and looks as if it is making a major contribution to economic growth.

The buildup of debt can initially lead to a substantial increase in demand, job creation, and economic growth. But as the era of global neoliberalism depended more on credit creation and leverage, the stimulus effect on growth diminished:

> Beyond home equity extraction and consumer credit, the US economy also received stimulus from incremental government spending on wars in Afghanistan and Iraq, and from the Bush tax cuts, which effectively transformed sovereign debt into consumer credit. Despite all this effort, the benefit [for the] US economy was a disappointment. The sum of tax cuts, war spending, consumer credit, and spending out of home equity extraction was in the range of 4% to 8% of GDP from 2002 to 2008. Nominal GDP growth was on average about two percentage points lower than the overall stimulus, even though the economy was operating below potential and experienced an unemployment gap and output gap during most of those years. (Mees 2011:4)

Foley's work is helpful in explaining what happened as finance grew to dominate the American economy, dramatically increasing in importance in the first decade of the new century. Foley developed an index he terms Material Value Added (MVA), which is calculated by removing the sectors that have the value-added method described (based on wages and profits). When comparing inflation-adjusted figures for nominal national income with this index, it turns out that his index better tracks changes in employment than the usual measure of national income. As he concludes, "The superiority of MVA as a business cycle and employment indicator is understandable because material value added is much more closely related to aggregate demand than the imputed value added in service industries like FIRE" (Foley 2011:6). Perhaps as important, Foley explains what the classical economists meant by the theory of value. The profits of financial capital from the classical economists' point of view are a share of the surplus value that takes the form of interest paid on borrowed capital. From this perspective "it is double-counting to 'impute' an imaginary produced 'financial service' as the counterpart of interest payments. Interest payments are a transfer of a part of the surplus value appropriated in production, not the purchase of a good or service" (8–9).

It may not be the case, as Paul Volker maintains, that the only clearly useful innovation the financial sector produced is the ATM machine, but the presumption widely made regarding the financial sector's contribution to well-being is misleading. Rather than adding to GDP (assuming, which is questionable, that GDP is a proxy for economic well-being), finance may merely be appropriating value produced elsewhere in the economy—thus Matt Taibbi's colorful description of Goldman Sachs as "a great vampire squid wrapped around the face of humanity, relentlessly jamming its blood funnel into anything that smells like money" (Taibbi 2009). Certainly not all finance is exclusively surplus redistributing. Much of what banks and other financial firms do involves providing positive services to the economic system, but the character of asset speculation and its contribution to the creation of bubbles and collapses to a significant extent is only redistributing surplus produced in other parts of the economy.

Karl Marx, the last of the great classical economists, offers a useful construct, the concept of fictitious capital—paper values that cannot be realized—to explain what we now know as the Keynes-Minsky understanding of business cycles. According to Marx, when the extent of fictitious capital so exceeds the potential output that people begin to doubt the plausibility of market valuations, the prices of assets can suddenly and dramatically fall.

Fictitious capital does not have a material basis in commodities or productive activity. Instead it relies on the anticipated future value that will be created to justify its exchange. This optimism prompts the extension of credit and, as Keynes, and before him Marx, explained, uncertainty is always present. The buying and selling of claims to wealth can, as discussed in chapter 3, become a self-levitation process in which, as prices of paper claims rise, the assets can be used as collateral to borrow still more and buy more assets, driving prices higher in a seemingly endless loop. It is endless, that is, until it unceremoniously ends and what is left are the many players who thought they would be able to sell and get out before the collapse, with the more naïve holding devalued assets and facing severe losses. Animal spirits lead to overextension of credit and then to collapse. While collateralized debt obligations and credit default swaps may be new, in their essence they would not have seemed strange to Marx, who wrote: "With the development of interest-bearing capital and the credit system, all capital seems to double itself, and sometimes treble itself, by the various modes in which the same capital, or perhaps even the same claim on a debt, appears in different forms in different hands. The greater portion of this 'money-capital' is purely fictitious" (1984: chap. 29).

In Marx's framework, an overaccumulation of capital results when capital cannot realize the expected profit rate and financial assets can only be sold at reduced profit or at a loss. Overaccumulation is also evident in empty shopping centers, idle factories, and unsold housing inventory. In Marx's way of thinking, this contradiction—between what could be used and the exchange value of commodities that cannot be sold at the expected profit—requires that the assets be written down, losses taken, and at some lower price markets clear. Both Austrian free-market economists and Marxists see this forcible reassertion of prices to reflect values as the function of economic crises in a capitalist system. Both reject the notion of neoclassical growth models of a steady-state growth from one equilibrium to the next with smooth, costless adjustments. Joseph Schumpeter's concept of creative destruction, in which waves of technological and organizational innovation change both what is produced and the way things are produced, is very Marxist—as Schumpeter, who was in implicit conversation with Marx, would be the first to recognize. (For a discussion of these economists as part of what I have called the mainline tradition as opposed to the mainstream approach to political economy, see Tabb 1999.)

Speculation in assets and productive capacity tends to get ahead of itself in waves of optimism, expected profit is not realized, overaccumulation occurs, and crisis follows. In this narrative, a Keynes-Minsky overextension leads to a correction, thence to a fall in asset prices, bankruptcies, falling wages and unemployment. At the same time globalization has vastly increased the size of the labor force upon which capital draws, which has led to a general increase in the share of output going to capital. As discussed in chapter 2, this process has been accompanied by stress on the maximization of shareholder value, further concentrating wealth, which seeks outlets in asset speculation, rather than in productive investment. The FIRE sector grows, but measured GDP growth is not matched by employment creation, and wages fall further behind productivity gains. This leads to the great and unsustainable creation of fictitious capital, and to crisis.

One can accept or reject Marx's explanations for why the capitalist system not only is prone to crises but can run up against diminished opportunities for profitable investment. However, it is clear that the current lack of sufficient attractive investment opportunities in the real U.S. economy (despite the rapid growth in emerging market economies) has fueled the growth of financialization and unsustainable debt creation—along with stagnant working-class incomes, higher unemployment, income inequalities, and social relations reminiscent of the nineteenth century's Gilded Age of robber barons and superexploited, disempowered workers. In a globalized economy the state has retreated from entitlement provision and protection of labor that was the basis of the American dream. For three decades debt creation put off crisis and provided the wherewithal for consumer spending. In the present period, we are told, the working-class standard of living must shrink, and realism demands less taxation of business and diminished production of public goods.

In a longer historical perspective, the stakes for the United States may be high indeed. While the framework here has been within the SSA approach, a longue durée perspective of the French Annales School suggests it is historically shortsighted to see the present era of financialization as an unprecedented occurrence in capitalist development. There have been other periods in which the decline of a global hegemon (the Dutch, the English) has coincided with the creation of an overabundance of money capital. Taking such an approach, Arrighi and Silver write that "in the past (although not yet in the current one), hegemonic crises eventually led to a complete hegemonic breakdown and 'systemic chaos.'" By systemic chaos they refer to a situation of "severe and seemingly irremediable systemic disorganization" (Arrighi and Silver 2001:271). While speculation on how such a transition will come out is well beyond the boundary of our ambitions, the framing these world-systems theorists offer underlines the extent to which the United States and the world economy may be in an extended period of major transformation and that the choices made in the current period will have significant historical resonance.

The Neoliberal Legacy

The idea that a rising tide lifts all boats may have made some sense during the national Keynesian SSA, but the global neoliberal SSA growth at the very top has come at the expense of the vast majority of Americans and their communities. Between 1976 and 2007 the average inflation-adjusted hourly wage declined in the United States by more than 7 percent (Saez 2010). Almost a third (32.9 percent) of gross pretax income went to the top 10 percent of all households in 1976. In 2007 the top 10 percent received half (49.7 percent) and the top 1 percent received half of the total going to the top 10 percent, an amount equal to a quarter of all household income by the later date. Very wealthy people were largely corporate executives receiving generous stock options and top earners at hedge funds, private equity firms, and investment banks. Returns from financial investments added more wealth and income at the top because the rich disproportionately owned such assets and many made their money on Wall Street. Moreover, as described in chapter 2, maximization of stockholder value resulted in greater income polarization by holding down working-class compensation. Such regressive developments reversed the patterns established during the decades of the national Keynesian SSA. This is the shift: from 1950 to 1980 the share of income going to those at the top declined, while the real income of the vast majority grew. However, from 1980 to 2008 the income share of the bottom 90 percent of Americans fell by 13.59 percent (Johnson 2010). Such trends provided the basis for much of the public outrage at the generous treatment of Wall Street.

By early 2011 a fifth of Americans qualified for food stamps (or the supplemental nutrition assistance program). The benefits, received by over forty-four million Americans, averaged $130 a month, not enough to sustain healthy nutrition levels. Many people ran out of food before the end of the month, then turning to food pantries and soup kitchens. The richest 10 percent of Americans received 100 percent of income growth between 2000 and 2007. In the national Keynesian SSA, the top 10 percent of families accounted for a third of income growth.

Even before the Great Recession, economic insecurity had been growing through the years of the global neoliberal SSA. An Economic Security Index (ESI) sponsored by the Rockefeller Foundation measures the share of Americans who experience at least a 25 percent drop in their available family income, whether due to a decline in income, a decline in net wealth from excessive medical spending, a drop in the value of retirement accounts, or other factors. The ESI increased by one-third between 1985 and the prerecession year of 2007. It increased by half between 1985 and 2009. In 2009 and 2010 one in five Americans experienced a 25 percent or greater decline in household income. Researchers found that it takes an average individual experiencing such an income shock six to eight years to recover economically. Understandably, many more Americans felt vulnerable and economically insecure in the aftermath of the Great Recession. After reviewing survey results, Hacker et al. (2010:19) found that "in short, economic insecurity appears more the rule than the exception in American life, and more so over time."

A group of McKinsey & Company researchers (Bisson, Kirkland, and Stephenson 2010:4) predict that "on average fifteen percent of US households can now expect their income to fall by as much as 50 percent each year." They urge that governments "ensure social stability and maintain social safety nets. What's more, they must accomplish these ends for citizens who continue to live within distinct national borders, even though those citizens' fortunes will be hugely influenced by transformative shifts in the flows of capital, goods, labor, and information that recognize no borders." They are certainly correct in their view that the response of Washington to these pressures "will do more to shape outcomes over the next decade than the actions of any other single economic actor." What Washington does will depend on the intensity of conflicting pressures exerted.

Faced with rising deficits, both Congress and state governments chose to dramatically cut government spending and to lay off public-sector workers rather than raise taxes on those individuals and corporations that had prospered over the decades of the neoliberal ascendancy. Blaming government spending for economic hardship misdirected people from the transformations produced by transnational capital and international finance that continued to shape the economic prospects for working-class Americans. It is difficult to disagree with William Lazonick (2009b:29) that "any government policy agenda that seeks to re-create the middle class in the United States needs to begin with an attack on the financialized corporation." More than this, it has to reject the constraints financialization places on a democratic society.

The consequences of three decades of the global neoliberal SSA—short-term profit maximization, lowered job security, rising income inequality and insecurity, privatization of government functions, and downsizing of the state to accommodate tax cuts—resulted in less infrastructure spending, a failure to keep up with the educational attainments of other countries, and a lack of government support for the industries that will shape twenty-first-century America. Extensive tax avoidance by transnational capital and internationally oriented financial institutions, as well as wealthy Americans, has produced a demonized government increasingly unable to meet its contractual obligations.

Addressing what was thought to be a tax gap (the difference between what should be paid under the law and what was paid) of a minimum $400 billion, the Internal Revenue Service stepped up its international tax compliance. The IRS created a Global High Wealth Industry Unit to better monitor tax compliance by high-income individuals and their related enterprises, and in an organizational shift it refocused and renamed its Large and Mid-Size Business Division as the Large Business and International Division to extend its international strategy for collecting taxes, giving it added resources to address this area of compliance (Internal Revenue Service 2010). Many in Congress supportive of the interests of high-wealth individuals argued for cutting the IRS budget to limit "extortion" by Big Government.

Those who blamed government spending for the nation's ills called for austerity measures. Those looking for deep cuts in federal spending as a proportion of GDP—back to what it had been fifty years earlier—required targeting Social Security and Medicare. Social Security was not actually in any great trouble; with small changes it could continue to self-finance for the next seventy-five years, even on conservative forecasts. Medicare was rising fast as a proportion of the federal budget, largely because per capita health-care costs in the United States were twice those of other advanced economies.

While people overwhelmingly support Social Security as it has existed, it offers a pot of money that could be raided to pay down federal debt. As one member of the president's bipartisan commission on debt reduction declared (like Willie Sutton when asked why he robbed banks), "it was where the money was." A cochair of the commission appointed by President Obama, former senator Alan Simpson, famously described Social Security as "like a milk cow with 310 million tits" in an e-mail he sent to the executive director of the National Older Women's League. Simpson was chosen by a White House that looked to the commission to give Washington cover to cut domestic spending, including Social Security and Medicare, instead of pursuing alternatives such as "weaning corporations—banks, insurance companies, war contractors—off the federal teat" (Skomarovsky 2010).

Social Security recipients were less able to do without their promised benefits. Among those sixty-five and older, Social Security provides the major source of income for 57 percent of families. For a third of beneficiaries, these transfer payments provide 90 percent or more of their income. The aging of America should not be confused with the inability of Social Security, modestly adjusted, to provide for America's retirees. The 2010 Social Security Trustees Report predicts that it should be possible to hold the tax at current levels until 2020, and between then and 2040 to raise the rate by a little under 1.5 percent (which would take up only 12 percent of the projected wage growth over that period), leaving "our children" more than 40 percent better off after the Social Security tax increase than Americans in 2009 (Baker 2010). While reducing retirement benefits is seen as "making the difficult choices," the really difficult choice would be to compel Wall Street—which benefited both from the activities that led to the crisis and from its rescue—to help pay to reduce the deficit.

In keeping with the concerns of this book, if more money for Social Security is needed, a financial speculation tax could be implemented. Taxing Wall Street could bring in a great deal of revenue while at the margin discouraging speculation. The United Kingdom has had a 0.25 percent tax on each side of a stock trade for some time now. The British Board of Inland Revenue collects it with very little difficulty at very low cost. If the United States had an equivalent tax it could bring in $40 billion a year. Dean Baker (2011) estimates that a financial speculation tax on options, futures, CDSs, and other products could bring in $150 billion a year (even assuming very substantial reduction in trading volume). Measures have been proposed that would not inhibit nonspeculative investment while raising as much as 1 percent of GDP, or twice the projected shortfall in Social Security.

While a small transaction tax might work at the national level without driving financial trading abroad, the long-term solution to the erosion of the tax base is to have the financial sector contribute more to the cost of government services through a global tax collected on all financial transactions and rebated to governments. Indeed, transnational corporate taxation (not just of the financial sector) could be assessed at the global level to prevent tax avoidance and reduce tax cheating, with proceeds given to national governments where production takes place, where products are sold, and perhaps with some portion allocated for the development needs of the poorest people in the global South. Transnational corporations and international finance have undercut the capacities of government to tax major sources of income. Addressing this tax avoidance in such ways would end the fiscal crisis of the state.

A great deal of revenue could be raised by taxing capital gains (including carried interest, the ruse used by private equity and hedge-fund partners to avoid income tax rates) as normal income. Over 80 percent of capital gains income went to the top 1 percent of earners, and over 90 percent to the top 5 percent. Such changes seemed fair, given that between 2001 and 2007 the income share of the four hundred richest taxpayers had doubled while their tax rates fell. Requiring that interest payments be made from after-tax income could not only raise revenues but limit the financial sector's self-leveraging at the expense of taxpayers, encouraging them instead to invest out of retained earning and from equity raised, a double benefit. This strategy would produce more tax revenue from the banks and make the financial system safer by discouraging leveraged borrowing. Such a change would affect private equity and hedge funds, limiting their activities. With tax revenues in the United States at a sixty-year low, and 56 percent of all income growth in the previous twenty years going to the top 1 percent of households, raising their taxes seems a reasonable alternative to savage service cuts.

As for cutting Medicare, the other big target for cost reduction, it is necessary to distinguish between the rising costs of health care, which is a serious problem, and proposals to address this budgetary burden by taking a scalpel to Medicare. While it is the case that Medicare costs are projected to rise significantly, this cost growth is not due to inefficiencies in the program. Compared with private health insurance, it is considerably more efficient. The public plan does not require a huge advertising budget, pay exorbitant salaries, pay dividends to stockholders, or spend large amounts to deny people coverage (except in cases of real fraud). Alternative systems— "socialized medicine" and single-payer approaches in Europe—cost half as much and have better health outcomes for their populations. Washington politicians prefer to cut entitlement programs rather than confront pharmaceutical companies and require them to bargain with Medicare, as the Veterans Administration does, or take on the political challenge of confronting insurance companies.

Could there be better places to cut federal spending than reducing Social Security and Medicare benefits? The total U.S. military budget is almost as large as those of the rest of the nations of the world put together. Pentagon spending has grown at an inflation-adjusted rate of 7 percent a year over the first decade of the new century (12 percent not adjusting for inflation). The Department of Defense consumes over half (56 percent) of all discretionary federal spending. It has accounted for close to two-thirds of the increase in annual discretionary spending since 2001. Pork and waste in the military budget are enormous. The bipartisan task force organized by the Project on Defense Alternatives details military spending cuts that would save $960 billion between 2011 and 2020 without reduction in the strength of the military needed to defend the country. The Congressional Research Service finds that the War on Terrorism, including the Iraq and Afghanistan wars, has been the costliest military venture in the history of the United States (after adjusting for inflation) except for the Second World War. In the manner of a much diminished Great Britain after World War II, the United States may be forced to conclude that it can no longer afford so costly a military. Other nations have learned to define their national security interests more broadly to include economic security. As Leslie Gelb argues, with the exception of the United States, nations calculate power more in terms of GDP than of military might. He argues that "in international affairs of the twenty-first century U.S. interest abroad cannot be adequately protected or advanced without an economic reawakening at home" (2010:43).

The intense frustration palpable in an America in prolonged recession, a frustration directed at incumbent elected officials, is rooted not only in present suffering, but in fear regarding the future. A great deal of the anger is targeted at bigness in all its forms, but particularly at Big Government. While Wall Street is blamed for creating the financial crisis and transnational corporations for sending jobs offshore, it is hard for people to see what might be done about them. One can vote out elected officials but not economic elites. Of course this is exacerbated by the fact that politicians are financed by, and may answer to, these same economic elites.

In rejecting state disciplining of irresponsible capitalists out of fear of government takeover, people were essentially thinking in terms of bringing back a presumed golden age of small towns, small business, and small government. Those Americans who wanted to take their country back to this largely mythical past may quite understandably not like what is happening to them and their country, but a backward-looking populism of this sort makes realistically facing the future more difficult. It is one thing not to like the choices one is given and another to denounce government and try to further weaken its capacities, rather than to redirect its priorities. The issue is not big or small government, but achieving a government that meets the needs of its people. The effort to stampede the country into drastic cuts in welfare-state health, retirement, and other programs seems yet another instance of the "shock doctrine": the use of the public's disorientation following massive collective shocks—wars, terrorist attacks, natural disasters, and deep economic crises—to achieve elite goals by imposing economic shock therapy (Klein 2007).

While people may be harmed by the changes in taxation and government expenditure patterns, the public generally has a limited understanding of the federal budget. Some 60 percent of Americans polled believe that the federal budget deficit can be fixed just by eliminating waste, fraud, and abuse. Voters do not casually agree with these untruths; at least 40 percent strongly agree. Americans have long held these optimistic views of how waste could be expunged from government and taxes reduced without any real loss to them. People elected on such a platform in office often do reduce taxes but usually do not pay for the loss of revenue, creating larger deficits. The two most egregious offenders in this regard are Ronald Reagan and George W. Bush. Following World War II, the national debt had fallen as a proportion of national income during the administrations of all presidents until Reagan. When he entered the White House, the federal debt was equal to 32.5 percent of GDP. By the end of the Reagan years it was 56 percent of GDP. When George W. Bush arrived in the White House the debt was likewise 56 percent of GDP. When he left office, it was 83 percent and the United States had gone from a structural surplus in 2000 to a structural deficit of 2.8 percent of GDP. (A structural deficit will remain even if the economy returns to satisfactory macro performance.) Thus the two most conservative presidents since the 1920s were the ones on whose watch the national debt dramatically increased. George W. Bush's two terms saw the biggest deficits in American history. It was the continuation of his tax cuts and the cost of the wars, not new programs introduced by President Obama, that accounted for the bulk of the increase in the national debt, worsened by the deep recession. The difficulty the feuding parties had in agreeing on how to reduce this deficit led to a warning that the credit rating of the U.S. government might be downgraded by Standard & Poor's in the spring of 2011.

When opinion polls ask Americans what they would cut from the federal budget (besides waste), their responses reflect a lack of accurate knowledge of government spending patterns. When people were polled in a January 2011 Ipsos/Reuters survey, 75 percent said foreign aid should be cut. (The only other cuts a majority approved were from the budgets of the IRS and the SEC, the agencies needed to enforce fair tax collection and honest business dealings under existing laws.) A 2010 national poll showed that Americans guessed, on average, that the United States spends 25 percent of the budget on foreign aid. They thought that given the U.S. financial situation, the amount should be reduced to be about 10 percent (Program on International Policy Attitudes 2010). The real figure for foreign aid is less than 1 percent of the budget, and much of this money is not foreign aid in the sense most Americans understand the term; rather, it funds military expenditures in countries of the global South, costs of the State Department, the Peace Corps, and so on (Birdsall 2011). If we look at the White House request to Congress for development aid in fiscal year 2012, we find that even generously defined, barely half the aid budget the administration requested would go to what we would think of as foreign aid. And certainly when we are concerned with development of poorer regions, the proportion would be far less than even this already small amount. Even using the largest estimate for U.S. foreign aid, it is far less than the amount given by almost all other aid givers as a proportion of GDP.

While Americans may not know that the defense budget rose by 80 percent between 2000 and 2011 (not including the cost of wars in Iraq and Afghanistan), when asked, they prefer cuts in military spending to reduction in domestic programs like Social Security and health care, even though they are confused about what the 2010 health care reform legislation actually included—as they are about so many other aspects of the budget. Polls show widespread belief that the rich have prospered while the rest of the country has not, an accurate perception. A Bloomberg poll from March 2011 finds that the most popular way to reduce the deficit is to let the Bush tax cut for the rich expire. An NBC-*Wall Street Journal* poll finds financing the deficit reduction with a surtax on millionaires popular (Klein 2011:8). That poll also shows that while a combined 22 percent name deficit reduction/government spending as their top issue, 37 percent believe that job creation/economic growth is the number one issue. Core Republicans and tea party supporters, not Democrats, independents, and swing voters, are most concerned about making more spending cuts (Murray 2011). How this plays out in future elections remains to be seen. Public philosophy regarding the role of government and the priorities of the country is mediated through media and Washington politics in ways that reflect not majority beliefs but economic elites (Bartels 2008).

It turns out, again if one can believe academic efforts to gauge such matters, that Americans of almost all political persuasions are in favor of fairness and a greater degree of equality in their society. They would appear to favor more progressive taxation in principle. Yet none of this is simple. A large number of Americans are convinced that since they may someday be rich and want to leave money to their children, the death tax (the inheritance tax) is objectionable. It is difficult for social scientists to sort through conflicting attitudes and values held by their fellow citizens.

Michael Norton and Dan Ariely (2011) asked a statistically significant random sample of Americans which of three pie charts displaying income distribution they would prefer if they did not know where their own income would fall. (This is called in the literature the Rawlsian veil of ignorance. They were told, "Imagine that if you joined this nation, you would be randomly assigned to a place in the distribution so you could end up anywhere in the distribution from the richest to the poorest.") The first pie chart was divided in equal fifths. Unbeknownst to the respondents, the second distribution by income quintiles was the wealth distribution of the United States, and the third the far more egalitarian distribution of Sweden. Only 10 percent preferred the (unlabeled) U.S. distribution, with 47 percent preferring the unlabeled Sweden and 43 percent choosing the equal distribution. These results suggest that Americans prefer some inequality to perfect equality, but not the extreme inequality found in the United States. The second and third steps were even more interesting. The questioners removed the "veil of ignorance" and asked what the respondents' ideal distribution of wealth would be for the United States—that is, how much wealth should go to each quintile. They also asked what the respondents thought the wealth distribution actually was in the United States. Respondents vastly underestimated the actual wealth inequality of their country, believing that the wealthiest 20 percent held 59 percent of the wealth; the actual figure is about 84 percent. They preferred that this top quintile have only 32 percent of the wealth (Norton and Ariely 2011:10). Interestingly, it didn't matter if people voted for Democrats or Republicans, whether they were male or female, or what they themselves earned—their agreement dwarfed these differences.

But, and it is a very big but, and a reason why understanding public opinion is so difficult, Americans do not hold attitudes on specific tax alternatives that reflect such seeming support for greater equality. Consider an explanation of a poll showing that most Americans supported the Bush tax cuts (in their entirety) and repeal of the inheritance tax:

[It was] not because they were indifferent to economic inequality, but because they largely failed to connect inequality and public policy. Three out of every four people in the NES survey said that the difference in incomes between rich people and poor people has increased in the past 20 years, and most of them added that that is a bad thing—but most of these people still supported President Bush's tax cuts and the repeal of the estate tax. People who wanted to spend more money on a variety of specific government programs were, if anything, more likely to support tax cuts than those who did not, other things being equal, while those who said that "people in the government waste a lot of money we pay in taxes" were markedly less supportive of the Bush tax cut than those with more optimistic views about government efficiency. Finally, and perhaps most strikingly, people's opinions about tax cuts were strongly shaped by their attitudes about their own tax burdens, but virtually unaffected by their attitudes about the tax burden of the rich—even in the case of the estate tax, which only affects the wealthiest one or two percent of taxpayers. (Bartels 2005:16)

In a November 2010 WorldPublicOpinion.org poll, a majority (53%) said they had paid "a lot" of attention to the debate over federal budget cuts. A mere 21 percent said the $60 billion in cuts that Congress was considering was too high. A plurality (36%) regarded the cuts as too low, and 31 percent found them about right. The political impact for a legislator who is in favor of the extending the tax cuts appears to be a net positive even though this would add to the deficit substantially, something people presumably opposed. A majority (52%) were more likely to support their member of Congress if he or she supported the tax cuts, while only 28 percent were less likely. Support for reelecting a member who voted in favor of the cuts was high among Republicans (67%) and reached majority support among independents (54%), explaining why Congress was flirting with not raising the debt ceiling and letting America's bills go unpaid, a reneging on bond commitments that would shake world financial markets. Continued debate over the extent of progressivity in the tax system is to be expected, a constant in American politics. The same is true on the spending side, given both attitudes toward the extent of wasteful spending and disagreement over the role of the federal government in spending that promises to promote growth.

Most voters are motivated reasoners who, believing what they believe, find reason in whatever information they are given to confirm their existing beliefs. This is a powerful psychological force (Redlawsk, Civettini, and Emmerson 2010). But these researchers also find that although voters interpret even negative information regarding their preferred candidates favorably, they do not do so ad infinitum. Eventually if enough disconfirming information builds up, after an extended period of increasing anxiety a tipping point is reached for most, and what the investigators call "more accurate updating" occurs (they change their minds). The difficulty is getting new information to people who rely on sources of news that only confirm their initial biases.

Replacing Dependence on Financialization

President Obama in his 2011 State of the Union address called on Americans to "out-innovate, out-educate, and out-build the rest of the world." More education, he reminded his listeners, helps students get better-paying jobs, helps their employers, and helps the country. A closer look at the need to "out-innovate/out-educate" that is more than a campaign line calculated to win applause requires facing the incentives of our economy that influence career choices and activities people choose since these have significant effect on the broader allocation of resources in the society. Economists understand that "when talented people become entrepreneurs, they improve the technology in the line of business they pursue, and as a result, productivity and income grow. In contrast, when they become rent seekers, most of their private returns come from redistribution of wealth from others and not from wealth creation. As a result, talented people do not improve technological opportunities, and the economy stagnates" (Murphy, Shleifer, and Vishny 1991:505).

Government can change incentives. The president, observing that government "planted the seeds for the Internet. That's what helped make possible things like computer chips and GPS," emphasized the positive externalities from government investments. It was not at all clear that Obama could convince the nation of the need for public investment and at the same time meet the commitments he had made to a sizable cutting of the federal budget deficit. Republicans were quick to say that what he called investment is really spending; they did not see the need for such spending. Yet, after decades of lack of replacement investment for basic infrastructure, the Federal Highway Administration judges 25 percent of the nation's bridges to be structurally deficient or obsolete. The Association of State Dam Safety Officials found thousands of dams unsafe and deficient, their numbers growing with each survey. America's water and sewage systems, some dating back to the Civil War, have been ignored, accustomed as we are to their functioning even without maintenance. But the McKinsey Global Institute (2011) warns us that "US infrastructure is inadequate to meet the needs of a dynamic, growing economy. At the same time, the quality of infrastructure from transportation to water systems has been in relative decline in the United States, which currently ranks 23rd in the quality of its overall infrastructure, undermining competitiveness." A decade earlier the United States ranked seventh. Another McKinsey study finds that infrastructure ranks among the top four criteria multinationals use to make decisions on where to invest (McKinsey 2010). While those opposing such initiatives said they are unaffordable under existing fiscal constraints, it will cost more to fix America's inadequate infrastructure problems next year than this, and far more in the years after that. Programs that would make sense, along the lines of the New Deal job creation of the 1930s, are not considered realistic while cities and states lay off hundreds of thousands of teachers, policemen, hospital workers, and others who provide our society with basic public services. Yet it was after all during the high-deficit years of the Great Depression that government built much of the infrastructure that has now fallen into disrepair.

On the other hand, it may be argued that reliance on the market, on the U.S. capacity for self-renewal, will unleash an era of growth and job creation in the country if only taxes are lowered and government gets smaller. However, one needs to ask why China is the leader in wind power and other emerging alternative energy technologies such as solar panels. The answer is its government subsidies and insistence of policy makers that the country's power grid utilize alternative energy before any other source and do so under long-term contracts that guarantee dependable markets for startups and their new technologies. Public financing for wind turbines, solar panels, and other low-carbon initiatives has also grown dramatically in European countries like Germany where government supports green technologies. China spends 9 percent of its GDP on infrastructure, Europe 5 percent, and the United States half of that—differences apparent to anyone who has traveled on European high-speed trains or landed at one of China's new, efficient airports.

While other countries pursue active industrial policies that facilitate gaining leadership in twenty-first-century industries, in the United States such investment is portrayed as un-American. Such criticism reflects the same nostalgia and desire to go back to the world of an imagined past, erasing the role that government has in fact played in promoting investment, from subsidizing the transcontinental railroad to supporting state research universities. It seems shortsighted to reject serious government encouragement of industries that could promote more sustained growth and create large numbers of jobs. The usual answer given is that the government cannot do this. But in other countries there is a clear record of constructive use of incentives.

People who have done the math tell us that $100 billion spent to directly hire American workers would create 2.6 million jobs over two years and an additional half million indirectly—far more jobs than when this kind of money is spent on tax cuts. Producing 8.2 million jobs needed to put Americans back to where we were has been costed out to be $235 billion (Harvey 2011). This is less money than the government spent continuing the Bush tax cuts. If they had been allowed to expire, the federal government would have collected $295 billion in additional revenues in 2011—more than enough needed to create those jobs. One can argue about the math, and about whether jobs should be created in the public sector or only with private employers, but in principle employment creation could be achieved if Americans were willing to accept a greater role for the federal government in this process and were confident that, as in the New Deal, Washington could sufficiently resist political pressures and backroom deals to do this efficiently. As an alternative to the renewal of asset speculation as the accumulation strategy, this would require a dramatic change in public perception and ideological commitment.

This is because the logic of investment in alternative energy, rebuilding infrastructure, and educating young people to a higher level of achievement would appear to be common sense to many, probably most, Americans, but people do not trust their government. There are right-wing and left-wing reasons for this. The Right fears a Big Government takeover reducing liberty, requisitioning taxation, and wasting money for poor return and the undermining of the free market. The Left sees the process overpowered by special interests, large corporations, Wall Street, and generally those who fund political campaigns to procure government contracts, with quiet changes in laws governing their economic interests and friendly regulatory (non)enforcement.

Economists and others who do not like large amounts of spending on public programs—infrastructure, health care, retirement, education, and income maintenance—take the occasion of increased public debt to blame spending and public employees who are too well paid and to demand deep cuts. Keynesians say that in a period of high unemployment, government spending stimulates growth and can be paid down as the economy expands. They point to the way the national debt in relation to a growing national income declined under all post–World War II presidents until Reagan. This debate is complicated by the need to take into account the impacts of globalization. Given the increased foreign competition from states that use industrial policy successfully, those who would rely on an unregulated market and no state involvement need to convince their fellow citizens that this can be a winning strategy in the new context. Keynesians must address the reduced impact of domestic stimulus in a globalized economy in which leakages from spending in the United States stimulate increased imports, produce jobs abroad, and can create or increase balance-of-payments deficits and more foreign borrowing to support consuming beyond our means. Further, larger corporate profits from increased exports do not automatically correspond to growth in government tax revenues given the ability of transnationals to designate earnings as taking place outside the jurisdiction, and given capital-intensive production techniques that do not lead to proportional job creation in the United States.

The Commerce Department reports that U.S. multinational corporations eliminated 2.9 million American employees over 2000–2010 while adding 2.4 million employees in other countries. These developments contribute to the declining share of personal income in the United States that comes from wages and salaries (which went from 68 percent in 1959 to 57.6 percent in 2007) while the share of income from dividends, capital gains, and interest rose (Economic Policy Institute 2011). The share of federal tax revenues from corporate income taxes fell from 4 percent of GDP in the 1960s to 2 percent in the 1990s and 1.3 percent in 2010 (Office of Management and Budget 2011: table 2.1). Corporate tax contributions to national budgets in most countries have fallen with the globalization of capital and the opportunities for tax avoidance, underlining the need to develop global-level taxation. Better policies at the national level are certainly possible, and necessarily come first, but they are constrained until they are supported at the level of the world system.

In the past a deep economic crisis typically coincided with the demise of a social structure of accumulation. Time is required during which the bases of a new SSA are built over the opposition of those who were the core of the older hegemonic block. Following an extended period of contention among differing public philosophies, a new SSA comes into existence. It is achieved by a coalition strong enough to win approval for its priorities. Such change takes time and will be preceded by a period of gridlock in Washington.

Protective measures against excessive risk in the financial system, limits to financialization, and taxation of finance could be part of a shift in systemwide norms. Such changes are unlikely to be adopted without the support and reinforcement of regulationist institutions in other areas, ranging from environmental and energy policies to health care, education, and labor relations. They will require a coherent alternative public philosophy embodied in a unified, widely embraced vision and a new hegemonic bloc.

It is possible that, as in the 1970s as the national Keynesian SSA was crumbling, there will first be a period of stagflation as neither labor nor capital will want to accept a decline in real income. The overhang of debt and the more rapid growth of emergent market economies add to these pressures. It will be quite remarkable if the needed adjustments and rebalancing occur smoothly and politicians prove to be visionary leaders. Across a range of policy issues, contending reform proposals will be supported by overlapping coalitions that confront many of the same opponents and ways of thinking.

If past is prologue, the political coalitions and economics that will rule the new social structure of accumulation will establish the norms of acceptable behavior in corporate governance, government activity, and the regulation of financial markets. The shape of the next social structure of accumulation is likely to be regulationist. The question is whether it will be a repressive regulation of a fearful society with a reduced public sphere limiting the life chances of Americans or one that restructures the citizen-state, labor-capital, government-corporate, and U.S.-global accommodations in ways that hold financialization in check and empower an inclusive, sustainable growth path. We make our own collective history. There are no answers at the back of the book.

Aaron, Kat. (2009). "Predatory Lending: A Decade of Warnings." Washington, D.C.: Center for Public Integrity, May 6.

Abreu, Dilip, and Markus K. Brunnermeier. (2003). "Bubbles and Crashes." *Econometrica* (January).

Acharya, Viral V., Moritz Hahn, and Conor Kehoe. (2010). "Corporate Governance and Value Creation: Evidence from Private Equity." February 17. http://ssrn.com/abstract=1324016.

Acharya, Viral V., Hyun Song Shin, and Tanju Yorulmazer. (2009). "Crisis Resolution and Bank Liquidity." August. http://ideas.repec.org/s/nbr/nberwo.html.

Ackerman, Frank. (2008). "The Economics of Collapsing Markets." *Real-World Economics Review* 48.

Adam, Christopher, and David Vines. (2009). "Remaking Macroeconomic Policy After the Global Financial Crisis: A Balance Sheet Approach." *Oxford Review of Economic Policy* (Winter).

Admati, Anat R., et al. (2010). "Fallacies, Irrelevant Facts, and Myths in the Discussion of Capital Regulation: Why Bank Equity Is Not Expensive." http://papers.ssrn.com/sol3/papers.cfm?abstract_id=1669704.

Adrian, Tobias, and Hyun Song Shin. (2010). "Liquidity, Monetary Policy and Financial Cycles." *Current Issues in Economics and Finance* (January/February). http://www.newyorkfed.org/research/current_issues/ci14-1.pdf.

Aglietta, Michel. (1976). *A Theory of Capitalist Regulation: The US Experience*. London: Verso.

Akerlof, George A., and Paul M. Romer. (1993). "Looting: The Economic Underworld of Bankruptcy for Profit." *Brookings Papers on Economic Activity* 2.

Akerlof, George A., and Robert J. Shiller. (2009). *Animal Spirits: How Human Psychology Drives the Economy and Why It Matters for Global Capitalism.* Princeton: Princeton University Press.

Akyüz, Yilmaz. (2000). "The Debate on the International Financial Architecture: Reforming the Reformers." United Nations Conference on Trade and Development, Discussion Paper no. 148.

Akyüz, Yilmaz, and Korkut Boratav. (2005). The Making of the Turkish Financial Crisis." In *Financialization and the World Economy.* ed. Gerald Epstein. Cheltenham, UK: Edward Elgar.

Alcaly, Roger. (2010). "How They Killed the Economy." *New York Review of Books.* March 25.

Alesina, Alberto F., and Silvia Ardagna. (2009). "Large Changes in Fiscal Policy: Taxes Versus Spending." NBER Working Paper no. 15438, October. http://www.nber.org/papers/w15438.

Alessandri, Piergiorgio, and Andrew Haldane. (2009). "Banking on the State." November. http://www.bankofengland.co.uk.

Almunia, Miguel, et al. (2009). "The Effectiveness of Fiscal and Monetary Stimulus in Depressions." November 18. http://www.voxeu.org/index.php?q=node/4227.

Ambit ERisk. (2002). "Case Study: US Savings & Loan Crisis." August. http://www.erisk.com/Learning/CaseStudies/USSavingsLoanCrisis.as

Anabtawi, Iman. (2003–4). "Secret Compensation." *North Carolina Law Review* 82:835.

Andersen, Torben M., et al. (2007). *The Nordic Model: Embracing Globalization and Sharing Risks.* Helsinki: Research Institute of the Finnish Economy.

Applebaum, Binyamin. (2011). "At Meeting of World Financial Bodies, a Sharper Focus on Middle East Inequalities." *New York Times*, April 15.

——. (2011). "Stimulus by Fed Is Disappointing, Economists Say," *New York Times*, April 24.

Argitis, George, and Christos Pitelis. (2008). "Global Finance and Systemic Instability." *Contributions to Political Economy.* http://www.ideas.repec.org/a/oup/copoec/v27y2008i1p1–11.html.

Armijo, Leslie Elliott. (2001). "The Political Geography of World Financial Reform: Who Wants What and Why?" *Global Governance* (November).

Armijo, Leslie Elliott, and David Felix. (1999). "Reform of the Global Financial Architecture: Who Wants What and Why?" Paper presented to the annual meeting of the American Political Science Association, Atlanta, September 2–5.

Arrighi, Giovanni. (2004). "Spatial and Other 'Fixes' of Historical Capitalism." *Journal of World-System Research* (Summer).

Arrighi, Giovanni, and Beverly J. Silver. (1999). *Chaos and Governance in the Modern World System.* Minneapolis: University of Minnesota Press.

——. (2001). "Capitalism and World (Dis)order." In *Empire, Systems and States*, ed. Michael Cox, Tim Dunn, and Ken Booth. Cambridge: Cambridge University Press.

Atkins, Paul, Mark McWatters, and Kenneth Troske. (2011). "TARP Was No Win for the Taxpayers." *Wall Street Journal*, March 17.

Atkinson, A. B. and Salvatore Morelli. (2010). "Inequality and Banking Crises: A First Look." http://isites.harvard.edu/fs/docs/icb.topic457678.files/ATKINSON%20paper.pdf.

Auerbach, Alan J., William G. Gale, and Benjamin H. Harris. (2010). "Activist Fiscal Policy." *Journal of Economic Perspectives* (Fall).

Baba, Naokiko, Frank Packer, and Teppei Nagano. (2008). "The Spillover of Money Market Turbulence to FX Swap and Cross-Currency Swap Markets." March. http://www.bis.org/publ/qtrpdf/r_qt0803h.pdf.

Bagehot, Walter. (1873). *Lombard Street, a Description of the Money Market*. London: Henry S. King.

Bailey, David, and Soyoung Kim. (2009). "GE's Immelt Says U.S. Economy Needs Industrial Renewal." http://www.reuters.com/article/2009/06/26/us-ge-immelt-idUSTRE55P4ZT20090626.

Baker, Dean. (2002). "The Run-Up in Home Prices: Is It Real or Is It Another Bubble?" Center for Economic Policy and Research. August. http://www.cepr.net/index.php/publications/reports.

——. (2010). "Seven Key Facts about Social Security and the Federal Budget." http://www.cepr.net/index.php/publications/reports/seven-key-facts-about-ss-and-federal-budget.

——. (2011). "The Deficit-Reducing Potential of a Financial Speculation Tax." Center for Economic and Policy Research. January.

Baker, Dean, et al. (2004). "Unemployment and Labor Market Institutions: The Failure and Empirical Case for Deregulation." http://www.cepr.net/documents/publications/unemployment_dereg_2004_09.pdf.

Baker, Dean, and Travis McArthur. (2009). "The Value of the 'Too Big to Fail' Big Bank Subsidy." Center for Economic and Policy Research Issues Brief. September. http://www.cepr.net/documents/publications/too-big-to-fail-2009–09.pdf.

Baker, Peter. (2011). "The White House Looks for Work." *New York Times Magazine*, January 23.

Baker, Russell. (2009). "A Revolutionary President." *New York Review of Books*, February 12.

Balakrishnan, Ravi, et al. (2009). "What's the Damage? Medium-term Output Dynamics after Financial Crises," *World Economic Outlook* (October). Washington, D.C.: International Monetary Fund. http://www.imf.org/external/pubs/ft/weo/2009/.

Balz, Dan. (2010). "Across the Country, Anger, Frustration and Fear among Voters as Election Nears." *Washington Post*, October 28.

Bank for International Settlements. (2010). "General Manager's Speech: Three Policy Challenges for the World Economy." Speech delivered by Mr. Jaime Caruana, General Manager of the BIS, on the Occasion of the Bank's Annual General Meeting, June 28. http://www.bis.org/speeches/sp100628a.htm.

Banker. (2009). "FSA Proposes Shake-up in Regulation," March 25. http://www
.thebanker.com/news/fullstory.php/aid/6492/FSA_proposes_shake-up_in_regulation
_.html.

Barberis, Nicolas, and Richard H. Thaler. (2003). "A Survey of Behavioral Finance."
In *Handbook of the Economics of Finance*, ed. George M. Constantinides, Milton
Harris, and René M. Stulz. Amsterdam: Elsevier.

Barro, Robert J. (2009). "Government Spending Is No Free Lunch." *Wall Street Journal*, January 22.

——. (2010). "The Stimulus Evidence One Year On." *Wall Street Journal*, February 23.

Bartels, Larry M. (2005). "Homer Gets a Tax Cut: Inequality and Public Policy in the
American Mind." *Perspectives on Politics* (March).

——. (2008). *Unequal Democracy: The Politics of the New Gilded Age.* Princeton: Princeton University Press

Bartiromo, Maria. (2009a). "Facetime." *BusinessWeek*, April 20.

——. (2009b). "Facetime." *BusinessWeek*, February 23.

Basel Committee on Banking Supervision. (2010). *An Assessment of the Long-Run Economic Impact of Stronger Capital and Liquidity Requirements*. August. Bank for International Settlements. http://www.bis.org/publ/bcbs173.pdf.

Bates, Thomas W., Kathleen M. Kahle, and René M. Stulz. (2009). "Why Do U.S.
Firms Hold So Much More Cash than They Used To?" *Journal of Finance* (October).

Bauer, Rob, Robin Braun, and Gordon L. Clark. (2008). "The Emerging Market for
European Corporate Governance: The Relationship Between Governance and
Capital Expenditures, 1997–2005." *Journal of Economic Geography* (July).

Bebchuk, Lucian A., Alma Cohen, and Holger Spamann. (forthcoming). "The Wages
of Failure: Executive Compensation at Bear Stearns and Lehman 2000–2008."
Yale Journal on Regulation.

Bebchuk, Lucian A., and Jesse Fried. (2004). *Pay Without Performance: The Unfulfilled
Promise of Executive Compensation*. Cambridge: Harvard University Press.

Bebchuk, Lucian A., and Holger Spamann. (2009). "Regulating Bankers' Pay." Harvard John M. Olin Discussion Paper Series. http://papers.ssrn.com/sol3/papers
.cfm?abstract_id=1410072.

Becker, Jo, and Gretchen Morgenson. (2009). "Member and Overseer of the Finance Club." *New York Times*, April 26. http://www.nytimes.com/2009/04/27
/business/27geithner.html.

Becker, Jo, Sheryl Gay Stolberg, and Stephen Labaton. (2008). "White House Philosophy Stoked Mortgage Bonfire." *New York Times*, December 21.

Berger, Allen N., Anil K. Kashyap, and Joseph Scalise. (1995). "The Transformation of
the U.S. Banking Industry: What a Long, Strange Trip It's Been." *Brookings Papers
on Economic Activity* 2.

Berle, Adolf A., and Gardiner C. Means. (1933). *The Modern Corporation and Private
Property.* New York: Macmillan.

Bernanke, Ben S. (1983). "Nonmonetary Effects of the Financial Crisis in Propagation
of the Great Depression." *American Economic Review* (June).

——. (2003). "Downside Danger; Why the World's Central Banks Must Be More Vigilant About Falling Prices." *Foreign Policy* (December).

——. (2004). "The Great Moderation." Eastern Economic Association, Washington, D.C., February 20. http://www.federalreserve.gov/BOARDDOCS/SPEECHES /2004/20040220/default.htm.

——. (2008). "Reducing Systemic Risk." August 22. http://www.federalreserve.gov /newsevents/speech/bernanke20080822a.htm

Bernanke, Ben S., and Alan S. Blinder. (1988). "Credit, Money and Aggregate Demand." *Papers and Proceedings of the American Economics Association* (May).

Bernanke, Ben S., and Mark Gertler. (1995). "Inside the Black Box: The Credit Channel of Monetary Policy Transmission." *Journal of Economic Perspectives* (Autumn).

——. (2001). "Should Central Banks Respond to Movements in Asset Prices?" *American Economic Review, Papers and Proceedings of the American Economic Association* (May).

Bernanke, Ben S., and Vincent Reinhart. (2004). "Conducting Monetary Policy at Very Low Short-Term Interest Rates." *American Economic Review, Papers and Proceedings* (May).

Bezemer, Dirk J. (2009). "'No One Saw This Coming': Understanding Financial Crisis Through Accounting Models." http://mpra.ub.uni-muenchen.de/15892/1 /PRA_paper_15892.pdf.

Bibow, Jörg. (2010). "Global Imbalances, the U.S. Dollar, and How the Crisis at the Core of Global Finance Spread to 'Self-insuring' Emerging Market Economies." Levy Economics Institute of Bard College, Working Paper no. 591.

Bikhchandani, Sushil, and Sunil Sharma. (2001). "Herd Behavior in Financial Markets." *IMF Staff Papers* 47:3.

Bird, Ron, Harry Liam, and Susan Thorp. (2010). "Hedge Fund Excess Returns under Time Varying Beta." Paul Woolley Centre Working Paper Series 9.

Birdsall, Nancy. (2011). "Divining (or Inferring) the Objectives of U.S. Foreign Aid." Center for Global Development. March 10.

Bisson, Peter, Rik Kirkland, and Elizabeth Stephenson. (2010). "The Great Rebalancing." *McKinsey Quarterly* (June).

Bivens, Josh, and John Irons. (2008). "A Feeble Recovery: The Fundamental Weaknesses of the 2001–07 Expansion." EPI Briefing Paper no. 214. Washington, D.C.: Economic Policy Institute. December.

Blackburn, Robin. (2006). *Age Shock: How Finance Is Failing Us.* London: Verso.

Blanchard, Olivier. (2008). "The State of Macro." NBER Working Paper no. 14259 (August). http://www.nber.org/papers/w14259.

Blanchard, Olivier, and Carlo Cottarelli. (2010). "The Great False Choice, Stimulus or Austerity." *Financial Times*, August 11.

Blanchard, Olivier, and Lawrence F. Katz. (1997). "What We Know and Do Not Know about the Natural Rate of Unemployment." *Journal of Economic Perspectives* (Winter).

Blanchard, Olivier, and Gian Maria Milesi-Ferretti. (2009). "Global Imbalances: In Midstream?" Research Department International Monetary Fund, December 22. http://www.imf.org/external/pubs/ft/spn/2009/spn0929.pdf.

Blanchard, Olivier, and John Simo. (2001). "The Long and Large Decline in US Output Volatility." *Brookings Papers on Economic Activity* 2. http://www.jstor.org/pss/1209161.

Blecker, Robert A. (2005). "Financial Globalization, Exchange Rates and International Trade." In *Financialization and the World Economy*, ed. Gerald Epstein. Cheltenham, UK: Edward Elgar.

Blinder, Alan S., and Ricardo Reis. (2005). "Understanding the Greenspan Standard." Working Paper no. 114. Brussels: Centre for European Policy Studies. September.

Blinder, Alan S., and Janet L. Yellen. (2001). *The Fabulous Decade: Macroeconomic Lessons from the 1990s.* New York: Century Foundation Press.

Blinder, Alan S., and Mark Zandi. (2010). "How the Great Recession Was Brought to an End," July 27. http://www.economy.com/mark-zandi/documents/End-of-Great-Recession.pdf.

Bluestone, Barry, and Bennett Harrison. (1982). *The Deindustrialization of America: Plant Closings, Community Abandonment, and the Dismantling of Basic Industry.* New York: Basic Books.

Board of Governors of the Federal Reserve System, Federal Deposit Insurance Corporation, Office of the Comptroller of the Currency, Office of Thrift Supervision. (2009). "Credit Quality Declines in Annual Shared National Credits Review." September 24. http://www.fdic.gov/news/news/press/2009/pr09175.html.

Boone, Peter, and Simon Johnson. (2010). "Will the Politics of Global Moral Hazard Sink Us Again?" In *The Future of Finance; The LSE Report*, ed. Adair Turner et al. http://www.futureoffinance.org.uk/.

Bogle, John. (2010). "Restoring Faith in Financial Markets." *Wall Street Journal*, January 19.

Bonaparte, Yosef, Alok Kumar, and Jeremy K. Page. (2010). "Political Climate, Optimism, and Investment Decisions." http://papers.ssrn.com/sol3/papers.cfm?abstract_id=1509168.

Boratav, Korkut. (2009). "A Comparison of Two Cycles in the World Economy: 1989–2007." IDEAs Working Paper Series no. 07/2009.

Bordo, Michael D., Michael J. Dueker, and David C. Wheelock. (2000). "Aggregate Price Shocks and Financial Instability: An Historical Analysis." http://www.nber.org/papers/w7652.

Borio, Claudio. (2009). "Ten Propositions about Liquidity Crises." BIS Working Paper no. 293. November. http://www.bis.org/publ/work293.htm.

Borio, Claudio, and Phillip Lowe. (2002). "Asset Prices, Financial and Monetary Stability: Exploring the Nexus." BIS Working Paper no. 114. July.

Bosworth, Barry, and Aaron Flaaen. (2009). "America's Financial Crisis: the End of An Era." http://www.brookings.edu/~/media/Files/rc/papers/2009/0414_financial_crisis_bosworth/0414_financial_crisis_bosworth.pdf.

Bowers, Tab, Olivier Hamoir, and Anna Marrs. (2010). "What Next for Global Banking." *McKinsey Quarterly* (March).

Bowles, Samuel, and Herbert Gintis. (1993). "The Revenge of Homo Economicus: Contested Exchange and the Revival of Political Economy." *Journal of Economic Perspectives* (Winter).

Bowles, Samuel, David M. Gordon, and Thomas E. Weisskopf. (1983). *Beyond the Wasteland: A Democratic Alternative to Economic Decline.* Garden City, N.Y.: Anchor Press/Doubleday.

Boyer, Robert. (1990). *The Regulation School: A Critical Introduction.* New York: Columbia University Press.

——. (2000). "Is a Finance-led Regime a Viable Regime Alternative to Fordism? A Preliminary Analysis?" *Economy & Society* 29 (February).

——. (2007). "Assessing the Impact of Fair Value upon Financial Crisis." *Socio-Economic Review* (October).

Braithwaite, Tom. (2011). "Elusive Information." *Financial Times*, February 16.

Braithwaite, Tom, and Kara Scannell. (2011). "SEC Faces Budget Crackdown." *Financial Times*, January 19.

Braithwaite, Tom, and Suzanne Kapner. (2011). "White House Accused of Regulatory 'Shakedown.'" *Financial Times*, March 10.

Brender, Anton, and Florence Pisani. (2010). "Global Imbalances and the Collapse of Globalized Finance." Brussels: Centre for European Studies.

Brenner, Robert. (2003). "Towards the Precipice." *London Review of Books*, February 6.

Brenner, Robert. (2006). *Economics of Global Turbulence* (London: Verso).

——. (2009). "What Is Good for Goldman Sachs Is Good for America; The Origins of the Current Crisis," April 18. http://www.sscnet.ucla.edu/issr/cstch/papers/BrennerCrisisTodayOctober2009.pdf.

Bresser-Pereira, Luiz Carlos. (2010). "The Global Financial Crisis and After: A New Capitalism?" http://www.networkideas.org/featart/jan2010/Global_Crisis.pdf.

Brown, Stephen J., William N. Goetzmann, Bing Liang, and Christopher Schwarz. (2008). "Mandatory Disclosure and Operational Risk: Evidence from Hedge Fund Registration." *Journal of Finance* (December).

Brunnermeier, Markus K. (2009). "Deciphering the Liquidity and Credit Crunch 2007–2008." *Journal of Economic Perspectives* (Winter).

Brunnermeier, Markus K., and Stefan Nagel. (2004). "Hedge Funds and the Technology Bubble." *Journal of Finance* (October).

Bucks, Brian, and Karen Pence. (2006). "Do Homeowners Know Their House Values and Mortgage Terms?" http://www.federalreserve.gov/Pubs/feds/2006/200603/index.html.

Buehler, Kevin S., Christopher J. Mazingo, and Hamid H. Samandari. (2010). "A Better Way to Measure Risk." *McKinsey Quarterly* (April).

Buiter, Willem. (2009a). "The Unfortunate Uselessness of Most 'State of the Art' Academic Monetary Economics." *Economist's View*, March 3.

——. (2009b). "Lessons from the Global Financial Crisis for Regulators and Supervisors." May 26. http://blogs.ft.com/maverecon/2009/05/lessons-from-the-global-financial-crisis-for-regulators-and-supervisors.

——. (2010). "Is Sovereign Default 'Unnecessary, Undesirable and Unlikely' for All Advanced Economies?" *Global Economics Views* 16.

Burnsa, Natasha, and Simi Kediab. (2008). "Executive Option Exercises and Financial Misreporting." *Journal of Banking & Finance* (May).

Buzenberg, Bill. (2009). "Commentary: The Mega-Banks Behind the Meltdown." Washington, D.C.: Center for Public Integrity, May 6.

Caballero, Ricardo J. (2006). "On the Macroeconomics of Asset Shortages." National Bureau of Economic Research, Working paper 12753. December.

——. (2006). "Macroeconomics after the Crisis: Time to Deal with the Pretense-of-Knowledge Syndrome." *Journal of Economic Perspectives* (Fall).

Caldentey Esteban Pérez, and Matías Vernengo. (2010). "Modern Finance, Methodology and the Global Crisis." *Real-World Economics Review* 52.

Calmes, Jackie, and Dalia Sussman. (2011). "Poll Finds Wariness about Cutting Entitlements." *New York Times*, January 20.

Calomiris, Charles, Daniela Klingebiel, and Luc Laeven. (2005). "Financial Crisis Policies and Resolution Mechanisms: A Taxonomy from Cross-Country Experience." In *Systemic Financial Crises: Containment and Resolution*, ed. Patrick Honohan and Luc Laeven. New York: Cambridge University Press.

Calvo, Guillermo A., and Enrique G. Mendoza. (2000). "Contagion, Globalization, and the Volatility of Capital Flows." In *Capital Flows and the Emerging Economies: Theory, Evidence, and Controversies*, ed. Sebastian Edwards. Chicago: University of Chicago Press.

Campbell-Meiklejohn, et al. (2010). "How the Opinion of Others Affects Our Valuation of Objects." *Current Biology* (June).

Cassidy, John. (2009). *How Markets Fail: The Logic of Economic Calamities.* New York: Farrar, Straus and Giroux.

——. (2010). "After the Blowup." *New Yorker*, January 11.

Cecchetti, Stephen G. (2009). "Crisis and Responses: The Federal Reserve in the Early Stages of the Financial Crisis." *Journal of Economic Perspectives* (Winter).

Centre for Tax Policy and Administration. (2011). "OECD Tax Database." HYPERLINK "http://www.oecd.org/dataoecd/13/38/46721091.xls"Tax Revenues as Percentage of Gross Domestic Product Table A. http://www.oecd.org/ctp/taxdatabase.

Cerny, Philip G. (1994). "The Infrastructure of the Infrastructure? Towards 'Embedded Financial Orthodoxy' in the International Political Economy." In *Transcending the State-Global Divide: A Neostructural Agenda in International Relations*, ed. Ronan P. Palan and Barry Gills. Boulder: Lynne Rienner.

Chailloux, Alexandre, et al. (2008). "Central Bank Response to the 2007–08 Financial Market Turbulence: Experiences and Lessons Drawn." IMF Working Paper WP/08/210. September. http://imf.org/external/pubs/ft/wp/2008/wp08210.pdf.

Chan, Nicholas, et al. (2006). "Do Hedge Funds Increase Systemic Risk?" Federal Reserve Bank of Atlanta, *Economic Review* (fourth quarter). http://www.frbatlanta.org/filelegacydocs/erq406_lo.pdf.

Chan, Sewell. (2010). "F.D.I.C. Outlines Path to Financial Repair." *New York Times*, October 12.

Chandler, Alfred D., Jr. (1986). "The Evolution of Modern Global Competition." In *Competition in Global Industries*, ed. Michael E. Porter. Boston: Harvard Business School Press.

Chanos, James S. (2009). "We Need Honest Accounting." *Wall Street Journal*, March 24.

Chapman, Peter. (2010). "Ten Lessons of a Banking Collapse, in Lehman's Terms." *Financial Times*, September 15.

Chari, V. V. (1999). "Nobel Laureate Robert E. Lucas, Jr.: Architect of Modern Macroeconomics." *Federal Reserve Bank of Minneapolis Quarterly Review* (Spring).

Cifuentes, Rodrigo, Hyun Song Shin, and Gianluigi Ferrucci. (2005). "Liquidity Risk and Contagion." *Journal of the European Economic Association* 3:2–3 (April/May).

Clark, Melanca, with Maggie Barron. (2009). "Foreclosures: A Crisis In Legal Representation." Brennan Center for Justice, New York University Law School. http://brennan.3cdn.net/a5bf8a685cd0885f72_s8m6bevkx.pdf.

Coffee, John C., Jr. (2003). "Gatekeeper Failure and Reform: The Challenge of Fashioning Relevant Reforms." Columbia Law and Economics Working Paper no. 237, September.

Colander, David. (2009). "The Risks of Financial Modeling: VaR and the Economic Meltdown." Testimony before Committee on Science and Technology, U.S. House of Representatives, September 10.

Colander, David, et al. (2008). "The Financial Crisis and the Systematic Failure of Academic Economics," (Dahlem Report). http://www.debtdeflation.com/ . . . /Dahlem_Report_EconCrisis021809.pdf.

Congressional Oversight Panel. (2009). *Report of the Congressional Oversight Panel on Troubled Asset Relief Program (TARP)*. January 9. http://ongressnow.galelrywatch.com/docs/2ndCOPTARP.pdf.

———. (2010). *Assessing the TARP on the Eve of Its Expiration*. September 16. http://cop.senate.gov/documents/cop-091610-report.pdf.

Connor, Gregory, Thomas Flavin, and Brian O'Kelly. (2010). "The U.S. and Irish Credit Crises: Their Distinctive Differences and Common Features." March. http://economics.nuim.ie/research/workingpapers/documents/N206–10.pdf.

Costello, Daniel. (2011). "The Drought Is Over (At Least for C.E.O.'s)." *New York Times*, April 10.

Cottarelli, Carlo, and José Viñals. (2009). "Looking Ahead." *Finance & Development* (September).

Coval, Joshua, Jakub Jurek, and Erik Stafford. (2009). "The Economics of Structured Finance." *Journal of Economic Perspectives* (Winter).

Cragg, Michael, and Joseph Stiglitz. (2011). "Should the Government Invest, or Try to Spur Private Investment?" *Economists' Voice* (April).

Creswell, Julie. (2009). "Profits for Buyout Firms as Company Debt Soars; Mattress Maker, Bought and Sold Six Times, Is a Casualty in Private Equity Boom." *New York Times*, October 5.

Crockett, Andrew. (2000). "Marrying the Micro- and Macroprudential Dimensions of Financial Stability." http://www.bis.org/review/rr000921b.pdf.

——. (2001). "Monetary Policy and Financial Stability." http://www.bis.org/review /r010216b.pdf.

Croft, Jane, George Packer, and Peter Thal Larsen. (2009). "UK Battle to Avoid RBS Ownership." *Financial Times*, January 20.

Crotty, James R. (1986). "Marx, Keynes and Minsky on the Instability of the Capitalist Growth Process and the Nature of Government Economic Policy." In *Marx, Keynes and Minsky on the Capitalist Growth Process and the Nature of Government Economic Policy*, ed. Suzanne W. Helburn and David F. Bramhall. Armonk, N.Y.: M. E. Sharpe.

——. (1999). "Was Keynes a Corporatist? Keynes's Radical Views on Industrial Policy and Macro Policy in the 1920s." *Journal of Economic Literature* (September).

——. (2000). "Slow Growth, Destructive Competition, and Low Road Relations: A Keynes-Marx-Schumpeter Analysis of Neoliberal Globalization." Joint Conference on the Future of the Korean Economy in the Context of Globalization at Suanbo, Korea, June 22.

——. (2008). "If Financial Market Competition Is Intense, Why Are Financial Firm Profits So High? Reflections on the Current 'Golden Era' of Finance." *Competition and Change* (June).

——. (2009a). "Structural Causes of the Global Financial Crisis: A Critical Assessment of the 'New Financial Architecture.'" *Cambridge Journal of Economics* 33, 4.

——. (2009b). "The Bonus-Driven "Rainmaker" Financial Firm: How These Firms Enrich Top Employees, Destroy Shareholder Value and Create Systemic Financial Instability." http://www.networkideas.org/featart/dec2009/Rainmaker.pdf.

Cuomo, Andrew M. (2009). "No Rhyme or Reason; The 'Heads I Win, Tails You Lose' Bank Bonus Culture." http://www.oag.state.ny.us/media_center/2009/july /pdfs/Bonus%20Report%20Final%207.30.09.pdf.

Dai Qingli. (2010). "Blaming China Exaggerates Her Power." *Financial Times*, September 16.

Dallery, Thomas. (2009). "Post-Keynesian Theories of the Firm under Financialization." *Review of Radical Political Economics* (September).

D'Arista, Jane. (2006). "Another Year Awash in Liquidity." *Capital Flows Monitor*, April 27.

D'Arista, Jane, and Korkut Alp Ertürk. (2010). "The Case for International Monetary Reform." *Real-World Economics Review* 54.

Davidson, Paul. (2008). "Is the Current Financial Distress Caused by the Subprime Mortgage Crisis a Minsky Moment? Or Is It the Result of Attempting to Securitize Illiquid Noncommercial Mortgage Loans?" *Journal of Post Keynesian Economics* (July).

——. (2009). "Alternative Exaltations of the Operation of a Capitalist Economy: Efficient Market Theory vs. Keynes's Liquidity Theory." *Real-World Economics Review* 50.

Davies, James B., et al. (2009). "The Global Pattern of Household Wealth." *Journal of International Development* (November).

De Antoni, Elizabetta. (2010). "Minsky, Keynes, and Financial Instability: The Recent Subprime Crisis." *International Journal of Political Economy* (Summer).

Demir, Firat. (2009a). "Financialization and Manufacturing Firm Profitability under Uncertainty and Macroeconomic Volatility: Evidence from an Emerging Market." *Review of Development Economics* (November).

——. (2009b). "Capital Market Imperfections and Financialization of Real Sectors in Emerging Markets: Private Investment and Cash Flow Relationship Revisited." *World Development* 37, 5.

Demirgüç-Kunt, Aslı, and Luis Servén. (2010). "Are All the Sacred Cows Dead? Implications of the Financial Crisis for Macro and Financial Policies." *World Bank Observer* (February).

Devereuz, Michael P., and Simon Loretz. (2008). *The Effects of EU Formula Apportionment on Corporate Tax Revenues*. Oxford University Centre for Business Taxation, Said Business School. January 31.

Dialynas Chris P., and Marshall Auerback. (2007). "Renegade Economics: The Bretton Woods II Fiction." October. http://media.pimco-global.com/pdfs/pdf/WP007–090607%20Renegade%20Economics%20FINAL.pdf.

Dichev, Ilia D., and Gwen Yu. (2011). "Higher Risk, Lower Returns: What Hedge Fund Investors Really Earn." *Journal of Financial Economics* (May).

Dionne, E. J., Jr. (2011). "A Broken Metaphor." *Washington Post*, March 13.

Dooley, Michael, and Peter Garber. (2009). "Global Imbalances and the Crisis: A Solution in Search of a Problem." http://www.voxeu.org/index.php?q=node/3314.

Dooley, Michael P., David Folkerts-Landau, and Peter Garber. (2003). "An Essay on the Revised Bretton Woods System." http://papers.ssrn.com/sol3/papers.cfm?abstract_id=447259.

——. (2009). "Bretton Woods II Still Defines the International Monetary System." http://www.nber.org/programs/ifm/ifm.html.

Dos Santos, Paulo L. (2009). "On the Content of Banking in Contemporary Capitalism." *Historical Materialism* 17.

Draghi, Mario. (2010). "To G20 Leaders Progress and Issues on the Global Regulatory Reform Agenda." June 24. http://www.financialstabilityboard.org/publications/r_100627a.pdf.

Draut, Tamara. (2010). "The Investment Deficit." *American Prospect* (November).

Drehmann, Mathias, et al. (2010). "Countercyclical Capital Buffers: Exploring Options." Bank for International Settlements Working Papers no 317. July. http://www.bis.org/publ/work317.htm.

Duménil, Gerard, and Dominique Lévy. (2004). *Capital Resurgent: Roots of the Neoliberal Revolution*. Cambridge: Harvard University Press.

——. (2005). "Costs and Benefits of Neoliberalism: A Class Analysis." In *Financialization and the World Economy*, ed. Gerald Epstein. Cheltenham, UK: Edward Elgar.

Dymski, Gary. (1994). "Asymmetrical Information, Uncertainty, and Financial Structure: 'New' Versus 'Post' Keynesian Microfoundations." In *New Perspectives in Monetary Microeconomics: Explorations in the Tradition of Hyman P. Minsky*, ed. Gary Dymski and Robert Pollin. Ann Arbor: University of Michigan Press.

——. (2001). "The Global Crisis and the Governance of Power in Finance." In *The Financial Crisis: Origins and Implications*. Houndmills, Basingstoke: Palgrave Macmillan.

——. (2009). "Racial Exclusion and the Political Economy of the Subprime Crisis." University of California Center Sacramento, Research on Money and Finance, Discussion Paper no. 2. February 15.

——. (2010). "Three Futures for Postcrisis Banking in the Americas: The Financial Trilemma and the Wall Street Complex." Levy Economics Institute of Bard College, Working Paper no. 604. June.

Eaglesham, Jean. (2011). "Banks Near Deal with SEC." *Wall Street Journal*, April 15.

Eichengreen, Barry. (2008). "Origins and Responses to the Crisis." October. http:// emlab.berkeley.edu/users/webfac/eichengreen/e183_sp07/origins_responses.pdf.

——. (2008). "The Last Temptation of Risk." *National Interest* (May/June). http:// www.nationalinterest.org/Article.aspx?id=21274.

Eichengreen, Barry, and K. Mitchener. (2003). "The Great Depression as a Credit Boom Gone Wrong." Monetary and Economics Department, Bank for International Settlements, BIS Working Paper no. 137. September.

Eichengreen, Barry, and Kevin O'Rourke. (2009). "A Tale of Two Depressions." http://www.voxeu.org.

El-Erian, Mohamed. (2007). "In the New Liquidity Factories, Buyers Must Still Beware." *Financial Times*, March 22.

——. (2009). "The New Normal." *Businessweek*, June 1.

Elmendorf, Douglas W. (2010). "Policies for Increasing Economic Growth and Employment in the Short Term." http://www.cbo.gov/ftpdocs/112xx/doc11255 /Unemployment_Testimony.shtml.

Elsby, Michael, Bart Hobijn, and Aysegül Sahin. (2010). "The Labor Market in the Great Recession." http://www.brookings.edu/~/media/Files/Programs/ES/BPEA /2010_spring_bpea_papers/spring2010_elsby.pdf.

Engelen, Ewald. (2008). "The Case of Financialization." *Competition and Change* (June).

Epstein Gerald A. (2003). "Financialization, Rentier Interests, and Central Bank Policy." In *The Selected Works of Gerald A. Epstein*. http://works.bepress.com/gerald _epstein/88/.

——. (2005). "Introduction: Financialization and the World Economy." In *Financialization and the World*, ed. Gerald Epstein. Cheltenham, UK: Edward Elgar.

Epstein, Gerald, and Jessica Carrick-Hagenbarth. (2010). "Financial Economists, Financial Interests and Dark Corners of the Meltdown: It's Times to Set Ethical Standards for the Economics Profession." http://www.peri.umass.edu/fileadmin /pdf/working_papers/working_papers_201–250/WP239.pdf.

Epstein, Gerald A., and Arjun Jayadev. (2005). "The Rise of Rentier Income in OECD Countries: Financialization, Central Bank Policy and Labor Solidarity." In *Financialization and the World Economy*, ed. Gerald A. Epstein. Cheltenham: Edward Elgar.

Ertürk, Korkut Alp. (2010). "Heterodox Lessons of the Crisis." *Real-World Economics Review* 54. http://www.paecon.net/PAEReview/issue54/Erturk54.pdf.

Ertürk, Korkut, and Gökcer Özgür. (2009). "What Is Minsky All about Anyway?" *Real-World Economics Review* 50.

Etzioni, Amatai. (2002). "Give Business Schools an 'F.'" *Washington Post National Weekly Edition*, August 12–18.

EuroMemorandum Group. (2008). *Democratic Transformation of Finance, a Full Employment Regime and Ecological Restructuring—Alternatives to Finance-Driven Capitalism*. Workshop of European Economists for an Alternative Economic Policy, September 26–28, Brussels.

European Central Bank. (2009). *Credit Default Swap and Counterparty Risk* (August). http://www.ecb.int/pub/pdf/other/creditdefaultswapsandcounterpartyrisk2009en.pdf.

European Commission. (2010). "Green Paper: Corporate Governance in Financial Institutions and Remuneration Policies." http://eur-lex.europa.eu/LexUriServ/LexUriServ.do?uri=COM:2010:0284:FIN:EN:PDF.

Fahlenbrach, Rüdiger, and Rene M. Stulz. (2008). "Managerial Ownership Dynamics and Firm Value." Ohio State University, Fisher College of Business Working Paper no. 2007–03–013. January.

Fama, Eugene. (1970). "Efficient Capital Markets: A Review of Theory and Empirical Work." *Journal of Finance* (May).

——. (1980). "Banking in the Theory of Finance." *Journal of Monetary Economics* (January).

Farrell, Diana, et al. (2008). *Mapping Global Capital Markets*. Fourth Annual Report, McKinsey Global Institute. January.

Farzad, Roben. (2007). "Let the Blame Begin." *Business Week*, July 27.

Federal Reserve Bank of Kansas City. (2008). Symposium on Maintaining Stability in a Changing Financial System. http://www.kc.frb.org/home/subwebnav.cfm?level=3&theID=10976&SubWeb=10660.

Federal Reserve Board. (2010). "Household Debt Service and Financial Obligations Ratios." Updated March 17. http://www.federalreserve.gov/releases/housedebt.

Felix, David. (1994). "Debt Crisis Adjustment in Latin America: Have the Hardships Been Necessary?" In *New Perspectives in Monetary Macroeconomics*, ed. Gary Dymski and Robert Pollin. Ann Arbor: University of Michigan Press.

——. (2005). "Why International Capital Mobility Should Be Curbed and How It Could Be Done." In *Financialization and the World Economy*, ed. Gerald Epstein. Cheltenham: Edward Elgar.

Ferguson, Thomas, and Robert Johnson. (2009a). "Too Big to Bail: The 'Paulson Put,' Presidential Politics, and the Global Financial Meltdown. Part I: From Shadow Financial System to Shadow Bailout." *International Journal of Political Economy* (Spring).

——. (2009b). "Too Big to Bail: The 'Paulson Put,' Presidential Politics, and the Global Financial Meltdown. Part II: Fatal Reversal—Single Payer and Back." *International Journal of Political Economy* (Summer).

Ferri, Pierro, and Hyman P. Minsky. (1991). "Market Processes and Thwarting Systems." November, Levy Institute Working Paper no. 64. http://www.levy.org/pubs/wp64.pdf.

Fich, Eliezer M., Jie Cai, and Anh L. Tran. (2009). "Stock Option Grants to Target CEOs during Private Merger Negotiations." http://papers.ssrn.com/sol3/papers .cfm?abstract_id=1392322.

Financial Crisis Inquiry Commission. (2011). *The Financial Crisis Inquiry Report: Final Report of the National Commission on the Causes of the Financial and Economic Crisis in the United States*. New York: Public Affairs.

Financial Stability Board. (2010). "Intensity and Effectiveness of SIFI Supervision; Recommendations for Enhanced Supervision Prepared by the FSB in Consultation with the IMF." http://www.financialstabilityboard.org/publications/r_101101.pdf.

Financial Times. (2011). "Living in a World of Rising Rates." April 9.

Fisher, Andrew Martin. (2009). "The Perils of Paradigm Maintenance in the Face of Crisis." United Nations Research Institute for Social Development. November.

Fisher, Irving. (1933). "The Debt-Deflation Theory of the Great Depression." *Econometrica* (October).

Fitoussi, Jean-Paul, and Francesco Saraceno. (2010). "Inequality and Macroeconomic Performance." Centre de recherche en économie de Sciences Po. July.

Foley, Duncan K. (2011). "The Political Economy of Output and Employment 2001–2010." Institute for New Economic Thinking. April.

Foster, J. D. (2009). "Keynesian Fiscal Stimulus Policies Stimulate DebtÐNot the Economy." *Heritage Foundation Backgrounder* 2302. July 27. http://www.heritage .org/Research/Economy/upload/bg_2302.pdf.

Friedman, Milton. (1953). *Essays in Positive Economics*. Chicago: University of Chicago Press.

Friedman, Milton, and Anna Jacobson Schwartz. (1963). *A Monetary History of the United States, 1867–1960*. Princeton: Princeton University Press for the National Bureau of Economic Research.

Froud, Julie, Leaver, Adam, and Karel Williams. (2007). "New Actors in a Financialised Economy and the Remaking of Capitalism." *New Political Economy* (September).

Furman, Jason. (2008). "The Concept of Neutrality in Tax Policy." Testimony before the U.S. Senate Committee on Finance hearing on Tax: Fundamentals in Advance of Reform. April 15.

Galbraith, James K. (2009). "No Return to Normal; Why the Economic Crisis, and Its Solution, Are Bigger than You Think," *Washington Monthly* (March/April). http://www.washingtonmonthly.com/features/2009/0903.galbraith.html.

——. (2010). "The Great Crisis and the American Response." *drx*, Levy Economics Institute of Bard College. http://www.levyinstitute.org/pubs/hili_112a.pdf.

Gamble, Andrew. (2006). "Two Faces of Liberalism." In *The Neo-liberal Revolution: Forging the Market State*, ed. Richard Robison. Houndsmills: Palgrave Macmillan.

Gapper, John. (2010). "Don't Turn Back on Financial Reform." *Financial Times*, November 3.

Geithner, Timothy F. (2006). "Hedge Funds and Derivatives and Their Implications for the Financial System." Distinguished Lecture, Hong Kong Monetary Authority and Hong Kong Bankers Association. September 14.

Gelman, Eric. (2008). "Fear of a Black Swan." *Fortune*, April 3. http://money.cnn.com/2008 /03/31/news/economy/gelman_taleb.fortune/index.htm?postversion=2008040305.

Gertler, Mark, and Nobuhiro Kiyotaki. (2010). "Financial Intermediation and Credit Policy in Business Cycle Analysis." http://www.columbia.edu/cu/economics/program /research/Gertler_Kiyotaki.pdf.

Gezici, Armaᴆan. (2010). "Distributional Consequences of Financial Crises: Evidence from Recent Crises." *Review of Radial Political Economics* (Summer).

Ghosh, Jayati. (2010). "Financial Euphoria and Aftershock." http://www.networkideas .org/news/feb2010/news22_Financial_Euphoria.htm.

Gjerstad, Steven, and Vernon L. Smith. (2009). "From Bubble to Depression?" http:// www.cato.org/pub_display.php?pub_id=10103.

——. (2010). "Why We're in for a Long, Hard Slog." *Wall Street Journal*, September 10.

Glyn, Andrew. (2009). "Functional Distribution and Inequality." In *The Oxford Handbook of Economic Inequality*, ed. Wiemer Salverda, Nolan, Brian, and Timothy M. Smeeding. Oxford: Oxford University Press.

Godley, Wynne. (1996). "Money, Finance and National Income Determination: An Integrated Approach." Working Paper Series no. 167. Annandale-on-Hudson, N.Y.: Levy Economics Institute. June.

——. (1999). "Seven Unsustainable Processes: Medium-Term Prospects and Policies for the United States and the World." Annandale-on-Hudson, N.Y.: Levy Economics Institute, January.

Godley, Wynne, and Mark Lavoie. (2007). "Fiscal Policy in a Stock-Flow Consistent (SFC) Model." *Journal of Post-Keynesian Economics* (October).

Godley, Wynne, Dimitri B. Papadimitriou, and Gennero Zezza. (2008). "Prospects for the United States and the World: A Crisis That Conventional Remedies Cannot Resolve." Levy Economics Institute of Bard College, December.

Goedhart, Marc, Timothy M. Koller, and David Wessels 1010). " How Inflation Can Destroy Shareholder Value." *McKinsey Quarterly* (February). https://www. mckinseyquarterly.com/Corporate_Finance/Capital_Management/How_inflation _can_destroy_shareholder_value_2520.

Goeas, Ed, and Nicholas Thompson. (2011). "Key Findings from National Survey." March 1. http://www.politico.com/static/PPM191_poll.html.

Goldman, Julianna, Hans Nichols, Mark Draiem, and Lizzie O'Leary. (2010). "Obama Wants a Detente with Business; Once the Midterm Elections Are Over, the President Plans to Make Up with Business." October 6. http://www.businessweek.com /magazine/content/10_42/b4199029119904.htm.

Goldstein, Jonathan P. (2010). "Introduction: The Political Economy of Financialization." *Review of Radical Political Economics* (September).

Goldstein, Morris. (2005). "What Might the Next Emerging-Market Financial Crisis Look Like?" Working Paper no. 05-7. Washington, D.C.: Institute for International Economics).

Goodman, Peter S. (2008). "Taking Hard New Look at a Greenspan Legacy." *New York Times*, October 8.

Gordon, David M., Richard Edwards, and Michael Reich. (1982). *Segmented Work, Divided Workers: The Historical Transformation of Labor in the United States*. New York: Cambridge University Press.

Gordon, David M., Thomas E. Weiskopf, and Samuel Bowles. (1996). "Power, Accumulation and Crisis: The Rise and Demise of the Postwar Social Structure of Accumulation." In *Radical Political Economy: Explorations in Alternative Economic Analysis*, ed. Victor D. Lippitt. Armonk, N.Y.: M. E. Sharpe.

Gorton, Gary. (1994). "Bank Regulation When 'Banks' and 'Banking' Are Not the Same." *Oxford Review of Economic Policy* (Winter).

——. (2010). *Slapped in the Face by the Invisible Hand: Banking and the Panic of 2007*. New York: Oxford University Press.

Gorton, Gary B., and Andrew Metrick. (2009). "Securitized Banking and the Run on Repo." NBER Working Paper No. w15223. August. http://www.nber.org/papers/w15223.

Gosselin, Peter. (2008). *High Wire: The Precarious Financial Lives of American Families*. New York: Basic Books.

Grabel, Ilene. (2010). "Not Your Grandfather's IMF: Global Crisis, 'Productive Incoherence' and Developmental Policy Space." August. http://www.peri.umass.edu/fileadmin/pdf/working_papers/working_papers_201–250/WP214_revised.pdf.

Gray, John. (2009). "The Way of All Debt." *New York Review of Books*, April 9.

Greenspan, Alan. (2004). "Understanding Household Debt Obligations." http://www.federalreserve.gov/boarddocs/speeches/2004/20040223/default.htm#pagetop.

——. (2010). U.S. Debt and the Greek Analogy." *Wall Street Journal*, June 18.

——. (2011). "Dodd-Frank Fails to Meet Test of Our Times." *Financial Times*, March 29.

Greenwald, Bruce C., and Joseph E. Stiglitz. (1990). "Asymmetric Information and the New Theory of the Firm: Financial Constraints and Risk Behavior." *American Economic Review* (May).

Greider, William. (1989). *Secrets of the Temple: How the Federal Reserve Runs the Country*. New York: Simon & Schuster.

——. (2009). "Dismantling the Temple." *Nation*, July 15.

Grow, Brian, Keith Epstein, and Robert Berner. (2009). "How Banks Are Worsening the Foreclosure Crisis." *Businessweek*, February 12. http://www.businessweek.com/magazine/ . . . /b4120034085635.htm.

Gungen, Ali Riza. (2010). Fictitious Capital Speculation and Financialisation: Critical Moments of Instability, Crisis and Intervention in the Turkish Experience." IIPPE Financialisation Working Paper no. 5. http://www.iippe.org/wiki/images/5/50/Fictitious_Capital_Speculation_and_Financialisation.pdf.

Guttmann, Robert. (2009). "Asset Bubbles, Debt Deflation, and Global Imbalances." *International Journal of Political Economy* (Summer).

Hacker, Jacob S., et al. (2010). *Economic Security at Risk: Findings from the Economic Security Index*. Rockefeller Foundation. July.

Haldane, Andrew G. (2009). "Credit Is Trust." Paper presented at the Association of Corporate Treasurers, Leeds, September 14. http://www.bis.org/review/r090917d.pdf.

——. (2010). "The Hundred Billion Dollar Question." March. http://www.bankofengland.co.uk/publications/speeches/2010/speech433.pdf

Haldane, Andrew G., and Piergiorgio Alessandri. (2009). "Banking on the State." Paper presented at the Federal Reserve Bank of Chicago Conference on International Financial Crisis: Have the Rules of Finance Changed? September 25. www.bankofengland.co.uk/publications/speeches/2009/speech409.pdf.

Haldane, Andrew, Simon Brennan, and Vasileios Madouros. (2010). "What Is the Contribution of the Financial Sector: Miracle or Mirage?" In *The Future of Finance; The LSE Report*, ed. Adair Turner et al. http://www.futureoffinance.org.uk/.

Hall, Peter A., and Daniel W. Gingerich. (2004). "Varieties of Capitalism and Institutional Complementarities in the Macroeconomy: An Empirical Analysis." MPIfG Discussion Paper 04/5. http://www-management.wharton.upenn.edu/guillen/Hall/Hall.MPIfGSpaper.pdf.

Hall, Robert. (2007). "How Much Do We Understand About the Modern Recession?" *Brookings Papers on Economic Activity* 2.

——. (2010). "Why Does the Economy Fall to Pieces after a Financial Crisis?" *Journal of Economic Perspectives* (Fall).

Haltiwanger John, Ron S. Jarmin, and Javier Miranda. (2010). "Who Creates Jobs? Small vs. Large vs. Young." http://ideas.repec.org/p/cen/wpaper/10-17.html.

Hannoun Hervé. (2010). "Information Gaps: What Has the Crisis Taught Us?" Paper prepared for the G20 Finance Ministers and Central Bank Governors, Basel, April 8–9. http://www.bis.org/speeches/sp100419.htm.

Hanson, Samuel, Anil K. Kashyap, and Jeremy C. Stein. (2010). "A Macroprudential Approach to Financial Regulation." July. http://www.economics.harvard.edu/faculty/stein/files/JEP-macroprudential-July22–2010.pdf.

Harper, Christine. (2010). "Banks 'Dodged a Bullet' as U.S. Congress Dilutes Trading Rules." Bloomberg.com, June 25.

Hart, Oliver, and Luigi Zingales. (2010). "How to Make a Distressed Bank Raise Equity." *Financial Times*, February 8.

Harvey, Philip. (2011). "Back to Work: A Public Jobs Proposal for Economic Recovery." Policy Brief, Demos. http://www.demos.org/pubs/BackToWork.pdf.

Haug, Espen Gaarder, and Nassim Nicholas Taleb. (2009). "Why We Have Never Used the Black-Scholes-Merton Option Pricing Formula." http://papers.ssrn.com/sol3/papers.cfm?abstract_id=1012075.

Haughwout, Andrew. (2011). "New Developments in Housing Policy." January 14. http://www.newyorkfed.org/education/pdf/Haughwout.pdf.

Haughwout, Andrew, Richard Peach, and Joseph Tracy. (2010). "The Homeownership Gap." *Federal Reserve Bank of New York Current Issues in Economics and Finance* (May).

Hays, Sharon. (1994). "Structure and Agency and the Sticky Problem of Culture." *Sociological Theory* (March).

Henderson, Brian J., and Neil D. Pearson. (2011). "The Dark Side of Financial Innovation: A Case Study of the Pricing of a Retail Financial Product." *Journal of Financial Economics* (May).

Henry, David. (2006). "Danger—Explosive Loans." *BusinessWeek*, October 23.

Hirshleifer, David A., and Tyler Shumway. (2001). "Good Day Sunshine: Stock Returns and the Weather." Dice Center Working Paper no. 2001–3.

Hodgson, Geoffrey M. (2008). "After 1929 Economics Changed: Will Economists Wake Up in 2009?" *Real-World Economics Review* 48, December 6.

Hoge, James F., Jr. (2004). "A Global Power Shift in the Making–Is the United States Ready." *Foreign Affairs* (July).

Honohan, Patrick, and Daniela Klingebiel. (2003). "The Fiscal Cost Implications of an Accommodating Approach to Banking Crises." *Journal of Banking and Finance* (August).

Hördahl, Peter, and Michael R. King. (2008). "Developments in Repo Markets During the Financial Turmoil." *BIS Quarterly Review* (December). http://www.bis.org/publ/qtrpdf/r_qt0812e.pdf.

Horn, Gustav, et al. (2009). "From the Financial Crisis to the World Economic Crisis: The Role of Inequality." Macroeconomic Policy Institute, Hans Böckler Stiftung. October. http://www.feps-europe.eu/fileadmin/downloads/political_economy/0910_FEPS_IMK.pdf.

Horton, Mark, Manmohan Kumar, and Paolo Mauro. (2009). "The State of Public Finance: A Cross-Country Fiscal Monitor." http://www.imf.org/external/pubs/ft/spn/2009/spn0921.pdf.

Hudson, Michael. (2006). "Saving, Asset-Price Inflation, and Debt-Induced Deflation." In *Money, Financial Instability and Stabilization Policy*, ed. L. Randall Wray and Matthew Forstater. Northampton, Mass.: Edward Elgar.

——. (2010). "The Transition from Industrial Capitalism to a Financialized Bubble Economy." October 20. http://papers.ssrn.com/sol3/papers.cfm?abstract_id=1695039.

Huffschmid, Jörg. (2008). "The Impact of Finance on the European Social Models." Paper presented at the Transform Conference, Stockholm, sponsored by the Rosa Luxemburg Foundation, June 13–14.

Hughes, Jennifer, and Christopher Swan. (2006). "'Culture' at Fannie Mae Led to Fraud." *Financial Times*, February 23.

Hume, Michael, and Andrew Sentance. (2009). "The Global Credit Boom: Challenges for Macroeconomics and Policy." Bank of England External MPC Unit Discussion Paper 27. June.

Ibbotson, Roger G., Peng Chen, and Kevin X. Zhu. (2011). "The ABCs of Hedge Funds: Alphas, Betas, and Costs." *Financial Analysts Journal* (March/April).

Institutional Risk Analyst. (2009). "Kabuki on the Potomac: Reforming Credit Default Swaps and OTC Derivatives." May 18.

International Monetary Fund. (2007). *Global Financial Stability Report; Market Developments and Issues*. September.

——. (2009a). "Initial Lessons of the Crisis for the Global Architecture and the IMF." Paper prepared by the Strategy, Policy, and Review Department. February 18. http://www.imf.org/external/np/pp/eng/2009/021809.pdf.

——. (2009b). "Lessons of the Global Crisis for Macroeconomic Policy." Prepared by the Research Department in consultation with the Fiscal Affairs and the Monetary and Capital Markets Departments. February 19. http://imf.org/external/np/pp/eng/2009/021909.pdf.

——. (2010). *World Economic Outlook; Rebalancing Growth*. April. www.imf.org/external/pubs/ft/weo/2010/01/index.htm.

International Monetary Fund and International Labor Organization. (2010). "The Challenges of Growth, Employment and Social Cohesion." Discussion paper. http://www.osloconference2010.org/discussionpaper.pdf.

Internal Revenue Service. (2010). "IRS Realigns and Renames Large Business Division, Enhances Focus on International Tax Administration." IR-2010-88. August 4.

Jacoby, Sanford M. (2008). "Finance and Labor: Perspectives on Risk, Inequality, and Democracy." http://papers.ssrn.com/sol3/papers.cfm?abstract_id=1020843.

Jenkins, Patrick, and Megan Murphy. (2010). "Goldman Warns Europe on Regulation." *Financial Times*, September 29.

Jensen, Michael C. (1978). "Some Anomalous Evidence Regarding Market Efficiency." *Journal of Financial Economics* (June/September).

——. (1989). "Eclipse of the Public Corporation." *Harvard Business Review* (September/October).

Johal, Sukhdev, and Adam Leaver. (2007). "Is the Stock Market a Disciplinary Institution? French Giant Firms and the Regime of Accumulation." *New Political Economy* 12, 3.

Johnson, David Cay. (2010). "Scary New Wage Data." October 25. http://www.tax.com/taxcom/taxblog.nsf/Permalink/UBEN-8AGMUZ?OpenDocument.

——. (2010). "Tax Rates for Top 400 Earners Fell as Income Soars, IRS Data Show." *Tax Notes*, February 18.

Johnson, Simon. (2009a). "The Quiet Coup." *Atlantic* (May).

——. (2009b). "The Defanging of Obama's Regulation Plan." June 18. http://economix.blogs.nytimes.com/2009/06/18/the-defanging-of-obamas-regulation-plan/.

——. (2009c). "Measuring the Cost of Not Fixing the Financial System." *Baseline Scenario*, December 5. http://baselinescenario.com/2009/12/05/measuring-the-fiscal-costs-of-not-fixing-the-financial-system/.

——. (2011). "The Bill Daley Problem." http://baselinescenario.com/2011/01/09/the-bill-daley-problem.

Johnson, Simon, and James Kwak. (2010). *13 Bankers: The Wall Street Takeover and the Next Financial Meltdown*. New York: Pantheon.

Kacperczyk, Marcin, and Philipp Schnabl. (2010). "When Safety Proved Risky: Commercial Paper During the Financial Crisis of 2007–2009." *Journal of Economic Perspectives* (Winter).

Kane, Edward J. (2008). "Ethical Failures in Regulating and Supervising: The Pursuit of Safety Net Subsidies." September. Networks Financial Institute Working Paper no. 2008-WP-12. http://ssrn.com/abstract=1273616.

——. (2010). "The Importance of Monitoring and Mitigating the Safety-Net Consequences of Regulation-Induced Innovation." January. papers.ssrn.com/sol3/papers.cfm?abstract_id=1507802.

Kannan, Prakash. (2010). "Credit Conditions and Recoveries from Recessions Associated with Financial Crises." March. http://www.imf.org/external/pubs/ft/wp/2010/wp1083.pdf.

Kaplan, Steven N., and Joshua Rauh. (2010). "Wall Street and Main Street: What Contributes to the Rise in the Highest Incomes?" *Review of Financial Studies* (March).

Kaplan, Steven N., and Per Strömberg. (2009). "Leveraged Buyouts and Private Equity." *Journal of Economic Perspectives* (Winter).

Kaufman, Henry. (2009a). "How Libertarian Dogma Led the Fed Astray." *Financial Times*, April 28.

——. (2009b). *The Road to Financial Reformation: Warnings, Consequences, Reforms.* New York: Wiley.

Kay, John. (2011). "The Beauty of Data Is in the Eye of the Beholder." *Financial Times*, April 16.

Keen, Steve. (1995). "Finance and Economic Breakdown: Modeling Minsky's Financial Instability Hypothesis." *Journal of Post-Keynesian Economics* (Summer).

——. (2009). "Mad, Bad, and Dangerous to Know." *Real-World Economics Review* 49.

Kessler, Adam. (2010). "Cognitive Dissonance, the Global Financial Crisis and the Discipline of Economics." http://www.paecon.net/PAEReview/issue54/Kessler54.pdf.

Keynes, John Maynard. (1920). "The Economic Consequences of the Peace." *The Collected Writings of John Maynard Keynes.* London: Macmillan.

——. (1921b). *A Treatise on Probability.* London: Macmillan.

——. (1931). "Consequences to the Banks of the Collapse of Monetary Values." *The Collected Writings of John Maynard Keynes*, vol. 21. London: Macmillan.

——. (1933). "National Self-Sufficiency," section 3, republished in *Collected Works*, vol. 11 (1982).

——. (1935). *A Treatise on Money*, vol. 1. London: Macmillan.

——. (1936). *The General Theory of Employment, Interest, and Money.* New York: Harcourt, Brace.

——. (1937). "The General Theory of Employment." *Quarterly Journal of Economics* (February).

——. (1943). "Proposal for the International Clearing Union." In *The International Monetary Fund, 1945–68*, vol. 3, *Documents*. Washington, D.C.: International Monetary Fund, 1969.

——. (1963a). "The Consequences to the Banks of the Collapse of Money Values." *Essays in Persuasion*. New York: Norton.

——. (1963b). "The Treaty of Peace." *Essays in Persuasion*. New York: Norton.

Keys, Benjamin J., et al. (2008). "Did Securitization Lead to Lax Screening? Evidence from Subprime Loans." December 25. http://papers.ssrn.com/sol3/papers.cfm?abstract_id=1093137.

Kindleberger, Charles. (1987). "Bubbles." In *The New Palgrave: A Dictionary of Economics*, ed. John Eatwell, Murray Milgate, and Peter Newman. London: Palgrave.

——. (1993). *A Financial History of Western Europe*. 2nd ed. New York: Oxford University Press.

Kirman, Alan. (1989). "The Intrinsic Limits of Modern Economic Theory: The Emperor Has No Clothes." *Economic Journal* 99, 395, Supplement: Conference Papers.

Klein, Ezra. (2011). "Washington's Suicide Pact." *Newsweek*, March 21.

Klein, Naomi. (2007). *The Shock Doctrine: The Rise of Disaster Capitalism*. New York: Metropolitan Books.

Knight, Frank H. (1921). *Risk, Uncertainty and Profit*. New York: Houghton Mifflin.

Kochhar, Rakesh, Ana Gonzalez-Barrera, and Daniel Dockterman. (2009). "Through Boom and Bust: Minorities, Immigrants and Home Ownership." May 12. http://pewhispanic.org/reports/report.php?ReportID=109.

Kocieniewski, David. (2011). "G.E.'s Strategies Let It Avoid Taxes Altogether." *New York Times*, March 24.

Koo, Richard C. (2010). "How to Avoid a Third Depression." Testimony before the Committee on Financial Services, U.S. House of Representatives, July 22. http://financialservices.house.gov/Media/file/hearings/111/Koo%207_22_10.pd.

Kose, M. Ayhan, Eswar S. Prasad, Kenneth Rogoff, and Shang-Jin Wei. (2006). "Financial Globalization: A Reappraisal." IMF Working Paper no. 06/189, August. http://www.brookings.edu/~/media/Files/rc/papers/2006/08globaleconomics_rogoff/20060823.pdf.

Kotz, David M. (2003). "Neoliberalism and the Social Structure of Accumulation Theory of Long-Run Capital Accumulation." *Review of Radical Political Economics* (Summer).

——. (2009). "Economic Crisis and Institutional Structures: A Comparison of Regulated and Neoliberal Capitalism." In *Heterodox Macroeconomics: Keynes, Marx and Globalization*, ed. Jonathan Goldstein and Michael Hillard. London: Routledge.

——. (2010). "The Financial and Economic Crisis of 2008: A Systemic Crisis of Neoliberal Capitalism." *Review of Radical Political Economics* (Summer).

Kotz, David M., Terrence McDonough, and Michael Reich, eds. (1994). *Social Structures of Accumulation: The Political Economy of Growth and Crises*. New York: Cambridge University Press.

Kregel, Jan. (2008). "Using Minsky's Cushions of Safety to Analyze the Crisis in the US Subprime Mortgage Market." *International Journal of Political Economy* (April).

——. (2009a). "The Natural Instability of Financial Markets." IDEAs Working Paper no. 04/2009. http://www.networkideas.org/working/jun2009/04_2009.pdf.

——. (2009b). "It's That 'Vision' Thing: Why the Bailouts Aren't Working, and Why a New Financial system Is Needed." *Real-World Economics Review* 50.

Krieger, Sandra C. (2011). "Reducing the Systemic Risk in Shadow Maturity Transformation." Remarks at the Global Association of Risk Professionals 12th Annual Risk

Management Convention, New York City. Federal Reserve Bank of New York. March 8.

Krippner, Greta R. (2005). "The Financialization of the American Economy." *Socio-Economic Review* (May). Data appendix http://www.soc.ucla.edu/faculty.php, 2005.

Krishnamurthy, Arvind. (2010). "How Debt Markets Have Malfunctioned in the Crisis." *Journal of Economic Perspectives* (Winter).

Krishnamurthy, Arvind, and Annette Vissing-Jorgensen. (2011). "The Effects of Quantitative Easing on Interest Rates." *Brookings Papers on Economic Activity* (Fall).

Kruger, Alan B. (2009). "Testimony before the National Association for Business Economics on 'Stress Testing Economic Data.'" October 12, TG-316. http://www.ustreas.gov/press/releases/archives/200910.html

Krugman, Paul. (2007). "Trade and Inequality, Revisited." June 15. http://www.voxeu.org/index.php?q=node/261.

——. (2009). "The Big Dither." *New York Times*, March 6.

——. (2010). "The '30s Feeling." *New York Times*, June 17.

Krugman, Paul, and Robin Wells. (2010). "The Slump Goes On: Why?" September 30.

Kunkel, Benjamin. (2011). "How Much Is Too Much?" *London Review of Books* (February).

Kuttner, Robert. (2005). "Bubblehead." *American Prospect* (August).

Laeven, Luc, and Fabian V. Valencia. (2008). "Systemic Banking Crises: A New Database." IMF Working Paper no. 08/224. September.

Laidler, David. (2009). "Lucas, Keynes, and the Crisis." Research Report #2009–2, Department of Economics Research Report Series, University of Western Ontario, July.

Lapavitsas, Costas. (2009). "Financialised Capitalism: Crisis and Financial Expropriation." *Historical Materialism* 17.

Lapavitsas, C[ostas], et al. (2010). "Eurozone Crisis: Beggar Thyself and Thy Neighbour." March.http://www.researchonmoneyandfinance.org/media/reports/eurocrisis/fullreport.pdf.

Lapham, Lewis H. (2009). "By the Rivers of Babylon." *Harper's Magazine* (January).

Lazonick, William. (2008). "The Quest for Shareholder Value: Stock Repurchases in the US Economy." http://www.ideas.repec.org/a/cai/reldbu/rel_744_0479.html.

——. (2009a). "The Buyback Boondoggle." *BusinessWeek*, August 24 and 31.

——. (2009b). "The New Economy Business Model and the Crisis of US Capitalism." *Capitalism and Society* 4, 2.

Lazonick, William, and Mary O'Sullivan. (2000). "Maximising Shareholder Value: A New Ideology for Corporate Governance." *Economy and Society* (February).

Levitt, Arthur. (2003). "Accountants Must Put Investors First." *Financial Times*, November 24.

Levitt, Arthur, with Paula Dwyer. (2002). *Take on the Street: What Wall Street and Corporate America Don't Want You to Know, What You Can Do to Fight Back*. New York: Random House.

Lewis, Michael. (2008). "The End." *Portfolio*, November 11. http://www.portfolio .com/news-markets/national-news/portfolio/2008/11/11/The-End-of-Wall-Streets -Boom/.

Lewitt, Michael. (2008). "The Risks of Systemic Collapse." *Market Oracle*, March 18. http://www.marketoracle.co.uk/article4049.html.

Lin, Justin. (2009). "Economist's View: Are Small Banks the Answer for Developing Countries?" *Economist*, July 10.

Lind, Michael. (2010). "Wall Street's Anti-Obama Strategy: Absurd Analogies Obama Is to Wall Street as . . . Hitler Was to Poland?" September 7. http://www.salon .com/news/opinion/feature/2010/09/06/obama_wall_steet_analogies/index.html

Lindgren, Carl-Johan, Gillian Garcia, and Mathew I. Saal. (1996). "Bank Soundness and Macroeconomic Policy." Washington, D.C. International Monetary Fund.

Lippitt, Victor D. (2010). "Social Structures of Accumulation Theory." In McDonough, Reich, and Kotz, *Understanding Contemporary Capitalism and Its Crises*.

Lo, Andrew W. (2008). "Hedge Funds, Systemic Risk, and the Financial Crisis of 2007–2008." Paper prepared for the U.S. House of Representatives Committee on Oversight and Government Reform November 13, 2008, Hearing on Hedge Funds. http://papers.ssrn.com/sol3/papers.cfm?abstract_id=1301217&rec =1&srcabs =978539.

——. (2009). "The Feasibility of Systemic Risk Analysis." http://www.papers.ssrn .com/sol3/papers.cfm?abstract_id=1497682.

Lohr, Steve. (2009). "Goodbye, Goodies? Wall St. Pay Moves in Cycles. Guess Where We Are Now." *New York Times*, February 5.

Lovallo, Dan, and Daniel Kahneman. (2003). "Delusions of Success: How Optimism Undermines Executive Decision." *Harvard Business Review* (July).

Lucas, Robert. (1980a). "The Death of Keynesian Economics." *Issues and Ideas* (Winter).

——. (1980b). "Methods and Problems in Business Cycle Theory." *Journal of Money, Credit and Banking* 12, 4.

——. (1981). *Studies in Business Cycle Theory*. Cambridge: Massachusetts Institute of Technology Press.

——. (2003a). "Macroeconomic Priorities." *American Economic Review* (March).

——. (2003b). "Keynote Address to the 2003 HOPE Conference: My Keynesian Education," April 26. http://homepage.ntu.edu.tw/~yitingli/file/Workshop/lucas%20 .pdf.

Luce, Edward. (2009). "America's Liberals Lay into Obama." *Financial Times*, March 28.

Lund, Susan, Charles Roxburgh, and Tony Wimmer. (2010). "The Looming Deleveraging Challenge." *McKinsey Quarterly* (January).

Mackintosh, James. (2008). "Hedge Funds Present Dilemma for Regulators." *Financial Times*, March 5.

——. (2010). "Hedge Fund Stars Shine above the Crowd." *Financial Times*, September 10.

——. (2011). "The Shorter View." *Financial Times*, March 11.

Macro Assessment Group. (2010). *Interim Report. Assessing the Macroeconomic Impact of the Transition to Stronger Capital and Liquidity Requirement.* August. http://www.bis.org/publ/othp10.pdf.

Maddison, Angus. (2001). *The World Economy: A Millennial Perspective.* Paris: Organization for Economic Cooperation and Development.

Magnus, George. (2007). "What This Minsky Moment Means for Business." *Financial Times*, August 23.

Malinowitz, Stanley. (2009). "Financialization and the Latin American Economies." http://lasa.international.pitt.edu/members/congress-papers/lasa2009/files/Malinowitz Stanley.pdf.

Malkiel, Burton G., and Atanu Saha. (2005). "Hedge Fund Risk and Return." *Financial Analysts Journal* (November/December).

Mallaby, Sebastian. (2011). "Goldman's Pieties Go Too Far." *Financial Times*, January 12.

Malmendier, Ulrike, and Stefan Nagel. (2008). "Depression Babies: Do Macroeconomic Experiences Affect Risk-Taking?" http://en.scientificcommons.org/40767240.

Marx, Karl. (1894). *Capital*, vol. 3. Chicago: Charles H. Kerr.

Masoud, Nadia, et al. (2011). "Do Hedge Funds Trade on Private Information? Evidence from Syndicated Lending and Short-Selling." *Journal of Financial Economics* (March).

Mayer, Christopher, Karen Pence, and Shane M. Sherlund. (2009). "The Rise in Mortgage Defaults." *Journal of Economic Perspectives* (Winter).

Mayer, Martin. (2009). "On Credit Default Swaps: Comments at AIER, June 25. http://us1.institutionalriskanalytics.com/pub/IRAstory.asp?tag=373.

McCormick, John, and Julianna Goldman. (2010). "Obama's Compromise on Extending Highest-Income Tax Cuts Unpopular in Poll." December 8. http://www.bloomberg.com.

McDonough, Terrence. (2010). "The State of the Art of Social Structure of Accumulation Theory." In *Understanding Contemporary Capitalism and Its Crises: Social Structure of Accumulation Theory for the Twenty-First Century*, ed. Terrence McDonough, Michael Reich, and David M. Kotz. New York: Cambridge University Press.

McDonough, Terrence, Michael Reich, and David M. Kotz, eds. (2010). *Social Structures of Accumulation Theory for the Twenty-First Century*. New York: Cambridge University Press.

McFerron, Whitney, et al. (2010). "Google Has Made $11.1 Billion Overseas Since 2007. It Paid Just 2.4% in Taxes. And That's Legal." *Bloomberg Businessweek*, October 25–October 31.

McKinley, Terry. (2009). "Will Pinning the Blame on China Help Correct Global Imbalances?" Center for Development and Policy Research, Policy Brief no. 2. June.

McKinsey & Company. (2006). *Mapping Global Financial Markets*. January. http://www.mckinsey.com/mgi/publications/mapping_global/executive_summary.asp

McKinsey Global Institute. (2011). *Growth and Renewal in the United States: Retooling America's Economic Engine*. February.

McMahon, Robert. (2009). "U.S. Trade Policy in Transition." February 10. http://www.cfr.org/publication/17859/us_trade_policy_in_transition.html.

McNally, David. (2009). "From Financial Crisis to World Slump: Accumulation, Financialisation, and the Global Slowdown." *Historical Materialism* 17.

Meads, Chris. (2011). "Opportunities for PE in a Changing World." *Financial Times*, April 4.

Mees, Heleen. (2011). US Monetary Policy and the Saving Glut." March 24. http://www.vox.org.

Mehrling, Perry. (2005). "The Development of Macroeconomics and the Revolution in Finance." *Fischer Black and The Revolutionary Idea of Finance*. Hoboken, N.J.: Wiley.

——. (2009a). "Credit Default Swaps: The Key to Financial Reform." Initiative for Policy Dialogue Conference Background Paper. June. http://www0.gsb.columbia.edu/ipd/programs/item.cfm?prid=133&iyid=13&itid=1335.

——. (2009b). "The Global Credit Crisis and Policy Response." May. http://www.econ.barnard.columbia.edu/faculty/mehrling/mehrling_credit_crisis.html.

Melloan, George. (2010). *The Great Money Binge; Spending Our Way to Socialism*. New York Simon & Schuster.

Meltzer, Allan H. (2003). "Rational and Nonrational Bubbles." In *Asset Price Bubbles: The Implications for Monetary, Regulatory, and International Policies*, ed. William Curt Hunter, George G. Kaufman, and Michael Pomerleano. Cambridge: MIT Press.

Micklethwait, John. (2007). "A Special Report on Religion and Public Life." *Economist*, November 3.

Mian, Atif, and Amir Sufi. (2008). "The Consequences of Mortgage Credit Expansion: Evidence from the 2007 Mortgage Default Crisis." National Bureau of Economic Research Working Paper no. 13936, April.

Michel, Lawrence, Jared Bernstein, and Sylvia Allegretto. (2007). *The State of Working America 2006/2007*. Ithaca: Economic Policy Institute and Cornell University Press.

Milbank, Dana. (2011). "Just How Powerful Is Elizabeth Warren?" *Washington Post*, March 16.

Milberg, William. (2008). "Shifting Sources and Uses of Profit: Sustaining U.S. Financialization with Global Value Chains." *Economy and Society* (August).

Milken, Michael. (2009). "Why Capital Structure Matters." *Wall Street Journal*, April 21.

Mills, C. Wright. (1956). *The Power Elite*. New York: Oxford University Press.

Minsky, Hyman P. (1982). *Can 'It' Happen Again? Essays on Instability and Finance*. Armonk, N.Y.: M. E. Sharpe.

——. (1986). *Stabilizing an Unstable Economy*. New Haven: Yale University Press.

——. (1990). "Schumpeter: Finance and Evolution." In *Evolving Technology and Market Structure: Studies in Schumpeterian Economics*, ed. Arnold Heertje and Mark Perlman. Ann Arbor: University of Michigan Press.

——. (1992). "The Financial Instability Hypothesis." Jerome Levy Economics Institute, Working Paper no. 74. May.

——. (1996). "Uncertainty and the Institutional Structure of Capitalist Economies." Jerome Levy Economics Institute, Working Paper no. 155. April.

Mishkin, Frederic S. (2010). "Over the Cliff: From the Subprime to the Global Financial Crisis." NBER Working Paper no. 16609. December.

Missal, Michael J., and Lisa M. Richman. (2008). "New Century Financial: Lessons Learned." *Mortgage Banking* (October).

Mitchell, Broadus. (1947). *Depression Decade: From New Era through New Deal, 1929–1941.* New York: Harper & Row, 1969.

Modigliani, Franco, and Merton Miller. (1958). "The Cost of Capital, Corporate Finance and the Theory of Investment." *American Economic Review* (June).

Mollenkamp, Carrick, Aaron Lucchetti, and Serena Ng. (2011). "Report Details Wall Street Crisis." *Wall Street Journal*, January 28.

Monk, Ashby H. B. (2009). "The Financial Thesis: Reconceptualizing Globalisation's Effect on Firms and Institutions." *Competition and Change* (March).

Morgenson, Gretchen. (2008). "The Fannie and Freddie Fallout." *New York Times*, July 13.

——. (2009). "Revisiting a Fed Waltz with A.I.G." *New York Times*, November 22.

Morgenson, Gretchen, and Louise Story. (2011). "A Financial Crisis with Little Guilt." *New York Times*, April 14.

Morris, Peter. (2010). "Private Equity, Public Loss?" Centre for the Study of Financial Innovation, July. http://www.csfi.org.uk/.

Mullins, Brody, Susan Pulliam, and Steve Eder. (2011). "Financiers Switch to GOP." *Wall Street Journal*, April 26.

Murphy, Kevin M., Andrei Shleifer, and Robert W. Vishny. (1991). "The Allocation of Talent: Implications for Growth." *Quarterly Journal of Economics* (May).

Murray, Mark. (2011). "NBC/WSJ Poll: Voters Deficit-Worried But Wary of Cuts." March 2. http://www.msnbc.com.

Mutti, Antonio. (2010). "Heterodox Reflections on the Financial Crisis." *Economic Sociology—The European Electronic Newsletter* (March).

Nayyar, Deepak. (2006). "Globalization, History and Development: A Tale of Two Centuries." *Cambridge Journal of Economics*, January.

Nersisyan, Yeva, and L. Randall Wray. (2010). "Does Excessive Sovereign Debt Really Hurt Growth? A Critique of This Time Is Different, by Reinhart and Rogoff." Jerome Levy Economics Institute Working Paper no. 603. June. http://www.levyinstitute.org/pubs/wp_603.pdf.

Ng, Serena, and Carrick Mollenkamp. (2010). "Fed Opens the Books on Bear, AIG Toxic Assets." *Wall Street Journal*, April 1.

Nichols, John. (2011). "Fed's 'Backdoor Bailout' Provided $3.3 Trillion in Loans to Banks, Corporations." *Nation*, December 2.

Niskansen, William A. (2008). "In Defense of Liberty." *Forbes*, November 10.

Nocera, Joe. (2011). "Letting the Banks Off the Hook." *New York Times*, April 19.

Norris, Floyd. (2009). "Problem For Bankers? The Rules." *New York Times*, March 13.

Norton, Michael I., and Dan Ariely. (2011). "Building a Better America—One Wealth Quintile at a Time." *Perspectives on Psychological Science* (January).

Norton, Robert E. (1984). "The Battle over Market Reform." *Fortune*, February.

Obstfeld, Maurice, and Kenneth Rogoff. (2009). "Global Imbalances and the Financial Crisis: Products of Common Causes." November. http://www.imf.org/external/np/res/seminars/2010/paris/pdf/obstfeld.pdf.

Obstfeld, Maurice, Jay C. Shambaugh, and Alan Taylor. (2008). "Reserve Accumulation and Financial Stability." October. http://www.voxeu.org/index.php?q=node/2361.

Obstfeld, Maurice, and Alan M. Taylor. (2004). *Global Capital Markets: Integration, Crisis and Growth*. New York: Cambridge University Press.

Ody, Elizabeth. (2010). "Interview: John Bogle; Owning Stocks Always Trumps Renting Stocks." http://kiplinger.com/magazine/archives/2009/08/john-bogle.html#ixzz10HSon2qP.

Office of Management and Budget. (2011). *Historical Tables; Budget of the Federal Budget for Fiscal Year 2010*. http://www.gpoaccess.gov/usbudget/fy10/pdf/hist.pdf.

O'Hara, Phillip Anthony. (2006). *Growth and Development in the Global Political Economy: Social Structures of Accumulation and Modes of Regulation*. New York: Routledge.

Ohlemacher, Stephen. (2011). "For Richest, Federal Taxes Have Gone Down; for Some in U.S., They're Nonexistent." *Washington Post*, April 17.

Orhangazi, Ozgur. (2008). Financialization and Capital Accumulation in the Nonfinancial Corporate Sector: A Theoretical and Empirical Investigation on the US Economy, 1973–2003." *Cambridge Journal of Economics* (April).

Orndorff, Mary. (2010). "Spencer Bachus Finally Gets His Chairmanship." *Birmingham News*, December 9.

Ortiz, Isabel, Jingqing Chai, Matthew Cummins, and Gabriel Vergara. (2010). "Prioritizing Expenditures for a Recovery for All, a Rapid Review of Public Expenditures in 126 Developing Countries." http://www.unicef.org/socialpolicy/files/Prioritizing_Expenditures_for_a_Recovery_for_All_October_11_final.pdf.

Ostry, Jonathan D., et al. (2010). "Capital Inflows: The Role of Control." IMF Staff Position Note, February 19.

Palley, Thomas I. (2007). "Financialization: What It Is and Why It Matters." Paper presented to the Conference on Finance-Led Capitalism? Macroeconomic Effects of Changes in the Financial Sector, Hans Böckler Foundation, Berlin.

——. (2009a). "After the Bust: The Outlook for Macroeconomics and Macroeconomic Policy." *Real-World Economics Review* 49.

——. (2009b). "America's Exhausted Paradigm: Macroeconomic Causes of the Financial Crisis and Great Recession." *Real-World Economics Review* 50.

——. (2010). " The Limits of Minsky's Financial Instability Hypothesis as an Explanation of the Crisis." *Monthly Review* (April).

Palma, José Gabriel. (2009). "The Revenge of the Market on the Rentiers: Why Neoliberal Reports of the End of History Turned Out to be Premature." *Cambridge Journal of Economics* (July).

Panetta, Fabio, Thomas Faeh, Giuseppe Granbe, Frederico M. Sigoretti, Marco Taboga, and Andrea Zaghini. (2009). "An Assessment of Financial Rescue Peogrammes." http://www.bis.org/publ/bppdf/bispap48.pdf.

Paredes, Tony. (2006). "On the Decision to Regulate Hedge Funds: The SEC's Regulatory Philosophy, Style and Mission." Washington University Law School Faculty Working Paper Series no. 06–03–02.

Patnaik, Prebhat. (2009). "The Global Financial Community." http://www.networkideas.org/news/apr2009/news21_Global_Financial.htm.

Patterson, Scott. (2009). *The Quants: How a New Breed of Math Whizzes Conquered Wall Street and Nearly Destroyed It.* New York: Crown.

"Paul Volker: Think Boldly." Interview with Alan Murray. *Wall Street Journal*, December 14.

Paulani, Leda Maria. (2010). "Brazil in the Crisis of the Finance-Led Regime of Accumulation." *Review of Radical Political Economics* (Summer).

Permanent Subcommittee on Investigations, United States Senate. (2011). *Wall Street and the Financial Crisis: Anatomy of a Financial Collapse*, April 13. http://hsgac.senate.gov/public/_files/Financial_Crisis/FinancialCrisisReport.pdf

Pew Research Center. (2010). "A Balance Sheet at 30 Months: How the Great Recession Has Changed Life in America." June 30. http://pewsocialtrends.org/assets/pdf/759-recession.pdf.

——. (2010). "Public Uncertain about How to Improve Job Situation." June 21. http://people-press.org/report/624/.

Phalippou, Ludovic, and Oliver Gottschalg. (2009). "The Performance of Private Equity Funds." *Review of Financial Studies* (April).

Philippon, Thomas, and Reshef, Ariell. (2009). "Wages and Human Capital in the U.S. Financial Industry: 1909–2006." *Review of Financial Studies* (April). http://ssrn.com/abstract=1433859.

Pike, Andy, and Jane Pollard. (2010). "Economic Geographies of Financialization." *Economic Geography* (January).

Piketty, Thomas, and Emmanuel Saez. 2007. "Income and Wage Inequality in the United States, 1913–2002." In *Top Incomes over the Twentieth Century: A Contrast Between Continental European and English-Speaking Countries*, ed. Anthony B. Atkinson and Thomas Piketty. Oxford: Oxford University Press. http://elsa.berkeley.edu/~saez/saez-UStopincomes-2007.pdf.

Pomerleano, Michael. (2009). "Another Crash Is Too Possible." http://blogs.ft.com/economistsforum/2009/09/another-crash-is-all-too-possible.

Posner, Richard. (2009). *A Failure of Capitalism: The Crisis of '08 and the Decent into Depression.* Cambridge: Harvard University Press.

Postrel, Virginia. (2009). "Macroeconomics." *Atlantic* (April).

Powell, Michael, and Janet Roberts. (2009). "Minorities Hit Hardest as New York Foreclosures Rise." *New York Times*, May 16.

Pozsar, Zoltan, et al. (2010). "Shadow Banking." Federal Reserve Bank of New York Staff Report no. 458. July.

President's Council of Economic Advisors (various years). Economic Report of the President. Washington, D.C.: Government Printing Office.

PricewaterhouseCoopers. (2006). *The World in 2050.* March. http://www.pwc.com/extweb/pwcpublications.nsf/docid/56DD37D0C399661D852571410060FF8B.

Prins, Nomi. (2010). "Shadow Banking." *American Prospect* (June).

Program on International Policy Attitudes. (2010). "American Public Vastly Over-estimates Amount of U.S. Foreign Aid." University of Maryland, November 29. http://worldpublicopinion.org.

Radelet, Stephen, and Jeffrey D. Sachs. (1998). "The East Asian Financial Crisis: Diagnosis, Remedies, Prospects." *Brookings Papers on Economic Activity* 1.

Rajan, Raghuram. (2009). "More Capital Will Not Stop the Next Crisis." *Financial Times*, September 2.

Rapaport, Michael, and Tom McGinty. (2010). "Banks Trim Debt, Obscuring Risk." *Wall Street Journal*, May 26.

Rasmussen Reports. (2009b). "51% Worry Government Will 'Help' Economy Too Much." September 23. http://www.rasmussenreports.com/public_content/politics/general_politics/September_2009/51_worry_government_will_help_economy_too_much.

Redlawsk, David P., Andrew J. W. Civettini, and Karen M. Emmerson. (2010). "The Affective Tipping Point: Do Motivated Reasoners Ever 'Get It'?" *Political Psychology* (August).

Reich, Michael, David Kotz, and Terrence McDonough, eds. (1994). *Social Structures of Accumulation: The Political Economy of Growth and Crisis*. Cambridge: Cambridge University Press.

Reich, Robert. (2010). "Inequality in America and What to Do about It," *Nation*, July 19–26.

———. (2011). "Why Our Sputnik Moment Will Fall Short." *Financial Times*, January 26.

Reinhart, Carmen M., and Vincent R. Reinhart. (2010). "After the Fall." September. http://www.nber.org/papers/w16334.pdf.

Reinhart, Carmen M., and Kenneth S. Rogoff. (2008a). "Is the 2007 U.S. Subprime Crisis So Different? An International Historical Comparison," *American Economic Review* 98:2.

———. (2008b). "The Aftermath of Financial Crises." Paper presented at the American Economic Association meetings, draft December 19. http://www.economics.harvard.edu/files/faculty/51_Aftermath.pdf.

———. (2009). *This Time Is Different: Eight Centuries of Financial Folly*. Princeton: Princeton University Press.

———. (2010). "Growth in a Time of Debt." *American Economic Association Review Papers and Proceedings* (May).

Riedl, Brian. (2009). "Why the Stimulus Failed; Fiscal Policy Cannot Exnihilate New Demand." *National Review Online*, September 7. http://nrd.nationalreview.com/article/?q=MTViNmZiZmQ4NmMxM2Y5NmEzNWIwYWRmNmNhMWJlY2I=.

Rochon, Louis-Philippe, and Sergio Rossi. (2010). "Has 'It' Happened Again?" *International Journal of Political Economy* (Summer).

Rockoff, Hugh. (1985). "On Monetarist Economics and the Economics of a Monetary History." *Journal of Monetary Economics* (January).

Rodrik, Dani. (2010). "Making Room for China in the World." *American Economic Review* (May).

——. (2011). *The Globalization Paradox: Democracy and the Future of the World Economy*. New York: Norton.

Rodrik, Dani, and Arvind Subramanian. (2009). "Why Did Financial Globalization Disappoint?" *IMF Staff Papers*. April.

Roe, Mark. (2010). "Can a Clearinghouse Really Stop the Next Financial Crisis?" Harvard Law School Forum on Corporate Governance and Financial Regulation. May 6. http://blogs.law.harvard.edu/corpgov/2010/05/06/can-a-clearinghouse-really-stop -the-next-financial-crisis/.

Rohatyn, Felix. (1994). "World Capital Markets: The Need and the Risks." *New York Review of Books*, July 14.

Romer, Paul M. (2010). "What Parts of Globalization Matter for Catch-Up Growth?" *American Economic Review* (May).

Rose, Andrew K., and Mark M. Spiegel. (2009). "Cross-Country Causes and Consequences of the 2008 Crisis: Early Warning." FRBSF Working Paper 2009–17. http://www.frbsf.org/publications/economics/papers/2009/wp09–17bk.pdf

Rossman, Peter, and Gerard Greenfield. (2006a). "Financialization: New Route to Profit, New Challenges for Trade Unions." *Labor Education, the Quarterly Review of the ILO Bureau of Workers' Activities*, no. 146.

——. (2006b). "New Routes to Profits, New Challenges for Trade Unions." *Labour Education*, ILO Bureau for Workers' Activities 1/2006, no. 142. http://www .iufdocuments.org/buyoutwatch/2007/02/financialization_new_routes_to.html.

Roxburgh, Charles, Susan Lund, Charles Atkins, Stanislas Belot, Wayne W. Hu, and Moira S. Pierce. (2009). *Global Capital Markets: Entering a New Era*. McKinsey Global Institute, September.

Roxburgh, Charles, et al. (2009). "The New Power Brokers: How Oil, Asia, Hedge Funds, and Private Equity Are Faring in the New Financial Crisis." McKinsey Global Institute, July.

Roxburgh, Charles, et al. (2010). *Debt and Deleveraging: The Global Credit Bubble and Its Economic Consequences."* January. McKinsey Global Institute.

Rubini, Nouriel, and Brad Setser. (2005). "Will the Bretton Woods 2 Regime Unravel Soon? The Risk of a Hard Landing in 2005–2006." http://pages.stern.nyu .edu/~nroubini/papers/BW2-Unraveling-Roubini-Setser.pdf.

Ruggie, John. (1982). "International Regimes, Transactions, and Change: Embedded Liberalism in the Postwar Economic Order." *International Organization* (Spring).

Saad, Lydia. (2010). "Americans See Economic Recovery a Long Way Off." Gallup, January 20. http://www.gallup.com/poll/125303/americans-see-economic-recovery-long -way-off.aspx.

Saez, Emmanuel. (2010). "Striking It Rich: The Evolution of Top Incomes in the United States (Updated with 2008 Estimates)." July 17. http://www.econ.berkeley .edu/~saez/saez-UStopincomes-2008.pdf.

Sapir, Jacques. (2009). "From Financial Crisis to Turning Point. How the US 'Subprime Crisis' Turned into a Worldwide One and Will Change the Global Economy." http://library.fes.de/pdf-files/ipg/ipg-2009-1/04_a_sapir_us.pdf.

Scardino, Albert. (1987). "What, New York City Worry." *New York Times*, May 3.

Scheer, Robert. (2009). "Living Large and In Charge." April 7. http://www.huffingtonpost.com/robert-scheer/living-large-and-in-charg_b_184459.html.

Schroeder, Susan K. (2002). "A Minskian Analysis of Financial Crisis in Developing Countries." CEPA Working Paper 2002–09 August.

Schumpeter, Joseph Alois. (1954). *History of Economic Analysis*. New York: Oxford University Press.

Schularick, Moritz. (2010). "The End of Financial Globalization 3.0." *Economists' Voice* (January).

Schularick, Moritz, and Thomas M. Steger. (2007). "Financial Integration, Investment, and Economic Growth: Evidence from Two Eras of Financial Globalization." April. http://www.jfki.fu-berlin.de/faculty/ecoomics/team/persons/schularick/International_Financial_Integration.pdf.

Schularick, Moritz, and Alan M. Taylor. (2009). "Credit Booms Gone Bust: Monetary Policy Leverage Cycles and Financial Crises, 1870–2008." NBER Working Paper no. 15512. November. http://www.nber.org/papers/w15512.

Schwartz, Nelson D. (2010). "Power Shift Is Expected By C.E.O.'s," *New York Times*, November 2.

Seib, Gerald F. (2009). "Obama Aspires to a 'Light Touch,' Not a Heavy Hand." *Wall Street Journal*, June 17.

Sender, Henry. (2007). "Inside the Minds of Kravis, Roberts." *Wall Street Journal*, January 3.

——. (2011). "Uncertain Prospects." *Financial Times*, April 18.

Sewell, William H., Jr. (1992). "A Theory of Structure: Duality, Agency, and Transformation." *American Journal of Sociology* 98.

Shefrin, Hersh. (2002). *Beyond Greed and Fear: Understanding Behavioral Finance and the Psychology of Investing*. New York: Oxford University Press.

Shenon, Philip. (2011). "Dirty Dictator Loot." *Newsweek*, March 21.

Shiller, Robert J. (2003). "Diverse Views on Asset Bubbles." In *Asset Price Bubbles: The Implications of Monetary, Regulatory, and International Policies*, ed. William C. Hunter, George G. Kaufman, and Michael Pomerleano. Cambridge: MIT Press.

——. (2009). "A Failure to Control the Animal Spirits." *Financial Times*, March.

Shin, Hyun Song. (2009). "Reflections on Northern Rock: The Bank Run that Heralded the Global Financial Crisis." *Journal of Economic Perspectives* (Winter).

Shleifer, Andrei, and Robert W. Vishny. (2010). "Unstable Banking." *Journal of Financial Economics* (September).

Singh, Manmohan, and James Aitken. (2010). "The (Sizable) Role of Rehypothecation in the Shadow Banking System." July. http://www.imf.org/external/pubs/ft/wp/2010/wp10172.pdf.

Skidelsky, Robert. (2005). "Keynes, Globalisation and the Bretton Woods Institutions in the Light of Changing Ideas About Markets." *World Economics* (January–March).

——. (2008). "We Forgot Everything Keynes Taught Us." *Washington Post*, October 14.

——. (2009). "The World Finance Crisis & the American Mission." *New York Review of Books*, June 17.

Skidelsky, Robert, and Felix Martin. (2011). "For a National Investment Bank." *New York Review of Books*, April 28.

Skomarovsky, Matthew. (2010). "Obama Packs Debt Commission with Social Security Looters." March 28. http://www.alternet.org/story/146183/obama_packs_debt_commission_with_social_security_looters.

Slack, Donovan. (2010). "Donations Poured in as Brown's Role Grew." *Boston Globe*, December 12.

Solow, Robert M. (2008). "Trapped in the New 'You're on Your Own' World." *New York Review of Books*, November 20. http://www.nybooks.com/articles/22080.

——. (2010). "Building a Science of Economics for the Real World." Prepared Statement for the House Committee on Science and Technology Subcommittee on Investigations and Oversight, July 20. ttp://democrats.science.house.gov/Media/file/Commdocs/hearings/2010/Oversight/20july/Solow_Testimony.pdf.

Sorkin, Andrew Ross. (2009). "Bank Profits Appear Out of Thin Air." *New York Times*, April 2.

——. (2010). "Regulators Tackle 'Carry Trades.'" *Financial Times*, February 11.

Soros, George. (1997). "The Capitalist Threat." *Atlantic Monthly* (February).

——. (2009). "My Three Steps to Financial Reform." *Financial Times*, June 17.

——. (2010). "America Must Face Up to the Dangers of Derivatives." *Financial Times*, April 23.

Spencer, Edson W. (1986). "The U.S. Should Stop Playing Poker With Its Future." *BusinessWeek*, November.

Steil, Benn. (2009). *Lessons of the Financial Crisis*. New York: Council on Foreign Relations. Special Report no. 45. March. http://www.cfr.org/publication/18753.

Stein, Jeremy C. (2010). "Monetary Policy as Financial-Stability Regulation." April. http://www.economics.harvard.edu/faculty/stein/files/MonetaryPolicyAsRegulation-8–2010.pdf.

Stewart, James B. (2010). "Where's the Goldman Sachs That I Used to Know?" *Wall Street Journal*, April 21.

Stiglitz, Joseph E. (2003). *The Roaring Nineties: A New History of the World's Most Prosperous Decade*. New York: Norton.

——. (2009). "The Current Economic Crisis and Lessons for Economic Theory." *Eastern Economic Journal* (Summer).

——. (2010a). "The Financial Crisis of 2007–2008 and Its Macroeconomic Consequences." Initiative for Policy Dialogue, Columbia University.

——. (2010b). *Freefall America, Free Markets, and the Sinking of the World Economy*. New York: Norton.

Stockhammer, Engelbert. (2004). "Financialisation and the Slowdown of Accumulation." *Cambridge Journal of Economics* (September).

——. (2008). "Some Stylized Facts on the Finance-Dominated Accumulation Regime." *Competition and Change* (June).

Stockman, David. (2010). "Taxing Wall Street Down to Size." *New York Times*, January 20.

Story, Louise. (2011). "JPMorgan Accused of Breaking Its Duty to Clients. *New York Times*, April 10.

Story, Louise, and Gretchen Morgenson. (2010). "In U.S. Bailout of A.I.G., Forgiveness for Big Banks." *New York Times*, June 30.

Strasburg, Jenny, and Susan Pulliam. (2011). "Hedge Funds' Pack Behavior Magnifies Swings in Market." *Wall Street Journal*, January 14.

Streitfeld, David. (2011). "Servicers Said to Agree to Revamp Foreclosures." *New York Times*, April 5.

Stulz, René M. (2010). "Credit Default Swaps and the Credit Crisis." *Journal of Economic Perspectives* (Winter).

Sum, Andrew, et al. (2008). "The Great Divergence: Real-Wage Growth of All Workers Versus Finance Workers." *Challenge* (May–June).

Swanson, Ian, and Jay Heflin. (2010). "'Fabulous Fab,' Goldman Offer Vigorous Defense before Senate." *The Hill*, April 27.

Sweezy, Paul M. (1994). "The Triumph of Financial Capital." *Monthly Review* (June).

Sweezy, Paul M., and Harry Magdoff. (1978). "Debt and the Business Cycle." *Monthly Review* (June).

Tabb, William K. (1999). *Reconstructing Political Economy: The Great Divide in Economic Thought*. New York: Routledge.

——. (2004). *Economic Governance in the Age of Globalization*. New York: Columbia University Press.

——. (2007). "The Centrality of Finance." *Journal of World Systems Research* 13 (August).

——. (2010). "Finance and the Contemporary Social Structure of Accumulation." In *Understanding Contemporary Capitalism and Its Crises: Social Structures of Accumulation Theory for the Twenty-First Century*, ed. Terrence McDonough, Michael Reich, and David M. Kotz. New York: Cambridge University Press.

Taibbi, Matt. (2009). "Inside The Great American Bubble Machine." *Rolling Stone*, July 2. http://www.rollingstone.com/politics/story/28816321/inside_the_great_american_bubble_machine.

Tang, Ke, and Wei Xiong. (2009). "Index Investing and the Financialization of Commodities." Working Paper, Princeton University. http://www.princeton.edu/~wxiong/papers/commodity.pdf.

Taylor, John B. (2007). "Housing and Monetary Policy." Federal Reserve Bank of Kansas City. *Housing, Housing Finance and Monetary Policy*.

——. (2008). "The Financial Crisis and the Policy Responses: An Empirical Analysis of What Went Wrong." http://www.stanford.edu/~johntayl/FCPR.pdf.

——. (2009). "Systemic Risk and the Role of Government." http://stanford.edu/
~johntayl/Systemic_Risk_and_the_Role_of_Government-May_12_2009.pdf.

——. (2010). ""The Dodd-Frank Financial Fiasco." *Wall Street Journal*, July 1.

Taylor, Lance, and Stephen O'Connell. (1989). "A Minsky Crisis." In *Financial Dynamics and Business Cycles*, ed. Willi Semmler. Armonk, N.Y.: M. E. Sharpe.

Telser, Lester G. (1989). "October 1987 and the Structure of Financial Markets: An
Exorcism of Demons." In *Black Monday and the Future of Financial Markets*, ed.
Robert J. Barro et al. Homewood, Ill.: Irwin.

Tett, Gillian. (2010). "Calls for Radical Rethink of Derivatives Body." *Financial Times*,
August 26.

Thaler, Richard H., and Cass R. Sunstein. (2009). *Nudge: Improving Decisions about
Health, Wealth and Happiness*. New Haven: Yale University Press.

Toporowski, Jan. (2008). "The Economics and Culture of Financialisation." Department of Economics, School of Oriental and African Studies, University of London, Working Paper 158. April.

Transparency International. *2008 Corruption Perceptions Index*. http://www.transparency
.org/news_room/in_focus/2008/cpi2008/cpi_2008_table.

Tropeano, Domenica. (2010). "The Current Financial Crisis, Monetary Policy, and
Minsky's Structural Instability Hypothesis." *International Journal of Political Economy* (Summer).

Turner, Adair. (2010a). "The Crisis, Conventional Economic Wisdom, and Public
Policy." *Industrial and Corporate Change* 19, 5.

——. (2010b). "What Do Banks Do? Why Do Credit Booms and Busts Occur and
What Can Public Policy Do About It?" In *The Future of Finance; The LSE Report*,
ed. Adair Turner et al. http://www.futureoffinance.org.uk/.

Tymoigne, Éric. (2007). "A Hard-Nosed Look at Worsening U.S. Household Finance." *Challenge* 50:4.

——. (2010). "Detecting Ponzi Finance: An Evolutionary Approach to the Measure of
Financial Fragility." Jerome Levy Economics Institute of Bard College, Working
Paper no. 605. June.

United States Department of the Treasury. (2009). "Principles for Reforming the U.S.
and International Regulatory Capital. Framework for Banking Firms." TG-274. September. http://www.treas.gov/press/releases/docs/capital-statement_090309.pdf.

United States Office of the Comptroller of the Currency (various). *Bank Derivatives
Report*. http://www.occ.treas.gov/ftp.

Valukas, Anton R. (2010). *Lehman Brothers Holdings Inc. Chapter 11 Proceedings Examiner's Report*. http://lehmanreport.jenner.com.

Van Treeck, Till. (2009a). "The Political Economy Debate on 'Financialization'—a
Macroeconomic Perspective." *Review of International Political Economy* (December).

——. (2009b). "The Macroeconomics of 'Financialisation' and the Deeper Origins of
the World Economic Crisis." Hans Böckler Foundation, Working Paper 9/2009.
http://www.boeckler.de/pdf/p_imk_wp_9_2009.pdf.

Veronesi, Pietro, and Luigi Zingales. (2010). "Paulson's Gift." *Journal of Financial Economics* (September).

Volker, Paul A. (1998). "Statement Before the Joint Economic Committee." May 5. http://www.house.gov/jec/hearings/imf-5-05.pdf.

——. (2010). "The Time We Have Is Growing Short." *New York Review of Books*, June 24.

Wachtel, Howard W. (1986). *The Money Mandarins: The Making of a New Supranational Economic Order*. New York: Pantheon.

Wade, Robert. (2004). *Governing the Market: Economic Theory and the Role of Government in East Asian Industrialization*. Princeton: Princeton University Press.

Wall Street Journal. (1934a). "Bankers Oppose Exchange Bill; Investment Group Says It Is Deflationary When Expansion Is Desired." February 28.

——. *(1934b)*. "Says Stock Bill Perils Markets; N.Y. Stock Exchange President Lauds Aims, but Calls Some Provisions Unworkable." February 14.

——. *(1934c)*. "Assure Capital, Kennedy's Aim; Exchange Commission Head Stresses Need for Sound and Broad Market." July 26.

Wallerstein, Immanuel Maurice. (1974). *Capitalist Agriculture and the Origins of the European World-System in the Sixteenth Century; The Modern World-System, Studies in Social Discontinuity*. New York, Academic Press.

Warfield, Terry, and Qiang Cheng. (2005). "Equity Incentives and Earnings Management." *Accounting Review* (April).

Warren, Elizabeth. (2011). Testimony of Elizabeth Warren, Special Advisor to the Secretary of the Treasury for the Consumer Financial Protection Bureau, Before the Subcommittee on Financial Institutions and Consumer Credit Committee on Financial Services, United States House of Representatives. March 16.

Warwick Commission on International Financial Reform. (2009). *The Second Warwick Commission Report*. http://www2.warwick.ac.uk/research/warwickcommission/report/uw_warcomm_intfinreform_09.pdf.

Watson, Matthew. (2009). "Investigating the Potentially Contradictory Microfoundations of Financialization." *Economy and Society* (May).

Weisbrot, Mark. (2010). "French Protesters Have It Right: No Need to Increase Retirement Age." October 20. http://www.guardian.co.uk/commentisfree/cifamerica/2010/oct/20/france-protest.

Weisbrot, Mark, Dean Baker, and David Rosnick. (2005). "The Scorecard on Development: 25 Years of Diminished Progress." Center for Economic and Policy Research. September. http://www.cepr.net/documents/publications/development_2005_09.

Weinstein, Neil D. (1980). "Unrealistic Optimism about Future Life Events." *Journal of Personality and Social Psychology* 39:5.

Weiskopf, Thomas E., Samuel Bowles, and David M. Gordon. (1983). "Hearts and Minds: A Social Model of U.S. Productivity Growth." *Brookings Papers on Economic Activity* 2.

Whitehouse, Mark. (2011). "Crisis Nudge Debt Loads to the Brink." *Wall Street Journal*, March 28.

Widmaier, Wesley W. (2003). "Constructing Monetary Crises: New Keynesian Understandings and Monetary Cooperation in the 1990s." *Review of International Studies* 29.

Williams, Karol. (2000). "From Shareholder Capitalism to Present-Day Capitalism." *Economy and Society* (February).

Williamson, John. (1993). "Democracy and the 'Washington Consensus.'" *World Development* (August).

Williamson, Oliver E. (1985). *The Economic Institutions of Capitalism*. New York: Free Press.

Winter, Caroline, David Glovin, and Jennifer Daniel. (2011). "The Insider's Guide to Insider Trading." *Bloomberg Businessweek*, March 14–20.

Wolf, Martin. (2008). "Why It Is So Hard to Keep the Financial Sector Caged." *Financial Times*, February 6.

——. (2009a). "Why Britain Has to Curb Finance." *Financial Times*, May 22.

——. (2009b). "Why Narrow Banking Alone Is Not a Solution for Finance." *Financial Times*, September 30.

——. (2010). "The Challenge of Halting the Financial Doomsday Machine." *Financial Times*, April 20.

Wolff, Edward N. (2010). "Rising Profitability and the Middle Class Squeeze." *Science and Society* (July).

Wolfson, Martin. (1994). "The Financial System and the Social Structure of Accumulation." In *Social Structures of Accumulation: The Political Economy of Growth and Crisis*, ed. David Kotz, Terrence McDonough, and Michael Reich. New York: Cambridge University Press.

——. (2003). "Neoliberalism and the Social Structure of Accumulation." *Review of Radical Political Economics* (Summer).

Wolfson, Martin, and David M. Kotz. (2010). "A Reconceptualization of Social Structure of Accumulation Theory," in *Understanding Contemporary Capitalism and Its Crises: Social Structure of Accumulation Theory for the Twenty-First Century*, ed. Terrence McDonough, Michael Reich, and David M. Kotz. New York: Cambridge University Press.

Woodford, Michael. (2003). *Interest and Prices: Foundations of a Theory of Monetary Policy*. Princeton: Princeton University Press.

——. (2010). "Financial Intermediation and Macroeconomic Analysis." *Journal of Economic Perspectives* (Fall).

Woolley, Paul. (2010). "Why Are Financial Markets So Inefficient and Exploitative—and a Suggested Remedy." in *The Future of Finance; The LSE Report*, ed. Adair Turner et al. http://www.futureoffinance.org.uk/.

Wray, L. Randall. (2007). "The Continuing Legacy of John Maynard Keynes," "Introduction." In *The General Theory after 70 Years*, ed. Mathew Forstater and L. Randall Wray. Houndsmills: Palgrave Macmillan.

——. (2009). "Money Manager Capitalism and the Global Financial Crisis." *Real-World Economics Review* 51.

Wriston, Walter B. (1992). *The Twilight of Sovereignty*. New York: Scribners.

Wyplosz, Charles. (2008). "Financial Crisis Resolution: It's All about Burden Sharing." Vox, July 20. http://www.voxeu.org/index.php?q=node/1431.

Young, Peyton. (2009). "Why Geithner's Plan Is the Taxpayers' Curse." *Financial Times*, April 2.

Zalewski, David, and Charles Whalen. (2010). "Financialization and Income Inequality: A Post Keynesian Institutionalist Analysis." *Journal of Economic Issues* (September).

Zibel, Alan, and Louise Radnofsky. (2011). "Only 1 in 4 Got Mortgage Relief." *Wall Street Journal*, February 28.

Zuckerman, Gregory. (2011). "Trader Racks Up a Second Epic Gain." *Wall Street Journal*, January 22.

Minsky understanding of, 85–86; H.
Minsky on, 75–76, 130; misdirected
blame for, 159–172; and nature
of capitalism, 77; and need for
governmental intervention, 6–7;
and overconfidence, 193; paying for,
7; prediction of 2008, 2; protection
from, 24; resolution of, 193–194; role
of markets in, 20; role of Wall Street
in, 249; speculation in, 260–261;
triggering, 135–144; in U.S., 60–61
Financial Crisis Inquiry Commission
(FCIC), 139; Goldman Sachs investigated by, 104; hedge funds report of,
114; SIVs investigated by, 97
financial firms, nonbank, 94
Financial Industries Regulatory
Authority, 139
financial industry: dominance of, 37; and
Obama administration, 198; political
power of, 206; profits of, 43; self-
imposed problems in, 52; and U.S.
government, 187. See also banking
industry
Financial Industry Regulatory Authority,
191
financial innovation, 133, 216;
consequences of, 66, 86; regulation
of, 130
financial institutions, 96; corrupt
practices by, 181; failure risk of, 2;
Fed's rescue of, 252–253; immunity
of, 251; inner circles of, 182–187;
interconnections among, 129, 218;
rescue of, 8–9; study of, 248; too-
big-to-fail, 197
financial instruments: and economic
efficiency, 196–197; increase in use of,
19. See also specific financial instruments
financial intensity, 13
financialization, 37; and commercial
banking, 38–43; definition of, 12–13;
dominance of, 249, 250; in Europe,
231; excessive, 1–2; expansion

of, 14; and globalization, 24;
globalization of, 219–224; in global
neoliberalism, 243; historical turn
to, 34–35; income and spending
changes driven by, 13; and income
distribution, 40; and inequality,
257; of internationalization
economy, 14; in long run, 17–19;
peak of, 97; pre-Great Recession,
71; and redistribution of profits,
11; as redistributive growth, 12;
replacing dependence on, 272–276;
restructuring of, 53–57; roots of,
54; in shadow banking system,
129–131; as social good, 219–220;
of society, 232; spreading, 224–
227; understanding, 10–11; and
unsustainable debt creation, 261; use
of term, 11
financial markets: faith in efficiency
of, 150; global rules for, 255;
government intervention in, 254;
high cost of free, 90–92; information
in, 63, 118; instability of, 79–80;
interconnectedness of, 207–208;
misguided behavior of, 254; modern,
9; power of, 255–256; regulation of,
276; safety of, 249; self-stabilizing
properties of, 248; structure of, 203;
unregulated global, 14; U.S., 14
financial meltdown, the poor as cause
of, 164
financial products: and globalization,
216; ratings of, 102; real cost of, 195;
riskier Western-style, 223. See also
specific financial products
financial reform, 1; domestic, 192–206;
P. Volcker on, 197
financial sector, 92; autonomy of, 186;
global tax in, 265; government credit
extended to, 159; and gross liability
of U.S., 138; growth of, 253; growth
of liabilities in, 250; and income
distribution, 40; pay

living standards: and financialization, 2; stagnation of working-class, 13

loans: buying and selling bad, 139; covenant-lite, 137, 179; "NINJA," 136; as perpetual earning asset, 40; "toggle-PIK," 179. *See also* mortgages

"loan to own" practice, 123

local government, reaction to austerity measures of, 175

London, as center of world finance, 230

Long Term Capital Management, 131

looting strategies, 23

losses, socialization of, 90

Lowe, Phillip, 207

Lucas, Robert E., Jr., 65

Luetkemeyer, Rep. Blaine, 195

MacKay, Charles, 63

macroeconomics: crisis in, 65; textbook Keynesian, 71

Madoff, Bernard, 117, 156

Malinowitz, Stanley, 11

Malkiel, Burton G., 119

Maloney, Rep. Carol, 111

Managed Funds Assoc., 192

management: lack of checks on, 46; megabonuses for, 85; pay structure for, 28; relationship with stockholders of, 43. *See also* executives, top; fund managers; money managers

managerial revolution, in U.S., 27

Mantega, Guido, 239

Manuel, Trevor, 217

manufacturing: impact of China on U.S., 238; measure of value added in, 258; refocusing on, 16; weakening American, 50

market data, probabilities calculated from, 64

market failures, disregard of, 73–74

markets: crises produced in, 66; faith in efficiency of, 23; faith in unregulated, 108–109; interconnections between

financial firms and, 208; primacy of, 227. *See also* mortgage market

markets, financial: deregulation of, 22; and GDP, 24

market signals, false, 63

market theories: efficient, 64–65; flaws in, 23

Markit's iTraxx Europe index, 212

Marx, Karl, 25, 76, 77, 259–260, 260, 261

Massoud, Nadia, 113

mass production, 27

Material Value Added (MVA) index, 259

Mayer, Martin, 107

McCain, John, 2008 campaign manager of, 161

McClendon, Aubrey, 45

McKinley, Terry, 237

McKinsey & Co. researchers, 207

McKinsey Global Institute, 273

Means, Gardiner C., 43, 52

media, 56; and public perception, 269

Medicare: costs of, 266; cutting, 266; rising costs of, 264

megabanks, 199; banking practices of, 251

Meltzer, Allan, 62

merchant banking, 15

mergers: and economics of scale, 38; to manipulate earnings and deductions, 48

Merkel, Angela, 115–116

Merrill Lynch, 5; BOA's purchase of, 158; bonuses of, 158; in CDO market, 109; creditors of, 142; insurance loses of, 152; mortgage-backed securities sold by, 147; tax losses moved across borders, 228–229

MERS Corp., 171

Mexico, foreign ownership in, 225

Micklethwait, John, 93

middle class: creation of, 27; re-creating, 263

Milberg, William, 11

Miliken, Michael, 52

neoclassical synthesis, 74
neoclassical theory, 61
neoliberalism, 37; legacy of, 262–272;
    misguided certainties central to, 254;
    trade-not-aid development approach
    of, 30; in U.S., 29–30
neoliberalism, global, 19, 20,
    26; dominance of, 249; large
    corporations in, 35; national
    Keynesianism compared with, 32;
    SSA of, 27
Netherlands: healthy economy of, 231;
    offshore subsidiaries in, 148
net stable funding ratio, 234
New Century: bankruptcy's final report
    of, 138; subprime mortgages from,
    151
New Deal, 28, 86
New Economy bubble, collapse of,
    133
New York Federal Reserve Bank, 168;
    and Citigroup, 140; deferral to banks
    of, 182; earnings study by, 48; and
    insider discussions, 184
New York Stock Exchange, hedge funds
    in, 113
New York Times/CBS poll, on taxes and
    benefits, 4
Nicaragua, CIA funding contras in,
    228
"NINJA" loans, as adequate collateral,
    136
Niskansen, William, 164
Nocera, Joe, 251
nonbanks: operations of, 94–95; and
    regulation, 96
Nordic countries, consistently
    egalitarian outcomes in, 257
norms: changes in, 276; ethical, 23;
    expectations for, 25
Norton, Michael, 270

Obama, Pres. Barack, 6, 16, 128, 246;
    address to bankers of, 173; on

Dodd-Frank bill, 204; focus on
    innovation of, 17; 2011 State of the
    Union address of, 272; on Swedish
    nationalization, 189
Obama administration:
    accommodationist minimalism of,
    193; banks supported by, 172, 177;
    Clinton administration retreads in,
    183; financial policies of, 195–196;
    foreclosure policies of, 170; home
    ownership supported by, 145;
    interference in market of, 189–190;
    mortgage relief plan of, 166; and
    nationalization, 141; policy toward
    Fannie and Freddie of, 162; programs
    chosen by, 8; and reliance on Fed,
    200; success of, 143; L. Summers in,
    184–185; Wall Street-friendly stance
    of, 194
obsolescence, planned, 54
OECD countries, 224
Office of Comptroller of the Currency
    (OCC), 165; and mortgage market,
    251
Office of Federal Housing Enterprise
    Oversight, 160, 161
Office of Financial Research (OFR),
    purpose of, 208
Office of Thrift Supervision, 111, 165
Ohio, state's retirement funds of, 137
Okun's Law, 257, 258
older Americans, in labor force, 41
omnibus financial reform (2010), 208
one price, law of, 37
OPEC governments, 240
opportunism, and Great Recession, 22
opportunistic agents, 63
options: and economic efficiency,
    196–197; history of, 99
Organization for Economic
    Cooperation and Development
    (OECD), 98
Organization of Petroleum Exporting
    Countries (OPEC), 29